Orson Squire Fowler

Life

Its Science, Laws, Faculties, Functions, Organs, Conditions, Philosophy...

Orson Squire Fowler

Life
Its Science, Laws, Faculties, Functions, Organs, Conditions, Philosophy...

ISBN/EAN: 9783337014476

Printed in Europe, USA, Canada, Australia, Japan

Cover: Foto ©Thomas Meinert / pixelio.de

More available books at **www.hansebooks.com**

LIFE:
ITS SCIENCE, LAWS, FACULTIES, FUNCTIONS, ORGANS, CONDITIONS, PHILOSOPHY,

AND

IMPROVEMENT:

INCLUDING THE

ORGANISM, HEALTH, SOCIAL AFFECTIONS, MORAL SENTIMENTS, INTELLECT, MEMORY, SELF-EDUCATION, AUTOBIOGRAPHY, MISCELLANY, &C.,

AS TAUGHT BY

PHRENOLOGY.

IN SIX VOLUMES.

I. Physiological Science.   IV. Religious Science.
II. Phrenological Science.   V. Intellectual Science.
III. Sexual Science.   VI. Autobiography and Miscellany.

BY

PROF. O. S. FOWLER,

PRACTICAL PHRENOLOGIST; LECTURER; FORMER EDITOR OF "THE AMERICAN PHRENO-
LOGICAL JOURNAL;" AUTHOR OF "FOWLER ON PHRENOLOGY;" ON "PHYSIOLOGY;"
"SELF-CULTURE;" "MEMORY;" "RELIGION;" "MATRIMONY;" "OFFSPRING, AND
THEIR ENDOWMENT;" "HEREDITARY DESCENT;" "LOVE AND PARENT-
AGE;" "MATERNITY;" "AMATIVENESS;" "SEXUAL SCIENCE," "TEM-
PERANCE;" "THE SELF-INSTRUCTOR;" "HOME FOR ALL;"
"CHEAP CISTERNS," "ANSWERS TO HAMILTON,
VINDEX," &C., &C.

WHAT IS LIFE?

BOSTON:
PUBLISHED BY O. S. FOWLER,
514 TREMONT STREET.

CONTENTS.

PHYSIOLOGICAL SCIENCE.

CHAPTER I.

THE FUNDAMENTAL PRINCIPLES OF LIFE.

SECTION I.

VALUE AND IMPROVEMENT OF LIFE.

Section IV.

How to Eat; or, Mastication, Quantity, Time, &c.

Section V.

The Digestive Process, and its Organs, the Stomach, Liver, Pancreas, &c.

CHAPTER IV.
FLUIDS; THEIR NECESSITY, OFFICE, AND SUPPLY.

Section I.

Fluids; their Necessity, Offices, and Kinds; Cisterns, &c.

Section II.

Stimulating Drinks. — Alcoholic and Malt Liquors; Wine, Tea, Coffee, Lemonade, &c.

Section III.

Fluid Excretions.

Section IV.

The Blood, and its Circulation; the Heart, and its Structure.

Section V.

Animal Heat; its Manufacture, Distribution, and Exit.

Section VI.

The Skin, Perspiration, &c.

Section VII.

Sleep; its Necessity, Office, Amount, Time, Promotion, &c.

CHAPTER V.

THE MOTIVE AND MENTAL APPARATUS, AND FUNCTIONS.

Section I.

The Osseous and Muscular Systems.

Section II.

Exercise; its Value, best Modes, and the Lifting Cure.

ERRATA.

Page 47, line 17 from top, for *acts* read *facts*.

Page 62, line 17 from top, for *legum* read *legium*.

Page 98, line 15 from bottom, for 19 *Temple Place* read 43 *West St*.

Page 105, line 20 from bottom, for *heat* read *heart*.

Page 125, line 21 from top, for *than* read *or*.

Page 162, line 6 from top, for *their* read *its*.

Page 198, line 6 from top, for *opart* read *a part*.

Page 219, line 7 from top, for *these* read *three*.

Page 247, line 13 from bottom, for *insane* read *inane*.

Page 269, line 4 from top, for 105 read 107.

Page 284, line 9 from top, for *pain* read *pains*.

Page 295–6, omit r in *reject, rejecting*, etc.

Page 298, line 4 from top, for ; *and* read . *The*.

Page 298, line 6 from top, for *and* read *or*.

Page 302, line 19 from top, omit *in*.

Page 303, line 8 from bottom, for *stirred* read *stived*.

Page 307, line 8 from bottom, for *praving* read *providing*.

Page 312, line 2 from top, for *sons* read *son*.

Page 312, line 16 from top, for *on* read *out*.

Page 318, line 17 from top, for *aggravates* read *aggravate*.

Page 318, line 20 from top, for *is* read *are*.

Page 319, line 6 from bottom, for *abbreviation* read *obviation*.

Page 327, line 18 from top, for *involuntary* read *voluntary*.

Page 327, line 19 from top, for *rouses* read *causes*.

Page 329–30, for *sash* read *sack*.

Page 341, line 6 from bottom, for *creates* read *create*.

Page 342, line 2 from top, for *build* read *cause*.

Page 342, line 8 from top, for *leads* read *lords*.

Page 342, line 16 from top, for *others* read *else*.

Page 346, line 19 from top, for *causes* read *cause*.

Page 346, line 20 from top, for *are* read *is*.

Page 346, line 20 from top, for *enter* read *enters*.

Page 346, line 2 from bottom, for *much* read *also*.

Page 347, line 14 from top, for *firm* read *force*.

Page 349, line 17 from bottom, for *such* read *seek*.

Page 357, line 19 from top, for *are* read *err*.

Page 357, line 3 from bottom, for *wash* read *watch*.

Page 359, line 18 from bottom, for *stuffed* read *sloughed*.

Page 361, top line, read *The most modern*, etc.

Page 361, line 13 from top, omit *ladies*.

Page 361, line 19 from bottom, for *they* read *it*.

Page 362, line 1 from top, for *b-th* read *now*.

Page 362, lines 15 and 16 from top, for *the* read *her*.

Page 367, line 15 from top, for *morbid* read *marked*.

Page 369, line 13 from top, for *is* read *are*.

Page 370, line 5 from top, for *prosecute* read *proscribe*.

Page 373, line 14 from top, for *tin* read *tree*.

Page 373, lines 4 and 5 from bottom, read, *Begin far below your strength, and work along up gradually to its meridian, but never stop suddenly*.

Page 375, line 6 from top, for *moods* read *moody*.

GENERAL PREFACE.

A RIGHT LIFE constitutes incomparably the most exalted achievement and attainment possible to man or angel. *Just how to live*, is the master problem, as yet unsolved, of all individuals, and all communities, throughout all climes and ages. Its *scientific* solution and application to all the relations of life, therefore, immeasurably transcends all other human ends and acquisitions, because it embraces all knowledge, all virtue, and all enjoyment. What is right, and what wrong? what we ought to do here, and *not* to do there? and how we shall guide our steps aright throughout all the every-day affairs of life? are perpetually recurring questions, requiring specific answers in action every hour of life. All subjects whatsoever have their right side and their wrong; and a correct and infallible decision as to which is right, and which wrong, is infinitely important, because all virtue and enjoyment on the one hand, and all vice and misery on the other, eventuate therefrom. How to derive from life and its surroundings all possible enjoyments, and avoid all possible sufferings, is the very highest aspiration of self-love, and the first instinct of all that lives, and should constitute the one great personal inquiry of every intelligent being all through life. Hence, that scientific exposition of the natural laws and facts of human existence taught by man's organic relations, and their application to the happiness and virtue of individuals and communities here proposed, surpasses all other subjects in practical importance.

3

PHRENOLOGY constitutes the teacher and text-book in this inquiry. Its discovery was by far the greatest, most profound and useful ever made, because this science unfolds creation's sublimest department,— *the* MIND, in which alone life inheres,— thereby seizing this problem of life at its very centre, and ramifying it throughout all its elements and their outworkings.

GALL, though he discovered the phrenological *fact* that each mental capacity manifests itself by means of one particular portion of the brain, called its organ, and that their different sizes, in different persons, cause and indicate the special talents and characteristics of each, as well as the location of most of the organs, yet he did little by way of developing its *science*, as such, or applying its doctrines to human improvement. Spurzheim, too, a close observer, and a deep thinker, added to Gall's discoveries, and made valuable applications of them to "education," &c.; while George Combe, a truly great man, and one of the profoundest reasoners of his own age, or of any other, superadded to the discoveries of both, besides applying them to " insanity," and several other important human interests; to which the Author has endeavored to contribute his mite in his works on " Phrenology," " Matrimony," " Self-Culture," " Memory," &c.

Yet these, and all its other applications, are only fragmentary; whereas the best interests of mankind demand a *comprehensive* and a *complete* exposition, not only of this science itself, including its history, faculties, organs, facts, combinations, &c., but likewise an application of its teachings to *all* the various departments of human life. To help supply this pressing public demand, are these volumes penned.

They describe the mental faculties in *five* different degrees of power, — *very large, full, average, moderate,* and *small,* — and show the different effects on character and conduct of their various COMBINATIONS, as causing that infinite *diversity* of disposition and talents existing among men — a new subject of great practical importance.

They also embrace all the works, writings, observations, and reflections of the Author, revised, enlarged, systematized, condensed, and embodied into one complete *series* of volumes, and presenting a summary of the results of almost *half a century* of his professional consultations, as applied to the distinguished personages of *four generations*, in *both hemispheres*, besides incorporating whatever is specially valuable from previous phrenological writings; thus becoming a *complete encyclopedia of whatever is known* respecting this science of man. It consists of exhaustive works on the following subjects: —

I. PHYSIOLOGICAL SCIENCE; or, HEALTH, its Value, Laws, Organs, Functions, Conditions, Preservation, Restoration, &c.

II. PHRENOLOGICAL SCIENCE; its Principles, Proofs, Temperaments, Cerebral Organs, Mental Faculties, Teachings, &c., as applied to Self-Culture. With a Steel Engraving of the Author.

III. SEXUAL SCIENCE; or, MANHOOD, WOMANHOOD, and their Mutual Inter-relations: LOVE, its Laws, Power, &c.; SELECTION, and Mutual Adaptation; COURTSHIP, or Love-making; MARRIED LIFE made Happy; REPRODUCTION, and Progenal Endowment, including Paternity, Maternity, Bearing, Nursing, and Rearing Children; PUBERTY; GIRLHOOD; SEXUAL AILMENTS Restored, and FEMALE BEAUTY Preserved and Regained, &c.

IV. RELIGIOUS SCIENCE; or, MAN'S MORAL NATURE and Relations, as proving the existence of a SUPREME BEING, and His Attributes, Philosophical Theology, &c.; IMMORTALITY, its Proofs, Conditions, and Relations to Time; NATURAL RELIGION, its Doctrines, Duties, &c.; Worshipping God in Nature, and by Obeying His Natural Laws; Future Rewards and Punishments; the Law of Love, "Faith," "Prayer," Rites, "Total Depravity," "Conversion," "Forgiveness," &c., as taught by Phrenology.

V. INTELLECTUAL SCIENCE; or, MEMORY, REASON, and their Culture; including "The Senses," Intellectual Faculties, Schooling, Self-Education, Mental Discipline, &c.

VI. AUTOBIOGRAPHY, Miscellaneous Writings, Quotations, &c.

While all these volumes are derived directly from Phrenology, yet a belief in this science, though desirable, is no more indispensable to the appreciation and adoption of their glorious teachings, than is a knowledge of the origin of luscious fruits to the enjoyment of their delicious flavors and grateful nutrition; so that "non-communicants" are cordially invited to partake at this banquet, if, perchance, they may thus be induced to examine this science itself, which is founded in the eternal ordinances of Nature. At all events, let both it and its doctrines be tested by that touchstone of all truth, *sound common sense.*

OBJECTORS are generally treated with that "dignified silence" justly due to their ignorance or misrepresentations; because, expounding truth effectually refutes error; so that proving the *truth* of Phrenology brings all its objectors face to face with their MAKER, with whom we leave them to settle their cavils.

Would Galileo, would the discoverers or expounders of any great truth, advance it by wasting on its bigoted opponents those precious energies required for its promulgation?

Pseudo-discoveries antagonistic to those of Gall, are ignored, because his are substantially correct. The Author has practised on other theories enough to know that they are unreliable; whereas, a minute inspection of the phrenological "developments" of a *quarter of a million,* of all ages and of both sexes, warrants this our most positive declaration, derived from all our experimental observations, that Gall's locations and descriptions are substantially correct, so that all in conflict with his are wrong.

If the *authorship* of this august subject falls below what is possible and desirable, let successors — of predecessors there are none — supply omissions and make required improvements. A subject *thus* vast and momentous demands a presentation more labored, yet it is at least clear. Philosophical authorship — that highest kind, because its mission is to *mould public opinion*, not to beguile a passing hour — should select the precise words required, yet not be florid. Striving mainly to render these works thoroughly *scientific*, a transcript from Nature, and an epitome of her human laws and facts, the Author has treated each subject concisely, and adopted a style mainly Saxon, more perspicuous than ornamental, laconic than diffuse, and direct than figurative; aiming mainly to convey the most thought possible in the fewest words, and laboring chiefly on its *subject-matter*, for which thank Phrenology. To make his ideas easily understood, and then to *brand them right into* the innermost consciousness of every reader, *hic labor, hoc opus est*. Every page was written to *do good*, and render every observant reader ever afterwards the better and happier, more successful, talented, and virtuous.

May they enable and inspire many fellow-mortals to so study and obey the laws of that one life entity conferred upon them as to redouble, many fold, all the powers and pleasures of their entire beings, throughout the infinite cycle of their terrestrial and celestial existence.

EXPLANATION.

To enable the Author to refer his readers from every part of each volume to all parts of all the volumes, without repetition, he gives each subject, principle, topic, thought, and idea presented, a numbered sub-head, to which he refers by those raised figures, called superiors, found throughout the text. Thus the idea that "Man is the Epitome of Nature," is numbered 2, and referred to by inserting 2 thus [2]. And often the first words of paragraphs will express their subject-matter.

Though each volume, section, and idea presented is complete in itself, and can be fully understood without making these references, yet each and all will be reimpressed by making them, which can be done easily by reading with the left hand kept on the "Contents."

GENERAL INTRODUCTION.

1. — NATURE IS INFINITELY SACRED, PERFECT, AND BEAUTIFUL.

ALL THE ATTRIBUTES AND WORKS of her Divine Author she embodies. Her laws are imperatively binding upon all His creatures, because they are the perpetual reiteration of His eternal commands. To obey *them* is to fulfil His imperial edicts, while their violation is rebellion against Him. *Thus saith God in Nature*, is paramount authority. To be her apostle is our highest vocation, and the acme of all learning, all goodness, and all piety. Let the study, obedience, and exposition of her holy ordinances constitute our chief delight, and persuading others to· "do likewise," employ tongue and pen, by night and day, in public and private, always and forever!

Is not Nature likewise the embodiment of all *truth?* for what is truth but the soul of Nature? and what is Nature but the incarnation of truth? Let us then learn universal truth at her sacred shrine.

Is she not also beauty personified? What beauties equal those of her flower-spangled lawns and star-spangled skies, of her vegetables and fruits, her birds and animals, her men and women, unless it be her higher beauties of poetry and song? of character and mind? Indeed, what *but* Nature is beautiful, or perfect, or altogether lovely, except her infinitely perfect Author? Then let us adorn and perfect ourselves by admiring and imitating her varied and exhaustless ranges of beauties and perfections, and worship her Author by following His will as expounded through her.

2. — MAN IS THE EPITOME OF NATURE.

Every law and fact of matter, every mechanical device, principle, and execution throughout the entire vegetable and animal kingdoms, every single want and instinct, faculty and function, indeed *everything, everywhere* in Nature, is

2

found embodied and perfected in him. Is "configuration" a primal element inherent in matter? and is not man endowed with a form the most superb and beautiful on earth? Are not magnitude and "divisibility" properties of both matter and of man? Color is a quality of Nature; but what colors lighted up by the god of day bear any comparison with those of the glowing, blushing maiden? Surely those of neither flowers, fruits, birds, nor animals. What terrestrial lusciousness or loveliness is half as luscious or lovely, as human children and the feminine graces and virtues? What adaptations throughout Nature bear any comparison with those of man in constructive skill, or in their marvellous efficiency? Is Nature poetical, and is not man likewise enamoured of poetry and song? Is Nature resistless in her winds and tides, her lightnings and earthquakes, and does not man harness both winds and tides into his triumphal car, and make the "forked lightning" his telegraphic messenger and page? What can stand before his tremendous power and energy? Does gravity govern matter, and does it not equally govern him? Is the arch a principle in mechanics, and is it not the *double* arch incorporated into the human feet and hands, ribs and skull? Is man poetical, and is not Nature *all* poesy? What instinct, animal or vegetable, but is wrought into his constitution? In short, "all Nature struggles to be man;" while man is the compendium of all that is. In fact, human life is that one grand *ultimate,* towards which universal Nature, throughout all her laws and facts, converges — an end how infinitely great and glorious?

3. — MAN IS THE EPITOME OF HIS MAKER.

"God created man *in His own image,* and after His own likeness." Is God infinitely merciful and benevolent, and is not man endowed with the milk of human kindness? Is God infinitely just and retributory, and is not this element also incorporated into man? Do not both sit in judgment? Is God unchangeable "from everlasting to everlasting," and is not persistency also a powerful human attribute? Are dignity and power Divine attributes, and are they not also human? What care, what loving tenderness equals that bestowed by doting parents on idolized children, unless it be that infinite parental kindness of the "Father of all" to all the children of His creative hand? Is God the great first Cause, and is not man profound in both casuistry, and the adaptation of ways and means to the attainment of ends? In short, every human attribute is a divine one, and every divine attribute, as far as finite mortals can discern, is inherent in man; so that human science, by unfolding the crowning work of our great Creator, expounds all His other works, together with all His attributes. How wonderfully perfect are all the parts of our entire being individually? Yet how incomparably more so are the specific adaptations of each and of all to each other, and of all collectively, to those grand and glorious RESULTS, functions, and enjoyments, of which our being, when fully developed, is capable? And since every part of man is adapted to all the parts and all the principles of Nature, and they to him, to learn man fully is to know all things, because all that is culminates in him.

ANTHROPOLOGY thus becomes universal *Philosophy* and universal *Theology*, and therefore, as far exceeds all other studies as man is superior to animal, vegetable, and thing.

4. — PHRENOLOGY ANALYZES MAN'S MIND.

THE HUMAN MIND is the ultimate end and goal of man, and of all things terrestrial; so that mental science constitutes the embodied summary of all science. To study it, is to study all things, besides being our only way to learn how to live aright. It is the philosopher's crucial test of all doctrines, all practices, ethical, moral, religious, social, educational, commercial, and governmental, and the summary of universal humanity in all conditions, climes, and centuries.

Phrenology alone enables us to identify, analyze, and ramify each of the constituent faculties of this mind, together with all their outworkings, by demonstration, by sight and touch, by admeasurement — that absolute test of truth.

As a *system* of mental philosophy, it alone is at all worthy of that exalted name. Though mental science has engrossed the profoundest researches of the mightiest intellects of the whole human family, before and since Aristotle, yet its last succeeding apostle demonstrates the utter fallacy of all his predecessors, only in turn to be overthrown by his successors, till Phrenology furnished the first clear and correct analysis of the primary mental faculties, and their laws and modes of action, ever promulgated; besides being easily and completely comprehended by child as well as savan.

"Phrenology appears to me to bear the same relation to the doctrines of even the most recent metaphysicians, which the Copernican astronomy bears to that of Ptolemy." — *Robert Chalmers.*

"Even if all connection between the brain and the mind were chimerical, the treatises of Phrenologists would be of great value from their furnishing a *metaphysical nomenclature* far more logical, accurate, and convenient than Locke, Stewart, and the other writers of their schools." — *Archbishop Whateley.*

Scores of other deep thinkers equally attest that this science furnishes the only tangible and lucid exposition of the mental faculties and functions ever propounded.

5. — MIND CAN BE STUDIED ONLY THROUGH ITS ORGANS.

Man is compounded of both mind and body, each acting only in and by means of the other. Beyond all question, ORGANISM is Nature's sole medium for both exercising the mind, and manifesting that action; and its organic relations constitute the controlling conditions of its action, as well as the only means of all life.

Mind and body should therefore be studied *together*, and in view of their *mutual* inter-relations. If they acted independently, they might be studied separately; but Nature, by establishing perfect co-operation between them, compels their *conjoint* investigation. So that the mind can be studied scientifically and practically only from the stand-point of its organism, as subservient to mentality, and as manifesting and modifying its action.

Heretofore man has been studied only by piecemeal. The anatomist has studied him structurally merely; the physiologist functionally simply; the metaphysician only psychologically; the theologian solely ethically; while all have overlooked or ignored the influences wielded by the bodily conditions over the mental, and the mental over the physical. They write and lecture as if no such natural laws existed. The mind has indeed been elaborately discussed *per se,* as if it were some vague, detached, ethereal entity, but, excepting by Phrenologists, it has never been treated as if it were affected by any organic conditions whatever; while physicians have constantly studied bodily ailments as if unaffected by mental states. Does Carpenter — do other physiological authors or lecturers — tell us WHAT bodily conditions induce given mental? or how to produce desirable intellectual or moral states by superinducing their corresponding organic conditions? Yet a knowledge of this reciprocal action is about the only practical advantage to be derived from this class of studies. Thus diet, breathing, exercise, the temperaments, health, disease, and all the other physical conditions, are far less important in *themselves*, than in their effects on our *virtues, vices, talents*, and *morals*. This marked omission in other works, Phrenology supplies, and it is here expounded.

6. — PHRENOLOGY IS MAN'S GREAT REFORMER AND SELF-PERFECTER.

Man was created just as perfect as the highest exercise of *all* the Divine atributes could possibly render him. Hence, all he requires in order to live a perfect life, is to live a *natural* one; for a normal life must needs be just as perfect as its original constitution. Hence a thorough knowledge of Human Nature in general, and especially of our own selves, becomes an absolutely indispensable prerequisite for living a natural, and therefore a perfect life. Instinct, if unperverted, might indeed guide us aright, but it is so generally perverted as oftenest to mislead. Yet were it actually perfect, should we not superadd wisdom? Fact and philosophy, conjoined with intuition, should be our constitutional pole star.

Now Phrenology analyzes man just as God made him. It unfolds him as he came forth pure and perfect from his Maker's divine hands; thereby showing all communities, all individuals, just how far and wherein they may have departed, in any particular respect, from this standard of perfection, besides likewise pointing out the pathway of return. Moreover, every single individual, all the way along up from the very cradle, perpetually requires some ultimate *tribunal*, some standard text-book, always at hand, to show just what should, and should not, be done in all matters affecting his present and future well-being. Now Phrenology furnishes this standard, by showing just what is right, and will therefore render happy, as well as what is wrong, and will cause misery, thus: Wherein, and as far as this, that, or the other doctrine, action, or feeling *accords* with the proper exercise of any of our phrenological faculties or functions, it is right, and will yield happiness; but wherein and as far as it *violates* any, it is wrong, and will inflict suffering.

SELF-CULTURE should also be the one great life-work of every single individual, and improving children the next. To render ourselves and them just as perfect men and women as possible, *pays* a larger dividend than any other labor or investment whatever, and is our *paramount* duty to ourselves, mankind, and God.   Yet all personal and juvenile improvement presupposes a correct *model* after which to pattern, without which all self-perfecting and educational efforts, like striking in the dark, must necessarily prove abortive, or else injurious.   Phrenology both furnishes such a standard, and likewise teaches each and all just wherein and how far their own and children's characters and conduct depart from, or conform to, this model; points out the specific excellences and defects of each one; shows what faculties are excessive and need restraint, what are deficient and require cultivation, and especially, which they are exercising *wrongly*, and need to rectify; as well as just what will stimulate and tone up defective, and how to offset and compensate for excessive, faculties.

UTILITY being the final tribunal of all things, and the only measure of their value, since Phrenology thus becomes by far the most *useful* of all modern discoveries, this application of it to human weal becomes commensurately valuable.

7.— LIFE MUST BE INVESTIGATED AS ONE GREAT WHOLE.

Since life consists in a great *variety* of faculties, functions, and organs, all interwoven together, and each, as in a complicated machine, dependent upon all the others, studying its *individual* departments,— anatomy, physiology, mentality, &c.,— furnishes but partial and sometimes erroneous views of it *as a whole.*   To obtain anything like a complete knowledge of him, it becomes indispensable that his constitution be studied in its COLLECTIVE capacity.   He must be known, not by sections, but as a UNIT; for in no other way can the reciprocal bearings and complex inter-relations of the multifarious laws of his being be understood.   How useless, how imperfect is a knowledge of anatomy, unless accompanied by that of both the physiology and the mentality! And the latter two without the former! And the latter without both the others! As in the body the lungs cannot be understood without studying the muscles, nor either independently of the brain, heart, viscera, &c.; so all the mental powers must be investigated, as they are ordained to act, in *concert* with all the others. Thus how could reason be investigated independently of those functions it was created to guide and govern? or *any* faculty by itself alone? The very attempt is preposterous, and must prove futile. This existing sectional mode of studying man deserves severe rebuke, while that UNITARIAN method of conducting this study proposed in these volumes merits public attention. All past and present fractional attempts to expound and improve humanity have signally failed, because devoted one to one and others to other sets of bodily organs and functions, or one to one, and another to some other doctrinal aspect of theology, or politics, or marriage, or education, or diet, &c. It is as if a fly, in one obscure corner of this great temple of life, were discussing its narrow corner of some one room among all of the thousands of the apartments which comprise this magnificent structure of humanity, yet none even attempting 'to present its outline as one great *totality.* To present this *embodied* aspect of human life throughout all its multifarious aspects and inter-relations, is the august object here attempted. How sublime the conception! and how infinitely desirable to every human being is its execution!

Since our theme is infinite, of course no finite mind can do it full justice. One might well feel abashed in making such an attempt, — in entering where angels should hardly dare to tread; but *some* one must at least *try,* for the entire race, in its every individual, if not making a complete wreck of this most precious entity existence, is falling almost infinitely below its inherent enjoyments and attainments, just for want of that COLLECTIVE knowledge of its elements, laws, and right management here attempted. The natural starting point of such an undertaking is

8. — The Physical Man.

The body, with its physical organs and functions, though not the man, as will yet be shown, is nevertheless the only medium for the terrestrial *manifestation* of life, and thereby becomes its neglected "chief corner-stone." How important this *base* of life and all its functions is, we shall soon see.[23] Appropriately, therefore, the exposition of life should begin with its material organs — with the science of *physical* life; with HEALTH, its laws, organs, faculties, functions, conditions, preservation, restoration, &c.; not only *per se*, as it is usually considered, but also as affecting and promoting each and all our *mental* capacities and functions. While treatises on health, as such, are valuable, how much more useful would they become if they showed how, by a right management of health, to modulate, purify, and enhance every single power and function of the mind? To this fundamental subject we consecrate the first of these volumes on life.

9. — Phrenology as analyzing the Mental Elements.

THE EXEGESIS, the *analysis* of things, is the most important fact concerning them; for by conveying a clear understanding of their *nature*, it unfolds all their relations, laws, right and wrong modes of action, and in fact whatever appertains to them.

Now Phrenology analyzes all the *primary faculties* of the human mind, those *originators* of all we desire, do, feel, and think, those *creators* of all our specialties, talents, and capabilities, those *constituents* of life, and everything human. They are those *springs* from which the river of life ushers forth. Their analysis alone analyzes the mind, and shows what life is, as well as how all its parts should be exercised.

In short, Phrenology is one of the *natural sciences* — the natural science of man in general, and of the human *mind* in particular. If, therefore, the study of nature is interesting and useful, then must the study of this her highest department, man's mind, be as much more so as its subject-matter surpasses all else terrestrial.

The works of Gall, Spurzheim, and Combe, are each valuable contributions to the sum total of human knowledge. Those who have not studied them are mere tyros in a knowledge of man. Though science is the same "from everlasting to everlasting," yet its *discoveries* are progressive. Since the death of these phrenological fathers many important discoveries have been made, at least in the *applications* of this science to human improvement. It is due that a new work, embodying all especially valuable in the older works, should superadd these recent advancements, and give a complete view of this science *as it now is*. Such a work would prove a *blessing to mankind without a peer.*

The second volume of this series attempts to supply this public want of a modern work on this subject. What the Author knows about Phrenology he embraces in these volumes, devoting VOLUME II. expressly to the exposition of this science *as such.*

10. — MAN'S SEXUAL AND FAMILY RELATIONS

Constitute as integral a department of his nature as gravity. God *sexes* every living thing He makes. "*Male and female* creates He" every worm and insect, fish and fowl, beast, and human being, throughout all His creative cycles.

This sexual element is no trifle. It was not ordained for nought. Instead, it embodies the only reproductive instrumentality of this entire universe. Undoubtedly new worlds are perpetually springing into existence throughout the boundless fields of space, generated by this element, just as it is peopling each of these worlds with all forms of individual life. But for gender, inexorable Death would, in one generation, lay waste all the domains of universal space and being. And you and I, O man, woman, child, and every living thing, owe our existence, together with all our capacities to enjoy and accomplish, immortality even superadded, to this sexual department of Nature.

By thus creating all either a male or female, and thus incorporating these masculine or feminine attributes into, and ramifying them throughout our whole beings, mental as well as physical, God *commands* us to exercise them, and to exercise them *right;* that is, in accordance with those natural laws of gender which He has instituted for their government.

This requires that we *understand* these laws, so that we may govern ourselves by them, and avoid violating them.

3

As by creating us with an eating nature, He requires that
we eat, and eat right, but not wrong; so by creating us a
male or a female, He commands every man and woman to
learn and fulfil the masculine or feminine *natural laws.*

THE GREAT SIN AND EVIL of the race originate, not in total
depravity, but in *ignorantly* violating Nature's *sexual institutes,*
which knowledge on this subject would obviate.

ALL THE DOMESTIC VIRTUES and enjoyments spring from this
same tap-root; so that sexual science teaches each individual
when and whom to marry, as well as how to conduct all
the conjugal and parental relations aright, throughout every
minute particular, besides forestalling all of those alienations,
infidelities, and vices, which originate in ignorance of this
subject.

OUR INNATE CONSTITUTION governs our character and talents,
virtues and vices, enjoyments and sufferings, together with
all there is of life, a thousand fold more than education, and
all surrounding conditions whatsoever. *How we were begotten
and born* mainly predetermines whatever appertains to us.

Hence, immeasurably the best way to improve mankind
consists in improving his *nativity.* These *ante*-natal conditions
affect us and our offspring a thousand times more than all
post-natal influences combined. Then, O prospective parents, as you would have children *worthy* of your whole-souled
affections and efforts, learn how to *start* their existence upon
the highest possible plane of physical and mental vigor and
morality. And ye philanthropists, intent on elevating humanity, go up to this *fountain.* First make good this *spring* of
existence, then shall its outgushings all through life be good
also. Is it not passing strange that a subject of such tran-
scendent importance has been so long overlooked, and even
tabooed?

VOLUME III. is consecrated to this sacred theme. Let the
following, from its preface, state its object:—

" Reader, go none of *these* subjects right *home* to the very heart's *core*
of your inner *life?* Have you no masculine or feminine nature to study,
direct, nurture, enjoy, or recuperate? Have you neither a conjugal mate,
nor any tender yearnings for some loved one to inspire hope, incite to
effort, share life's joys and sorrows, and tread with you the pathways
of earth and heaven? Have you no children, and no wish for any, to
inherit your mentality and physiology, as well as patrimony? to do and
care for, and to care and do for you? to close your eyes in death, and

after it to repeat your virtues? In fine, are you listless, aimless, forlorn *drift*-wood, left by the retiring current of time, sinking and decaying in the mire of inanity, none caring for you, and you for none? for if not all these, and much more, then should the subject-matter of this volume stir your soul to its innermost depths, and sweep whatever life-chords remain unpalsied within you. Nothing else lies quite as near the focal centre of human existence as do our *affections*, and this treatise shows all how to derive from them the most enjoyment possible, with the least suffering. It is a thoroughly scientific and purely philosophical work on this whole subject of man's domestic, social, sexual, and parental constitution and relations.

"Special attention is invited to its three great points — the mighty power wielded by gender and love over man, and especially woman, to Nature's reproductive . institutes, and to sexual preservation and restoration."

In short, RIGHT SEXUAL DOCTRINES and practices create a very large proportion of human virtue and happiness, while most of man's vices and miseries originate in wrong sexual and domestic ideas and usages; so that the true sexual THE-OLOGY, so to speak, becomes as immeasurably important to mankind as are sexual purity and power to individuals, and right family relations to communities.

Yet who but phrenologists have ever treated this subject scientifically or practically, by showing inquirers how either to form or conduct these relations aright? A lyceum lecture on marriage, lauded as if really a great original, is at last found, on being epitomized, to consist in portraying the evils of celibacy, the sacredness and advantages of wedlock, the superiority of a good domestic wife over a fashionable one, and like general platitudes, but without one single principle to guide to its correct formation or management. A million like it would never teach a single matrimonial candidate either how to make a right marital. selection, or evolve mutual affection, or how to derive from a given marriage the greatest amount of good, and the smallest sum of evil possible. And yet these heart-core problems, of the gravest practical importance to all who contemplate marriage, are solved in this work.

Beginning with gender, it analyzes the male and female *elements*, expounding all their mutual inter-relations, "woman's rights" included, discusses love, its laws, facts, and effects on human life and character, from its first dawnings to its marital consummation, including selection, or

20 PHYSIOLOGICAL SCIENCE.

mutual adaptation, showing who can and cannot live affectionately together, and why; follows with courtship and married life, their errors and right management, so as to render all loves and marriages only happy; and "reproduction," or the creation, carriage, birth, nursing, and rearing of children, to puberty; and closes with sexual restoration and female beauty, its analysis and perpetuity included; thus furnishing the only complete and scientific treatise on this entire range of sexual, affectional, domestic, and family subjects ever promulgated. ·And all from the stand-point of man's social *faculties* and sexual *constitution.* What public problem is equally important? Its *completeness,* as covering this entire sexual subject, from its Alpha to its Omega, is one of its excellences. It is, as its title implies, an elaborate treatise on "SEXUAL SCIENCE."

11. — RELIGIOUS SCIENCE.

MORAL TRUTH touching the being and attributes of God, natural theology, immortality, its proofs, conditions, relations to time, future rewards and punishments, &c., constitutes another great section of humanity, and range of problems. Yet all is chaotic uncertainty throughout this whole field of religious dogmatism. Men are rushing to and fro, half delirious, with these and kindred inquiries:—

"Did all that is, come by chance? or exists there, in very truth, a God, the Great Creator and Governor of this magnificent universe? And if a God exists, what of His attributes, laws, government, works, worship, and the allegiance due from man to his Maker? That is, *What is the true* THEOLOGY?"

"Is death our last? or is man indeed immortal? And if so, what of that immortality? Are this life and that to come antagonistic? And if so, should we sacrifice the pleasures of this life on the altar of the best interests of that, or those of that for those of this? Or are both states so inter-related that whatever promotes or curtails the pleasures of either, thereby similarly affects the other also? And if so, then *what* life is best for us, both here and hereafter?"

"Is man totally depraved by nature? And if so, has this depravity any antidotes or palliatives? Must he be born again? What of Faith, Prayer, Worship, Rites, Forgiveness, &c.?"

These and like problems, O man, which have puzzled the race throughout all ages, are among the most practically important mankind can ever ask or answer, because there impinge upon them eventualities so much farther reaching and more momentous than upon any others whatsoever, that it becomes us, as intelligent, self-interested beings, to obtain answers so absolutely reliable that we can well afford to live and die by them. Religion has engrossed human attention ever since long before Confucius, Moses, the Parsees, Brahmins, Druids, Christ, Mohammed, Luther, etc., until now, with less and still less prospect of any reliable or generally conceded doctrines or practices. How much has been written, preached, printed, said, thought, and felt respecting mythology, the Bible, Koran, sectarianism, infidelity, etc.?

Then, is man indeed doomed to religious uncertainty forever? By no means. Exist there any natural moral *formula*, or fundamental principles, by which to test religious doctrines, creeds, and conduct? Most assuredly there does.

But where can we *find* answers and formulas thus reliable? *In the structure of the human* MIND. Since man is the epitome of all that is,[2] the grand summary of the universe, and since the human mind is the ultimate end of all things,[4] and therefore adapted to everything else in nature; therefore if there is a God, and if man is immortal, the mind of man will be adapted to both. And if it is thus adapted, they of course exist.

But where can we find this mind so expounded as to solve these and like problems scientifically? for religious truth is just as demonstrable as any other.

In and by the science of PHRENOLOGY. Its analysis of the mental faculties expounds all their adaptations and dependencies, together with all those ranges of truths they involve. In short, man's mind is the storehouse of all truth, religious included, which Phrenology unlocks, and which this volume applies to its moral and religious elucidation. Its Author understands both this science, and that subject of religion to which he thus applies it. Its line of argument discusses the following among many kindred subjects: —

Man is created with moral and religious faculties. This his religious department must have its laws, which render religion one of the natural and demonstrable sciences. Religious truth is the same throughout all times and places. Hence the thousand and ten conflicting religious creeds and sects prove that all but one are wrong. The location of these moral organs on the top of the head proves that their faculties control human character and destiny, and should be supreme in conduct; while their joining the reasoning organs shows that both should be exercised *together*, not by proxy, but by every one being his *own* priest.

VENERATION, the centre organ of this group, worships a Supreme Being; therefore a God exists, adapted to this worshipping instinct. All are born with it, and therefore bound to exercise it in worshipping their Creator. Devotion yields man his richest pleasures, besides sanctifying all his other enjoyments. Promoting piety by studying God in His works, and obeying His natural laws. Loving Him renders us like Him. Analysis of the Divine attributes. Prayer benefits us, not Him. How it is answered. Religious creeds, rites, the Sabbath, etc. Sects accounted for. A new sect proposed. The true theology.

SPIRITUALITY proves immortality. This mental faculty adapts man to it. The law of progress, general and individual. Age ripens, improves, and spiritualizes. Death as proving a futurity. The life to come is but a continuation of this. All we do and are here affects us forever, just as youthful conduct does all after-life. Memory never forgets, but is "fact-tight." Life is a system of causes which produce eternal effects. Little things are most eventful. What causes here produce what effects there. Phrenology furnishes an infallible guide to the best life here and there.

CONSCIENTIOUSNESS. Right and wrong are *inherent*, and created by natural laws. Obedience to them is a divine duty, infinitely obligatory on all. Right rewards, wrong punishes, irrespective of faith, prayer, or persons. Christians should obey the natural laws. Use of punishment. All evil causes good. Penitence demands and implies forgiveness, as well as stops further sin and suffering. The teachings of Phrenology as compared with those of Christ. Summary application of this whole subject, etc.

In fine, man's *moral constitution* is that chit, from which emanate the tap-root and rootlets, the trunk, bark, branches, twigs, leaves, and fruit of all religious emotions, actions, and doctrines. Whatever it teaches is divine truth, and infinitely obligatory on all, because it thus becomes a fundamental part of our very being; whilst all other teachings are so strongly tinctured with the errors and prejudices of their individual authors as to be unreliable. Now Phrenology, by analyzing man's moral faculties, discloses a complete *system* of NATURAL THEOLOGY, by showing just what his moral nature is, and thereby what it teaches, and Volume IV. unfolds religious truth from this, the highest of all platforms.

Should not the purely scientific discussion of these and analogous subjects from the standpoint of the structure of the human mind, command the attention of Christian, savant, infidel, and all?

12. — INTELLECTUAL SCIENCE.

The analysis of all the intellectual faculties, of the senses, memory, reason, judgment, etc., and their culture, together with mental discipline, schooling, self-education, etc., occupy Volume V. MIND controls matter. INTELLECT should be installed supreme judge and lord over all human actions and feelings. *Knowledge* is power, and *reason* is man's constitutional guide and governor in all things. Those alone may justly exult who elect *sense* as their President. *Mental discipline* is man's highest attainment, because it crowns all others. Teaching men the natural laws, and the consequences of their obedience and infraction, enlists their very *self-interest* in leading right lives. Whatever *disciplines the intellect* improves the individual and community more than all else.

MEMORY is one of man's most valuable possessions. What *rent* could a lawyer, a business man, a scholar, everybody well afford to pay, to be enabled to recall and apply to any case in hand *all he ever knew?* How many daily losses are consequent on a poor memory, which a good one would convert into gains? REASON is still more valuable, while eloquence and the other intellectual endowments are scarcely less so.

A RIGHT EDUCATIONAL PHILOSOPHY is also immeasurably important. Parents annually expend millions of money along with untold anxieties in scholastic education, without any guiding first *principles,* often even killing their darlings by well-meant but ill-directed efforts, actually making them *worse* while attempting to make them better. All parents need some text-book to teach them how to eradicate the faults and develop the virtues of those thus near and dear to them, as well as how to make them the best possible.

All adults also need scientific directions for *self*-education — the only kind of real value — yet can nowhere find them, because they presuppose an analytical exposition of each of the intellectual *faculties,* which Phrenology alone gives to perfection. To analyze and show how to cultivate each and all our intellectual capacities, accomplishments, and talents, musical, conversational, scientific, and all others, as well as how to conduct self-education and mental culture in general, including the scholastic education of children, is this work written. It both discloses the true educational *system,* and shows how to accelerate our own and children's intellectual advancement many times faster than can be done by present methods. •

13. — PHRENOLOGY EXPOUNDS HUMAN SCIENCE THROUGHOUT ALL ITS ASPECTS.

LIFE HAS ITS SCIENCE. As mathematics, astronomy, anatomy, vegetation, gravity, and every other department of Nature has each its own "exact science;" so has life. It, equally with them, forms an integral part of Nature, and is as much regulated by those *natural laws* which render all they govern both exact and scientific. As the science of astronomy unfolds the laws and facts of the heavenly bodies, so Phrenology unfolds the laws and facts of life, its faculties, functions, organs, conditions, &c.; and this science is as exact as any other; only that since life is the ultimate of all things, and human life the climax of all life, of course its science is as much more complicated and ramified than they, as human life is more exalted than inert matter.

All these, and all other subjects appertaining to man, Phrenology expounds in the broadest aspect of their first principles, as well as in their minute details, besides applying that exposition to all the every-day affairs of life. It must, therefore, soon become the great study of the entire race, and so remain till "time shall be no longer."

Some standard work on this Science of Man, which shall thus expound and apply it throughout, becomes the greatest possible benefaction to the whole human family, and deserves to be *studied* as well as read. These infinitely important ends and objects, these works attempt to accomplish.

Well might even an archangel falter before so vast an undertaking, were not the lights shed by Phrenology distinct and luminous. Claiming no extraordinary ability for this labor of love, and supplicating "aid from on high," the Author consecrates to it all the energies of his entire being.

LIFE:

ITS SCIENCE, LAWS, FACULTIES, FUNCTIONS, ORGANS, CONDITIONS, PHILOSOPHY,

AND

IMPROVEMENT:

INCLUDING THE

ORGANISM, HEALTH, SOCIAL AFFECTIONS, MORAL SENTIMENTS, INTELLECT, MEMORY, SELF-EDUCATION, AUTOBIOGRAPHY, MISCELLANY, &C.,

AS TAUGHT BY

PHRENOLOGY.

IN SIX VOLUMES.

I. Physiological Science.
II. Phrenological Science.
III. Sexual Science.

IV. Religious Science.
V. Intellectual Science.
VI. Autobiography and Miscellany.

BY

PROF. O. S. FOWLER,

PRACTICAL PHRENOLOGIST; LECTURER; FORMER EDITOR OF "THE AMERICAN PHRENO-
LOGICAL JOURNAL;" AUTHOR OF "FOWLER ON PHRENOLOGY;" ON "PHYSIOLOGY;"
"SELF-CULTURE;" "MEMORY;" "RELIGION;" "MATRIMONY;" "OFFSPRING, AND
THEIR ENDOWMENT;" "HEREDITARY DESCENT;" "LOVE AND PARENT-
AGE;" "MATERNITY;" "AMATIVENESS;" "SEXUAL SCIENCE," "TEM-
PERANCE;" "THE SELF-INSTRUCTOR;" "HOME FOR ALL;"
"CHEAP CISTERNS," "ANSWERS TO HAMILTON,
VINDEX," &C., &C.

WHAT IS LIFE?

BOSTON:

PUBLISHED BY O. S. FOWLER,
514 TREMONT STREET.

CONTENTS.

PHYSIOLOGICAL SCIENCE.

CHAPTER I.

THE FUNDAMENTAL PRINCIPLES OF LIFE.

SECTION I.

VALUE AND IMPROVEMENT OF LIFE.

i

Section II.
Ventilation, its Necessity, Means, &c.

CHAPTER III.
FOOD; ITS NECESSITY, SELECTION, MASTICATION, DIGESTION, APPROPRIATION, AND EXCRETION.

Section I.
Necessity and Office of Food.

Section II.
Is Man naturally Graminivorous, or Omnivorous?

Section III.
The Preparation of Food by Cooking, &c.

Section IV.

How to Eat; or, Mastication, Quantity, Time, &c.

Section V.

The Digestive Process, and its Organs, the Stomach, Liver, Pancreas, &c.

CHAPTER IV.

FLUIDS; THEIR NECESSITY, OFFICE, AND SUPPLY.

Section I.

Fluids; their Necessity, Offices, and Kinds; Cisterns, &c.

Section II.

Stimulating Drinks. — Alcoholic and Malt Liquors; Wine, Tea, Coffee, Lemonade, &c.

Section III.

Fluid Excretions.

Section IV.

The Blood, and its Circulation; the Heart, and its Structure.

Section V.

Animal Heat; its Manufacture, Distribution, and Exit.

Section VI.

The Skin, Perspiration, &c.

Section VII.

Sleep; its Necessity, Office, Amount, Time, Promotion, &c.

CHAPTER V.

THE MOTIVE AND MENTAL APPARATUS, AND FUNCTIONS.

Section I.

The Osseous and Muscular Systems.

Section II.

Exercise; its Value, best Modes, and the Lifting Cure.

CHAPTER VI.

RESTORATION FROM DISEASES.

SECTION I.

HYGIENE BETTER THAN MEDICINES.

SECTION II.

THE VARIOUS PATHIES; ALLOPATHY, HYDROPATHY, ELECTROPATHY,
BREATHING-PATHY, BATHING-PATHY, FOOD-PATHY, TERRA-PATHY,
SOLAR-PATHY, AND AN "UNKNOWN"-PATHY.

SECTION III.

CURES FOR SPECIAL AILMENTS.

GENERAL PREFACE.

A RIGHT LIFE constitutes incomparably the most exalted achievement and attainment possible to man or angel. *Just how to live*, is the master problem, as yet unsolved, of all individuals, and all communities, throughout all climes and ages. Its *scientific* solution and application to all the relations of life, therefore, immeasurably transcends all other human ends and acquisitions, because it embraces all knowledge, all virtue, and all enjoyment. What is right, and what wrong? what we ought to do here, and *not* to do there? and how we shall guide our steps aright throughout all the every-day affairs of life? are perpetually recurring questions, requiring specific answers in action every hour of life. All subjects whatsoever have their right side and their wrong; and a correct and infallible decision as to which is right, and which wrong, is infinitely important, because all virtue and enjoyment on the one hand, and all vice and misery on the other, eventuate therefrom. How to derive from life and its surroundings all possible enjoyments, and avoid all possible sufferings, is the very highest aspiration of self-love, and the first instinct of all that lives, and should constitute the one great personal inquiry of every intelligent being all through life. Hence, that scientific exposition of the natural laws and facts of human existence taught by man's organic relations, and their application to the happiness and virtue of individuals and communities here proposed, surpasses all other subjects in practical importance.

3.

PHRENOLOGY constitutes the teacher and text-book in this inquiry. Its discovery was by far the greatest, most profound and useful ever made, because this science unfolds creation's sublimest department, — *the* MIND, in which alone life inheres, — thereby seizing this problem of life at its very centre, and ramifying it throughout all its elements and their outworkings.

GALL, though he discovered the phrenological *fact* that each mental capacity manifests itself by means of one particular portion of the brain, called its organ, and that their different sizes, in different persons, cause and indicate the special talents and characteristics of each, as well as the location of most of the organs, yet he did little by way of developing its *science*, as such, or applying its doctrines to human improvement. Spurzheim, too, a close observer, and a deep thinker, added to Gall's discoveries, and made valuable applications of them to "education," &c.; while George Combe, a truly great man, and one of the profoundest reasoners of his own age, or of any other, superadded to the discoveries of both, besides applying them to "insanity," and several other important human interests; to which the Author has endeavored to contribute his mite in his works on "Phrenology," "Matrimony," "Self-Culture," "Memory," &c.

Yet these, and all its other applications, are only fragmentary; whereas the best interests of mankind demand a *comprehensive* and a *complete* exposition, not only of this science itself, including its history, faculties, organs, facts, combinations, &c., but likewise an application of its teachings to *all* the various departments of human life. To help supply this pressing public demand, are these volumes penned.

They describe the mental faculties in *five* different degrees of power, — *very large, full, average, moderate,* and *small,* — and show the different effects on character and conduct of their various COMBINATIONS, as causing that infinite *diversity* of disposition and talents existing among men — a new subject of great practical importance.

They also embrace all the works, writings, observations, and reflections of the Author, revised, enlarged, systematized, condensed, and embodied into one complete *series* of volumes, and presenting a summary of the results of almost *half a century* of his professional consultations, as applied to the distinguished personages of *four generations*, in *both hemispheres*, besides incorporating whatever is specially valuable from previous phrenological writings; thus becoming a *complete encyclopedia of whatever is known* respecting this science of man. It consists of exhaustive works on the following subjects: —

I. PHYSIOLOGICAL SCIENCE; or, HEALTH, its Value, Laws, Organs, Functions, Conditions, Preservation, Restoration, &c.

II. PHRENOLOGICAL SCIENCE; its Principles, Proofs, Temperaments, Cerebral Organs, Mental Faculties, Teachings, &c., as applied to Self-Culture. With a Steel Engraving of the Author.

III. SEXUAL SCIENCE; or, MANHOOD, WOMANHOOD, and their Mutual Inter-relations: LOVE, its Laws, Power, &c.; SELECTION, and Mutual Adaptation; COURTSHIP, or Love-making; MARRIED LIFE made Happy; REPRODUCTION, and Progenal Endowment, including Paternity, Maternity, Bearing, Nursing, and Rearing Children; PUBERTY; GIRLHOOD; SEXUAL AILMENTS Restored, and FEMALE BEAUTY Preserved and Regained, &c.

IV. RELIGIOUS SCIENCE; or, MAN'S MORAL NATURE and Relations, as proving the existence of a SUPREME BEING, and His Attributes, Philosophical Theology, &c.; IMMORTALITY, its Proofs, Conditions, and Relations to Time; NATURAL RELIGION, its Doctrines, Duties, &c.; Worshipping God in Nature, and by Obeying His Natural Laws; Future Rewards and Punishments; the Law of Love, "Faith," "Prayer," Rites, "Total Depravity," "Conversion," "Forgiveness," &c., as taught by Phrenology.

V. INTELLECTUAL SCIENCE; or, MEMORY, REASON, and their Culture; including "The Senses," Intellectual Faculties, Schooling, Self-Education, Mental Discipline, &c.

VI. AUTOBIOGRAPHY, Miscellaneous Writings, Quotations, &c. While all these volumes are derived directly from Phrenology, yet a belief in this science, though desirable, is no more indispensable to the appreciation and adoption of their glorious teachings, than is a knowledge of the origin of luscious fruits to the enjoyment of their delicious flavors and grateful nutrition; so that "non-communicants" are cordially invited to partake at this banquet, if, perchance, they may thus be induced to examine this science itself, which is founded in the eternal ordinances of Nature. At all events, let both it and its doctrines be tested by that touchstone of all truth, *sound common sense.*

OBJECTORS are generally treated with that "dignified silence" justly due to their ignorance or misrepresentations; because, expounding truth effectually refutes error; so that proving the *truth* of Phrenology brings all its objectors face to face with their MAKER, with whom we leave them to settle their cavils.

Would Galileo, would the discoverers or expounders of any great truth, advance it by wasting on its bigoted opponents those precious energies required for its promulgation?

Pseudo-discoveries antagonistic to those of Gall, are ignored, because his are substantially correct. The Author has practised on other theories enough to know that they are unreliable; whereas, a minute inspection of the phrenological "developments" of a *quarter of a million,* of all ages and of both sexes, warrants this our most positive declaration, derived from all our experimental observations, that Gall's locations and descriptions are substantially correct, so that all in conflict with his are wrong.

If the *authorship* of this august subject falls below what is possible and desirable, let successors — of predecessors there are none — supply omissions and make required improvements. A subject *thus* vast and momentous demands a presentation more labored, yet it is at least clear. Philosophical authorship — that highest kind, because its mission is to *mould public opinion*, not to beguile a passing hour — should select the precise words required, yet not be florid. Striving mainly to render these works thoroughly *scientific*, a transcript from Nature, and an epitome of her human laws and facts, the Author has treated each subject concisely, and adopted a style mainly Saxon, more perspicuous than ornamental, laconic than diffuse, and direct than figurative; aiming mainly to convey the most thought possible in the fewest words, and laboring chiefly on its *subject-matter*, for which thank Phrenology. To make his ideas easily understood, and then to *brand them right into* the innermost consciousness of every reader, *hic labor, hoc opus est*. Every page was written to *do good*, and render every observant reader ever afterwards the better and happier, more successful, talented, and virtuous.

May they enable and inspire many fellow-mortals to so study and obey the laws of that one life entity conferred upon them as to redouble, many fold, all the powers and pleasures of their entire beings, throughout the infinite cycle of their terrestrial and celestial existence.

EXPLANATION.

To enable the Author to refer his readers from every part of each volume to all parts of all the volumes, without repetition, he gives each subject, principle, topic, thought, and idea presented, a numbered sub-head, to which he refers by those raised figures, called superiors, found throughout the text. Thus the idea that " Man is the Epitome of Nature," is numbered 2, and referred to by inserting 2 thus [2]. And often the first words of paragraphs will express their subject-matter.

Though each volume, section, and idea presented is complete in itself, and can be fully understood without making these references, yet each and all will be reimpressed by making them, which can be done easily by reading with the left hand kept on the " Contents."

possibly *could* obtain from it, not merely by what we do derive.
None fully appreciate the enjoyments taken in eating; and yet who
receive from it a hundredth part as much as they could take if their
digestion were perfect and taste exquisite, and always regaled
with just what is relished best?

How much more pleasure could you *have* taken in your first
love, than you actually did take? Can the fledgling soar highest
or furthest at its *first* flight? Much as you actually did enjoy,
you took but a tithe of the joy you know you were capable of
experiencing. Your love barely began to be developed before it
was either blighted, or else turned into downright disgust. Suppose, instead, you had known, from the first, just how to perfect
this element; had chosen the very one above all others precisely
adapted to your specific tastes and wants, and each had done just
what was requisite to completely develop the other's affections,
besides forestalling all discordant feelings; had superadded all
the exquisite emotions of just your required number of beau-ideal
children; had possessed home and surroundings precisely to your
tastes, and neighbors exactly to your liking; had been honored
and trusted among men; possessed enough, but not too much,
of this world's goods; and completely developed and gratified
every single want, desire, and capacity of your entire being, all
the way along up from childhood; enjoyed all the books, teachers,
educational and literary advantages, lectures, conversation,
&c., requisite for your fullest intellectual cultivation; been an
honored member of your beau-ideal church; and every life-mo-
ment had been crowded with all those varied delights of which
your entire being, fully developed, is capable, and reincreasing
with years, how much could you *then* have enjoyed all through
life?

"Ah, if we could only always *remain* young. But palsied old age, and
that 'grim monster,' SPOIL this beautiful picture. What we enjoy at all,
must be enjoyed before seventy. After that, life is only dreary December."

Are you quite sure? Hear that cherub child shout with merry
glee. Why should not age increase his enjoyments *pari passu*
with his capacities? How happy is that tottering child in tottering! Yet is it not afterwards immeasurably happier in running
and gambolling? and happier still in athletic sports? and yet far

6

more so in the intellectual and moral pleasures of life's meridian?
and in its afternoon and evening than noonday? Some elderly
people grow happier as they grow older. Then why is not this
possible to all? Life's decline, in its calm, quiet, serene enjoyments and "dignified ease," can be happier than even the stalwart
strugglings of mature years, and these than childhood.

Beyond question, we are all adapted to be just as happy as
we can endure to be, happy almost to bursting, at least to overflowing, throughout every department of our entire being, all the
way along up from infancy through adolescence, maturity, and
old age, clear up — not down — to death. No imagination can
even begin duly to estimate either the number, the variety, or
the extent of life's enjoyments possible to us all. Possible? Ay,
inherent, and constitutional. In what a perfect paradise does
man's primitive constitution place him!

Yet what are all the actual and possible pleasures of *this* life
compared with those of the life to come? Immortality is no *ignis
fatuus.* "Religious Science" proves it to be an immortal reality,
and a necessary component of being; and that the powers and
enjoyments of the world to come as immeasurably surpass all
those of this life, as the ocean exceeds the rivulet!

But why mock our subject by these futile attempts to admeasure the actual and possible pleasures, and therefore value,
of existence? Only eternal *experience* can do it justice.

THE PURSUIT OF HAPPINESS, that first tap-root instinct of universal life, in which all other instincts originate, should therefore
constitute the paramount *life-study* and *object* of every human
being. How can I make myself and others the happiest, is the
sole problem of existence. Those lead the truest and best lives
who enjoy the most. Our duties and pleasures are identical.
Those who enjoy the most please their Creator the best, because
they best fulfil the specific mission of their creation. The Epi-
curean philosophy is the true one, — "Whilst we live, let us live."
Let us secure the fullest gratification of all our faculties, which
God created only to be gratified, but not to be denied. Let us
make every new day, hour, and moment of life one ceaseless round
of perpetual delight.

Let children be made just as happy as possible; for making
them happy develops their being, while whatever causes their

misery, injures their life-principle. Let young people be allowed
to make themselves just as happy as possible; because for this
alone were they created. God delights to see all His creatures
enjoy themselves.

The pious doctrine of self-denial and self-crucifixion outrages
every instinct, animal and human, and thwarts every primitive
end and adaptation, of universal being. It had its origin in sacri-
ficing human beings to appease the supposed wrath of infuriated
Jupiter, and later in animal sacrifices, of which it is the last relic,
and unworthy of enlightened human belief. It is, indeed, barbarous. Let those who advocate it duly consider the god they
worship.

"But your revolting doctrine contravenes all discipline of ourselves
and others, all restraints whatsoever, even all 'law and order,' and
throws wide open all the floodgates of all the passions and appetites;
besides paying a premium to unbridled lust, and unmitigated selfishness.
A worse doctrine, one more contrary to religion and public and private
good, could hardly be promulgated."

Indeed! Then has God made a great creative *mistake?* Has
He indeed blundered in creating this "master passion" for happiness, only to oblige each and all to "crush it out"?' Not He.
Must we war forever with this basillar principle and instinct of
life? this corner-stone, in fact, this foundation of all existence?
We shall yet make qualifications which completely obviate this
seemingly plausible objection. Suffice it here to give this general answer: —

"All *wrong* exercise of our passions and appetites causes misery.[20] Only their *right* exercise makes us happy.'[18] Thus, not
only gluttony, drunkenness, &c., but *all* wrong alimentary habits
impair future gustatory enjoyments. The highest enjoyment of
Alimentiveness is obtainable only by obeying its natural laws.
The highest, most exquisite, and only true amatory enjoyments
are to be found, not in unbridled sensualities, but in obeying the
sexual laws of *one* love in marriage, as shown in "Sexual Science,"
417 to 424. All other appetites and passions are governed by
this same law. Virtue is enjoyment, and enjoyment is virtue.
We should not seek the pleasures of to-day, but of a lifetime, and
that of life *eternal*. And yet those same conditions which cause
the highest happiness of to-day, also cause those of all after existence. Yet after doctrines specifically refute this objection."

17. — IMPROVING LIFE OUR PARAMOUNT DUTY AND SELF-INTEREST.

THE GREAT INQUIRY of old and young, each and all, from the cradle to the grave — *forever* — should therefore be, how can I make the uttermost *possible* out of a behest thus infinitely precious? How can I turn it to the best account? How derive from it all those rich and varied enjoyments of which it renders me capable? How so "invest" it as to obtain from it the greatest "income" of pleasure possible? Not only is no "income tax" levied on this income, but Nature rewards its improvement with the richest bounty possible to receive. Only one life-lease is granted us. It can have no substitute. This lost, our *all* is lost. Hence man never propounded, never answered any other question a thousandth part as practically important as — How can we derive the very utmost possible enjoyment from this life-entity, and escape all its miseries?

We instinctively strive to enhance whatever we consider valuable. As iu proportion to our estimate of property, reputation, &c., we seek to augment them; so should not our utmost exertions be directed towards promoting this life-force, that is, towards self-development? The value of life inheres in its functions, individually and collectively. Your eyes are the more or the less valuable in exact proportion to the amount of vision they put forth. If they could see as well again as now, they would be worth twice as much; or, if your visual powers should be diminished one half, their value would be equally lessened.

How MUCH then is your power to see worth? Ten thousand dollars? Would you be wise to accept that sum, on condition that you remain in total darkness till you die? Of course doubling the vigor and power of every individual function of the body doubles their value.

EVERY MENTAL capacity is governed by this law. How much would pay you to let your memory be blotted out forever? What sum of money could give you as much pleasure as does your power of recollection? Surely not ten times ten thousand dollars. Then doubling its efficiency would double its value, and make it worth more than two hundred thousand dollars. How much does that girl lose who loses her *virtue*, her moral purity, or he who loses a clear conscience for life? How much is your sense worth? How much could you afford to take, and be deprived of it forever? Dollars furnish but a miserably poor measure of the value of any of our mental capacities.

Then how much are they worth *collectively?* How much is each, how much are all of your mental capacities and virtues worth? Set your own estimate; and you cannot overrate either or all. A million pounds? Would you drive a sharp bargain by agreeing, on receipt of a million, to *cease to be?* Pray how much good would your million do you?

How much is your child worth to *you?* to its other parent? to grandparents, relatives, and mankind generally? Then how much to *its own self?* The fact is, the value of money, of diamonds, of every terrestrial good, is as nothing in comparison with that of life and its functions. All other values sink into insignificance when compared to the superlative value derived from improving each and all our life-functions.

ETERNITY awaits us. And all improvement, all deterioration, of ourselves in this life are translated with us to the other side of death, besides being immeasurably magnified thereby. Thus, a given amount of self-culture or self-deterioration here, becomes the means of a hundred or a thousand *fold* greater there. Of course this law applies with redoubled force to children and youth.

By whatever is sacred in life, death, and eternity, then, should we make the improvement of this life-entity our one great paramount work.

OUR FIRST DUTY to God and man centres in this same self-development. As children honor their parents the most effectually by perfecting themselves; so we "glorify our Father in heaven" in proportion as we purify and perfect our own selves.

Obviating our own faults, and improving our own excellences, likewise benefits our fellow-men more effectually than anything else we can possibly do to or for them.

In fine, self-interest, duty to God and man, love of happiness,[16] and all the great motives of existence, inspire the eventful inquiry, *How can this life-entity be improved?* Nature answers, "*By fulfilling its conditions.*" Then in what do they consist?

18. — LIFE AND ALL ITS FUNCTIONS GOVERNED BY NATURAL LAWS.

THE PARAMOUNT fact of all life obviously is, that every single one of all its functions, throughout all their phases, are governed by natural laws. In fact, universal Nature is thus governed, even down to every mote of matter throughout all its mutations, forever. The axiom, " Every effect has its specific cause, and every cause always produces its own legitimate effect," is but the summary fact of Nature, the governing condition of all things, and too apparent, as well as too generally admitted, to need proof or amplification.

SOME RATIONALE must needs call for this arrangement of the natural laws. Nothing exists for nought. Whatever is, has and must needs have, its *why and wherefore*. An institute of Nature thus universal and potential, must needs execute some great trust, some necessary work, some end every way *commensurate* with this cause and effect executor.

HAPPINESS is that end.[16] How could we be happy unless there pre-existed certain conditions which always result in happiness? If Nature were all haphazard and chaotic — if the same things gave us pleasure to-day but pain to-morrow — how could we render ourselves happy, or avoid becoming miserable? We could only passively enjoy or suffer whichever might *happen* to us. All efforts to render ourselves or others happy, or prevent misery, would be absolutely futile, and life itself worthless; so that Nature, in order to achieve her one great end,[16] must needs first pre-establish certain *rules*, which, when observed, secure enjoyment. In short, " law and order" must take the place of chaos; yet this would have been nugatory unless happiness *always* resulted from their observance.

At all events, such laws *do* exist, and enjoyment always *does* and necessarily must flow from their obedience, just as surely as water runs downwards. This is the first fact, the first condition, and the first lesson of life — is to it what the sun is to the earth.

These natural laws are the foundation and motive-power of all that is. In and by means of them alone do " we live, move, and have our being." They pervade, permeate, and govern all things. They originate all power, and then apply it to the production of all results. All science consists in them and their outworkings.

Thus the science of astronomy consists solely in those natural laws which govern the heavenly bodies, and their operations. The science of chemistry consists in those natural laws which govern this department of Nature, and their workings. This is equally true of each and all the other natural sciences. In fact all Nature is wholly *made up* of these natural laws and their operations. What would she be but for them? Only chaos personified. What ends does she accomplish except by their instrumentality? Absolutely none. They embody the live principle, and the quintessence of all that is, the binding power of all our duties and obligations to God and man, the means of all our enjoyments, and the soul of all goodness and philosophy.

ALL KNOWLEDGE likewise consists in a knowledge of these identical laws, and their effects. A knowledge of history is only a knowledge of what the laws which govern human nature are, and have effected. A knowledge of mathematics consists solely in understanding numerical laws and facts; and so of all the other sciences.

HE ALONE IS LEARNED, therefore, who knows these laws and their operations, though ignorant of ancient mythology and languages; while all who do *not* understand them are in that proportion practical ignoramuses, however good linguists, mythologists, &c., they may be. Even all art and all poetry are but the expression of these identical laws.

19. THEY EMBODY THE DIVINE WILL AND MANDATES.

ALL GOODNESS likewise consists in conforming to, and all badness in violating them; for they alone *constitute* all right, and their infraction creates all wrong. They are God's tribunal of whatever is right and wrong throughout His universe.

The Decalogue itself is indeed infinitely obligatory, yet not at all because issued amidst Sinai's thunderings and lightnings, but solely because it is a rescript of these natural laws, in which all right, and by converse, all wrong, inhere; whilst all other inherent rights and wrongs are no less binding because omitted in this moral formula. They constitute that *lex legum*, that "higher law," which declares what is virtuous and what vicious.

LOVE of these primal institutes of Nature should therefore be our first love. As we love our very being and our happiness, as we love God and His commandments, let us love these His edicts, written, not on tables of stone, but throughout all His universe, and interwoven into all our desires and instincts. If David could exclaim "O, how love I Thy" (Jewish) "commandments," much more should we all exclaim, perpetually, "O, how love I Thy Natural Laws! They are my meat and my drink. Whatever I enjoy, I enjoy through them alone. Their Author is my Author, and their commands are His eternal rules of action, sent out unto all he creates. Let all nurseries and legislative halls, all schools and colleges, all churches and human institutions, resound with these laws, and all whom God hath made, press all their energies into their fulfilment."

20. ALL PAIN IS CONSEQUENT ON THEIR VIOLATION.

PAIN EXISTS. It even constitutes as integral a department of Nature as happiness, besides embodying as mighty a moral; namely, to *compel* obedience to His laws. The pleasures attached to their fulfilment, though the most powerful incentive thereto which their divine Author could devise, embody only *half* His means of enforcing their obedience. He persuades us, by proportionate happiness, to obey them, but dissuades us from their disobedience by all those penalties He has attached to their violation. Pain is constitutionally abhorrent to man — is the only groundwork of all dislike. By an arrangement living back in his very nature, he instinctively and universally shrinks from it as from poison; as well as avoids its cause. He shuns only what occasions it, and for no other reason, and dislikes all things in PROPORTION to the pain they give him, as well as wholly because of such pain. Hence he instinctively avoids violating law, because such violation occasions that suffering which he dreads ; and seeks in obedience that pleasure to which he is constitutionally so powerfully attracted. To obey them is to be happy in and by means of such obedience, whereas to violate them is to incur proportionate misery. Our enjoyments admeasure our obedience, and our sufferings our transgressions. No man or woman, youth or infant, not even beast or reptile, can violate any one of them, anywhere or at any time, without suffering proportionate misery. Learned and ignorant, great and small, Christian and infidel, prince and peasant, stand alike amenable to them, and are equal

subjects of their rewards and punishments. They are "no re-
specters of persons." "Obey and be happy, or disobey and
suffer," is their universal watchword, throughout all times,
climes, and persons. They *will not be* trifled with, but are stern,
sovereign, and immovable; without fear, favor, or sympathy.
"Without sympathy?" By no means. Instead, they are sympathy personified. Their only intent and operation is to do good.
Their underlying *principle* is to promote happiness by promoting
obedience, and prevent subsequent suffering by preventing further
sinning. Their very inflexibility is notice to all *never* to trans-
gress them. If they ever gave an inch, man would take an ell;
hence they never deviate one hair's breadth.

TOM PAINE superficially argued that if the Deity is all-wise,
all-powerful, and all-good, He could and would have excluded
pain from this universe. He virtually argues, —

"How comes it that so many suffer all the misery they can endure
and yet live? Must we charge all this actual and possible suffering to
divine malignity? Has God missed His mark? or been thwarted and
outwitted by some cunning spirit of evil? or by 'total depravity?'
Have His benign plans miscarried? Why must man suffer all this?"
"To PROMOTE THEIR HAPPINESS."
"What? must Nature do evil that good may come? Must we suffer
in *order* to enjoy? This is like burning with ice, and freezing with fire;
like falling down in order to rise up; like blending natural antagonisms."

No, indeed. This is utterly impossible. Our world is, indeed,
full of suffering and woe ! Pandora's box, filled with all manner
of diseases and miseries, has been opened upon man ! He literally groans in agony ! Poverty, wretchedness, loathsome diseases, distressing sickness, the heart-rending decease of friends,
children, and companions, and even premature death itself, tearing
its victims from life and all its pleasures, torment most mankind !
Millions suffer beyond description, and millions of millions are or
have been tortured into the wish that they had never been born,
or that death, with all its horrors, would hasten to their relief;
while most consider our world, though so perfectly adapted to
promote human happiness, only a path of thorns, and life itself a
lingering, living DEATH !

And yet suffering forms no NECESSARY part of any constitutional
arrangement or function of man. Teeth are created and adapted
to masticate food, not to ache; nor need they ever. The stomach

7

is not made to occasion griping pains, nor in any way to distress us; nor the lungs to torture while they waste away in
lingering consumption, blasting all our hopes and happiness.
Neither malignant fevers, nor distressing rheumatism, nor torturing gout, nor loathsome life-eating cancers, nor any other kind or
degree of disease or suffering form any part of man's original
constitution, or of Nature's ordinances; but all are utterly repugnant to both.[16]

Was Benevolence created to torment us with the sight of
pain we cannot relieve? or Combativeness to brawl, quarrel,
and fight? or Destructiveness to devastate whole nations with
woe and carnage, making loving wives lonely widows, and happy
children desolate orphans, by the MILLION; besides all the horrors
of the battle-field itself? or Appetite to gormandize till it offers
up all that is virtuous and happy at the shrine of beastly gluttony
and drunkenness? or Approbativeness to pinch the feet of the
suffering Chinese, or flatten the head of the savage Indian, or
deform the waists of fashionable would-be beauties? or Self-
Esteem to wade through seas of blood to thrones of despotism?
or Veneration to create all the abominations of Paganism or the
bigotry of Christendom? or Constructiveness to make implements
of torture and death? or Acquisitiveness to cheat and rob? or
Causality to plot mischief and devise evil? or Adhesiveness to
mourn in hopeless grief the loss of near and dear friends? or
Parental Love to torture us with inexpressible anguish by the
death of a dearly-beloved child, or perhaps entire groups of beautiful and happy sons and daughters? or Connubial Love to weep
disconsolate and distracted at the grave of a dearly-beloved
wife, or devoted husband — perhaps after every means of support
has been exhausted, every child buried, every earthly hope
blasted, and while torturing disease preys upon life itself, and opens
the yawning grave at our feet? No, NEVER! Cold and heat are
not more antagonistic than these results are contrary to all Nature's adaptations. Nor is there a single physical organ, nor
mental faculty, nor human function, whose normal product is
pain, nor anything but pleasure. Any other doctrine contradicts
universal fact, attests the ignorance of its advocates, and libels
Infinite Goodness!

Even the devil himself, if a personal devil exists, must needs fulfil this same benevolent mission; for he can tempt *only* those who are in a sinful, and therefore temptable *state;* and by enticing them to burn their fingers to-day, he keeps them out of greater fires of sin to-morrow.

Our world is one great round of beneficent provisions for human virtue and happiness, but this punishing the infraction of natural law is the Alpha and Omega of them all; the great teacher and moralizer of the race in each of its members, as well as the master contrivance of the Almighty.

All hail, then, this institution of pain! But for it we could only half live. How powerful, how perpetual a *practical* teacher of righteousness it becomes! But for it how could we know whether or when we were freezing, or burning, or bruising, or cutting, or injuring, or destroying any part of our bodies, or be kept from killing ourselves; whereas, this ever-present, sentient sentinel stands forever "on guard" all over our bodies, outside and inside, compelling us to note what gives us pain, so as not to repeat it.

It stands equal sentinel over every emotion of our minds, paining us in and by means of every single evil thought and feeling, desire and passion. Divine goodness and wisdom ordained it as His messenger of universal good. Gravity is no more useful in the material world than is suffering in the moral. With one hand God is forever holding forth the rewards of obeying his laws, while with the other He is promoting this identical end by the terrible lashings of pain for violating them.

21. — Every Law is Self-rewarding and Self-punishing.

In the way thou sinnest, thou shalt surely suffer. Obeying one law creates one kind of enjoyment, and another law another kind; while violating one law inflicts one kind of pain, and another another. Those who obey the affectional laws, but violate the dietetic, enjoy domestic felicity, but suffer from dyspepsia, and *vice versa*. Those who obey the parental law in loving their children, but violate the conjugal by hating their companion, enjoy in their children but suffer in their consort; and the converse. One may obey the law of Benevolence, yet break that of Acquisitiveness, as did Gosse, by giving away two fortunes, and suffer ever after from poverty; whilst a miser obeys the former in acquiring money, yet robs Benevolence, and most of his other faculties, by miserly penuriousness. Hence many are very happy in some respects, because they obey some laws, yet suffer inexpressibly in other respects, because they violate other laws.

This arrangement enables all to trace their enjoyments and sufferings up to the *precise* laws they are obeying and transgressing, and thus ascertain exactly *wherein* they are sinning and suffering, so as to repeat the former, but avoid the latter.

Thus Mrs. A. thinks the world of her church, attends its every meeting, is a missionary of good, and really enjoys religion exceedingly, because she fulfils the natural laws of veneration ; and yet is nervous, dyspeptic, weak, and often down sick, as well as suffers excruciating torture from neuralgia or sick headaches, &c., because she has outraged the laws of health. Now, by seeing in what respects she enjoys, and in what she suffers, she can ascertain just *what* particular laws she is fulfilling, and what breaking ; so that, by fulfilling the physical, she can become as happy physically as she now is religiously.

Please consider how excellent a Preceptor, Teacher, and Professor of the natural laws this arrangement becomes. Though its instructions are often costly, yet they always teach effectively, by rendering "experience the best of schoolmasters." As a moralizer, a practical instructor in righteousness and all the human virtues, as well as a solemn warning against sins and vices of all kinds and degrees, it as far exceeds in eloquence and power the most gifted pulpit orators as Divinity exceeds humanity. If preachers would show just what obeyed laws cause these enjoyments in this sermon, and what breaches of natural law cause those sufferings in another, they would soon reform all their " hard cases," by arraying their very *self-interest* on the side of virtue and goodness.

But till then, let each become his and her *own* preacher, by studying out the *causes* of each and all his joys and sufferings as they transpire, thus : — this twinge of mental anguish came from my having broken this law, and that thrill of pleasure from my having fulfilled that natural requirement. And those must be genuine dolts, "dyed in the wool," whom this does not "convert from the error of their ways."

In the DAY thou sinnest, thou shalt suffer. As short settle-

ments are best, but long pay-days are almost worthless, is it any
wonder that so many sleep and sin on over those they are told are
payable *after death?* This natural law account is payable *at
sight*, and cannot possibly be avoided. Nature is her own law-
giver, court, judge, jury, sheriff, and executive officer; besides
being omniscient and omnipresent, to see that exact justice is
meted out to the last iota. No ends of the earth are far enough
away, no hiding-places are hidden enough, no one is high or low
enough, to allow of escape.

How MUCH enjoyment obeying these laws bestows, but violating
them inflicts, we little realize. This depends partly on our
capacities to enjoy and suffer, and partly on the relative value of
each law. Thus a most affectionate woman breaks the law of
love, — whether ignorantly or knowingly matters not, — by cause-
lessly discarding one she tenderly loves; she suffers as much
more than one with little affection as she is the most loving : and
her sufferings begin with the violation, but end *never!* Every
subsequent moment of her life, asleep and awake, she suffers
throughout her entire being, and more excruciatingly than any
can imagine who have not suffered similarly. The ultimate sum
total is really inconceivable. It may prevent her marrying at
all, or eventuate in an unhappy marriage, and this impair her
health, and this cause the death of children, besides inducing
innumerable miseries otherwise unknown; whereas, if she had
obeyed this love requirement, she would have been immeasurably
happy in both her conjugal and maternal affections, and in all
these other respects ; so that the difference between obeying and
violating is really incalculable and eternal. None of us can at all
afford to forego the one, or incur the other. The sacrifice
"doesn't pay."

SINS AND VIRTUES MULTIPLY, and their *effects spread* like fire on
the prairie. Fulfilling or transgressing one law, induces that of
many other laws. Mythology relates that a man, compelled to
choose between drunkenness and matricide, chose the former as
the lesser evil, and while drunk murdered his mother. One sin
induces many sins with their sufferings, and one virtue begets
many virtues with their enjoyments. Then by our love of enjoyment and dread of suffering, let us make ourselves just as
happy, by obeying just as many laws, as possible.

22. — IMPORTANCE OF STUDYING THESE LAWS.

To KNOW them is the first step towards their obedience. True, our various instincts prompt and aid us therein, but we require the guidance and assistance of *knowledge* besides. A law of mind causes intellect intuitively to take the helm of actions, and guide them at its will.

These instincts often become perverted by previous wrong habits, and of course mislead. Beyond all question, they are constituted to work in harmony with natural laws, and impel and guide us in their observance, besides being infallible; so that all should be careful to nurture, and not to pervert them; but we violate most of them so continually from the cradle, that we need intellect to bring us back to Nature.

GOD PUBLISHES these laws throughout all his domains, thereby virtually commanding all His creatures to learn them. They are not occult, nor hidden in labyrinthian mazes, ready to spring on us by stealth, but are like a city set upon a hill, discernible far and near. No mist, no uncertainty, beclouds any of them. They are open, palpable, and lighted up by the full blaze of both philosophy and perpetual experience. None of them need ever be misapprehended. Those who cannot discern them, not as in a glass, darkly, but clearly and fully, as in the noonday sun, are either blind or stupid. Such cognizance is even THRUST continually upon us.

To EXPOUND THESE LAWS and enforce their observance, should therefore be the one distinctive end and drift of all education, domestic, common, and classical. As happiness is the only "end of man," all education should be directed to its attainment. Otherwise it is useless. It should then teach first and mainly the NATURE OF MAN, and other studies only as collaterals. Yet how utterly foreign to this object is it as now conducted! Pupils are taught scarcely anything concerning themselves, physically or mentally, or how to render themselves happy, or avoid pain.

But ignorance is no excuse. None have any right to be ignorant. God Himself is their Preceptor. All are sacredly bound to heed those lessons of experience He is constantly inculcating. Those who cannot learn from books and teachers, must learn by experience, or suffer.

Section II.

ORGANISM AND ITS CONDITIONS, AS MANIFESTING AND INFLU-ENCING LIFE.

23. — ALL LIFE'S FUNCTIONS MANIFESTED ONLY BY ORGANS.

LIFE'S FIRST LAW, its *tap-root* condition, that from which emanate most of its other laws, that fundamental *sine-qua-non* means of all terrestrial functions, obviously is that it manifests itself *only through* ORGANS. No form of life, no one of all its multifarious operations, is ever put forth by any other means. In fact, life is *composed* of these two things — primary *faculties*, which originate all functions, and those *organs* by means of which they express themselves. Neither ever exists except in conjunction with the other, but both co-exist and act *together*, throughout all departments of Nature.

EACH PARTICULAR faculty is likewise exercised always and only by means of its *own* organ, never by any other. Each organ is specifically *adapted* to exercise its specific function, but no other. Thus the eyes are precisely adapted to see, but to do nothing else; and all seeing is executed by them. No other organs except the eyes ever see; nor do the eyes do anything but see. Their structure renders seeing alone possible to them, and all else, except what contributes to sight, impossible; while that of the ears executes, and can alone execute, hearing, &c. Was any function ever manifested except through its own individual organ? This arrangement is necessary. No other could secure efficiency of function, or prevent confusion, while this can, and does.

But this truth is so perfectly apparent throughout every single organ and function everywhere, that it needs neither proof nor amplification; for, like the sun, it proves itself, ramifying itself throughout universal space and being.

24. — ALL ORGANIC STATES SIMILARLY AFFECT THEIR FUNCTIONS.

IF man had been created a purely physical being, without any mind, he could have accomplished nothing, could have enjoyed nothing; or if he had been created a purely spiritual being, without a material organization, this world, with all its adaptations for promoting human happiness; the glorious sky over our heads and the flower-spangled lawn under our feet, the life-giving sun and health-inspiring breeze, the rains and dews of heaven, and all the fruits, bounties, and luxuries of earth, as far as they concern man, would have been made in vain. But he is created a *compound* being, composed of flesh and blood, on the one hand, and of mind and soul on the other; and both are so closely inter-related that every action and condition of either exert a perfectly reciprocal influence on the other.

What means it that an organ is an organ, but that all its states affect all its operations? that the eyes are the organs of vision, the stomach of digestion, &c., but that all existing *states* of these, of all other organs, similarly affect their respective functions? How *could* the eyes see unless they were in perfect sympathy and rapport with the visual *faculty?* How could weak organs manifest strong functions? or slow organs execute rapid functions? or *vice versa?* In the very fitness and necessity of things, only powerful organs could possibly manifest powerful functions, and rapid acting organs rapidity of function. This principle governs every other state of all the other organs and functions. This reciprocal sympathy between all organs and their functions is both universal and perfect — is alike a fact and a necessity, throughout Nature. Its philosophy is apparent. Let us canvass some of its facts.

WOOD is strong because its office is to execute this most potential function: Leaves, performing an indispensable office, must have free access to air; hence trees must grow to a great height. There immense canvas of leaves and fruit must be sustained aloft in proud defiance of surging winds and raging storms, winter and summer, through centuries. This sustainment requires an immense amount of power, which is effected by their trunk and roots. A hundred feet of purchase renders the strain, great all along their trunk, at their roots really tremendous. Wood is made hard, stiff, and strong of texture to meet this want, and is much the largest and toughest between the trunk and roots, and at the junction of the limbs, where the most power is required. Supplying this power by bulk, by consuming material and space, would prevent Nature's making many trees, whereas her entire policy is to form all she can; hence she renders the organic *texture* of wood as solid and powerful as its function is potential. And the more solid its structure, the more powerful is its function, as seen in comparing oak with pine, and lignum-vitæ with poplar.

All powerful animals are also proportionally powerful in texture. Thus the elephant, one of the very strongest of beasts, is so powerful in dermis, muscle, bone, and entire structure, that bullet after bullet shot against him, flatten and fall, harmless at his feet. The lion, too, is as strong in texture as in function. Only those who know from observation can form any adequate idea of the wiry toughness of those muscles and tendons which bind his head to his body, or of the solidity of his bones; corresponding with the fact that, seizing a bullock in his monster jaws, he dashes with him through jungle and over ravine, as a cat would handle a squirrel; and when he roars, the city trembles. The structures of the white and grizzly bear, of the tiger, hyena, and all powerful animals, and, indeed, of all weak ones, in like manner correspond equally with their functions.

In short, this correspondence between all organic conditions and functions is fixed and absolute; is necessary, not incidental, universal, not partial; is a relation of cause and effect, and governs every organ and function throughout universal life and nature. Our organism is the basis of all our mental and moral functions. It so. is in the very constitution of things, that mind can be put forth *only* in and by its material organs, and is strong or weak, quick or sluggish, as they are either.

Of course man, throughout all his functions, is governed by this organic law. Not only is all walking done only by the lower limbs, but it is rendered light or heavy, elastic or logy, full of snap or wanting in it, &c., in proportion as one's walking *organs* are either.

Digestion is performed by the stomach, all the states of which, such as its strength, weakness, temperature, inflammation, abuse, &c., similarly affect that digestion, and all the digestive functions. Thus over-eating, not eating at all, eating right or wrong kinds of food, eating irregularly, &c., similarly affect the stomach. The importance of this law is well nigh infinite, and yet it is so obviously both a fact and a necessity that to amplify it seems superfluous. The *fact* of this sympathy between all organs and their

8

functions is apparent. All that lives attests it in all their experiences every moment of life, asleep and awake.

25.—THE BODY, BRAIN, AND MIND ARE IN RECIPROCAL SYMPATHY.

· THE BRAIN is both the organ of the mind, and the great focal
organ of life. This doctrine is assumed here, but proved in Volume II. Of course all its states similarly affect both the mind,
and all the life functions. Its strength or weakness renders all
its operations correspondingly strong or weak. This vital truth
is established by the perpetual *experience* of every member of
the human family.

Even the little finger nail lives and acts only by means of its
nervous connection with the brain. Sever this connection and it
dies. A neighbor, by a fall, broke his back just above the junction of the sciatic or lower limb nerves with the spine; thus severing 'the nervous connection between these limbs and the brain.
Of course they died; yet he would not believe they were dead till
he made us *brand his feet with red hot irons*, so that his still
living eyes could *see* those irons scethe his own flesh. But they
were actually dead, not because any damage had been done them,
but solely because their nervous connection with his brain had
been severed.

ALL OPIATES, ALL ALCOHOLICS affect the mind and body equally
and similarly, first exhilarating, then stupefying both; and each
through the other.

Cold and warm mornings produce directly opposite effects on the
mind by differently affecting the body. Fevers enhance, and often
derange the action of the mind by augmenting that of the brain;
while hunger, fatigue, debility, and the like, enfeeble the former
by diminishing the action of the latter. Dyspepsia induces gloom
and mental debility, by deranging the physical functions — rendering its victims irritable, misanthropic, wretched, disagreeable,
and utterly unlike themselves. Physical inaction induces mental
sluggishness, while bodily exercise quickens intellectual action
and promotes happy feeling. Excess and deficiency of food and
sleep affect the mind powerfully, yet very differently. Experience has taught many of our best speakers to prepare their
minds for powerful effort by *physical* regimen. Certain kinds
of food stimulate some of the propensities, while other kinds aug-

ment our ability to think and study. Fasting promotes piety, but "fulness of bread" augments sinful desires. Bodily sickness enfeebles the mind, but health strengthens it; while inflammation of the brain causes insanity, and its inaction, as in fainting, mental stupor. Both morality and talent are affected by food, drinks, physical habits, sickness, health, &c. When the devout Christian or profound thinker has eaten to excess, or induced severe colds or fevers, or in any other way clogged or disordered his physical functions, the former can no more be "clothed with the spirit," or "soar upon the wings of devotion," nor the latter bring his intellectual energies into full and efficient action, than arrest the sun. Indeed, most of our constantly recurring transitions of thought and feeling are caused by physiological changes. "A sound mind in a healthy body" expresses this great truth, which the practical *experience* of all mankind confirms.

That the ancients understood this principle, and applied it to education, is proved by their christening their schools of learning "Gymnasia," in accordance with this fundamental principle, that promoting bodily strength promotes mental vigor. In short, we may as well dispute our own senses as controvert this doctrine, that both mind and body powerfully and reciprocally affect each other.

This reciprocity is effected by means of the *brain*, that great focus of the system, which experiences all sensation, and issues all mandates.

The various conditions of the mind and brain must therefore, in the very nature of things, sympathize perfectly with each other. The mind cannot act except in conjunction with the brain, nor can the brain act without causing mental action. Of course all their other states must and do also sympathize. This mutuality is what renders it the organ of the mind.

The brain is also in perfect rapport with every part and parcel of the body, by means of that perfect tissue of nerves which ramify from it through every iota of the body. This puts the brain into perfect reciprocity with the body, and the mind with the brain; so that all the conditions of the body, brain, and mind *permeate each other*. Every throb of either produces a corresponding pulsation in both the others. No part of the body can be affected in any way without similarly affecting the mind; and all

mental operations, such as bad news at table, by destroying the
appetite, correspondingly affect all parts of the body.

UNIVERSALITY governs this reciprocity.   Nature never does
things by halves.   Governing a part of the functions of vision by
the laws of optics, compels her to govern *all* the former by the
latter.   And thus of every conceivable application of this principle.   That same utility which renders it best to throw law over
a part of any class of her operations [18], renders it equally useful to extend that same law over this entire class.   How unjust
if a part were thus governed, and a part left wholly at random?
Does Nature ever adopt this piecemeal plan?   Is Causality a
nullity?   Is God irregular?

This sympathy is effected by these two palpable facts, that the
brain is the organ of the mind, and also inter-related to the body.
To question the latter is to dispute an anatomical fact, and to
deny the former is equivalent to denying that the mind has any
connection with the body, or with matter.   But mind *is* affected
by organic conditions.   Therefore all is cause and effect.   We
know, for we feel, that *some* bodily states affect the mental;
therefore *all* do; and hence to excite, or invigorate, or debilitate,
or disease, or derange, or restore either, similarly affects the
other.   Both are as effectually interwoven as are warp and woof,
and this interweaving constitutes the warp and woof of life.

26. — ABNORMAL PHYSICAL CONDITIONS CREATE SINFUL PRO-CLIVITIES.

Do not opiates almost frenzy their victims with wrath?   Does
not drunkenness demoralize and vitiate?   The same man who,
while temperate, is an excellent husband, father, neighbor, and
man, by becoming intemperate is rendered improvident, sensual,
a fiend in his family, and a low-bred, swearing, fighting desperado,
and sometimes even a murderer; but, restoring him physically reinstates him morally.   That cherub child, perfectly well
day before yesterday, was as amiable as an angel, because well,
but yesterday, fevered by sickness, was too cross and hateful to
be endured; whereas, restoring him to health by to-day, has
restored his angelic loveliness.   Many a poor, sickly child is
punished unmercifully because it is cross, yet is cross because it
is sick; whilst, curing its body would obviate its ugliness.

Most women, however amiable by nature, when they become nervous, thereby become bad-tempered, hating and hateful; and the only way to cure their temper consists in curing their nervousness. Many a superb wife and mother, from the very excess of her love for husband and children, works on, on, ou, day and night, year after year, in doing for them, till her health fails, which throws her into a fevered, cross-grain, ugly mood, so that she scolds them right and left, blaming everybody for everything, besides maligning her neighbors, solely because of her *physical* prostration; and yet, restoring her health would make her the same family angel she was at first. Her scolded husband should *pity*, not upbraid her; while all concerned should do all they can to obviate her fretfulness by removing its physical cause.

Why do mad dogs attack and bite even their best friends, but because their physical inflammation inflames their Combativeness and Destructiveness?

Why are dyspeptics always irritable, but because a sour stomach sours the temper? And the only way to sweeten their temper consists in sweetening their stomachs. One of the ablest, best, and most scientific of men, when attacked by indigestion, was accustomed to shut himself up in his studio, lest he might vent his spleen on some innocent person. The Bible justly ascribes the wickedness of Babylon to her gluttony and drunkenness, and prescribes fasting, that is, a given physical condition, as a means of grace and goodness. Paul, too, who rarely ever says anything without saying something important, begins one of the most expressive passages of the Bible with, " Brethren, I beseech you, by the mercies of God," — would Paul begin a text *that* way which meant little?—" that ye present your *bodies* a living sacrifice, holy, acceptable unto God." What is "holy and acceptable"? The body. Now since it can be holy, it can therefore be *un*holy, and if it can be acceptable unto God, it can therefore be *un*acceptable to Him. If it can be "a meet temple for the indwelling of the Holy Ghost," it can also be an *un*meet temple —"which is your reasonable service." The Greek word here translated "reasonable" should have been rendered "spiritual," and would, properly transposed, then have read thus: " Brethren, your *spiritual* service consists in presenting your *bodies* holy, acceptable unto God, which is your spiritual service, and which I entreat you by His

mercies to do." The Bible is full of like passages, declaring that
piety and the moral virtues are materially influenced by the
physical conditions, — a doctrine the progressive pulpit is just
beginning to proclaim under the phrase, "*muscular* Christianity."
Why did they wait for *Phrenology* to enforce it? Why should
a biblical doctrine so patent, and so promotive of piety and goodness, slumber on thus unheeded century after century? Com-
mentators, where have been your eyes, that a biblical as well
as natural truth thus universal, and illustrated by every single
physical condition of every human being and animal, should have
been overlooked?

But our whole world is *full* of like illustrations of this great
organic law, that the entire physiology and mentality are in
reciprocal rapport, and mutually act and react upon each other.
All living beings perpetually experience it every instant of their
existence. Life is even *made up* of this reciprocity. It constitutes not a primal, but *the* primal *lex legum* of Nature, instituted
for the best good of His creatures; to ignore which is folly, but
to practice which promotes our highest happiness.

But this natural truth needs no comments from us. It is its
own commentator. It is a *law of things*, self-rewarding its
obedience, and self-punishing its infractions and neglect,[21] and
ramifying itself upon every minute state of body and mind. As
gravity governs equally all the ponderous heavenly bodies, and
all the minutest particles of matter, so this law governs all the
minutest manifestations existing between the body and mind.[24]
"*All*, when any," is a natural law.

THIS GREAT ART OF LIVING, therefore, consists in learning
what bodily states cause given mental, and what mental states
produce given physical. · How strange that an art which is to life
what foundation is to superstructure, should have thus been completely ignored till enforced by Phrenology?

27. — ITS MATERIALISTIC OBJECTION ANSWERED.

"But, sir, this doctrine not only inculcates materialism, but it *is* rank
out and out materialism itself, and that in its strongest form. It makes
mind wholly dependent on matter, and only its outworkings. No
materialist before or since Voltaire, himself included, has stated, or can
state it in a stronger light. If it is true, then farewell to immortality;
for the death of the body presupposes and proves the concomitant death
of the soul; because, if they are thus intimately related in life, in death
they cannot be divided."

Carry *that* objection up to the throne of the almighty *Creator* of all things, and settle your hash with Him; for thus, and thus *only*, hath *He* seen fit to ordain all the mighty works of His almighty hands. If, therefore, you have any objections, just make them at *headquarters*, and propound a better plan. You object against a *fact*, against what *is*, against what *you your own self* and all other living beings perpetually *experience*. This huge earth, and these huger sun and stars, these great mountains, plains, rivers, and oceans, these trees, vegetables, flowers, fruits, grains, and animals, along with these wonderfully constructed bodies, with all their bones, muscles, tissues, and organs, were not made for nought. An arrangement thus stupendous has its commensurate *purpose*. Matter was obviously created solely to supply organs for the manifestation of *mind;* and most admirably does it subserve this purpose. The all-wise Architect and En-gineer of this universe undoubtedly understood Himself and His work when He saw fit to create matter, and then fashion it into organs for manifesting functions. If He could have devised any better plan, He would doubtless have done so, but "foresaw" that this was the most feasible, and the best. We might wonder how, after having created that limestone rock, He could make from it these beautiful and serviceable bones and joints; but *He does* it, and we, yes *you*, self-stultified objectors, are the gainers; for it makes all its possessors happy.

Is it not strange, almost ludicrous, to see otherwise sensible men, after eating a breakfast "material" in more senses than one, use material lungs, throats, mouths, muscles, and brains, to decry materialism, then go to a "material" home to recuperate with a "material" dinner, only on returning to take a "material" dose of "blue mass," and consider themselves smart and *consistent?* Is it not, at least, ungenerous to use material organs for abusing materialism? Let none preach against what they cannot do without. Stop objecting against material organs, or else stop using them. Yet you had better learn how to "use them as not abusing them," with gratitude to their Divine Author. And let minister and people shout eternal hosannas for an ordinance which thus introduces us upon the plane of eternal existence and enjoyment.

But the *determining* question is whether life consists in the *organs* themselves, or in that *spirit* principle which uses them? Which is the lord, and which the vassal? Which was created for the other? Which enjoys and suffers? The MIND. Was man created mainly to eat, sleep, breathe, labor, glitter, and die?. No, but to *feel and think*. And what constitutes his identity and personality — his essence, *himself?* His dress, or even body? Is it not his SOUL? This embodies the manhood of man. All else is extraneous. Cut from him, if that were possible, limb after limb and organ after organ, till all shall be removed, but leave his mind entire, and he remains the same being still; but his body, separated from his immortal spirit, is not himself. Does sight inhere in the eyes, or in that seeing mental *faculty* which uses them in effecting sight? Obviously in the latter; for, let the former be ever so perfect, the moment the latter leaves them, they can see no more. And yet those whose eyes have been destroyed, *remember* what they have seen. Now if the eyes constitute sight, their destruction must destroy both it and all its memories. Eyes are to sight what the tool is to its handle — simply its`means of action*, but· not itself. Sight is as different from its eyes as cotton cloth is from that cotton factory which manufactured it. As the factory is only a means to a desirable end, and useless but for this end ; so the body is only the means for executing that life which constitutes that one ultimate end of this material department of Nature. Then why object to it? Is it so poor, so objectionable an arrangement that you thus cry out against it? Our organs, like an outer garment, are a means of enjoyment, which we lay off when we are done using it ; yet it forms no necessary part of *ourselves*. Our identity and personality inhere in our *spirit-principle*, our intellect and soul, not in our bodies. Their being in rapport does not render them identical, any more than is a man and his shadow. Both philosophy and the intuition of all mankind consider the mentality as the man, and the organism as only its servant.

The Author is a positive believer in immortality, and as much expects to live after the death of his body as he expects the sun will rise to-morrow morning ; and yet he as firmly believes in this doctrine of mutual sympathy between the body and the mind.

At all events the latter is an experimental *fact*, of which all organized beings are perpetual living attestations. If this sympathy between the body and mind proves the materiality of man and the death of the body and soul together, then that doctrine is true; for this is certain, yet this inference is doubtful.

Let objectors beware lest they make converts to this materialistic doctrine they oppose. When they convince an intelligent man that this alleged rapport between the body and mind really does prove the death of the soul with that of the body, they make him a materialist. Does that benefit him or them? The *fact* of such a reciprocity still exists all the same, while they become propagandists of materialism. The less materialism you infer from this great institute of Nature, and the more you study and apply it to the improvement of the life, happiness, and morality of yourself and fellow-beings, the more true sense and philanthropy will you evince.

But "Religious Science" will discuss this whole subject of materialism, immortality, &c., from first principles. Suffice it here that material organs are created, that they embody Nature's *only* means of manifesting each and all of her functions, and that the reciprocity between all the existing states of all organs and their functions is both a necessity and a fact, and that either can be thrown into any given state by throwing the other also into its corresponding one.

28.—Value of a good Constitution.

Since life is thus valuable,[16] and organism its only medium of manifestation,[23] and since all its organic states affect all its functions,[24] a *good constitution* becomes about as valuable as that life it manifests. Since good eyes are as valuable as are all the knowledge and happiness they impart, and thus of all the other integral organs, of course the value of a good body over a poor one is measured by all the increased powers to enjoy and accomplish it gives. By over-driving, or foundering, or injuring a splendid horse, you take his zest and snap out of him ever after. Before, he needed no whip, after, he performs much less *with* one than before without. That one injury cut down his *power* to accomplish one half or two thirds, and made him an old horse in constitution, though young in years. So when your own constitution is once sapped, farewell to half or more of your life zest,

9

capacities, and enjoyments. A prime body is everything. Ho!
thoughtless youth, take good care of your eyes, teeth, muscles,
lungs, and especially *nerves* and *brain*, your entire organism,
before you learn their worth by their impairment. None are
quite *as* poor as those who have poor bodies, nor any quite as
" well off in the world " as those who have good ones. No strong
and healthy poor man or maiden need envy their rich peers who
have poor bodies.

Ladies, *first* see to it that you have good bodies *to* dress, for
a good body poorly dressed is worth a thousand fold more than
a poor one splendidly attired. And the time is " at hand " when
a lady's " ton " will depend far more on how good her body is,
than on how well she dresses it.

Business men, speculators for a rise, know ye that a splendid
physique is the finest *piece of property* you will ever possess,
while injuring it will entail on you a loss far greater than any
other ever can be. This year you have added fifty thousand dollars to your coffers, but in doing so have worn in on your organism, and thereby lost more than twice fifty thousand dollars
worth of life-force. A little animal power is worth more than
dollars can admeasure, and yet men and women treat it as they
do sole leather — to be worn out by all manner of hard usage,
and worth no more than old boots.

To preserve and improve a good organism, if we have one,
and to recuperate and reinvigorate whatever we do have, be it
more or less, is the great art and elixir of life, and should take
precedence over every other life end and pleasure. Stop instantly whatever interferes with it, and do anything, everything
to augment it. This then is that august subject we now approach.

Section III.

HEALTH, ITS VALUE AND ATTAINABILITY.

29. Definition and Value of Health.

" The poor man's riches, the rich man's blessing."

The normal 'and vigorous action of all the physical organs and functions, creates and constitutes health; while disease consists in their imperfect, feeble, and abnormal action, and death in their suspension. Life and health are proportionate to each other. Viewed in any and all aspects, health is life.

The value of health therefore equals that of life,[16] and exceeds that of all else. It is our richest possession, because it alone imparts the greatest attainable zest and relish to whatever we possess. Without it, what can man, woman, child, or even bird or beast do, become, or enjoy? Other things being equal, our capacities for accomplishing and enjoying are proportionate to its vigor, but become enfeebled as it declines. No attainable amount of wealth, or honor, or learning, or anything else whatever can make us happy any further than we have *health* with which to enjoy them; and the value of all we possess diminishes in proportion as we become sickly. With how keen a zest those in health relish delicious foods and fruits, which only nauseate those whose diseases have destroyed their appetite. The rich invalid is pitiably poor, because he cannot enjoy his possessions, while all who are healthy are therefore rich, because their fund of life turns all surroundings into means of enjoyment.[16] The healthy servant is richer, because happier, than his feeble millionaire master, and the robust peasant, than his infirm king! Those who have always enjoyed health, little realize its uses or its value. As we admeasure time only by its loss, so none duly prize the worth of health till it declines. Brought to the gates of death, our last hour come, what would we give — what *not* give — for another year of life and health, with all their pleasures? *Millions* would be cheap, because health is so immeasurably more promotive of happiness — that only measure of all values[16] — than riches, than all else combined.

To all in all conditions it is the pearl of greatest price.

Then how consummately foolish is this trifling with health so almost universal? Esau's folly was wisdom in comparison with theirs who, in sheer carelessness, exchange a lifetime of vigor for one of feebleness? And some barter away life itself for some momentary indulgence! A foolish ambition breaks down constitutions by the thousand. Unwilling to be outdone, they work at the top of their strength just as long as they can stand, or overheat themselves, or drink cold water while too warm, or in one way or another bring on in a day or week complaints which debilitate them for life, and hurry them into premature graves.

An ambitious young man, just to finish cradling before his neighbor, worked to complete exhaustion and finished a few hours the soonest, but in doing so *lamed his side for life*, contracted a two months' sickness, from which he barely recovered with his life, but with a *broken down constitution*,[28] so that he has since been able to do but little work, and many kinds not at all; besides suffering perpetual pain these thirty years since. That single day's' work did him vastly more injury than any fortune could ever do him good, because it inflicted on him vastly more pain than any amount of money could ever give him pleasure.[16] It weakened all his capacities to do and enjoy, besides enhancing all his sufferings, for life, which it will shorten many years. Yet he received no extra pay for this destruction of health. He sacrificed an incalculable amount of happiness and life on the altar of a foolish emulation. Yet like instances of like folly — folly? the worst form of *wickedness* — are common. What reader of thirty, if not of twenty, but has, by some abuse of health, impaired it forever? How many, in how many ways, wickedly squander it, without receiving any return for this choicest of all our life possessions?

Health is like a fortune at interest, the income from which, economically used, will support you; but it cannot be squandered at any period through life, without being brought into the account, and shortening and enfeebling it in exact proportion. Spending foolishly draws on the principal, and every draft, great and little, must be reckoned into that final settlement which every draft hastens. As the faster you draw the sooner you exhaust it, so all over-eating, over-working, loss of sleep, improper habits, colds, and whatever injures health, is a draft on the constitution cashed at a hundred per cent. discount, till, when your life-fund is expended, but not till then, death summons you to your final reckoning. Every abuse of health enfeebles it for life, and hastens its close. Ho! O youth! ho all, be entreated to consider the infinite value of health, and the proportionate importance of its preservation. Compared with it, millions are trash. Even all else without it is dross. Gain whatever you may by impairing it, you are an infinite loser, but lose what you may in its preservation or restoration, you gain more than by acquiring fortunes, or even crowns, and worlds.

If you would succeed in life, PRESERVE HEALTH.

If you would get rich, make HEALTH PARAMOUNT.

If you would enjoy animal life, PRESERVE HEALTH.

If you would acquire knowledge, TAKE NICE CARE OF HEALTH.

If you would become great or good, vigorous health is indispensable.

If you live to do good, preserve health, for what good could you do if sick or dead?

If you would always be "on hand" for business, pleasure, work, whatever may turn up, secure PERFECT HEALTH.

Whatever may be your life-end, or motive, make the PRESERVATION OF HEALTH your FIRST BUSINESS, as it is your indispensable instrumentality.

SICKNESS IS COSTLY. As a pecuniary investment, nothing *pays* the right way like health, nor the wrong like disease. Sickness both stops your wages, if you labor; or if in business, takes you from it and compels you to intrust it to others — always disastrous — besides creating heavy expenses for doctors, nurses, medicines, and a thousand incidentals. How many, now poor, would have been rich, if they and their families had always been well.

SICKNESS IS PAINFUL. See that sick child. How forlorn and woe-stricken its looks! Mark those rheumatic or gouty subjects. Every motion is painful, and most of their sources of pleasure are converted into wormwood. Behold that wretched victim of disease lying prostrate on a sick bed! Torn from business, society, and all the enjoyments of life, and racked with pain! The boiling blood courses through his veins, swollen almost to bursting.

4

Hear his piteous wail — "My head, O my head !"   See those eyes rolling in agony. Open the windows of his soul, and behold his struggle for life in the midst of death, his horrid dread of which far exceeds the torturing pains of disease. Hear him pant for breath ! Witness that gurgling in his throat. Behold the last agonizing struggle between life and death, and that final giving up of the ghost ! What is more dreadful than sickness ? What horror of horrors at all compares with that most awful scene experienced on earth, premature death? from which may God deliver us. Rather let us all deliver *ourselves*, by PRESERVING OUR HEALTH !

30. HEALTH ATTAINABLE : THE AMOUNT POSSIBLE.

Health is *spontaneous*, is our normal state. To preserve it, we are not obliged to do some great thing, go on a painful or costly pilgrimage, nor even to practise the least self-denial, but only not to *abuse* it. Let Nature "have her perfect work," and she will furnish it all ready at our hands. Perfect health is simply the perfect operation of all her organs and functions. This she has taken the utmost pains to secure. Behold the labor she has bestowed to construct the body with a degree of perfection attainable only by infinite skill and power ! Since these organs are thus infinitely perfect, are their functions less so ? Was not this structural perfection devised expressly to secure corresponding perfection of function? Else what is its use? Unless deranged or prevented by violated law, every organ will go on from the beginning of life, until worn out by extreme old age, to perform its office with all the regularity of the sun, and with a power commensurate to any demand compatible with the laws of our being. To argue that health is *spontaneous*, and as natural as breathing, or eating, or sleeping, is, in fact, only these and other functions in their natural and vigorous action, is attempting to prove an axiom, or that we see what we see. Allowed their natural play, all the organs will go on perpetually to manufacture life, health, and happiness, which, unless their flow is arrested by violated law, will flow on as freely and spontaneously to every human being as the river to its own ocean home. A boy once inadvertantly whistled in school : —

"*Angered teacher.* 'John, you rogue, what made you whistle?'
"*Boy.* 'I didn't, master; IT WHISTLED ITSELF.'"

It breathes itself, sees itself, moves itself, sleeps itself, digests
itself, thinks and feels itself, *everything itself;* and breathes, sees,
thinks, feels, everything exactly *right,* if the proper food and
stimuli are present. Is it difficult to breathe? or to breathe
right? or enough? or wholesome air? Rather, it is exceedingly
difficult *not* to breathe, or to breathe too little, or a noxious
atmosphere. Is it hard to eat? or to eat enough? or to eat what
is healthy? Yet the converse is always difficult. These illustrations apply to every other function of the body. Every organ
is constituted to commence its normal and healthy action from the
first, and perform it spontaneously throughout life; and that to a
much greater age than any now attain. Indeed, it requires great,
or else long-continued *violence,* to arrest their healthy and pleasurable functions at any time between birth and death. Hence there
is no more need of our becoming sick, or of these functions being enfeebled or disordered, than of our shutting our eyes for
weeks together, or refusing to breathe, or move, or preventing
any other function by force. The power of the human constitution to resist disease is perfectly astonishing. How many readers
have abused their health outrageously, hundreds of times, with
comparative impunity; and even after they have thus broken it
down, have still endured sickness and suffering till they wonder
that they yet live? What would yours now have been if you had
promoted instead of abusing it? How many hardships could you
once endure? How much it took to break you down? None
realize how much we abuse it. Every day and·night, almost
hour, we do something more or less detrimental to it — stay in-
doors too much; or remain much in heated rooms; or exercise
too little; or else labor too much, or not exactly right; or sleep
in close rooms; or eat too much, or what is injurious, or at
least a diet less beneficial than other things we might eat;
or overtax the mind, or perhaps exercise it too little; or sit
in an unwholesome posture; or neglect the skin; or dress too
warm; or take cold; or one or another of those ten thousand
kindred things, more or less injurious to health, which all perpetrate almost perpetually. All this, in addition to those extreme imprudences of which almost all are more or less guilty

every little while. And yet, in spite of all this abuse of it, see how healthy many continue to·be, often for eighty or a hundred years. Alcohol poisons the human constitution, yet see how many drink it daily, often to drunkenness, for thirty, and even fifty years, without destroying their health, though they greatly impair it. See what poisonous drugs some will take, yet live. In short, Nature has done her utmost to bestow vigorous and uninterrupted health on every member of the human family, and to ward off disease and prolong life. Behold and wonder at the physical stamina and energy provided for by her, and then say whether every human being is not constituted for health. Even admitting that children often inherit diseases from parents, yet the fact that parents have health sufficient to become parents, is abundant proof that their offspring, by a careful observance of the health laws, can both ward off their inherited predisposition —directions for doing which are given hereafter [128] [129] — and enjoying excellent health to a good old age.

Behold that fallow-deer, or moose, or reindeer! Far to the north; the winter temperature generally below zero, and often below forty; without shelter or fire; the snow many feet deep, and his food poor and scant; what physical stamina is required even to keep him alive through an eight months' winter! And yet, attacked by that fierce pack of ravenous wolves, he bounds off, seemingly as light as a feather. He runs many miles per hour. They chase him day in and day out, night in and night out. He finally stands at bay, and smites now one and then another of his fierce pursuers dead with one blow of his still powerful fore leg. And if at last,·taken unawares, he succumbs, how perfectly amazing the energies he first puts forth! as is also that of his hungry pursuers. And a like illustration holds true of all wild animals, lions, tigers, hyenas, wildcats, elephants, zebras — but why specify any, since all are about equally robust? And our domestic animals, despite all the abuses suffered at the hands of careless or heartless taskmasters, endure and accomplish wonders.

Then does God deal out this "greatest good" more bountifully to beast than to man? Every single fact and principle in the natural history of both, thunder "No." Is not his entire physical organism better, and every way more perfect, than theirs? In what else is he their inferior? Then why should he be in health? Is he not God's special *favorite?*

HUMAN FACTS shall decide. Are wild Hottentots, Moors, Arabs, Indians, &c., less powerful or enduring than the moose? Let Blackhawk's account of his long marches, and his feats of endurance and privation, answer. Keokuk had a physique of marvellous power and endurance. What splendidly "made up" men are the Camanches? We shall yet give facts bearing on this subject,[103] but the point we are making, the natural robustness of the human constitution, is apparent without. All children having sufficient natural health to be born alive, can grow stronger and more healthy every year, up to life's full meridian; and then retain it till they die of sheer old age. Only a long outraging of the health laws ever prevents this delightful result. Sickness and premature death constitute no part of Nature's ends. Instead, both are abnormal, are *punishments* for infringements of the laws of health, and, of course, avoidable by obeying these laws. No wonder that men, women, and children are sick, and die thus suddenly and early, considering how perpetually they violate the health prerequisites. Their enduring so much with comparative impunity, only shows how perfectly healthy conformity to them would render all.

31. — SICKNESS AND DEATH NOT PROVIDENTIAL, BUT GOVERNED BY LAW.

"O! but health and sickness, life and death, are wise but mysterious dispensations of PROVIDENCE. 'The LORD killeth, and maketh alive; HE bringeth down to the grave, and bringeth up.' Our days are all numbered, so that we *must* die at our appointed time."

Do we live in a world of law, or of chance?[18] Does every effect have its cause, and every cause its effect? or do the most important of all effects occur without cause, by "Providential interposition," perhaps in the very teeth of causation? Does God violate His own laws? Preposterous! This doctrine is false in fact, injurious in its consequences, subversive of all causation, conceived in ignorance, and brought forth by bigotry! Our world is governed throughout *only by law*. *All* is cause and effect.[21] We see, feel, and know that *some* causes promote health, while others retard it. Certain causes always occasion death, and others avert it. If sickness and death are providential, why ever give medicine to remove the former, or prevent the

10

latter? What! vainly and impiously attempt to arrest by medicine a dispensation of an all-wise *Providence!* Fear and tremble
lest He smite you dead, for giving medicine to thwart His unchangeable decrees!

Irony aside, sickness and death are no more providential than
the rising of the sun, or any fixed operation of nature, but the
legitimate and necessary *effects* of their procuring causes. None
consider them as providential, but all treat them practically as
effects in their very attempts to obviate them by removing their
causes. All mankind *do* something — apply *causes* to the relief
of pain and prevention of death, as spontaneously as they breathe.
What stronger evidence could be required or had that all instinctively *feel and know* them to be *effects* governed by causation? Are deaths caused by poisoning or shooting providential?
Then are all the operations of nature equally providential. Call
them *caused* providences; better call them *effects*. We often
know by what causes certain sickness and deaths were produced,
and are all internally conscious — the highest order of proof —
that they *are* effects, equally with all the other operations of nature. To argue this point is to argue what is self-evident; and
to suppose that a single glow of health or twinge of pain is not
an effect, but a providence, is supposing that this incalculably
important department of nature is without the pale of causation
and law — a doctrine utterly untenable.[18] His Causality must be
feeble, and mind weak or unenlightened, who entertains a doctrine thus hostile to all order, and to universal Nature.

The doctrine that they are sometimes providential, and sometimes caused by violating the organic laws, is no less irrational
than supposing that the sun rises one day in obedience to the
fixed laws of gravity, and another day by "special providence,"
wholly without means; and thus of all the other operations of
nature. Does the Deity trifle thus? Does He half do, and then
undo? Does He ever begin without completing? Does not that
same utility and even constitutional *necessity of things* which renders it best that sickness and health, life and death, should be
caused in *part* — as we know they are — should also be caused IN
WHOLE? The principle that whenever a part of a given class of
operations, as of seeing, motion, and the like, are governed by
causation, that entire class is governed by the same law, is a uni-

versal fact throughout nature.[19] That causation governs sickness and death in part is self-evident : therefore all sickness, all death, premature and natural, are equally the legitimate and invariable effects of violated physical law. In one sense they may be called " divine chastisements," because they are chastisements consequent on breaking the divine laws, but in no other. Both reason and fact impel us to this conclusion. No middle ground remains ; in fact, no ground but to ascribe all health and sickness, life and death, to inflexible causation. How strange that moral and intellectual leaders and teachers, pseudo "*educated*" men even, should entertain and promulgate a doctrine as injurious and as utterly absurd as that sickness and premature death are providential?

Countless thousands kill themselves or children, often with kindness, and then throw all the blame off from their own guilty heads, by ascribing all to "divine Providence"! What downright blasphemy ! Though being clerically exhorted to "submit to this afflictive dispensation meekly, trusting that this chastening rod of your Heavenly Father may teach you resignation to His will," may console the sick more than being reproved for their having inflicted this distress on themselves and inconvenience on others by breaking Nature's health laws, yet the latter would tend to *prevent* future sickness by inculcating subsequent obedience.

"But, Professor, these views really shock our most sacred feelings."

Then *rectify* your "most sacred feelings," till they will not be thus shocked by truth. Telling the Turk that Alla is no God, would shock his "most sacred feelings," because they are wrong. Telling the idol-worshipping Chinese that their brazen images are *only* brass, would shock their sacred feelings. Our sacred, and all our other feelings, should be guided by *reason*. All "sacred" prejudices *ought* to be shocked, till they are abrogated.

A little girl in Baltimore, told if she would hang up her stocking, Santa Claus would fill it with good things, did hang it up, and · Santa Claus, or other claws, did fill it. Calling for her stocking the moment she awoke, it was tossed upon her bed, when she greedily ate down its entire contents of almonds, raisins, nuts, candies, cakes, &c. ; ate a hearty breakfast, was plied with titbits between breakfast and dinner, and an hour after was taken with convulsions, and in another hour died. Though a post-mortem examination demonstrated that the unchewed raisins eaten in the morning had swollen and caused her death, yet the pious Rev. Dr. Musgrave preached her funeral sermon from the text, "The Lord gave, and the Lord hath taken away" — probably from evils to come, ascribing this afflictive bereavement to a merciful *Providence*, sent to wean stricken parents from earth, and prepare them for heaven! What sacrilege, what falsehood, thus to charge the Almighty with killing this dear child, when the post-mortem examination proved that its careless *parents killed their own child* by giving it the raisins, just as much as if they had unwittingly given it arsenic. If, after stating the coroner's verdict, he had said, substantially, "Behold, O weeping parents, and all, in this cause of this child's untimely death, a warning to feed your other children aright, so as to save them from premature death" — if all ministers would make any apparent causes of the early death of the corpse before them an occasion for warning the living not to hasten their own death by a like disease, there would be few deaths this side of a worn-out old age. Teaching men that nothing but violated law can possibly occasion sickness or premature death, especially juveniles, will enforce, by the most powerful of all motives, the study and observance of those laws, and thus ward off sickness and preserve life, while these false consolations lull parents and destroy children by scores of thousands annually. Mankind need, and *will some day have*, a new set of funeral sermons, *instructing the living how to live.*

After a public lecture, in which the preceding story was told, with comments, the Author was introduced to a listener, the Rev. Dr. Reese, Methodist Episcopal Bishop of Maryland, when the following dialogue occurred : —

"I fear, Bishop, that these views of special Providence conflict with your own religious ideas and feelings on that subject."

"Not at all, Professor, for I believe many delicate ladies, accustomed to high dresses and covered arms, array themselves for a ball or party in low dresses, short sleeves, and thin slippers ; dance to complete exhaustion ; carelessly expose themselves while going home tired after profuse perspiration ; catch a severe cold, which of course strikes to the throat and lungs ; and die of quick or slow consumption in consequence ; when the Lord's will sermon is preached at their funerals, whereas it should be — *committed suicide* with low dresses and thin slippers. Natural effects are not special providences."

At all events, all concerned should be especially careful, first, to ascertain whether "the Lord" did kill a given child or an adult before they thus *accuse* Him of doing it. To charge Him with killing those whom they themselves kill, or who killed themselves by breaking His health laws, is pious yet profane blasphemy, as horrid as man can well perpetrate. Hear Mrs. Sedgwick on this point : —

"WAS IT PROVIDENCE? Take, for example, a young girl bred delicately in town, and shut up in a nursery in her childhood, — in a boarding school through her youth, — never accustomed to air or exercise, two things that the law of God makes essential to health. She marries; her strength is inadequate to the demands upon it. Her beauty fades early. She languishes through her hard offices of giving birth to children, suckling and watching over them, and dies early. ' What a strange Providence that a mother should be taken in the midst of life from her children!' Was it Providence ? No! Providence had assigned her threescore years and ten ; a term long enough to rear her children, and to see her children's children ; but she did not obey the laws on which life depends, and of course she lost it.

"A father, too, is cut off in the midst of his days. He is a useful and distinguished citizen, and eminent in his profession. A general buzz arises on every side: ' What a striking Providence!' This man has been in the habit of studying half of the night; of passing his days in his office or in the courts; of eating luxurious dinners, and drinking various kinds of wine. He has every day violated the laws on which health depends. Did Providence cut him off? The evil rarely ends here. The diseases of the father are often transmitted ; and a feeble mother rarely leaves vigorous children behind her.

"It has been customary in some of our cities, for young ladies to walk in thin shoes and delicate stockings in mid-winter. A healthy, blooming young girl thus dressed in violation of Heaven's laws, pays the penalty — a checked circulation, colds, fever, and death. ' What a sad Providence!' exclaim her friends. Was it Providence, or her own folly? A beautiful young bride goes night after night to parties, made in honor of her marriage. She has a slightly sore throat; perhaps the weather is inclement ; but she must go with her neck and arms bare ; for who ever saw a bride in a close evening dress ? She is consequently seized with an inflammation of the lungs, and the grave receives her before her bridal days are over. ' What a Providence !' exclaims the world. ' Cut off in the midst of happiness and hope!' Alas, did she not cut the thread of life *herself?*

"A girl in the country, exposed to our changeful climate, gets a new bonnet instead of getting a flannel garment. A rheumatism is the consequence. Should the girl sit down tranquilly with the idea that Providence has sent the rheumatism upon her, or should she charge it on her vanity, and avoid the folly in future? Look, my young friends, at the mass of diseases that are incurred by intemperance in eating and in drinking, in study or in business; by neglect of exercise, cleanliness, and pure air; by indiscreet dressing, tight-lacing, &c. ; and all is quietly imputed to Providence! Is there not impiety as well as ignorance in this? Were the physical laws strictly observed, from generation to generation, there would be an end to the frightful diseases that cut life short, and of the long list of maladies that make life a torment or a trial. It is the opinion of those who best understand the physical system, that this wonderful machine, the body, this 'goodly temple,' would gradually decay, and men would die as if falling asleep."

LORD PALMERSTON, the great English Premier, when petitioned by the Scotch clergy to appoint a day for fasting and prayer, to avert the cholera, replied, in effect, —

"Clean and disinfect your streets and houses, promote cleanliness and health among the poor, and see that they are plentifully supplied with good food and raiment, and employ right sanitary measures generally, and you will have no occasion to fast and pray; nor will the Lord hear your prayers while these His preventives remain unheeded."

The truth is, that life and health, sickness and death, are invariably the legitimate *effects* of their specific causes. Nature's health laws reign as supreme as.any other. From them there is no appeal, and to them no exception. Given physiological causes always and necessarily produce their own legitimate effects, but no others. Observing the health laws renders health just as sure as the rising of the sun, because both are equally governed by infallible causation.

32. — HEALTH A DUTY : SICKNESS AND PREMATURE DEATH SINFUL.

Since, therefore, health is attainable, spontaneous, and can be destroyed only with difficulty; and especially, since it is thus infinitely valuable,[20] is it not the solemn and imperious *duty* of all to preserve it if good, and regain it if impaired? If not, then there is no such thing as obligation; because we can discharge no duty and accomplish no end without it, and only in proportion to its vigor. Is it not our duty to do good, worship God, love and provide for family, reason, enjoy the bounties of Nature, and exercise all the powers and faculties God has graciously bestowed upon us? If it is not sinful to impair these divine gifts by debility, or bury them in a premature grave, then nothing can be sinful. Is it not our duty to give our fellow-men pleasure instead of pain? Is it not then wrong to subject them to all the care and weariness of watching around our sick bed, and to all the anxiety consequent on our sickness? And is it not almost the climax of crime to break down the spirits of dear friends, especially of our own families and companions, with anguish by our death, whereas we might, by obeying the laws of health, gladden them with our friendship, support them by our labor, sustain them by our sympathies, and guide them by our counsels?

THE PAINS accompanying disease and death, constitute the highest order of proof that they are sinful; because no pain can ever exist except induced by violated law,[20] and violating law is sin itself. Avoid sinning and you escape suffering, but all suffering is the consequence of sinning. The very painfulness of sickness is therefore the witness of its sinfulness. Sickness is caused by violating the laws of health. Such violation, *all* violation, of law, is wrong. Therefore all sickness is sinful, and the consequent pain is its penalty. Health is the ordinance of nature, and the great instrumentality of every other duty, and therefore our first and highest duty to our fellow-men, ourselves, and our God; to our fellow-men, because we cannot discharge our obligations to them without it, and if sick, we wrong them by occasioning them pain; to ourselves, because we can perform no duty, and enjoy no blessing, without it; and to our God, because we are under the most imperious obligation to obey His laws,[19] those of health, of course, included. Ye who demur, say what " divine right " have you to violate God's laws? Show " indulgences " from the court of heaven, granting permission to trample on divine ordinances, or else admit such trespass and its consequent sickness to be wicked. None have any business to be sick.

PREMATURE death is still more sinful, because occasioned by a still greater violation of law; is indeed the chief of crimes. Is not suicide most wicked? Yet it consists in the same breach of these same laws, which broken, cause premature death. As to shorten life by self-murder is a sin of the highest grade; so to shorten it by injuring health, is equally wicked; because both result precisely alike, namely, in the destruction of life, and by similar means, namely, a breach of the health laws. Unless we have a divine "right" to commit suicide, gradual or sudden, we have none to incur premature death; and inasmuch as suicide is most heinous, by so much, and for precisely the same reason, is it equally wicked to induce death by the careless exposure or wanton injury of health. The extreme painfulness, too, of premature death, is Nature's proclamation that its cause is propor-

tionately sinful. Fraud, robbery, and the like, are as trifling sins
in comparison to the destruction of health, as life is more valuable
than property. It is high time that we considered sickness as
it actually is, *high-handed rebellion* against God, and a crime
against man:

EXCEPTIONS indeed occur, whenever unavoidable accidents, or
causes beyond our control transpire, but they do not invalidate
this doctrine. Then let old and young, one and all, take every
possible pains to *preserve* and *improve* health. Behold the infinite perfection of these bodies! Behold the variety and power of
their functions. Be astonished at their almost angelic capabilities
for enjoyment![16] O, who can contemplate this highest piece of
divine mechanism without overflowing wonder and gratitude?
And was *such* a structure made to be abused? Shall we bandy
about so delicate, so complicated, so infinitely valuable a gift as
if an old box? Shall we undo all He has done to secure the in-
valuable blessings of health and happiness? Shall we impair,
vitiate, or break down functions thus inimitably perfect in themselves, thus laden with all the enjoyments of life? Shall we not
rather cherish and enhance them? Shall we nurture our land and
trees, and neglect our own bodies? Shall we not love and keep
a present thus divine, on account of its own intrinsic worth, and
of its Bountiful Giver? Shall we cherish rich earthly legacies, yet
abuse a divine legacy which is perpetually bringing forth, from its
exhaustless store-house, every enjoyment, actual and possible,
of life? Shall we love earthly donors the more the greater their
gifts, and not worship, with our whole souls, the Author of that
life so infinitely above all other bestowments? Life, O, how precious![16] Its wanton waste, how infinitely foolish and wicked!
Let others do as they list, but let our great concern be to OCCUPY
this Heaven-conferred talent while it lasts, and to guard against
its injury with Argus vigilance. God forbid our doing or allowing the least thing to impair its efficacy, or neglecting any means
of enhancing its capabilities. This sacred duty, this paramount
obligation to God and our own soul, let us study and fulfil. O,
thou Bestower of this "pearl of great price," grant or deny
whatever else Thou wilt, give us intellect to know, and the inflexible determination to practice, *the laws and conditions of
health and life.*

33. — HEALTH RESTORABLE; DISEASE CURABLE.

ABNORMAL action always flexes towards normal. Nature invariably seeks to *right up* all wrong functions. Pain itself is a curative process.[113] The existence of remedial agents is not a matter of doubt, but is an experimental *fact*. Nature might justly have left all broken bones, severed nerves and blood vessels, and all other results of violated natural law, in whatever state they might have occurred; whereas our infinitely benevolent Father has instituted a *remedial principle*, and made provision for reuniting broken bones, and ruptured blood vessels, repairing lacerated muscles and nerves, and restoring debilitated and disordered functions. Regaining health is possible, though much more difficult than its preservation. Whilst an ounce of preservation of health is worth more than pounds of cures of disease, yet Nature's recuperative provisions are indeed marvellous. Her restoratives are neither few, nor feeble, nor restricted. Though she punishes some violations of her health laws, such as an amputated head, a pierced heart, &c., with death; yet most diseases, if taken in season, and managed rightly, can be cured or mitigated. Rank poisons can be neutralized or expelled. Fevers are a curative process.[113] In fact, pain signifies that the system has life enough left to undertake restoration. "While there is life, there is hope." The restorative effects of cundurango, this new cancer cure, imported from Mexico, are said to be efficacious. Doctors often pronounce death on patients who afterwards recover. Nature has taken the utmost pains to so vary her remedies as to heal most of the ills to which man is subject. Some restoratives act as if by magic; and in most cases these remedies are found in those particular *localities* where the diseases they cure abound. As, wherever any poisonous serpent crawls, there grows some weed specifically adapted to cure the venom of its bite; so we may look for some antidote to fever and ague, rheumatism, consumption, &c., in the localities which give rise to these diseases; so that *home* remedies will generally be found better than imported.

These medicines abound in the vegetable kingdom, and since some are there, why not *all ?* Since Nature has prepared them all ready at our hands, why resort to art? Can man compound

11

and prepare them better than his Maker? The simple fact of the existence of vegetable remedial agents already prepared, shows that we must not take Nature's work out of her own hands. Does the laboratory of art surpass that of Nature?[112]

And since she has undertaken to cure, why not *trust* to her mainly? Why not, after furnishing her with the right materials and conditions, *let her mostly alone?* She does well whatever she undertakes.[113]

Of course this recuperation depends mainly upon the power of constitution yet remaining; those having first-rate constitutions obviously recovering much faster and more fully than those with weak. But our present purpose is rather to state the *possibility* of such restoration than to discuss its "ways and means," which will be done hereafter.[112-130]

SECTION IV..

PROPORTIONATE AND CO-ORDINATE ACTION A LAW OF NATURE: AND ITS PROMOTION.

34.— NATURE DEMANDS EQUILIBRIUM IN ALL THINGS.

WHAT KEEPS the earth in its orbit, and times all its motions to a second? Proportionate and co-ordinate action between the forces of gravitation and repulsion. Nature is all made up of this proportion. The more or the less of any one function, the more or the less of all its co-ordinate functions, is a universal law of things. Its philosophy is self-evident, and its necessity absolute.

As A FACT, it is universal. All roots of trees and vegetables are in proportion to the tops they nourish, and all tops are larger or smaller according as their roots are either; and amputating either, requires the equal amputation of the other also. Hence cutting off a large part of the tops or of the roots of any tree or vegetable without cutting off the other in proportion, injures or else kills it. Cutting down a tree kills its roots, because it destroys this proportion between its roots and top. The roots continue to eliminate their wonted nutrition, but its having no top to consume it, gorges them to death. Hence transplanted trees should have as much of their tops cut off as they lose of their roots by being taken up; while cutting off most of the top of trees is about sure to well nigh or quite kill them.

THE BODILY organs and functions furnish innumerable illustrations of this natural law. Can a small heart serve a large body as well as a large one could? Can a weak stomach digest for an athletic and powerful frame as well as could a strong one? Would not a powerful stomach with weak lungs be like yoking an elephant with a sheep? Since a given amount of oxygen inhaled through the lungs can combine with *only* its "fixed" equivalent of carbon supplied by the stomach, a predominance of either over the other is inimical to life, by leaving a surplus to clog and derange the whole system.[119] The supply of vitality must needs equal its expenditure, or exhaustion must follow; whereas when its supply exceeds its consumption undue corpulency and obesity supervene. Hence extra lean persons need to manufacture more vitality, but consume less; while extra fat ones should consume more, or manufacture less, or both, or else become diseased.

ACCELERATING any function accelerates all the other functions. Nature requires and compels us to breathe the more, the more we exercise. In all cases, increasing muscular action by running, or lifting, or walking fast up hill, endoubles the breathing, circulation, perspiration, digestion, &c., in a like proportion; whereas soon after we stop any violent exercise, we cease laboring for breath, and the pulse runs down to its natural level. Let universal fact attest the truth of this law.

MOST DISEASES are also consequent on the predominance or deficiency of one or another of our functions. Consumption consists in the deficiency of lung action,[125] and dyspepsia in excessive nervous and cerebral action over that of the stomach; [120] so that its chief cure consists in diminishing brain action, and promoting muscular; that is, in restoring a balance of action between all the functions.

FEVERS are caused by a surplus of alimentation over its consumption and evacuation, and a consequent thickening of the blood; and by burning up this surplus *within* the system promote subsequent health.

THAT BELLE, rendered delicate, nervous, sickly, and miserable, by excessive nervous and cerebral derangement consequent on novel-reading, parties, amusements, and all the excitement of fashionable life, can never be cured by medicines, but can by work. Her malady consists in a predominance of nerve over muscle, and her remedy in restoring the balance between them. She is doomed either to wear out a miserable existence, or else to *exercise her muscles;* nor can salvation come from any other source. And one of the great reasons why journeyings, visits to springs, voyages, and the like, often effect such astonishing cures is, that they relieve the nervous system, at the same time that they increase muscular and vital action. The same exercise taken at home, would cure quite as speedily and effectually by the same means — a restoration of proportion between their functions. Nine invalids in every ten are undoubtedly rendered feeble by this one cause, and can be cured by labor. How many thousands, so weakly and sickly that they begin to despair of life, finally give up their business, move upon a farm, and soon find themselves well? Exercise has often cured those who have been bedridden many years.

A DOCTOR in Lowell, Mass., was called thirty miles, in great haste, to a sick woman, whose case had baffled all medical treatment, and was regarded as hopeless. All expected was merely to mitigate a disease of long standing : recovery being considered out of the question. The doctor saw that she was very nervous, and had been dosed almost to death, and told her that if she would follow his directions *implicitly,* he could cure her ; for he had one kind of medicine of great power, but which was useful only in cases exactly like hers, in which it was an infallible cure. After telling her how often she must take it, he added, that she must get up and *walk* across the room the second day, and *ride* out the third.

" O, that was impossible, for she had not been off her bed in many years, and was so very weak," &c.

" O, but this medicine will give you so much strength that you will be *able* to do both, and it will prevent any injurious consequences arising therefrom. Besides, it will not operate unless you stir about some. Do just as I tell you, and you will be off your bed in ten days."

She sent an express (the medicine being so rare that he did not take it with him) (?) after his bread pills rolled in aloes, to make them taste like medicine, took them, and *exercised* as prescribed, and the third day she actually got into a carriage, in ten days was able to leave her bed, soon after was able to work, and yet lives to be a blessing to her family, and to pour upon the doctor a literal flood of gratitude for performing so wonderful a cure, which nothing but restoring the lost proportion between her nerves and muscles could have effected. Nineteen twentieths of the invalids, especially females, of our land become so mainly by excessive nervous and deficient muscular and vital action, and can be cured by exercise in the open air, because many are rendered invalids less by insufficient exercise, than by insufficient *breath*. Females, and those who work hard in-doors perpetually, such as clerks in packing, unpacking, etc., often lose their health because they inhale rarefied air, and thus do not obtain a supply of oxygen adequate to its consumption. The reason why we breathe the more the more we exercise, is, that we need the more oxygen. Breathing copiously without obtaining a due supply of oxygen, is analogous to a proportionate suspension of breath. Such should work less, and thus preserve the proportion between the consumption and the supply of oxygen.

CONSUMPTIVE PATIENTS furnish another illustration of this principle. Why are they consumptive? Because their brains and nerves predominate over their vital and muscular apparatus; as is evinced by their being slim, sharp-featured, small-chested, and having small muscles, great sensitiveness, intense emotions, clear heads, and fine feelings.[125] This *disproportion* of function constitutes their consumptive tendency. Their lungs are too small for their brains. Restoring the balance obviates the tendency. Apoplexy, gout, obesity, corpulency, and the like, are caused by the opposite extreme, and can be cured by eating less and working more.

PRECOCIOUS children and youth furnish another illustration. How common the expression "that child is too smart to live;" because general observation attests the premature death of most brilliants. Hear that broken-hearted mother enumerate the virtues of her departed child — tell how fond of books, how quick to learn, how apt in remarks, how sweet-dispositioned and good — all produced by excessive cerebral action. Its death was caused by the *predominance* of mind. Its head ate up its body. As the vital energies cannot be expended twice, and as an extremely active brain robs the muscles and vital apparatus, the lat-

ter become small' and feeble, are attacked by disease, and die,
and of course the brain with it. Such parents, ignorant of this
principle, too often ply such prodigies with books and mental
stimulants, and thus aggravate this disproportion, and hasten
death; whereas they should pursue the opposite course; should
use every exertion to restrain cerebral, and promote muscular
action. The order of Nature requires that the great proportion
of their vital energies should be expended in laying a deep and
broad foundation for a corresponding superstructure of mental
greatness, and every item of vitality required by the body but
expended on the mind only weakens both. The great fault of
modern education is robbing the body to develop the mind —
trying to make learned babies and nursery prodigies at the expense of health. In doing this, parents often make them simpletons for life, or else youthful corpses. As when the miser had
learned his horse to live without eating, it died; so just as these
children become extra smart, they die. Where are those poetic
geniuses, the Misses Davidson? · In their graves at fifteen! What
folly parental vanity often perpetrates! No education is better
than such robbing of the body, ruin of the health, and destruction of life.

Extra talented and lovely youth are also more mortal than
others. The flower of both sexes are more liable to die young
than those more coarsely organized; because of this same preponderance of cerebral over muscular and vital power. Many of
those who take our first college appointments die soon after they
graduate, because they have studied, studied, studied, night and
day, year in and·year out, thus keeping their brains continually
upon the stretch, yet using their muscles little more than to go
to and from their meals and recitations. Is it any wonder that
they pay the forfeit of impaired health in blighted prospects and
premature death? Why should their entire range of classical
studies not embrace as important a natural law as this?

WORKING MEN furnish a converse illustration of this law.
They exercise their muscles too much; and brains too little. They
labor, eat, and sleep, but that is about all. To those crowning
pleasures, the exercise of mind, they are comparative strangers.
Their muscles rob their brains as effectually as the heads of the
literati rob their bodies. If they sit down to read or listen, they

fall asleep. Their finer sensibilities become blunted by inaction, just as those of the fashionable classes become morbid by over action. Their minds are sluggish, thinking powers obtuse, feelings hard to rouse, and all their capabilities of enjoyment partially palsied, because most of their energies are directed to their muscles. Besides this loss of enjoyment, they are much more subject to actual disease than they would be if they labored less and studied more.

This principle applies still more forcibly to the working classes of the old world. Laborers generally might live many years longer, and much more happily, if they worked less and studied more.

UNHEALTHY TRADES, as shoemaking, saddlery, drawing, painting, sewing, etc., are generally rendered so by exercising only a portion of the system, and can be rendered salubrious by exercising the dormant limbs and muscles an hour or two per day. To seamstresses this advice is particularly applicable and important. Sitting for months together in one posture, arched inwardly and their shoulders thrown forward, thus doubly impeding respiration, digestion, and all the vital functions, at the same time taking next to no exercise, no wonder that so many of them break down even while learning their trade, and work in misery for life. Let such walk at least two miles per day, or dance an hour before retiring, and also sit up straight, and sewing will not injure them. They should also restrict their diet.

THE INSTITUTIONS of society are most unfavorable to this required proportion of muscular, vital, and mental action. As things now are, those who work at all, work excessively; and as labor is considered a disgrace, all who can, are straining every nerve to live without it. Society should be so constructed as to require laborers to work only about half the day, and allow them the balance for mental and moral cultivation; while the literary, sedentary, and fashionable classes should labor several hours every day, if not for wages, at least for health. The fullest measure of personal happiness requires that all should appropriate about eight hours in every twenty-four to the vital apparatus, to sleep, food, and the supply of exhausted animal energy; about eight hours more to muscular exercise, mostly in the form of manual, productive labor; and about eight more to mental cultivation and moral improvement. "All work and no play," cuts off that vast range of pleasure designed and adapted to flow into the soul of man through the channel of mind; and continued mental application, by concentrating vitality in the brain, withdraws it from the muscles, stomach, and heart, thus impairing respiration, circulation, and all the vital functions, and of course curtails talent and even life itself; while epicures, gentlemen and ladies of leisure, and all fashionable idlers, rob both muscle and brain, so that all these classes fail to obtain the great end of life— happiness; [16] whereas, if all would labor several hours per day, so as to promote all the animal functions and insure health, they would thus furnish the brain and nervous system with an abundant supply of that animal energy so indispensable to mental power, and thus vastly enhance clearness of thought, retentiveness of memory, intellectual attainments, and moral excellence. None can become great or good without *manual labor*. Man must exercise if only to keep his brain in working order; it being to the brain what the sharpening of his tools is to the workman. Laborers plead that they have no time to study, yet they should *take* time. They were created to *enjoy;* and since they can enjoy much more by commingling study with labor, practical wisdom requires that they make mental culture as much a part of their business as work. Business and professional men, lawyers, ministers, bankers, brokers, merchants, clerks, editors, artists, etc., again say they have no time for exercise; but let such remember that this is the very way to *gain* time, by augmenting mental efficiency, and especially prolonging their lives. The result is that our business, fashionable, and sedentary classes have a great preponderance of the mental temperament over the vital and muscular, and hence are delicate, sharp-favored, homely, excitable, dyspeptic, nervous, melancholy invalids, living but a short and miserable life; while the working classes, though endowed by nature with excellent heads, yet lack that cultivation requisite to the development of their natural talents and virtues.

Those whose sole life-object is to see how long they can live, or how happily, should divide each twenty-four hours into three parts, and devote eight hours to sleep, rest, and meals; eight more to vigorous exercise or recreation; and the balance to the exercise of mind, uniting the last two whenever practicable.

Those whose object is to become intellectually great or learned, or gain or retain health, or all these combined, should pursue the same course. Burritt, the learned blacksmith, is often referred to as an intellectual prodigy. He certainly is the wonder of the learned world. Besides understanding more than fifty languages, he has accumulated a richer treasure of historical and miscellaneous information than probably any man living; and yet, in his letter to Edward Everett, he states that his poverty compelled him to labor at the anvil *eight hours* daily. This is the main secret of his greatness. "Go thou and do likewise," and train up your children, too, in harmony with this principle.

GROWING YOUTH require a great expenditure of vital energy during adolescence. Their vitality should predominate over their mentality. Especially it is better to ripen too late than early. As early fruits soon decay, but late ones keep all winter, and as the poplar tree, and all vegetables which grow fast, die soon, while the slow-growing oak and pine last long, and do much more service; so it is much better that children ripen late than early. So certain and uniform is this law, that the length of life of all animals can be calculated from the age at which they come to maturity. This law governs all that grows, man as a race, and every individual included. Accordingly, long-lived persons mature late, and our most talented men were backward boys. Adam Clarke was a very blockhead at school — an eyesore to his teacher, and a butt among his mates. What was young Patrick Henry? The dullest of the dull. Most distinguished men of all ages were backward boys; and in general, they entered on their career of greatness late in life Let children be children till out of their teens, and enter too late upon the business of life rather than too early. This eagerness of our youth to begin life early occasions immense misery. Do not leave the minds of children an uncultivated waste, yet expend only their *surplus* vitality in either study or labor. Sacrifice not one iota of health to mental acquirements. The brains of children are soft, and their nerves less sensitive to burns, bruises, colds, and hurts than those of adults. The nervous system is the last to mature, and last to yield to the approaches of age and of a natural death. Hence little pains should be taken to cultivate the intellect until Nature has fully matured the brain and nervous system. Some species

12

of animals are born blind. What consummate folly to cut open their eyes, or put on glasses, or attempt to *make* them see by artificial means before their natural time! Let Nature have her perfect work. Follow where she leads; but never precede her. Let your first labor be to give them strong *constitutions*, and to lay in as large a supply of physical energy as possible. Let intellectual attainments be what Nature has made them, *secondary.* Would you not lose by hurrying your fruit trees into bloom so early that the frosts of spring would certainly nip the bud?

35. — Exhaustion as inviting Disease.

Fatigue, temporary and permanent, physical and mental, consists in a deficiency of vitality as compared with its expenditure, and hence is a violation of this law of balance; and occasions an almost incalculable amount of disease. Vitality resists disease in proportion to its abundance. As an active skin nullifies exposures to colds which overcome a feeble one, so strong constitutions withstand exposures which would break down weak ones. While full of vitality and animal vigor, say in the morning, wet feet, malaria, noxious gases, contagion of various kinds, extreme cold, or exposures are resisted with impunity, yet when fatigued, deprived of sleep, or hungry, comparatively trifling causes, otherwise innoxious, prostrate the system with sickness, whereas keeping a full supply of vitality would have resisted the disease. Hence few persons sicken suddenly, but most are ailing more or less for days and weeks beforehand; because debility, by cutting off the supply of vitality, leaves the system too feeble to resist renewed exposures. Even in apoplectic, and other sudden attacks, disease has been undermining the system perhaps for years. Most forms of disease, taken in season, can be thrown off at once, and protracted illness averted. Extreme and protracted exhaustion generally precedes and induces consumption; many of its victims having first worn themselves completely out just before being taken down; whilst but for such exhaustion they would have escaped. Many a one has been prostrated by disease after having watched day and night around the sick bed, not, as generally supposed, because the disease was contagious, but because their exhaustion left the gates of life open to the ingress of the enemy. That excessive labor invites disease is a matter of general experience and observation. Our army abundantly proves that clerks and professional men, who before lived mostly within doors, could march farther, endure more hardships, and accomplish more hard army work, fighting included, than farmers and lumbermen, whom previous labors had broken down. How many, after seasons of unusually protracted and arduous labor, first became debilitated and then sick! American females, in particular, contract many of their diseases in consequence of previous exhaustion, occasioned by undue confinement within doors, late hours, restless children, and consequent deprivation of sleep, perpetual kitchen drudgery, unintermitting toil, and kindred causes; and many chronic invalids can be cured simply by rest and recreation, whose case medicines can never reach. They have expended animal energy faster than supplied it, become debilitated, are thus exposed to disease, and can be restored only by restoring the equilibrium of the system. Special attention is invited to the absolute necessity of providing a re-supply of vitality.[37] Exhaustion, so fatal to health, so prolific of disease, is not generally occasioned by too great an *expenditure* of vitality, as much as by its *non*-supply. Invalids might expend much more than they now do with impunity, provided they would re-supply more by obeying the recuperative laws. Like a poor farmer, they take all off, but put nothing on.

In short, if any one function runs down to a given level, *all* the functions must run down to the same level. As in case of a dozen vessels filled with water connected at the bottom, when either is tapped one foot or five feet from the bottom, *all* must sink to the level of the lowest; so if all your vital functions but one are six in the scale of seven, while that one is only two, none can be exercised above two, unless this weak one is first restored. Invalid men and women by millions, all of whose functions but one, their liver, or heart, or lungs, or kidneys, &c., are in perfect working order, wear out an inert and miserable existence, or die, who, by restoring this *one* weak function, could work on, enjoy on, a score or two of years longer. For such no help, no salvation, remains but to learn *what* function is weak, and restore it. And almost all are more or less impaired in some one respect, and thus maimed in all respects; whereas restoring this weak one would restore all the others.

These proofs of our doctrine of proportion might be extended illimitably, but is it not too obvious to require it? Does it not unfold a *fundamental* condition of health, and cause of disease? Is any other equally essential to mental or physical capability? If physicians understood this law, and labored to restore that lost balance which occasion diseases, instead of dosing down powerful drugs, they would save a large proportion of those patients they now lose; and if mankind in general would preserve or restore this proportion — if the sedentary and fashionable would study and fret less, but take more exercise, laborers rest and read more, those who have over-eaten would fast, and those who sit much in-doors would exercise much in the open air — the great majority of chronic invalids would soon be gladdened by returning health; that most dreadful penalty of violated law, death, be postponed a score or two of years; every faculty of body and mind be incalculably enhanced; and their pains supplanted by pleasures. Proportion between our eating and breathing, and between these two and muscular action, and between all three and the exercise of mind and feeling, will insure the observers of this law a high order of intellectual capability, moral excellence, and a long and happy life. The application of this law to the mental faculties will constitute much of the framework of Volume II.

Is it not strange that a condition of life and health thus apparent and fundamental, should have been wholly overlooked by all writers and lecturers on life and health? And yet it has been.

36. — Strengthening weak Functions by their Exercise.
" There is that giveth, and yet increaseth." — *Christ.*

Practice makes perfect. Culture improves. Use strengthens. Exercise develops. Those oaks which grow up alone in the field, are stronger than those which grow in the forest, because the former are perpetually obliged to put forth far more power to resist the surging winds than do those protected by each other in the forest; while those nailed to a wall always remain small and weak from disuse. Working horses aright strengthens them. Training racers increases both their speed and bottom. Wild lions, &c., are stronger than tame, because they take more exercise. The training of walkists, pugilists, dancers, acrobats, &c.,

redoubles their performing powers. All laborers labor with the more skill, ease, and power, the more they become accustomed to their work. Gymnasts increase their weights at every day's trial, yet lift them, thus increased, easier and easier every day of training. A gymnast developed his muscles to extraordinary size and power, but this robbed his stomach so that he became a confirmed dyspeptic; that is, the vigorous culture of his muscles rendered them most powerful, while the non-culture of his stomach enfeebled it. Did not a like disproportion cause the death of that champion oarsman Renforth? Literary men generally have larger heads and smaller muscles than laborers, while the latter have larger muscles and smaller heads than literati. When Dr. Windship first began to lift, he could raise only four hundred pounds, though he had practised gymnastics four years; but towards the end of his second year of training in lifting, he could raise *seven* hundred, and went on increasing every year, to ten, twelve, fifteen, twenty, and *twenty-four* hundred, till he can now raise *twenty-seven hundred pounds!* In 1852 he thought he should be able some day to raise a ton, but never more; whereas he now confidently expects to be able to lift *three thousand* pounds. Yet he is not naturally stronger than the average of men, except that he has simply developed by *culture* the strength inherent in him by nature. , None of us at all realize how strong we could render ourselves by right exercise.

D. P. BUTLER, of 43 West Street, Boston, in 1860, was coming down with consumption, took the lifting cure as his only remedy, recovered, and though at first he fell below two hundred pounds, yet he can now lift and hold with his hands probably *more than any other living man*, and his consumption is all gone. He is curing invalids by thousands solely by lifting.

A LITTLE GIRL, six years old, put under his training for a curvature of the spine, could raise only fifty-six pounds; but after practising just one year, could lift and hold *two hundred and thirty-six pounds;* and her spinal flexure straightened thereby!

PROFESSOR HITCHCOCK, who superintends the gymnastic department of Amherst College, attests how wonderfully his pupils improve in size and power of muscle, lungs, &c., by training.

THE HANDS and arms of sailors, and the feet and legs of expert dancers and pedestrians, are larger, relatively, than their other

organs, not thus especially exercised. Rowing enlarges the chest
and arms. Swinging the sledge enlarges and consolidates the
muscles of the arms. The right hand is generally larger than
the left, obviously because used the most; and its fingers than the
corresponding ones of the left.

LIONS are largest and strongest in their fore quarters, which
they use most in seizing and tearing their prey; but kangaroos
in their hind quarters, their main means of locomotion.

THIS LAW applies equally to all the other bodily organs. The
lungs can be enlarged and strengthened equally by culture.
What stentorian voices street pedlers acquire, even though once
delicate females, by crying "strawberries," "charcoal," and other
articles, resounding throughout our innermost chambers, and dis-
turbing our late slumbers. Twice during his collegiate course
the Author was obliged to fall back on account of consumptive
proclivities, but lecturing every evening, and talking professionally all day, soon not only arrested this consumptive tendency,
but rendered his lungs, then his weakest part, now his strongest,
for he lectures two, and often four hours, in every twenty-four,
besides talking very loudly in his office from eight A. M. to ten
P. M., except when lecturing or eating, without one thought of
lulling fatigue. But for this extra *use* of his lungs, he should
have been in his grave thirty-five years ago. Baron Cuvier, and
many other public speakers, have staved off consumption by
public speaking.

THE STOMACH is governed by this law; so is the skin. Those
who are so *very* particular as to what they eat usually have
weak stomachs. Those who want good, lusty digestive powers
must *tax*, not favor, yet not abuse them. Those catch côlds most
easily who *bundle up* the most. Exposing the system to the cold
fortifies it against them. Those children guarded the most tenderly and assiduously against exposure to the air, catch ten colds
while barefooted and ragged urchins, out in all weathers, and
wet through in all rains, catch none.

Another still stronger proof of this law is, that Nature does her
utmost to *restore* the balance whenever it is impaired. Those
children born with too much head for body instinctively race and
tear around incessantly, but are averse to study; because exercise
tends to restore this balance, which study prevents. Children

and adults often *grow out* of this and that ailment. Vigorous exercise of mind or body redoubles appetite, breathing, &c. That is, increasing any of our functions increases them all. Cutting off half or so of the roots of any standing tree, either kills about half its top, or else arrests its growth. An overloaded stomach draws on all the other organs for help; and so of weak or oppressed lungs, heart, &c.

Yet why labor farther, even thus far, to prove a fact and a law as obvious as that right exercise strengthens all organs, and their functions? As well labor to prove that the sun shines. Please think in how many thousand forms this great truth is admitted and practised.

Its personal application to the improvement of our own individual health, therefore, becomes as important as health is valuable.[29] Each reader should inquire, in the name of whatever value he puts upon his own or family's life and health, which of his or their organs are weak, so that, by restoring them, he can improve the efficiency of all the others. No other knowledge is more important, nor is ignorance on any other subject equally fatal. Hence learning how to cultivate these weak organs takes the first step towards success, health, and happiness.

CHAPTER II.

RESPIRATION; ITS LAWS, ORGANS, AND PROMOTION.

SECTION I.

THE LUNGS; THEIR OFFICE, STRUCTURE, ETC.

37.— VITALITY THE FIRST PREREQUISITE OF LIFE.

MANUFACTURING VITALITY is life's first and greatest work. Man, and all animated beings, are so constituted that every exercise of all muscles, nerves, and organs, whatever we say, do, and are, and all the operations of our entire and complicated mental and physical nature, *expend vitality.* As no machinery can be propelled without consuming that power which impels; so that wonderful mechanism which manifests life, mind included, cannot move one iota, in whole or in part, without thereby *using up* that vitality or animal energy which constitutes its motive principle. And since life consists in a vast variety and complication of functions, some of which are often most powerful and intense, of course its consumption of vitality must be proportionally great; even though individual functions expend but little. And this consumption is in the exact ratio of that life which it propels; because the latter *consists* in the former. We sometimes think, feel, do, and therefore live more in one hour than at other times in ten or twenty hours; and of course consume vital energy proportionally faster.

Moreover, all these functions are performed with as much more rapidity and efficiency when this supply is abundant, than when it is reduced, as machinery works when the "head" of steam or water is great, than when it is low; and for a kindred reason. Except in cases of corpulency, we think, feel, perform, and therefore live more or less easily, vigorously, and effectually in proportion as this supply is abundant; but become enfeebled in proportion as it declines.

It is therefore perfectly obvious that unless this great and con-

stant consumption is re-supplied, exhaustion must inevitably
follow ; which of course proportionally reduces life, and invites
disease,[36] and if carried too far, suspends life altogether.

THE GREAT ART of living and working then, consists in *keeping
up* a full supply of this vital force. Many break down seemingly
from over-work, but really from want of vitality, who could have
done all they did do, and twice as much more, with perfect ease,
and without sustaining the least injury, if they had simply taken
fair care of their *re-supply* functions. Both the preservation and
the restoration of health depend more on this vital re-supply than
on all other causes combined. What would you think of that
teamster who should work his team up to the top of its strength
without ever stopping to rest and feed, until they thus became
unable to work any longer? Then what do you think of yourself
for pursuing a like course? As the very *way* to get the most work
out of his team consists in keeping it in good working order ; so
the great art of doing the most work possible with head or hands
consists in keeping on a full head of life-power with which *to*
work. As the best way to "whip up" a jaded horse is to give
him food and rest ; so the best way to urge on any work in hand
is to put and keep yourself and workmen in good working *order*.
On no account work when "all tired out." Few things are equally
injurious. Keep on a full head of vital *steam*. As that engineer
would be foolish who should run his engine away out upon the
prairie, far from wood and water, till he had used up all of both,
so that he could go neither way ; so many men and women work
on with all their might till they can work no longer, without
taking any time to recuperate. The secret of Benton's extraordinary working capacity consisted in his having a vital laboratory of marvellous size and efficiency, and then in his *taking good
care* of it besides. As, though you had a machine the most perfect possible, it would be useless without motive power ; so,
though you have an organism and a brain of the very best quality,
it is useless except as far as it is supplied with that vitality which
sets and keeps it at work. It is to life and all its functions what
capital is in business, indispensable. No comparisons, no ampli-
fications, can possibly do justice to this important subject. Why
has it been so long overlooked?

PROMOTING this re-supply, therefore, becomes the first, as it is
13

the most neglected, art of living; and of course the primary topic of this volume.

The vital organs, those located within the ribs and pelvis, are ordained solely to manufacture this vitality. Of course the most important work of the physiologist consists in showing how to promote this manufacture. This is that most important subject to which we now proceed. Its first function is, —

38. — BREATHING A PARAMOUNT LIFE NECESSITY.

All that lives breathes, and must keep on breathing till death. Breathing is as necessary to vegetable life as to animal, and to fish, as to fowl and man. Trees, vegetables, mosses, &c., breathe through their leaves, or those blades of grasses, grains, &c., which subserve the same breathing purpose. Fish fulfil this identical function by respiring water instead of air, through gills instead of lungs. The first post-natal function of every new-born babe, is to take a good long electric breath; which sets the blood bounding off through its system with a rush, and starts every other function into instantaneous action. It so is that the most important function of terrestrial life, from first to last, is deep, copious respiration; and some would live on longer if they could only keep on breathing still longer.

THE ELEMENTS furnished to the blood by the breath are more, and more perpetually, indispensable to life than those derived from digestion, because we can live longer without food than air. Starvation is terrible, and soon fatal; but suffocation is worse, and despatches its victims a hundred fold more quickly and certainly. Indeed, mankind can live but a few minutes without breath; and those deprived of it die the soonest who are the most active. Thus the slow-moulded Malay can stay under water seven and eight to ten minutes, and then rise without injury, whereas the more active Caucasian suffocates if he remains under five or six minutes — the difference being one quarter in favor of the sluggish; because the more active the subject the more rapidly he consumes the energies derived from breath, and therefore the more frequent and copious must be this re-supply. The faster we live, the more and oftener we must breathe. As the snake, frog, alligator, and other cold-blooded, sluggish animals can live a long time without breath, especially while torpid; so the more stupid the human animal the less breath he requires. Hence, ability to hold the breath a great length of time is a poor recommendation.

OXYGEN, in large and perpetually renewed quantities, is the first prerequisite of the vital process. Without it, all the materials of life furnished by digestion would be of no avail. They are the timber and the tools of the vital organs; while oxygen is the master workman, the grand motive-power of the animal economy, indeed, of universal nature. The vital process closely resembles combustion, of which oxygen is the great agent and promoter. Even cotton, combustible as it is, cannot be ignited when well baled with iron hoops, because they keep it so closely packed together that the air, and therefore oxygen, cannot well penetrate it; whereas, when the bands burn off, so that the cotton is opened up to the air, it burns fiercely. As fire goes down with the scarcity of oxygen; and goes out when it disappears; so the fire of life wanes in proportion as this supply is diminished, and death supervenes almost immediately when it disappears. This imperious demand of the system for it renders the requisition for breath absolute, and its suspension soon fatal. A demand thus imperious signifies that its office is equally absolute.

From what source is oxygen obtained? From breath. Air always contains it, being composed of twenty-one parts of oxygen to seventy-eight of nitrogen; the other hundredth being carbonic acid gas, and going to support vegetation. Air, wherever found, and under all circumstances, is composed of these substances always in the same proportion. Any variation destroys it, or makes it into something else. Air, and of course oxygen, abound wherever man can go, unless artificially excluded. Being highly fluid, it can penetrate the least possible crevice, and even some solid substances. It not only surrounds the earth, extending some forty-two miles, and probably many more, above it in all directions, but its great heaviness presses with immense weight upon every part of the surface of the body. Its quantity is, therefore, as illimitable as its demand is imperious.

39. — THE LUNGS, THEIR STRUCTURE, LOCATION, &c.

LUNGS execute this all important breathing function. They are located in the very top of the chest, extending from beneath

the first rib downward about one third the length of the body proper, occupying most of the chest. They are composed of two hemispheres, the right containing three lobes, as seen in engraving
No. 2, while the left has only two; it being scooped out in the
middle, so as to allow the heart to be partly enveloped in it.

THE TRACHEA, or windpipe, is an air tube, connecting between
the mouth and nose above, and the lungs below, branching at its
bottom into the bronchia; the inflammation of which causes bron-
chitis, while consumption consists in the inflammation and suppuration of the lungs. This trachea conducts the air into and
out of the lungs.

IT BRANCHES into the right and left hemispheres of the lungs,
and then re-branches in-
to each lobe, and con-
tinues to bifucate and
ramify into cells smaller
and still smaller, until
they become too small
to be seen by the naked
eye, amounting to *six
hundred million* in a
single pair of lungs!
This air-cell branching
is evinced in the right-
hand hemisphere of en-
graving No. 2, and the
three lobes of the right
lung, as well as their
general external appear-
ance, are shown in the
left hand.

BLOOD-CELLS also
ramify throughout these
same lungs; each set of
cells occupying about
half of them. These

NO. 2.—SHAPE AND STRUCTURE OF THE LUNGS.

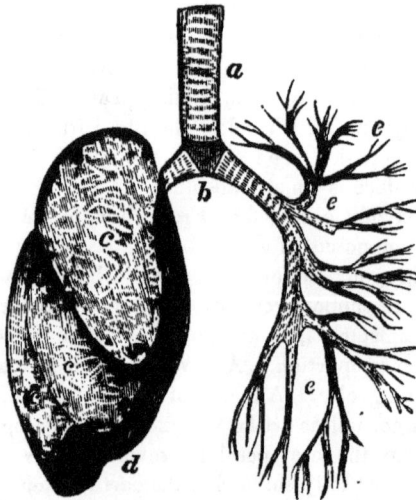

a,   The trachea, or windpipe.
b,   Its branch to the right and left lung.
c c c, The three lobes which compose each right lung.
e e e, The air cells of the lungs dissected.
d,   The pulmonary arteries, or entrance and egress of
        the blood from and to the heart.

blood-cells have their entrance from behind, at *d*, and 14 and 15
in engraving No. 3, which ramify like the air-cells into the minutest conceivable cellules, and lie along, side by side, with the
air-cells.

THE OBJECT of the lungs is to bring the air in the air-cells just as closely alongside of the blood in the blood-cells as possible, and yet keep them separate. The main body of the lungs themselves consists of a gauze membrane, containing, if spread out, from *fifteen to twenty thousand* square inches, according as the lungs are larger or smaller in different persons. This membrane is folded up so as to form two sets of tubes or cells by means of cartilage, on one side of which the blood, and on the other the air, are constantly rushing in and out, by inspiration, expiration, and palpitation.

Nature is a great economist in everything, space included; and by this folding contrivance of this membrane, presents a large amount of surface in a small compass — a contrivance akin to that by which she has folded the intestinal canal, and still further folded its mucous surface, so that a great amount may be contained within a small compass.[1] But for this arrangement, the size of the lungs must have been immense; just as, but for the similar structure of the intestines, mankind must have been six or eight times taller for the same weight than now. A large surface is thus provided for the juxtaposition of the air in the air-cells, side by side with the blood in the blood-cells. The right lung is somewhat larger than the left, and the two envelope the heart; so that this juxtaposition may facilitate their combined functions.

THEY RESEMBLE the finest gauze membrane, the interlacings of which are *so* fine that the *oxygen*, or electricity of the air, but not the air itself, can pass *through* it into the lungs, and the carbonic acid gas pass out through it, but not the blood; nor can the two commingle. It resembles a strainer so fine as to keep the air in its air-cells, and yet allow the gases, oxygen and carbonic acid gas, to pass in and out at pleasure.

MUSCULAR FIBRES ramify throughout all these cells to contract and expand them; while cartilage is employed to form tubes, and embody them into lobes.

ENGRAVING No. 3, after Bourgery, gives a *posterior* view of the heart and its blood-vessels entering and returning from the lungs. It is well worth studying sufficiently to understand this wonderful process, the arterialization of the blood.

No. 3. — POSTERIOR VIEW OF THE HEART, LUNGS, TRACHEA, AND LARYNX.

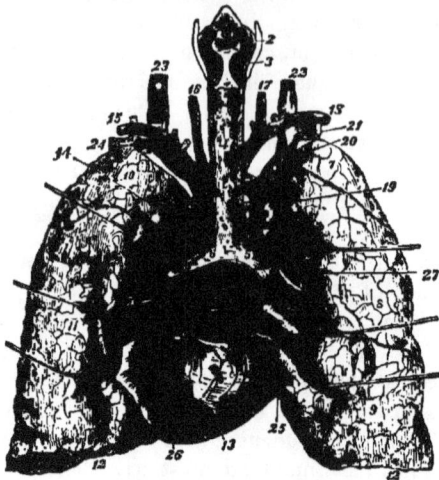

1. Epiglottis cartilage.
2, 3. Arytenoid muscles.
4. Trachea, with its mucous follicles.
5, 6. Right and left bronchi.
7, 8, 9. Right lobes of the lungs.
10, 11. Left do.
12, 12. Their base.
13. Heart.
14. Aorta.
15. Left subclavian artery.
18. Right do.
16. Left primitive carotid do.
17. Right do. do.
19. Vena cava descendens.
20. Right vena innominata.
21. Right subclavian vein.
24. Left do.
22, 23. Right and left jugular veins.
25, 26. Pulmonary do.
27. Pulmonary artery bifurcating as it enters the left lung.

These lungs must next be filled with air, and emptied every few seconds, or from eight to fourteen times per minute, from birth to death, so as to introduce this oxygen into their air-cells.

40. — MEANS BY WHICH THE LUNGS ARE INFLATED.

A VACUUM, made by the contraction of the diaphragm and hoisting of the ribs, introduces this air, freighted with oxygen, into the lungs. Air is neither stringy nor solid, so that we cannot get hold of it to draw it in; but its great weight, caused by its great height, presses it against all it touches at the rate of about fifteen pounds per every square inch, which of course crowds it into all crevices and openings. All required is to make an opening for it into the lungs, when this pressure drives it in.

THE DIAPHRAGM AND RIBS produce this required vacuum or opening, into which this atmospheric pressure pushes it, thus: The diaphragm is a thin, broad, dome-shaped muscle, located between the heart and lungs above, and the stomach, liver, and visceral organs below, attached across the back posteriorly, and to the abdominal muscles anteriorly, represented in engraving No. 4, by that rainbow-shaped body, D D, as it appears when cut down through its middle from right to left.

Suppose a broad, strong, dome-shaped muscle should be thrown over a head, and attached around at the chin, jaws, ears, and nape of the neck, thus covering the face and whole head; and suppose this head to be taken out, leaving this muscle in the same shape, fastened only at its bottom, or lower edges, and you have the shape of the diaphragm.

ALL muscles, diaphragm included, contract. The contraction of the diaphragm hauls its upper portion downwards till it brings it nearly on a level with its lower fastenings.

The base of the lungs (12 in engraving No. 3) fits right down all around the top of this diaphragm, the contraction of which causes what would be a

No. 4.—THE LUNGS, DIAPHRAGM, STOMACH, LIVER, GAUL-BLADDER, AND INTESTINES.

R,   Right, and L, left hemispheres of the lungs.
H,   Heart, being between them, but most on the left side.
D,   Diaphragm, or midriff, below, and separating them from L, the liver.
G,   The gaul-bladder.
Stm., Stomach.
I, I, I, Intestines.

vacuum, only that the atmospheric pressure pushes that portion of the air nearest to the mouth and nose into the lungs. The diaphragm inflates the lower, which is by far the larger portion of the lungs; while their upper part is worked by muscles between the ribs, called intercostal, the contraction of which lifts the ribs, which removes all pressure from the upper and outer portion of the lungs; thus allowing the air to rush in and fill up these upper and outer portions, as the simultaneous contraction of the diaphragm fills their lower portion. Yet these intercostal muscles do not sustain the ribs in this hoisted condition long. They hoist them at every inspiration, but soon leave them to drop back into their normal position, which presses the spent air out of the lungs

again ready for another inflation, at the same time that the diaphragm springs back to its place, and then takes a nap, — a very
short one, though, — to enable it to contract again. These muscles,
the diaphragm and intercostal, cause that heaving motion of the
chest seen in breathing.

ONE FIFTH only of the air in the lungs is expired. An ordinary
pair of lungs, when inflated, contains about one hundred cubic
inches, while the amount expelled at each expiration is generally
about twenty cubic inches; so that only about one fifth of the
air in the lungs is changed at each breath. The object of this
large remainder is probably twofold — to prevent the collapse of
the lungs, and to keep a perpetual supply of oxygen in them.

41. — HOW OXYGEN IS INTRODUCED INTO THE CIRCULATION.

BY WHAT MEANS is the oxygen thus introduced into the lungs,
induced to leave the air it loves, and enter into the blood? What
coaxes it through this lung membrane from the air-cells into the
blood-cells? But for some *efficient* means of such transfer, blood
and air might lie side by side on a surface of twenty million,
instead of twenty thousand, square inches, and forever, instead
of a few seconds, without the transfer of this oxygen from the
air, from which it cannot part without destroying that air, into
the blood. How, then, is this blood oxygenated?

BY IRON in the blood. Its red globules contain so much iron
that many of the ex-French nobility were wont to wear rings
made from the iron extracted from the blood of their friends, for
the same keepsake purpose for which we wear rings enclosing a
lock of our friend's hair. Now, though the oxygen of the air
loves its mate, nitrogen, right well, yet it loves iron better; so
that, when the oxygen contained in the air in the air-cells of the
lungs is brought alongside of the iron contained in the blood in
the lungs, the two rush into each other's arms. But the blood
being unable to pass through this membrane which separates them,
while the oxygen is able to do so, the oxygen jilts its mated
nitrogen, and elopes with the iron into the blood, changes that
blood from its dark venous to a bright red color, thins it, and
inspirits it with life and action; so that it is now all prancing with
vitality, eager to rush throughout the system on its mission of
life. As the powerful Achilles, having seized the beautiful Helen,

carried her off from Troy; so the iron of the blood, having loaded itself with all the oxygen it can carry off, employs the heart and lungs as its coach-and-four to transport its new bride through the arteries into the capillary system, there to deposit this instrumentality of heat.

That oxygen is thus transferred from the air in the lungs into the blood is rendered certain by the fact that when air is inspired, it contains twenty-one per cent. of oxygen, while expired air contains only twelve per cent.; it having lost nine per cent. of its oxygen, but none of its nitrogen. Not till thus supplied with oxygen, is the blood completely freighted with the materials of life. Though it derives from food fibrine, bone, hydrogen, nitrogen, carbon, &c., yet all these are of no avail until it adds to its cargo this grand motive principle of the animal economy. This oxygen, thus obtained, goes frothing, and rushing, and bounding throughout the system, on its life-imparting mission. By what means is the blood circulated?

42. — The Circulation of the Blood effected mainly by Breathing, instead of by the Heat.

Blood is the grand porter of the system — that transfer agent which supplies all parts of the body with required life materials, and also takes up and carries to their outlet all its waste or used up materials. Its presence is life, its absence death, and its rapid circulation a paramount condition of all life and all functions.

Breathing propels this blood. The received theory is that the blood is propelled by means of the *heart*. This is erroneous. Let us show first that the blood is *not* propelled mainly by the heart; next that it *is* propelled chiefly by the breath.

Intelligent readers will at once perceive the immeasurable importance of this problem — just what propels the blood? It vitally concerns all human beings throughout all times and places, in order that they may promote this function by aiding its agent. And all who think will eagerly search out the *philosophy* of the circulation as one of the most wonderful operations of Nature.

And the advancement made in modern science demands that it be applied, *de novo*, to this, as well as to all other questions and theories handed down from former generations. To allow their mere antiquity to overawe or impede their canvass, and, if needs

14

be, their overthrow, is both self-injurious, and unworthy this age of progress; to which we are immeasurably indebted. Surely we can well afford to look new problems squarely in the face, and canvass their intrinsic merits.

The modern theory is that the heart, by mere muscular contraction, furnishes motive-power sufficient to *push* the blood, by *vis a tergo*, or pressure from behind, on through the arteries, through the long, fine capillary blood-vessels, and then through the veins *back* again to the heart. It is estimated that, in effecting this herculean task, the heart exerts a power at every pulsation equal to fifty pounds, varying in different persons, degrees of health, labor &c. ; and therefore equals some three thousand five hundred pounds every minute, *two hundred thousand* pounds every hour, awake and asleep, and *five million* pounds per day. This amount is absolutely impossible. The energy put forth by the heart is reputed to be sufficient to raise its own weight *twenty thousand feet every hour*, whereas, an active pedestrian can raise himself only about one twentieth of that distance, and a locomotive only twenty-seven hundred feet. All such estimates refute themselves, by their own sheer impossibility. Think of the heart putting forth twenty times more relative energy than an active pedestrian climbing a mountain, and a third more than a racing boatman's arm, which is ten times as heavy !

These estimates are deduced, not from the size of its muscles, nor from what it is actually known to accomplish, but from what is *necessary* in order to propel the blood throughout the system as fast as we know it actually does circulate. That all this amazing force is *required* in order to accomplish this circulation, is admitted ; but that the *heart* does not accomplish it is evinced by its* size. Beyond all question, size, other things being equal, is a measure of power. Thus bolts and shafts of iron, timber, ropes, animals, men, &c., are generally the stronger or weaker in proportion as they are the larger or smaller. Then why should a half-pound heart put forth as much muscular force perpetually as an arm weighing ten times more, while taxed to its utmost during a short boat-race? No argument is necessary to prove that this is not, and *cannot* possibly be true. The more so since the heart, like every other muscle, must and does take about a quarter of its time for rest. It lies down and takes a nap after every pulsation, to enable it to execute the next.

That whatever force propels the blood is really *tremendous*, and quite equal to preceding estimates, is rendered obvious by the force with which this blood spirts forth a yard or more, and flies all around, when arteries or veins are punctured, as in bleeding, stabbing, cutting the throats of animals, &c. This shows that the force from behind is really immense; even after the power just previously expended in forcing it through those long and infinitesimal capillary blood-vessels, too fine to be seen by the naked eye.

Besides, of what are arteries and veins made that they can withstand all this dynamic pressure from birth till death, and yet *grow* besides? No, medical savans, your theory is preposterous. What life-fountain could supply all the vital force requisite for all this perpetual effort; and what machinery could endure all this terrific strain? Sensible men should cast about to see whether Nature has not provided some *other* means, less absurd and more rational, less liable to derangement and less affected by other derangements, as well as not contradicted by every known law of dynamics.

THIS RATIONAL THEORY of the circulation we propound. .

The office of the heart is to regulate, cut off, and *admeasure* the blood, not to create its propelling power. Such regulation requires no little propulsive force, of which the heart has considerable, as is evinced by the size of its muscles, and power of its pulsations, as proved by external observations, and in other ways. Yet its main office is *regulatory*, not propulsive; its propelling power barely sufficing for such regulation, yet little more.

Then since the heart does not, pray what *does* generate that tremendous power necessary to propel the blood throughout the system?

BREATHING. The lungs, not the heart, generate this motive power, thus, —

ELECTRICITY constitutes this motive agent; besides being the great generator of the motive powers of the universe, that of the muscles included. The *modus operandi* of that generation, as applied to the blood, is this : —

All bodies electrically charged *positively*, proportionally *repel* each other, while all negatives and positives *attract* each other. This is both a fundamental law of electricity, and a generator of illimitable motive power throughout Nature — is self-acting "perpetual motion" personified, and undoubtedly can and will be employed to generate any required amount of motive-power, at little cost, just when and where men require it for use. It furnishes propulsion to the blood thus : —

Breathing introduces a vast amount of oxygen or electricity, that chief agent and means of life, into the system. Indeed, *it does nothing else*. That is, it charges the *air cells* of the lungs with electricity to their fullest extent.

THE IRON in the blood attracts about half of this electricity through that thin film which separates the air cells from the blood cells. This charges *both* sets of cells *positively*, which generates a powerful self-acting *propulsive* force by the electricity in each repelling that in the other. *This electricity*, not the muscular contractions of the heart, generates that tremendous power necessary to push the blood along through all that inconceivably fine network of long capillary blood-vessels throughout the body ; besides stimulating the heart to put forth whatever muscular efforts it does put forth. And this force, unlike dynamic pressure, does not strain or burst the heart, because it works on a different principle — that of *mutual electric antagonism*, not of pressure.

"But why should the electricity in the air cells drive off that in the blood cells? Why not that in the blood cells drive off that in the air cells?"

Because *drawing in* the breath keeps *crowding* electricity into the lungs, and *holding* it there for the instant, keeping the "better half" of this electricity in the filling air cells, at the same time that the electrified blood *moves off*, or rather *rushes away* from this air-cell electricity, just as fast as it gets charged positively; this repulsion being instantaneous when the breath strikes the lungs. In other words, breathing first crowds the *air* cells full of electricity, which keeps passing through into the blood cells, yet is held there whilst we are *drawing in* the breath. This leaves no escape for the electricity in the air cells, while that in the blood cells has full liberty to rush away from that in the air cells, and does rush on to the extremities of the system. Doubtless those rings found throughout the whole arterial system,[83] are stimulated by this electricity to contract, and so aid this rush of blood along through them.

THE MUSCLES AND NERVES now seize this electricity thus brought to their hands, and consume it in carrying on the various operations and functions of the life process, which leaves this blood *negative* by the time it gets through these capillaries into the veins. Of course this negative state of the venous blood now *attracts* or draws it *back* to the lungs. That is, this very electricity in the air cells which drives off the arterial blood freighted with life, at that very instant *as* powerfully *draws in* this venous or negative blood, only to recharge it positively, and send it off again on its life-sustaining circuit; thus "killing two birds with this one stone," and "making each hand wash the other."

How much more rational and obvious is this theory than that the heart furnishes *all* this force!

Think what a vast amount of power is required, not only to propel the blood to the surface through these long infinitesimal capillaries; but also to overcome all the obstacles it has to encounter! Thus, think of the pressure of a person weighing two or more hundred pounds when sitting on a board, all this weight pressing upon a few square inches perpetually, for hours, and yet the blood must be pushed along through this point of pressure, between board and bone, in spite of this heavy, steady weight, else its death and mortification must ensue; and thus of thousands of like obstructions. What an amount of internal circulatory power becomes necessary to resist a lady's tightly drawn stays, for example, or even a man's suspenders; or to keep the blood flowing through the soles of the feet while we stand; or even to resist the pressure of the air on the body, which is fifteen pounds per square inch, or *over one ton on every square foot* of the body's whole surface! Yet this electric principle furnishes power enough for all this, without any bursting of blood-vessels, or strain anywhere. The old theory, taught by these medical schools which oppose Phrenology, is both obviously absurd and an absolute physical impossibility. Jefferson College, why have you taught these absurdities thus long? Why have you not discovered this new principle, which is right in your line, before? Because you did not *know* enough. You don't *think;* for if you did, you would neither teach such nonsense, nor oppose Phrenology.

But this new theory, however plausible, demands *proof*, and has it in any required amount, and as patent as the unclouded noon-day sun, in the following *ranges* of facts.

Those who are well, breathe enough at each inspiration to last them till the next breath, and therefore have a pulse perfectly *regular;* whereas those any way ailing, show it by a pulse ren-dered *irregular*, thus : The moment the air strikes their lungs, it creates a strong, quick pulse, while the next is lower and slower, and the third still feebler and longer; till the instant the next breath strikes the lungs it sends off the blood in another rapid and powerful pulsation. What evidence could or need be stronger in proof that this propulsive force is derived from the *lungs*, not heart, than this *fact*, which all can perceive in their own persons?

Holding the breath furnishes this same proof, by this same means. The longer it is held, the slower and feebler the pulsa-tions become in every single person, well and sickly, in every single instance. Try it, but not too long, and note the diminu-tion of the pulse, till a full breath restores it. Is not the heart's force as great just *before* the breath as after?

Drowning is effected by depriving the lungs of air, and thus arresting the circulation, and the way to resuscitate those almost dead is to inflate their lungs; which restores life by reinstating the circulation. Where have medical professors, doctors, and others kept their eyes and senses, not to have long ago discovered a principle and its proofs so obvious, and established by facts so patent and universal?

The office of leaves in trees and vegetables also proves that the lungs mainly propel the blood. All concede that sap is to vegetable life precisely what blood is to animal, while leaves are to the former what lungs are to the latter. Assuming what all concede, that leaves and lungs fulfil the same office, we assert that *leaves circulate the sap;* therefore the lungs circulate the blood. It must take immense power to draw maple, and all other sap, along up under the tight-pressing bark. This power must be put forth by its own agent or organ.[23] But trees have no heart, actual or rudimental. Roots do not propel it, for their sole office is to supply nutrition. Then, since heart does not, what does propel this sap?

Leaves. This is proved by this fact, that though, as in start-ing hot-house grapes, the ground around their roots is frozen, yet the hot-house *heat* starts action and growth in the leaves, and these *leaves* it is which propels the sap down to the roots, and back again to these leaves. Maple sap, in running freely while the ground is yet frozen two feet deep, proves this same theory. If these horticultural facts, patent to all, do not prove, they at least strongly confirm our theory, that the main circulatory agent is the lungs instead of the heart.

43. — INCREASING RESPIRATION BY DIAPHRAGM BREATHING.

PROMOTING respiration promotes every life capacity, function, and enjoyment. Yet many breathe so little that the heaving of their chests is scarcely perceptible, while their abdominal motion is imperceptible. They seem "too *lazy*" to breathe deeply, apparently intent on doing with as *little* breath as possible. How amazing, when breath is so important, and cheap! And most of us might live many times faster and better, solely by redoubling our breathing. How can this be done?

BY DIAPHRAGM breathing. All animals, without any exception, breathe with their diaphragms, even more than with their ribs; while most men, and nearly all women, breathe almost wholly with the ribs, but scarcely at all with their diaphragms. This is consequent mainly on sitting bent forward in the school-room, and on females suspending their apparel mostly from their hips, by bands which press just *below* the diaphragm, so as to prevent its easy downward motion, till they fall into the *habit* of breathing without it. All apparel of men, women, and children should depend from the *shoulders*, not hips; and their weight should be made to pass down more behind than before, so as to help keep the body *straight*, not bend it forward.

MOST LADIES, by noticing their own chests as they disrobe, will see that their breath goes down only five or six inches; whereas every breath should move their whole chest, bowels included. Learn, then, to fill the lungs *full*, as in taking a long breath; that is, make *every* breath a long one.

This experiment will tell all whether and how far they breathe with their diaphragm : —

Press your hand on the *lower* part of your bowels, and note whether, and how far, they heave at every breath; for in *right* breathing they heave as much as the chest. Those in whom they do not heave thus should breathe full, deep, long breaths till their bowels *do* move; and keep on trying and observing till they have formed the *habit* of breathing as *deeply* as possible. That is, they should press in, and press out, all the air they can at every breath. See how horses with heaves heave their abdomens! Please observe that the lower lobes of the lungs are by far the largest; so that diaphragm-breathing gives twice or thrice more breath than rib-breathing. We all need all the breath we can get from *both* sources.

THE BOWELS also require motion, in order to help push the food forward through them. Their dormancy renders all the other functions dormant, while their action vivifies all.[71] Diaphragm-breathing also prevents and cures dyspepsia, which mere rib-breathing occasions.

BREATHING THROUGH THE NOSE is far better than through the mouth. Any dust in the air lodges in the nose, whence it is easily expelled. What animal ever breathes through the mouth, except in lolling? or almost overcome from heat.

INDIAN mothers are very particular to teach their children to breathe only through their nose; and Indians consider those antagonists who breathe with open mouths weak, and easily conquered.

OPEN MOUTHS look badly. Please note how awkwardly and badly gaping mouths do appear.

NOSE BREATHING catches and appropriates all fragrance, which undoubtedly, as it were, *electrifies* the system with odors, good, bad, and indifferent. Breathe bad-smelling air through your mouth, and then spit right afterwards.

SECTION II.

VENTILATION, ITS NECESSITY, MEANS, ETC.

44. — REQUISITION FOR FRESH AIR.

WELL-OXYGENATED AIR is alone fit for breathing; which is necessary chiefly because oxygen is necessary. But breathing consumes about half its vitalizing properties; besides charging it with carbonic acid gas. About five sixths of the oxygen imbibed is excreted in this gas, which is most deleterious. A good pair of lungs, in average action, consumes about two hundred and fifty cubic feet of air every twenty-four hours, and expires about *eighteen thousand* cubic inches of carbonic acid gas; enough to make *five and a half ounces* of solid carbon! Breathing both oxygenizes and *decarbonizes* the blood. Arterial blood contains of oxygen $\frac{23}{100}$, carbonic acid only $\frac{63}{100}$, while venous blood contains of oxygen but $\frac{15}{100}$, yet of carbonic acid $\frac{71}{100}$. These figures show how great is the consumption of the vitalizing properties of the air breathed, as well as how great its vitiation by breathing; while the perpetual experience and instinct of all human beings and animals attest the absolute necessity for constant and copious re-supplies of fresh and well-oxygenated air. How dull and stupid all feel after sitting a while in a hot room, especially if heated by an air-tight stove, which is unfit for use; because, while it rarefies the air so that we can breathe but little, it prevents its circulation in the room, so that we soon breathe out most of its oxygen. Hence the accompanying stagnation of the blood, and lethargy of body and mind. But strike out into the fresh air, and how differently you feel? How lively the body? How brisk all the feelings? How clear the mind? How happy the whole man? Every human being ought to spend several hours every day, cold and warm, in the open air, coupled with much bodily action. Four hours of outdoor breathing daily, is the least time compatible with health for adults, though ten are better; while children require a greater amount of both, because they have, or ought to have, a *higher temperature* and greater circulation, which has more to do in them than in adults — has to *build* up, as well as sustain their system. This shutting them up in the house, even in cold weather; this being so afraid of a little fresh, cool air, is consummate folly — is downright murder; for there is no numbering the deaths this extra carefulness occasions. Cool air is not poisonous, but more healthy than warm; because, for its bulk, it contains more oxygen, that great quickener of the blood, and stimulator of muscular, nervous, and cerebral action.[88] If a heated atmosphere had been best for man, Nature would have heated it; but it relaxes. All the inhabitants of the tropics are indolent, mentally and physically. All northerners, however active, are rendered indolent in warm climates. Hence the requisition of more or less cold to stir up the system. Unless

you would make inert blockheads of your children, do not keep
them shut up in a hot-stove room. However cold it is, let
them go out, as all children delight to, and their lungs will soon
warm them up and keep them warm. If your dear, darling,
delicate, puny child is indeed so weak that fresh air gives it a
cold, you ought to be sent to prison for rendering it thus tender;
rather, ought not to have any child.

SCHOOLS are great disease breeders. Children require an
abundance of exercise and fresh air, instead of being packed into
small and over-heated rooms, just to "sit on a bench, and say A."
To keep them thus panting for breath and action *one quarter* of
their lives, and the balance hardly better, signs, seals, and delivers
the death-warrant of many a fond and lovely bud of humanity.
Our children do not get half air enough. This occasions their
being puny, sickly, and mortal. No wonder that half of them
die in childhood. The wonder is that more do not. All children
should be rosy; while most juveniles, in these days, look pale
and haggard. The city is no place to bring up children. They
cannot go out of doors for fear of getting lost or run over; nor
play within, because ma, grandma, or aunt is sick. Nor can
they obtain fresh air in coal-heated nurseries or kitchens. God
made the country, man the city. The country is the place for
them. But, parents, whether you inhabit city or country, see to
it that your children have a full supply of fresh air *daily and
perpetually.* Hear Andrew Combe on this subject of ventilation : —

"The fatal effects of breathing highly vitiated air may easily be made
the subject of experiment. When a mouse is confined in a large and
tight glass jar full of air, it seems for a short time to experience no inconvenience; but in proportion as the consumption of oxygen and the
exhalation of carbonic acid proceed, it begins to show symptoms of uneasiness, and to pant in its breathing, as if struggling for air, and in a
few hours it dies, convulsed exactly as if drowned or strangulated. The
same results follow the deprivation of air in man, and in all animated
beings; and in hanging, death results not from dislocation of the neck,
as is often supposed, but simply because the interruption of the breathing prevents the necessary changes from taking place in the constitution
of the blood.

"The horrible fate of the one hundred and forty-six Englishmen who
were shut up in the Black Hole of Calcutta, in 1756, is strikingly illustrative of the destructive consequences of an inadequate supply of air.
The whole of them were thrust into a confined place, eighteen feet

square. There were only two very small windows by which air could be admitted, and as both of these were on the same side, ventilation was utterly impossible. Scarcely was the door shut upon the prisoners when their sufferings commenced, and in a short time a delirious and mortal struggle ensued to get near the windows. Within four hours, those who survived lay in the silence of apoplectic stupor; and at the end of six hours, *ninety-six* were relieved by death! In the morning, when the doors were opened, twenty-three only were found alive, many of whom were subsequently cut off by putrid fever, caused by the dreadful effluvia and corruption of the air.

"But, it may be said, such a catastrophe as the above could happen only among a barbarous and ignorant people. One would think so; and yet such is the ignorance prevailing among ourselves, that more than one parallel to it can be pointed out even in our own history. Of two instances to which I allude, one has lately been published in the 'Life of Crabbe,' the poet. When ten or eleven years of age, Crabbe was sent to a school at Bungay. 'Soon after his arrival, he had a very narrow escape. He and several of his school-fellows were punished for playing at soldiers, by being put into a large dog-kennel, known by the terrible name of the "Black Hole." George was the first that entered, and the place being crammed full with offenders, the atmosphere soon became pestilentially close. The poor boy in vain shrieked that he was about to be suffocated. At last, in despair, he bit the lad next to him violently in the hand; "Crabbe is dying, Crabbe is dying!" roared the sufferer; and the sentinel at length opened the door, and allowed the boys to rush out into the air. My father said, 'A minute more and I must have died.' " — *Crabbe's Life, by his Son.*

"The other instance is recorded in Walpole's Letters, and is the more memorable, because it was the pure result of brutal ignorance, and not at all of cruelty or design. 'There has been lately,' says Walpole, 'the most shocking scene of murder imaginable: a parcel of *drunken* constables took it into their heads to put the laws in execution against *disorderly* persons, and so took up every person they met, till they had collected five or six and twenty, all of whom they thrust into St. Martin's round-house, where they kept them all night, with doors and windows closed. The poor creatures, who could not stir or breathe, screamed as long as they had any breath left, begging at least for water; one poor wretch said she was worth eighteen pence, and would gladly give it for a draught of water, but in vain! So well did they keep them there, that in the morning four were found stifled to death; two died soon after, and a dozen more are in a shocking way. In short, it is horrid to think what the poor creatures suffered : several of them were beggars, who, from having no lodging, were necessarily found on the street, and others honest, laboring women.'   .   .   .

"I do not mean to say, that in all the above instances the fatal results were attributable exclusively to vitiation of the air by breathing. Fixed air may have been disengaged also from some other source, but the deteriorating influence of respiration, where no ventilation is possible, cannot be doubted. According to Dr. Bostock's estimate, an average sized man consumes about 45,000 cubic inches of oxygen, and gives out about 40,000 of carbonic acid in twenty-four hours, or 18,750 of oxygen, and

16,666 of carbonic acid in ten hours, which is nearly the time during
which the sufferers had remained in the cabin before they were found.
As they were two in number, the quantity of oxygen which would have
been required for their consumption was equal to 37,500 cubic inches,
while the carbonic acid given out would amount to upwards of 32,000
inches — a source of impurity which, added to the constant exhalation
of waste matter and animal effluvia from the lungs, was manifestly quite
equal to the production of the serious consequences which ensued from
it, and which no one, properly acquainted with the conditions essential
to healthy respiration, would ever have willingly encountered. Even
supposing that the cause of death was some disengagement of gas within
the vessel, it is still certain that, had the means of ventilation been adequately provided, this gas would have been so much diluted, and so
quickly dispersed, that it would have been comparatively innocuous.

"The best and most experienced medical officers of the army and
navy, are always the most earnest in insisting on thorough ventilation
as a chief preservative of health, and as indispensable for the recovery
of the sick. Sir George Ballingal recurs to it frequently, and shows the
importance attached to it by Sir John Pringle, Dr. Jackson, Sir Gilbert
Blane, and others of equally high authority. Sir John Pringle speaks
of hospitals being, in his day, the causes of much sickness, and of frequent deaths, 'on account of the bad air, and other inconveniences
attending them;' and Dr. Jackson, in insisting on 'height of roof as a
property of great importance in a house appropriated to the reception of
the sick of armies,' adds as the reason, that 'the air being contaminated
by the breathings of a crowd of people in a confined space, disease is
originated, and mortality is multiplied to an extraordinary extent. It
was often proved in the history of the late war, that *more human life
was destroyed by accumulating sick men in low and ill-ventilated apartments, than by leaving them exposed, in severe and inclement weather, at
the side of a hedge or common dike.'*

"In the same volume (p. 114) the reader will find another example
not less painful than instructive of the evils arising, first, from crowding
together a greater number of human beings than the air of the apartment can sustain, and, secondly from the total neglect of scientific rules
in effecting ventilation. In the summer of 1811, a low typhoid fever
broke out in the 4th battalion of the Royals, then quartered in Stirling
Castle. In many instances violent inflammation of the lungs supervened, and the result of the two diseases was generally fatal. On inves-
tigating the circumstances of this fever, it was found that rooms of
twenty-one feet by eighteen were occupied by *sixty* men, and that others of thirty-one feet by twenty-one were occupied by *seventy-two* men!
To prevent suffocation the windows were kept open all night, so that
the men were exposed at once to strong currents of cold air, and to 'the
heated and concentrated animal effluvia necessarily existing in such
crowded apartments; thus subjecting them to the combined effects of
typhus fever and of pneumonic inflammation. In the less crowded
apartments of the same barrack no instance of fever occurred.' The
men who were directly in the way of the current of cold air, were of
course those who suffered from inflammation.

"Mr. Carmichael justly regards impure air as one of the most powerful causes of scrofula, and accounts for the extreme prevalence of the disease in the Dublin House of Industry at the time he wrote (1809), by mentioning, that in one ward of moderate height, sixty feet by eighteen, there were *thirty-eight* beds, each containing *three* children, or more than one hundred in all! The matron told Mr. Carmichael, that 'there is no enduring the air of this apartment when the doors are first thrown open in the morning; and that it is in vain to raise any of the windows, as those children who happened to be inconvenienced by the cold, close them as soon as they have an opportunity. The air they breathe in the day is little better: many are confined to the apartments they sleep in, or crowded to the number of several hundreds in the school-room.' Can any one read this account, and wonder at the prevalence of scrofula under such circumstance?"

45.—THE VENTILATION OF DWELLINGS, DORMITORIES, CHURCHES, LECTURE-ROOMS, &c.

CITIZENS spend a large part of their time within doors, in domiciles and places of business, amusements, &c., and country-men average over half; while the ladies of both city and country live mostly within their own homes or churches; and many children are perpetually housed. All this, though wrong, is a *fact*, and likely to *continue*.

THE VENTILATION OF HOUSES, then, becomes as important to those who live mostly within doors, as good breathing timber is valuable.[88] This subject is beginning to engage public attention, but by no means in proportion to its intrinsic merits. All the rooms in all houses should be furnished at their top with a ventilator for the escape of *foul* air, which will allow fresh air to enter; while the bad air which settles at their bottom can easily be drawn off by suction, and made to support the combustion of the fires used about the house. We shall treat the *means* of effecting these desirable ends under "Inhabitiveness," in Vol. II., but simply show its importance here. He will prove a great public benefactor who propounds some simple yet efficacious means of domiciliary ventilation; and all architects should give this subject their special attention.

DORMITORY ventilation is of course equally important, yet more neglected. Opening outside doors often by day helps to change the air of sitting-rooms in the daytime, but not of bed-chambers.

SMALL BED-ROOMS, ten feet square and seven high, contain seven hundred cubic feet of air. Two persons sleeping together in it consume about one hundred and sixty feet in eight hours sleep, and probably more; for we naturally breathe deeper and more when asleep than ordinarily when awake. The two have in-haled about *one fourth* of its air, excreted *about twelve thousand square inches* of carbonic acid gas, or nearly enough to make *four ounces of solid carbon!* Carbonic acid gas is a deadly poison. This it is which kills those suffocated by the burning of charcoal in close rooms; and what turns the venous blood dark. Perhaps a light burning for hours in your bedroom has already both con-sumed its oxygen, and loaded it with carbonic acid gas. Perhaps others have been sleeping in it night after night for months with little ventilation; so that its stench is intolerable till you become accustomed to it. On no account sleep in a dark bed-room, nor in one which does not allow of *through* ventilation, by windows and fireplace, if not by one or more doors and windows, so as to keep *changing* your air perpetually during the night. Make am-ple provision for this change before you retire. Most persons spend *one third of their lives,* two in a bed, in little eight by ten bedrooms, containing only five or six hundred cubic feet of air, and that vitiated to begin with, and stuff every crevice and key-hole besides; breathing over one third of the poor air, making it almost thick with carbonic acid gas, and then wonder why they fall sick,— perhaps ascribing to divine Providence what belongs to foul air!

Six factory operatives often sleep all night in a little room not exceeding ten feet square and seven high! No wonder their vo-cation is unhealthy. How repulsive the smell of bedrooms gen-erally in the morning, observable on quitting them a few minutes and returning. Instead of being thus miserably supplied with fresh air, they should be large, and especially high, and arranged so as to admit free ventilation. A draught directly upon you may be objectionable, yet even this is far better than confined air, and can be rendered harmless by a good supply of bed-clothes — though the less of these, and keep comfortable, the better. Large, airy sleeping apartments would add one fourth to the aggregate duration and efficiency of life. They should be the largest rooms in our houses.

The general idea obtains that night air is unwholesome, and often pestilential; than which nothing is more unfounded. What! the Deity render night air unwholesome, and yet compel us to breathe it! This supposition conflicts with the whole economy of nature. If night air had been really injurious, she would have allowed us to sleep without breathing; for she never compels the least thing injurious. Night air is equally as wholesome as day air. It may be damper, but that does not hurt it for breathing. It is usually cooler, and, therefore, contains more oxygen, and hence is even better than day air, at least for sleeping purposes. Why are we so restless in hot summer nights, and why do we sleep so sweetly, and wake up so invigorated in cold fall nights, but because the needed supply of oxygen is so much greater in the latter? So far from its being injurious, sleeping with open windows greatly promotes health, even in stormy, boisterous weather. Many who sleep thus summer and winter are remarkably robust and healthy. Yet this practice should be adopted by degrees, so as not to give cold.

Let us apply these data to churches, lecture-rooms, theatres, vestries, billiard-rooms, depots, and places of public resort. A public place, forty by sixty, ten feet high, containing twenty-four thousand cubic feet of perhaps poor air, is packed for two hours with a thousand persons. This gives twenty-four square feet to each one, barely enough for *one hour's* breathing timber. If it is fifteen feet high, it contains only enough for an hour and a half. And all are breathing over and over again the identical air just expired by their tobacco and rum-feted listeners on both sides. Each person expires about *three thousand* cubic inches of carbonic acid gas, — *three hundred thousand* in all, — enough to make *seventy-five ounces* of solid carbon! All this, besides all the other fetid and noxious gases emptied into the room from foul breaths, and still fouler stomachs! To eat and drink after others, even though tidy, is considered really vulgar; but to *breathe* after others, however reeking with tobacco and bad whiskey, is "all right;" while, in point of fact, to breathe the foul, spent air, just robbed and vitiated by another, is far more utterly "*nasty*"_than to eat out of their unwashed dishes.

46. — BLUE VEINS SIGNIFY INSUFFICIENT BREATH : POSTURE.

The darker the blood, the greater the amount of carbon it contains. Now this carbon should pass off through the lungs, and it will do so when we breathe abundantly. But when too little nitrogen is brought alongside of the carbonic acid contained

in the blood to carry it off, it must return with the blood into
the system; and, being a rank poison as well as stagnating, it
poisons and prostrates the vital organs, diminishes life, and engenders disease. Blueness of veins in children or adults is a sure
index of the superabundance of this poison, that is, of insufficient
breathing. Let such both eat less and breathe more, so as to
thin and redden their blood. True, the blood in the veins should
be dark, but not dark enough to show through. And when
visibly dark, see to it, as you value life, that this powerful disease-
breeder is removed.

We should attend to breathing even more than to eating; and
make provision for a constant re-supply of fresh air even more
than for good food. And parents, see that your children have it
in luxurious abundance, night and day.

POSTURE then becomes immeasurably important. Sitting, walking, working, &c., bent forward, presses the shoulders and
ribs in upon the lungs, which of course so cramps them as to
retard their full inflation; for one in an erect posture will naturally breathe about one fourth more continually than in a stooping,
and of course live, enjoy, and accomplish that much more. Think
what a difference! See that it makes *for* life in your case, not
against it.

LOOKS, in these days, too, are everything. Think what men,
and especially women, spend solely on appearances in dress,
furniture, style, &c.; and then think how immeasurably *better* the
same person looks when erect than when bent forward. Erectness signifies nobleness and pride, while crouching expresses
either humility or feebleness, as in declining age.

SIT, STAND, WORK, WRITE, LIE, and WALK ERECTLY always; and
train your children up in this habit. The author has known many
dyspeptic and consumptive ladies *cured* solely by wearing suspenders which attached their apparel to their shoulders, and
passed back down over their shoulder-blades, thus pressing
them inwards. Only seeing or experiencing the different effects
on the mind and body of different postures, can at all impress the
practical importance of a position permanently erect, especially
in juveniles.

TIGHT-LACING is of course condemned by our subject, but is
treated elaborately in " Sexual Science." [606]

CHAPTER III.

FOOD; ITS NECESSITY, SELECTION, MASTICATION, DIGESTION, APPROPRIATION, AND EXCRETION.

SECTION I.

NECESSITY AND OFFICE OF FOOD.

47. — RE-SUPPLY OF ORGANIC MATERIAL THROUGH ALIMENTATION.

SINCE all functions are carried forward only by organs,[23] and since the states of all organs affect their functions similarly,[24] Nature must first make some absolute provision for *manufacturing* just such organs as she needs. From the first dawn of existence, *material* out of which to make these organs is a primal requisition for developing life. Its germ must *make* organs before it can use them, and be furnished with the organic material requisite for their manufacture before it can construct them. The necessity for this material is equal to that for organs.[23] Where and how is it supplied?

FITNESS is the first organic prerequisite. The life force cannot use any and everything; but must have just *the precise* materials necessary for manufacturing bones, muscles, brain, nerves, tissues, skin, hair, nails, &c. Where can they be obtained? Nature has laid up no specific storehouse where alone they can be had; unless all Nature is such a store. They must be *brought to* the life germ, all solved, and ready to be made into organs, and then made up, before it can put forth functions. Parental agency supplies enough merely to *start* its first rude tenement, till it can construct one more perfect than finite minds can imagine. Babes are a constructive marvel. What human workmanship bears any comparison with their organic construction?[633]

But Nature's policy of *individual* life, in which each one is allowed to go, come, and do, *in propria personœ*, necessitates an early parental separation, which presupposes a supply of the raw organic material to each human being. An entire chapter in

16

"Sexual Science," Vol. III., is devoted to the proper *feeding* of children.[633-647]

ALBUMEN contains most of these ingredients. Dirt, stones, minerals, earth, glass, &c., do not, but vegetables eliminate them from the soil by means of light, heat, air, moisture, &c., and thus become edible; because they possess the organic ingredients needed in the human mechanism.

ONE KIND of vegetable contains, as one kind of animal requires, one *proportion* of these ingredients, and another another; so that each kind of animal, fish, fowl, reptile, worm, insect, &c., is thus supplied with a kind of food exactly adapted to its specific needs. If all kinds of eater's ate but one kind of food, only a few, comparatively, could be fed; whereas, this vast diversity in both animal wants and their vegetable supply, feeds all animals on something, and allows all kinds of vegetables to be food for one or another kind of animals.

THE REPAIR of organs is as important as their manufacture. All use, whether of tools, apparel, or bodily organs, *wears* them out — fritters away their materials. Every function of the body and mind *uses up* its organ. If all organs wore on forever, remaining just as good as new, they would never need repair, but every organ is perpetually *consuming* its materials, and must be perpetually "undergoing repairs."

A perpetual supply of food, first to manufacture organs, then to keep them in perfect "running order," all through life, therefore, becomes, next to breathing, "first among equals" in the life process.

48. — NORMAL APPETITE NATURE'S FEEDING INSTRUMENTALITY.

To ASSURE a supply of food to the system, and that of the right kind, becomes as necessary as eating is important. No casual or temporary provision will at all answer this great purpose. It must accompany life everywhere, and even constitute an integral *part* of it, as well as be inseparable from it — must needs form a constituent of the *mind*, and be carried forward by one of its primary *Faculties*. And it *is*.

APPETITE is that faculty. Phrenology calls it ALIMENTIVENESS. See its definition in [14]. It creates a relish for food, hankers after it; and when denied it, begets *hunger*, one of the fiercest and

most resistless of all the human desires and passions. Without
it, little eating would ever be done. Neither reason nor observation, not even experience, could ever *guarantee* the proper feeding of the body. Only a powerful *propensity* to eat could possibly render this feeding sure, and predetermine its best time,
amount, kinds, &c.

DESIRE to eat must needs be commensurate with the system's
need of food. This need is as important as is that life it sustains,[20] [47] and accordingly the cravings of unsatisfied appetite are
beyond description. We call them hunger, which is caused by
the accumulation of gastric juice in the cells of the stomach.
They cannot discharge except when food is deposited in it.
When the system needs aliment it forewarns the nerves, which
telegraph to the stomach, and excite the manufacture of this gastric juice, which seeks that food which alone can discharge
this fluid. Undischarged gastric juice creates hunger, which,
however, differs materially from relish of food. Most have experienced more or less of the gnawings of hunger, even in this
land of alimentary abundance; then how much fiercer must it become in cases of protracted fasting from famine, imprisonment,
&c. In such cases, fine-grained, good men lose all their higher
refined sentiments, and become like famished wolves; oblivious
of the sufferings and rights of others. Eye-witnesses attest that
prisoners too feeble to scramble or even crawl for their scant rations, would *pick beans from the excrement* of fellow-soldiers,
which, swallowed unchewed, had been voided whole. Cats,
dogs, &c., often evince an almost· ravenous appetite, and the
fierce voracity of famishing wolves is proverbial. Even men
have been known, in the extremity of their hunger, to *put their
own teeth* into their *own flesh, gnaw their own bones*, and *lap their
own blood!* Think how ravenous they must first become! Yet
all this only admeasures the necessity of food, and the proportionate importance of eating right.

SUBSTANCES PREVIOUSLY ORGANIZED are alone edible, alone can
feed man, beast, fish, fowl, and insect. Rocks are formed from
gases, a cubic foot of limestone rock containing fifteen thousand
cubic feet of various gases. Rocks, decomposed by time and
atmospheric agencies, make soil, from which vegetables derive
their growth and properties. Rocks compose and feed the soil,

which feeds vegetables, and they support animals and man. Worms, grasshoppers, &c., feed on vegetables, fowls on them, and man on fowls: all food being derived from the vegetable kingdom. Of course vegetable seed, such as grain, nuts, &c., constitute the highest kind of vegetable food. Nearly all that grows feeds something; for Nature is a great practical *economizer* of all her time, space, materials, resources, and everything.

EATING, including raising, marketing, cooking, serving, and partaking of food, constitutes a *staple* provision of society.

49. — THE NATURAL FOOD OF EACH SPECIES FEEDS ITS OWN SPECIALTIES.

Why should or does one kind of animal relish one kind of food, and another another, but because the natural food of each sustains and develops its own specialties? The *end* of all eating is the nutrition of the eater's specialties. *Fitness* appertains to all Nature does and requires. Lions love raw flesh, and horses grain, because raw flesh is precisely adapted to sustain and develop the peculiarities of the former, as grain is of the latter. One animal relishes that peculiar kind it needs, while another loathes this same food, but enjoys what the other loathes. Thus the lion craves raw meat, warm with life, but loathes vegetable food; while the horse loathes flesh, but craves vegetables. Could grass nourish the physiology and mentality of the hyena, eagle, and whale, or flesh those of the sheep and ox, equally as well as the converse now does? Is not flesh adapted to sustain the functions of carnivorous animals, herbage that of herbivorous, nuts of the rodentia, insects and seeds of birds, and so of all that eats? Else why their respective *appetites* for their natural diets? What stronger proof could be required or had that the natural food of all animals is constitutionally calculated to nourish their respective characteristics, mental and physical, than that furnished by this law of adaptation? To argue a principle thus self-evident, the truth of which is guaranteed by Nature's universal economy, is like arguing an axiom. It is obviously a dietetic law and guide.

This principle is still further proved by the fact that the food of all animals bears a close resemblance to their natures. Thus, sprightly animals generally live on a sprightly diet; as the cat on mice, the tiger and lion on the antelope, &c. Tall animals, as the giraffe live on what grows high, and moles on what grows close to or in the ground. Fish live mostly on what swims, and the swallow on flying insects; whereas birds which fly less live more on worms and seeds, and domestic fowls, which fly little, live mainly on what flies but little. The natural diet of swine is chiefly roots — a coarse animal feeding on coarse food. Strong animals, as the mastodon, moose, elephant, elk, &c., live much on the ends of limbs, about the firmest food eaten; while horses and cattle relish hay, which is fibrous and tough, as its consumers are hardy and muscular. Strong and fleet sharks feed on other fish next in speed and strength to themselves. Monkeys, confessedly the highest order of animals except man, feed on fruit and nuts, obviously the best of vegetables except grains and the first class of fruits, reserved for man. The nutrition of nuts, too, is highly concentrated.

Mark one more universal illustration of this law. Animals are confessedly higher in the scale of capacity and enjoyment than vegetables, and accordingly must feed on what has already been organized; whereas vegetables, being lower in structure and function, can sustain themselves by a far lower order of nourishment than that drawn from the earth, organized too low to support animal life. And, in general, the higher the grade of any animal, the higher the order of its food. Even the vegetable kingdom observe this law of correspondence with their food. Thus the grape, an exceedingly juicy fruit, seeks a humid atmosphere, and so do pears and plums; whereas apples, less juicy, thrive best on dry soils. Though apparent exceptions may perhaps be cited, yet the general law is perfectly obvious, that there is something in the natural diet of all that eats or grows peculiarly adapted to sustain both the physical and mental characteristics of its consumer.

50. — NORMAL APPETITE AND SMELL THE ULTIMATE ARBITERS OF WHATEVER APPERTAINS TO ALIMENT.

"But all this leaves us about as much in the dark respecting our food as it found us. Though it sheds some dietetic light, yet it is often self-contradictory, and befogs about as much as it enlightens. Does not Nature provide some *infallible* guide to right eating, which tells us not only what is *generally* best, but always *just* what is required at any and all times? Our systems need one thing to-day, another to-morrow, and still other kinds at other times; then does Nature provide a sure *feeding formula* adapted and applicable to all cases?"

Indeed she does. Would she, after having predetermined every minute particular, throughout all her vast domains, leave a matter thus important at loose ends? Surely not. If appetite simply created an indiscriminate greed for any and all kinds of food, it would often lumber up the system with gross materials, the digestion and expulsion of which would exhaust its energies. Instead, each individual requires to eat just what, and *only* what, but no more than is then and there required for special and immediate use. This same alimentary instinct which preinclines us to eat, must also *select* just *the* kind, quality, and amount of food thus needed, and eschew all else.

NORMAL APPETITE accomplishes all this, by creating a special hankering and *relish* in each species, and in all individuals of each, for just that aliment demanded by each at that particular time. This feeding institute, without this provision, would be most imperfect; but with it, like all else in Nature, becomes perfection personified. Hence appetite is a *specific* as well as general dietetic guide. It not only creates in carnivorous animals a relish for flesh, in graminivora for grains, &c. ; but if, at any particular time, any one individual of any species, man included, needs any *special* aliment, each will experience a *craving* for the kind of food which contains the ingredients required. This is equally true of liquids — is a law of all alimentation. Whatever eats needs it, and Nature thus furnishes to each an *infallible* directory, which rightly applied, will select the best kinds of food in *detail*, as well as in general, and tell all just *what* to eat, when, how much, how, and everything appertaining to a perfect diet.

INSTINCTS are as destinies. Every animal, every human instinct, subserves some necessary purpose ; and every necessary end is carried forward by some instinct. Appetite is expressly adapted to execute whatever is necessary to perfect nutrition.

SMELL constitutes another reliable umpire in selecting our food. All animals smell of their food before they venture to taste it, and predetermine its utility as food by its smell. The universal contiguity of the mouth and nose, and their nerves, signifies that they should work in concert. Smell detects incipient decomposition even sooner and more effectually than either sight, touch, or taste. If smelling of food is not polite, it is at least natural to man and beast.

THIS EXPERIMENT will show how important a dietetic part smell plays. Let one accustomed to drink liquors, or taste of fruits, or anything, close eyes and nose, and taste of this and that without seeing or smelling of them, and he can scarcely tell whether he is tasting of brandy, or whiskey, or rum, or of this, that, or the other kind of fruit.

Smell should obviously be brought into perpetual requisition in selecting our food, and also as assiduously *cultivated*.

51. — THE DISCIPLINE OF APPETITE.

CULTURE improves all to which it is rightly applied. It increases the size and lusciousness of wild fruits; makes wild animals tame; augments the products of fields; beautifies flowers; redoubles the size and efficiency of the muscles, and all other physical organs; [30] and will yet be shown to improve each of the mental faculties, Alimentiveness included. Assuming here the improvability of functions by culture, let us apply this principle to the discipline of appetite. Men properly expend a great amount of time and pains in cultivating memory, language, reason, taste as applied to beauty, &c., but none whatever in cultivating taste as applied to food; excepting those who make a *business* of tasting teas, liquors, and other articles of diet in order to their purchase. Is Alimentiveness less important than these other faculties? Does not its right exercise by feeding the body in the best manner, redouble the vigor and efficiency of all the other functions of the body and mind? One can live twice as long, and fast, and well, with as without a discriminating appetite. Its right exercise promotes, while its wrong impairs, every life function, as it were by magic; but indiscriminate eaters can hardly half live, enjoy, or accomplish.

GREED AND FLAVOR constitute the two phases of Alimentiveness; greed securing *some* kind of edibles, and flavor selecting the *best* attainable. The first is the most important, and therefore universal. All possess the second, yet it increases in proportion as its possessors advance. Coarse-grained persons eat almost anything, intent chiefly on getting *enough;* while those of refinement become proportionally fastidious in their choice, and *being* particular promotes refinement.

To CULTIVATE flavor, eat *discriminatingly.* That is, " *Smack your lips*" over this, that, the other kind of food, to see which has the genuine flavor *ring;* and partake only of those kinds for which you have a keen relish. Eat what you eat, not as the gormond eats pork and beans, but just as the epicure eats woodcock, as if bound to obtain from it whatever gustatory relish it possesses. Most persons eat as the hen eats beans, with a grab and swallow, without once stopping to enjoy its flavor. Many eat like coarse-grained swine under a pear-tree, from one limb of which have fallen delicious Seckles, and from another hard, sour-pucker pears, craunching both equally, without noting any difference in their flavor, although one-Seckle pear contains more genuine lusciousness of flavor than a whole bushel of choke pears. Deposit in your stomach only what "goes just to the right spot." Horses are very particular as to what they eat; then why should not man be far more so? All we eat must permeate our entire system, and exert its legitimate effects upon every fibre of the body, every emotion and action of the mind; so be careful what you eat.

GOOD TASTING ORGANS are of course indispensable to right eating. None can feed themselves properly without keeping the *nerves* of the tongue and mouth in a sensitive, susceptible, exquisite, tasting *state;* the best way to do which is to keep the mouth *full of tobacco!*

Irony aside; none who chew, smoke, or dip, can possibly feed themselves discriminatingly, or keep their functions in the best working order. Keeping these tender mouth-nerves soaking in this pungent narcotic must *needs* blunt them, and thus impair the taste, and thereby the alimentation; and of course every function of their mind and body. Tobacco chewers, smokers, and dippers chew, smoke, and dip *that*, and then *stop* chewing, smoking, and dipping; and you will experience a "revival" throughout all your functions.

In short, there is just as much a *science* of alimentation as of mathematics, because both are governed by natural laws; and an unperverted appetite expounds these laws.

Then why is not this science of right eating *taught*, along with the other sciences? Is it less important than they? or less promotive of life than grammar, than school studies? Yet what physiologist or teacher teaches, what preacher preaches, this science as such?

SECTION II.

IS MAN NATURALLY GRAMINIVOROUS, OR OMNIVOROUS?

52. — HUMAN TEETH NOT CARNIVOROUS.

WHAT FOOD IS BEST for human development, physical and mental, therefore, becomes a problem as practically important to every man, woman, and child, as is life itself,[18] which depends much on what we eat.[49]

Though appetite when normal will settle this issue correctly, yet it is so universally perverted, by both hereditary entailments and wrong habits from the cradle, that it needs to be aided by philosophy. Indeed, all our propensities require the guidance of reason, man's highest tribunal. What, then, is its dietetic verdict?

The first point to be decided is, whether man is *naturally* adapted to eat vegetables alone, of course including grains, nuts, fruits, gums, vegetable oils, sweets, and all farinaceous edibles; or whether a mixed diet, including flesh, fowl, fish, &c., is best? And if so, mixed in what *proportions?* That is, what are the respective effects, on his mind and body, of a diet wholly vegetable, as compared with a mixed?

THE TEETH of all animals are adapted in structure to their natural food. As the structure of fish adapts them to swim, of birds to fly, of animals to walk, &c., and as every *part* of each is expressly adapted to its specific phase of function, — as all of Nature's structures specifically adapt them to the ends she thereby effects, — of course the teeth of all flesh-eating animals expressly adapt them to seize, hold, and tear their prey; while those of grass and all grain-feeding animals fit them to bite off and crush grasses and grains. The former should be, and are sharp, tho latter flat. The eye teeth of the former are by far the largest, besides projecting much farther than the others, and being very sharp, so as to grasp and hold their prey. Touching this adaptation of teeth to the natural food of all animals, President Hitchcock, the highest geological authority, observes, —

" From a single bone or tooth of any animal, its character, food, habits, haunts, and all the circumstances of its existence may be correctly in-

17

ferred.   Comparative anatomists have, from a single tooth, described, and made drawings of the extinct creature to which it belonged, which have been found to agree exactly with a skeleton afterwards discovered."

NO. 5. VIEW OF THE HUMAN TEETH.

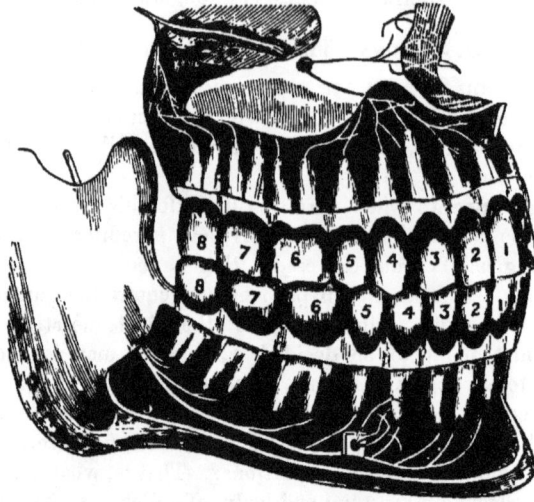

NAMES OF THE HUMAN TEETH.

1, 1. Middle Incisors.	4, 4. First bicuspidate.
2, 2. Lateral Incisors.	5, 5. Second bicuspidate.
3, 3. Canine.	6, 6, 7, 7. Molars. 8, 8. Wisdom.

That the teeth of every animal, known and unknown, accord perfectly with its natural food, is universally admitted; so that the form of the human teeth will determine, with absolute certainty, the natural dietetic character of man.   If constituted to eat meat, the shape of his teeth will approximate towards that of lions and tigers.   His front teeth will be small and sharp; his eye teeth, which correspond with the tusks, hooked, long, and enormously large; and his back teeth sharp for tearing, instead of broad for crushing; whereas, if his natural diet is vegetable and farinaceous, his back teeth will be adapted to grinding, and his eye teeth not longer than their neighbors.

The following engraving of the cow furnishes a standard sample of herbivorous teeth, as do those of the tiger of the teeth of the carnivora.

These teeth are composed of bone, cased with the hardest substance in the human body, called ENAMEL, to prevent their

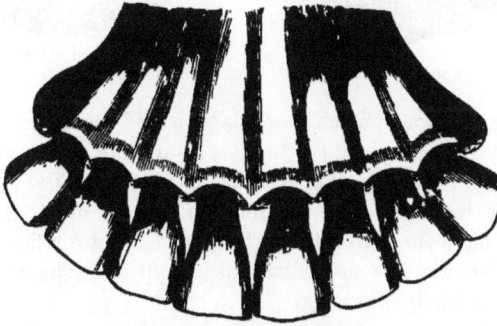

NO. 6. UNDER JAW OF THE COW.

breaking. They are kept in their places by prongs and muscles, and rendered sensitive by nerves shown in engraving No. 5, which pass into them by fissures or holes in the centres of their prongs. The inflammation of these nerves occasions the toothache.

NO. 7. JAWS OF THE TIGER.

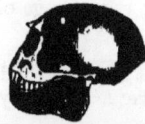

NO. 8. MONKEY.

NO. 10. FOX.

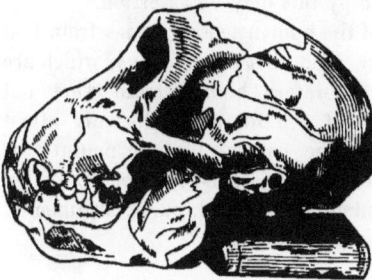

NO. 9. BABOON.

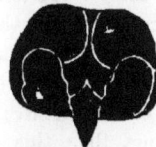

NO. 11. OWL.

NO. 12. CAT.

NO. 13. HYENA.

NO. 14. ICHNEUMON.

Reader, see for yourself towards which of these two forms the teeth of man approximate — that his front teeth are usually larger than his eye; and his double teeth flat for grinding, instead of sharp for tearing.   Not one index of the carnivorous form is found in his teeth.   Now this principle constitutes a final umpire, from which there is no philosophical appeal.   The absence of claws has a kindred bearing.

To render assurance doubly sure, let us contrast the teeth of the monkey tribes with those of man.   Though they will eat flesh rather than starve, yet flesh is not their natural diet, else they would kill and eat animals.   Now the form of their teeth, as seen in engravings Nos. 8 and 9, approximates towards that of the carnivora much more nearly than that of man does, the preceding engravings of the monkey, baboon, or ourang-outang fully evince.

"But man has hands and tools with which to kill, and sense to supply by knives and cookery his want of claws and teeth."

This leaves the teeth argument wholly untouched.   It simply excuses the admitted omission of carnivorous teeth and claws. As far as it has any anti-meat eating force, it makes against the obvious and conceded *principle* that the forms of the teeth of animals indicate their natural kinds of food — a principle too firmly established to be shaken by this may-be assertion.

Since, therefore, the form of the human teeth recedes from that of the carnivora far more even than that of monkeys, which are confessedly not carnivorous; therefore human teeth were not made to eat meat.   What proof can more conclusively attest anything, than this establishes the natural diet of man to be herbivorous?   Nearly every sound physiologist has been impelled to this conclusion by this dental, and other kindred arguments. The immortal Linnæus sums them up thus : —

"Fruits and esculent vegetables constitute the most suitable food for man."

"The natural food of man, therefore, judging from his structure, appears to consist of fruits, roots, and other succulent parts of vegetables; and his hands offer him every facility for gathering them. His short and moderately strong jaws on the one hand, and his cuspidati being equal in length to the remaining teeth, and his tubercular molars on the other, would allow him neither to feed on grass nor devour flesh, were these aliments not prepared by cooking." — *Cuvier.*

"The teeth of man have not the slightest resemblance to those of carnivorous animals, except that their enamel is confined to their external surface. He possesses, indeed, teeth called canine, but they do not exceed the level of the others, and are obviously unsuited for the purposes which the corresponding teeth execute in carnivorous animals." "Whether, therefore, we consider the teeth and jaws, or the immediate instruments of digestion, the human structure closely resembles that of the semiæ or monkeys, all of which, in their natural state, are completely frugivorous." — *Lawrence.*

"Every fact connected with human organization goes to prove that man was originally formed a frugivorous animal." — *Dr. Thomas Bell,* "*Physiological Observations on the natural Food of Man, deduced from the Character of his Teeth.*"

Cullen and Lamb take similar ground, and the Abbe Galani ascribes all crimes to animal destruction. Pope protests against "kitchens sprinkled with blood," and insists that animal food engenders crime. Plutarch tells us that Pythagoras ate no pork, and wondered what first "led man to eat carcass."

These conclusions, however unpopular, have been extorted from every rigid physiologist who has ever examined this subject, and are confirmed by the length of the alimentary canal, which is short in the carnivora, long in the herbivora, and long in man — about six or seven times the length of his body.

These two arguments, derived from the structure of the teeth and alimentary canal, of themselves completely establish the dietetic character of man to be mainly vegetable.

53. — A MIXED DIET CAN FEED THE GREATEST NUMBER.

Whatever diet will sustain the greatest number of human beings is therefore the best. That our earth is destined to be crowded with as dense a population as its utmost capacities for sustaining human life, combined with the most rigid husbandry of its necessaries, will support, is undoubtedly the economy of Nature. Hence, since a given amount of land will sustain more human beings, by about ten to one, if its products are consumed directly by man than when fed to animals, and they eaten as food; the economy of Nature could never have ordained this *thousand per cent. loss* in order to sustain flesh-eaters; unless one of them enjoys as much as ten vegetable-eaters. If Nature really requires and favors a flesh diet, she would have arranged to support a far greater number of flesh-eaters than vegetable-eaters; whereas, since she can sustain ten times as many exclusively vegetable-eaters as exclusively flesh-eaters, therefore an exclusively flesh-diet is in opposition to Nature's general economy.

A given amount of territory will sustain probably a thousand Anglo-Americans by agriculture, to one Indian by the chase. Suppose the earth already fully stocked with human beings, shall this one Indian be allowed to engross what would support a thousand human beings better than he is sustained? If he is content with this thousandth part of his territory, let him remain; but he has no right to prevent the existence of nine hundred and ninety-nine human beings, still better capacitated to enjoy life than himself. Hence Nature compels him to recede before the march of civilization, unless he incorporates himself with it. And his punishment is just.

Carnivorous animals furnish another illustration. To support one lion requires thousands of acres. Hence, since Nature abhors prodigality as much as vacuums, she ordains that lions and all beasts of prey shall retire at the approach of man; that is, yield their dominion to him as fast as he requires it, because he puts it to so much better use than they. The principle here stated is a law of things. Shall, then, one flesh-eater be allowed to keep ten vegetable-eaters from enjoying all the luxuries of life? Human happiness is Nature's paramount object.[16] To this, numbers are indispensable. Since, therefore, ten vegetable-eaters can enjoy more than one flesh-eater, they should take the precedence; hence flesh-eating must decrease as population increases. In fact, since one of the former enjoys much more than one of the latter, this waste of the necessaries of life by flesh-eating, and this deterioration of human enjoyments, therefore clash fundamentally with human numbers and happiness; which condemns an exclusively flesh diet as contrary to the nature of man.

A MIXED diet, however, will sustain more than a diet composed

exclusively of either flesh or vegetables. A diet almost all vegetables, but with a little animal, the latter including the products
of the dairy, poultry, and eggs, will sustain the most, and is
therefore the best. A few, yet not many, domestic animals and
fowls can be kept on offal food, unfit for man, and their manure
can be made to increase the productiveness of land more than
they diminish its products, so that they augment the *aggregate*
supply of human food. Grasses and vegetables also grow on salt
and other untillable marshes, on which a few cattle can be kept,
and their flesh, butter, and cheese be made to increase human
sustenance. This argument favors eating some meat, but not
much.

FISH, which by culture can be obtained in great quantities from
both salt water and fresh, can be made to add materially to human
food; besides containing.that phosphoric element which promotes
cerebral action, and sustains the mental manifestations.

54. — FRUITS AND GRAINS MORE PALATABLE THAN MEAT.

Man should subsist on *fruits and farinaceous food, mainly*, in-
terspersed with vegetables, nuts, eggs, and the products of the
dairy. The unbolted flour of wheat, rye, oats, barley, corn, buckwheat, &c., made into bread and puddings in various forms, and
seasoned with fruits and sweets, should constitute the main bulk
of his diet; and to it should be added potatoes, beans, peas, beets,
carrots, turnips, parsnips, nuts, and a limited supply of milk,
cream, butter, cheese, and some meat. The warrant for this
dietetic system is, first, its far greater *palatableness* than flesh.[50]
That it is relished better, is evident in our always reserving the
best part of our meals for the dessert — though we ought to eat
the best first — which consists of fruit, pies, puddings, cakes,
oranges, nuts, raisins, apples, peaches, pine-apples, berries, and
the like, but rarely of meat — never except in minced pies, from
five sixths to nine tenths of which are composed of flour, apples,
sugar, cider, and spices. Flesh is almost excluded from our list
of desserts, because less palatable than flour and fruit. We para-
phrase good living by "roast beef and plum pudding." Why
place the plum pudding last? Because it is best, and therefore
brought on *after* the roast beef; yet it is composed of flour and
fruit sweetened. Similar remarks apply to all other kinds of

puddings.   In extra good dinners, almonds and raisins are
brought on last, because best of all.   How much better fruit and
flour desserts relish than meats and gravies even after the appetite is glutted with the latter?   But bring on meats, and they
would scarcely be touched.   We all know how much keener the
appetite is at the beginning of meals than at the close; and yet a
sated appetite likes the flour and fruit preparations last, much
better than the meat dishes first.   Hence, as that tastes best
which is best,[50] fruits and flour constitute the natural diet of man.

Vary the experiment.   Set bread, berries, and milk, and also
meat, before children, and after telling them to make their meal
wholly of the one they like the best, yet partake of but one,
all will prefer the bread, milk, and berries.   This is true of most
adults.   Many readers can testify that suppers composed of milk,
bread, and fruit relish better than any other meal.   Peel, cut,
and sweeten peaches, and tell children they can eat them with
bread and butter, or that they can have meat and butter with
bread, but if they choose the meat, must not have the peaches,
and not one in hundreds will prefer the meat.   Not one in millions
prefer all meat to all vegetables and fruit.[50]   So of dried peaches
or apples, stewed with raisins, and sweetened.   Many kinds of
pears are still better.   Give adults the same choice, and in spite
of their perversion of appetite consequent on eating so much
meat, most prefer the bread and fruit.   Or set apple-dumplings
and good sauce upon the table with meat, it being understood
that boarders can have their choice, but must partake of only one
dish, and most will relish the fruit and flour preparations better
than the meat.   Or make a stew pie of flour and apples, cherries,
berries, peaches, green or dried pears, raisins, or any other kind
of fruit, well sweetened, and most people prefer it to all other
edibles; while all would eat a much greater proportion of these
various preparations of fruit and flour than they now do, but
that they are considered too *choice* and *scarce* to constitute a full
meal; and thus of nuts and raisins.   But for the impression that
these desserts are not substantial enough for laboring men,[38-40]
and that they are the most expensive, that is, if appetite had its
choice, it would eschew meat, and prefer sweetened preparations
of bread and fruit almost altogether.

Contrast the relish with which most people eat short-cake and butter, or buckwheat cakes and molasses or honey, as compared with meat and gravy. Not that these cakes are recommended, yet they show that preparations of flour and fruit *relish* better, especially with children, than meat.

Cake still further proves this. We make supper our most dainty meal, and cake is to it what desserts are to dinner, namely, the very climax of all. This is doubly true of *wedding* cake. Weddings are among the most important events of life, and nuptial suppers are important items of weddings;[537] and hence no expense or pains are spared to render them the very acme of luxurious eating. Do they consist in roast beef? or in any preparation of flesh? No; but in wedding *cake*. If meat were generally esteemed to *taste* the best, the married pair would send out cuts of meat instead of cake. These tests are infallible, though so common as to have escaped general observation. What supper can relish better than bread, butter, and honey, except it be short-cake, or some other cakes in place of bread? How insignificant is meat in comparison!

Finally, after we have eaten our buckwheat and molasses breakfast, our fruit and flour or meat dinner and dessert, and our short-cake-and-butter supper, "topped off" with preserves and cake, we stroll out in the evening with some loved one, and wishing to heighten our friendship by partaking together the very daintiest morsel known, we step into a confectionery, the sole object of which is to gratify the palate, and call for what? Meat in any form? No, but *ice creams*, &c., or *strawberries and cream*, or other berries in their respective seasons; because they furnish the highest gustatory enjoyment known, not to a few, for then they would not be kept, but to *all*, because preparations of meat are rarely kept by confectioneries proper, and when kept, are designed for *food*, not as a relish merely. Who loves roast beef better than rich Vergaloo pears, golden apricots, Morris White peaches, and other delicious fruits? If meat tasted best to the many, it would be the "crack dish;" but ice creams, berries and cream, berry short-cake, jellies, preserves, cakes, custards, macaronis, floating-islands, blanc-mange, candies in various forms, oranges, lemon pie, and like preparations of flour, sugar, eggs, nuts and fruit, make up what all regard as the real *dainties* of the palate, to the exclusion of flesh preparations.

18

The Bible says, "Butter and honey shall He eat," because these were the daintiest luxuries it could name, and Christ's prophetic feeding on such dainties indicated His super-royal rank. "What is sweeter than honey?" Many kindred allusions show that it considered farinaceous food and grapes far more delicious than meat. THIS EXPERIMENT shall be the final umpire. Strawberries, mashed, sweetened, and watered, with unleavened bread, make as delicious a breakfast as one can well eat. Black and red raspberries, dewberries, blackberries, peaches, pears, sweet apples, baked or raw, eaten with milk and sugar, are equally delicious; as are potato starch puddings, jelly cake, Washington pie, &c. Prunes, stewed in considerable water, with bread crumbed in, furnish another variation, as do bread crumbed into the juice of delicious grapes. Neither beeksteaks, chops, ham and eggs, fowls, pigeons, canvass-back ducks, quails, woodcocks, &c., yield more gustatory relish, or more substantial food. Make *meals* of them, not-desserts merely, and eat them with the keen relish of a fresh, not with a sated appetite.

EXPENSE favors a mainly vegetable and farinaceous diet. Fruits, grains, and vegetables can be raised far more easily and cheaply than meat; and grain would be much cheaper still if less were fed to stock and distilled. Though expense is nothing where health is concerned, and that diet is cheapest, in the end, be its first cost what it may, which feeds mind and body the best; yet meat is annually growing scarce and dearer, and when the West and South become well settled up, must be so *very* dear as to preclude its use by all but the wealthy few; as many readers will live to see.

55. — ANIMAL FOOD PROMOTES THE ANIMAL PROPENSITIES.

. The natural food of the lion and tiger, and carnivora generally, feeds and develops their specialties.[40]   Accordingly all flesh-eating animals, without one single exception, are fierce, savage, remorseless, devoid of all kindness, treacherous, stealthy, cunning, rapacious, selfish, malignant, and ferocious; while graminivora are usually docile and servile. Compare felines with bovines, hawks with hens, weasels with squirrels, wolves with sheep, sharks and alligators with turtles, and learn therefrom that, in proportion as man eats meat, he develops those selfish qualities

which always attend it; but that a vegetable diet fosters goodness. This inference cannot be controverted. All that eats
attests that animal food constitutionally develops Combativeness,
Destructiveness, Secretiveness, &c. The very existence of carnivorous animals depends upon and requires their predominance.
Without it their sharp claws, hooked tusks, and powerful muscles, all adapting them to pounce upon and slay their prey, would
be as useless as swords accompanied with cowardice. What could
a sheep do with claws and tusks? or lions and tigers without Destructiveness? Would Nature create these instruments of death
without also creating predominant Destructiveness to accompany
them? Destructiveness and a flesh diet are as universal concomitants as fire and heat; else Nature is not adapted to herself.
Separating them destroys both.

How frightful is the roar of chafed lions? How terrific the
horrid yell of exasperated tigers? because the expressions of
their terrible Destructiveness. You provoke them at your peril.
Is there a reasonable doubt that warm blood and raw flesh, still
quivering·with life, are constitutionally adapted to enhance animality?[49] Does not this concomitance carry its warrant upon its
very front? Animal food, therefore, stimulates animal propensity.

FACTS, those stubborn way-marks of first principles, also still
further attests this concomitance. Thus feeding a dog for
months or years on vegetables alone, increases his docility; but
exclusively on raw flesh, renders him fierce and dangerous; because meat inflames his Destructiveness. Hence the known ferocity of butchers' dogs. Slaughter-houses are often left with both
doors wide open to air the meat, yet our arrant thieves are kept
at bay as effectually as if an unchained tiger guarded the premises. The ferocity of meat-glutted, blood-fed dogs is proverbial.
Not so with those fed on vegetables. Why is this known difference? Our principle answers.

But a tiger, caught while young and fed on farinaceous diet,
became so tame that it was allowed to go unchained about the
premises, and ate its food from the hand, even after it was grown
up. Yet this taming of that fiercest of all animals, by a vegetable
diet, is no more extraordinary than its converse of increasing the
ferocity of the dog by animal food, which all can see daily. Both
are counterparts of each other, and of this same great dietetic law.

This is equally true of man. The ancients, in training their public fighters for their bloody arenas, in which strength and ferocity were mainly required, fed them chiefly on raw flesh; and at the fiendishness thereby produced, all after ages have been and will be shocked. Diversified experience taught them that the diet of the lion and tiger kindled in the man a ferocity like that which predominates in beasts of prey.

This experiment might seem too restricted for reliance if it had not been tried, in every variety of modification, over and over again, thousands of times, on the largest and most extensive scales, from the earliest records of humanity to the present time. Contrast the peaceable, life-sparing Egyptians, throughout their entire history, with the animal and man-slaughtering Jews. The former considered the killing of animals a crime, the latter a religious ordinance. The former ate little or no meat, and were amiable and harmless, throughout their entire history, while the latter, from pastoral Abraham, shepherds throughout all their generations, lived mainly on the flesh of their flocks; besides slaughtering immense herds of cattle and sheep on their altars, and then consuming the greater part of their sacrifices for food; and a more warlike race is not on record. Look at David, truly "a man of blood;" at their ravaging wars, internal and external, throughout their national history; including that terrible carnage which accompanied their final overthrow. Was ever the "trump of war" sounded, from the time Abram armed "his own household" and slaughtered five kings at once, till the destruction of Jerusalem, without being re-echoed throughout hill and dale, till it swept the entire land, and brought together old and young, in martial array, eager to rush upon the field of deadly combat?

Is there no cause-and-effect relationship between this peaceable character and the vegetable diet of the Egyptians on the one hand, and the carnivorous diet and destructive disposition of the Jews on the other? especially since a flesh diet is constitutionally promotive of ferocity, and a vegetable of docility.

The Greeks and Romans ate meat in abundance, and the terror of their arms attests a corresponding ferocity of temper. The ancients generally lived on animal food, and accordingly were exceedingly sanguinary. A similar contrast of those who inhabit the middle and northern latitudes, who generally eat meat freely, with the inhabitants of the tropics, who eat little flesh, establishes a similar conclusion.

But we need not look to other climes or eras for "evidence strong as Holy Writ" that animal food excites the propensities, and especialy Destructiveness. Savages generally live mostly on meat; hence, to a great extent, their savage disposition. The war-loving Indian lives mainly by the chase; and behold his unrelent-ing revenge! See him bury his teeth in the live flesh of his captured enemy, and, tiger-like, suck out his warm blood, exult-ingly exclaiming, "The sweetest morsel I ever tasted"! Hear him powwow around his helpless victims, and, fiend-like, torture them slowly to death, by the most excruciating cruelties possible to inflict. Revenge is the food of the mind whenever flesh is that of the body. Savage ferocity,is the natural product of animal food. Point to the flesh-eating nation, now or ever, not destruc-tive. And those are the most so who live the most on flesh. Does not "John Bull's" "roast beef" bear some cause-and-effect relationship to his warlike valor on the field of slaughter, as well as to his domination at home?

Look, in contrast, at vegetable-eating nations. Hindoos nei-ther eat meat nor love war; and Chinese eat but little meat, and are inferior fighters. Hence their unprecedented numbers. Con-trast the amiable Japanese, who eschew meat, and rightly consider the slaughter of animals a sin, with the New Zealand cannibal, who eats little but meat, and even *his own species*. The fact is no less remarkable in itself than true to this principle, that all savage nations are flesh-eaters, and the more ferocious the more exclu-sively they live on meat; whereas, all humane, good-dispositioned, peaceable nations, live on farinaceous food. As in all carnivorous animals, Destructiveness predominates, in head and character; so all flesh-eating nations have likewise great Destructiveness in organ and disposition; while, as this organ is small and faculty weak in herbivorous animals, so are they also deficient in grami-nivorous nations. In short, Destructiveness is the *constitutional* concomitant of animal food; and necessary in procuring meat.

Animal food also *inflames* Destructiveness, rendering it morbid as well as large; so that a given amount of it is proportionally far more destructive. Thus, this organ is relatively less in the Anglo-American head than in that of the Germans, Scotch, Russians, and many others; yet it is relatively more *excitable*, as is evinced by the greater harshness, hatred, and severity of temper, in the former than latter.   Behold how all the different facts and bearings of this great truth correspond with all the others.

"But animal food at least promotes force, one of the most important of all the human attributes.   Shall we make ourselves like the Hindoo and Chinese, pusillanimous, by abstaining from flesh, or robust and efficient by its use?   George Combe lived almost wholly on rare meat during his production of his great work, 'The Constitution of Man.' Meat is absolutely necessary in order to impart great power to human effort."

Meat does indeed promote force, yet force also accompanies a vegetable diet.   How much more forcible are lions than elephants, or tigers than buffaloes?   How much more do meat-eating Laplanders and Indians *accomplish* than vegetarian Chinese?   One John Chinaman will achieve more *work* than a score of Indians. What have these forest meat-eaters ever accomplished, except with the tomahawk and scalping-knife?

If meat alone gives force, one Indian should master two "pale-faces;" whereas, one white man is equal to a score of red ones. White men eat less meat, yet, under every disadvantage, have driven the Indian back and back again, farther and still farther upon the setting sun, till they bid fair — foul? — to exterminate his race.   Or is the Indian character in itself desirable?   Is it not, in common with that of all other flesh-eaters, hateful? ‚Are the New Zealanders so very forcible, at least for *good?* or the Chinese so pusillanimous, except in war?   If China is not forcible in butchery, human included, yet is she wanting in any of the essential elements of energy?   Look at her canals, commerce, and products.   To call her inefficient is to missupply terms. · Knock off those shackles of antiquity which bind her hand and foot to past ages, and she would soon vie with our own nation in energy and productiveness.   Or hamper us with her fetters of more than three thousand years, and see how every species of public and private enterprise would be held stationary as in a vice.   Feeding all China on meat, would undoubtedly cripple instead of excite; might, indeed, render the masses too turbulent to submit to authority; might engender private animosities, and foment public rebellions, and by thus changing their government and laws, promote ultimate energy, yet this effect would be incidental, not legitimate. The turbulence of our ancestors, fostered by flesh-eating, has so changed the governments and institutions of antiquity, as to have ultimately substituted our own republican instead of their druidical, narrow, and restrictive; but we owe our energy to these governmental changes, not directly to meat.

Admitted that meat gives force, yet the *kind* of force it imparts is analogous to that of the tiger and wolf—force to dare and *kill* rather than to do. Is the wild bull tame or feeble? Do not both the strongest and the fleetest of animals live on vegetables? The elephant and rhinoceros eat no meat, yet their muscular power and endurance far transcend those of the lion and tiger. The deer, antelope, and gazelle feed on herbage, yet distance all flesh-eating animals in the open chase. What carnivori is more sprightly and nimble than the gazelle and chamois? Since, therefore, the fleetest and the strongest of animals eat no meat, must man eat it or else be weak or sluggish?

Apply this principle directly to man: Is the Highland Scotchman, who was brought up on oatmeal, and tasted meat no oftener than the moon quartered, so very inefficient? Are the potato-fed Irish weak? Can our own beef-gourmands dig or carry more? The strength-champion of Philadelphia, in 1839, had never tasted meat. The rice-fed Chinese will outdo "John Bull" and "Uncle Sam," except in shedding blood. So will the herbivorous inhabitants of the Pacific isles. But if man's *constitution* demands meat, those who fulfilled this ordinance of Nature would far exceed those who do not; whereas, the fact is the reverse, which proves a meat diet unnecessary to strength.

Not that animal food does not develop muscular strength. Carnivorous animals are strong, but herbivorous are stronger, yet have less propensity. Hence, since meat is not necessary to either strength or force, since it animalizes and depraves, and thus does a positive damage but not a necessary good, why injure ourselves by its consumption?

56. — ANIMAL SLAUGHTER BLUNTS THE MORAL SENTIMENTS.

ACTIVE Benevolence shudders to see calves, and sheep, and fowls tied by their feet, and tumbled together into carts, on top of each other, banged about as if only boxes, kept for days without food, and, after all this living death, hung up by their hind

legs in excruciating torture, their veins punctured, faint with loss
of blood, struggling for life, yet enduring all the agonies of a
lingering death for hours, meanwhile pelted, so as to render their
meat white and tender, every blow extorting a horrid groan, till
tardy death finally ends their sufferings! All this perpetrated on
helpless, unoffending beasts, agonizing only to blunt Benevolence.
Hear the piteous wails of these wretched animals, on their passage
from the farmyard to the slaughter-house; see their up-turned
eyes rolling in agony; witness the desperate struggles, and hear
the terrible bellowings of the frantic bullock who apprehends his
fate, as he is drawn up to the fatal bull-ring; or even look at the
awful expression of all amputated heads, as seen in market, or
carted through the streets, and then say whether the slaughtering
of animals is not a perfect *outrage* on every feeling of humanity.
What well-organized child ever beholds an animal slaughtered for
the first time, without almost an agony of sympathy? Or can any
highly-benevolent adult, especially female, endure the distressing sight, unless accustomed to it? How tender-hearted woman
shudders thereat, and shrinks therefrom! Yet she is not unduly
sympathetic. If animals must die, at least let them suffer as *little*
as possible; and their meat will taste and nourish much the better,
the better they are cared for up to the last.

MEAT BLUNTS the moral sentiments, but inflames the propensities, whereas human perfection requires the converse. Man is
almost all propensity now. His animality vastly predominates
over his morality; whereas, to be happy, morality must predominate. All justly complain of the evils of society. The best are
depraved enough, and the worst almost devils incarnate. What
but *perverted* propensity causes the aggravated evils under which
society groans? In what else does depravity consist? Or how can
human wickedness and woe be obviated, except by subjugating and
purifying propensity by intellect and promoting moral sentiment?
How despicable the disposition of the tiger, the hyena, and shark!
Does man require to approximate himself thereto? Would becoming more tiger-like render humanity more perfect? Is predominant propensity human glory and happiness? Would you
have your children become more turbulent, quarrelsome, fierce,
revengeful, hating, and hateful; more like beasts of prey? Then
give them the more meat. Would you not rather render them
more lamb-like? then feed them the more on a vegetable diet.

"But brute kills brute. Then why not man kill beast? Has God denied us a privilege he accords to brutes?"

As those coarsely organized, can do many things which excite disgust and repugnance in those keenly sensitive and fine-feeling; so brutes can do what would shock the keener susceptibilities of humanity. Beasts of prey have little Benevolence, hence violate none when they slay to eat, but fulfil one. If man had no sympathy for distress — yet what would he be better than beast without it — he, too, might prey upon brute and man; but he has, and therefore must not abuse it by butchering inoffensive animals.

"But flesh-*eaters* neither kill nor blunt their moral sentiments."

As the "bloody Mary" did not bind the martyrs, nor light the fires of Smithfield, yet signed their death-warrants, and as Robespierre only *ordered* the beheading of the victims of the French revolution, yet both were the virtual executioners; so flesh-*eaters* are the real slaughterers, because they give the *order*. The butcher is to the slaughtered what the torch-carrier was to the martyrdom of John Rogers, and the hired servants employed to ply the guillotine are to the execution. All these are only the paid *agents*, whereas the responsibility falls mainly on those who *order*, not who execute under authority. The butcher kills mainly by proxy. The *consumer* is the virtual butcher; because he both requires the slaughter itself, and directs its kind, time, quantity, manner, and everything about it. Unless he demanded it, the poor beast would not bleed. He is the "Mary" and the "Robespierre" of the slaughter-house; because every pound of flesh he eats increases the demand, and thus becomes a virtual death-warrant issued against helpless brutes.   .

"If man did not raise beasts for slaughter he would raise but few; and those raised and slaughtered enjoy much more from birth to death than they suffer in their slaughter; so that being raised and killed is better than neither.

"Besides, man's Destructiveness was created to be exercised, and by placing Alimentiveness at its side, Nature says, "Slay all you need to eat," while Benevolence says, "Cause them as little *pain* as possible."

Since beasts and all else terrestrial were created for man, in case his best good demands flesh, let them die. He has a better *natural right* to kill and eat fowls than they worms. Destructiveness forms as constituent a department of Nature and of man

19

as does Benevolence, and therefore has its right sphere. Animals preyed on are usually so prolific that, unless Destructiveness killed them off, they would soon so exhaust their food as to starve to death, and starve man; just as the excess of canker-worms over leaves sometimes exterminates the worms by starvation.

PROCURING vegetable food, as in farming, also promotes morality and goodness, as well as intellect; while killing animals for food promotes the propensities. Still, these propensities constitute an integral part of man, and their legitimate exercise is as right and proper in its place as is that of his moral sentiments.

57. — VEGETABLES CONTAIN ALL THE NUTRITIOUS ELEMENTS REQUIRED TO SUSTAIN LIFE.

LIEBIG'S ANIMAL CHEMISTRY, one of the most profound and philosophical works on this subject, completely settles this point thus : —

"Two substances require especial consideration as the chief ingredients of the blood; one of these separates immediately from the blood when withdrawn from the circulation. It is well known that in this case blood coagulates, and separates into a yellowish liquid, the SERUM of the blood, and a gelatinous mass, which adheres to a rod or stick in soft, elastic fibres, when coagulating blood is briskly stirred. This is the FIBRINE of the blood, which is identical in all its properties with muscular fibre, when the latter is purified from all foreign matters.

"The second principal ingredient of the blood is contained in the serum, and gives to this liquid all the properties of the white of eggs, with which it is identical. When heated, it coagulates into a white, elastic mass, and the coagulated substance is called ALBUMEN.

"Fibrine and albumen, the chief ingredients of blood, contain, in all, seven chemical elements, among which nitrogen, phosphorus, and sulphur are found. They contain also the earth of bones. The serum retains in solution sea salt and other salts of potash and soda, in which the acids are carbonic, phosphoric, and sulphuric acids. The globules of the blood contain fibrine and albumen, along with a red coloring matter, in which iron is a constant element. Besides these, the blood contains certain fatty bodies in small quantity, which differ from ordinary fats in several of their properties.

"Chemical analysis has led to the remarkable result, that fibrine and albumen contain the same organic elements united in the same proportion; so that two analyses, the one of fibrine and the other of albumen, do not differ more than two analyses of fibrine or two of albumen respectively do, in the composition of one hundred parts.

"Both albumen and fibrine, in the process of nutrition, are capable of being converted into muscular fibre, and muscular fibre is capable of being reconverted into blood. These facts have long been established by physiologists, and chemistry has merely proved that these metamorphoses can be accomplished under the influence of a certain force, without the aid of a third substance, or of its elements, and without the addition of any foreign element, or the separation of any element previously present in these substances.

"The nutritive process in the carnivora is seen in its simplest form. This class of animals lives on the blood and flesh of the graminivora; but this blood and flesh are, in all its properties, identical with their own. Neither chemical nor physiological differences can be discovered.

"In a chemical sense, therefore, it may be said that a carnivorous animal, in supporting the vital process, consumes itself. That which serves for its nutrition is identical with those parts of its organization which are to be renewed.

"Chemical researches have shown, that all such parts of vegetables as can afford nutriment to animals contain certain constituents which are rich in nitrogen; and the most ordinary experience proves that animals require for their support and nutrition less of these parts of plants in proportion as they abound in the nitrogenized constituents. Animals cannot be fed on matters destitute of these nitrogenized constituents.

"These important products of vegetation are especially abundant in the seeds of the different kinds of grain, and of peas, beans, and lentils; in the roots and the juices of what are commonly called vegetables. They exist, however, in all plants, without exception, and in every part of plants in larger or smaller quantity.

"When the newly expressed juices of vegetables are allowed to stand, a separation takes place in a few minutes. A gelatinous precipitate, commonly of a green tinge, is deposited, and this, when acted on by liquids, which remove the coloring matter, leaves a grayish white substance, well known to druggists as the deposit from vegetable juices. This is one of the nitrogenized compounds which serves for the nutrition of animals, and has been named VEGETABLE FIBRINE. The juice of grapes is especially rich in this constituent, but it is most abundant in the seeds of wheat, and of the cerealia. It may be obtained from wheat flour by a mechanical operation, and in a state of tolerable purity; it is then called GLUTEN, but the glutinous property belongs, not to vegetable fibrine, but to a foreign substance, present in small quantity, which is not found in the other cerealia.

"The second nitrogenized compound remains dissolved in the juice after the separation of the fibrine. It does not separate from the juice at the ordinary temperature, but is instantly coagulated when the liquid containing it is heated to the boiling point.

"When the clarified juice of nutritious vegetables, such as cauliflower, asparagus, mangel-wurzel, or turnips, is made to boil, a coagulum is formed, which it is absolutely impossible to distinguish from the substance which separates as coagulum, when the serum of blood or the white of an egg, diluted with water, are heated to the boiling point. This is VEGETABLE ALBUMEN. It is found in the greatest abundance in certain seeds, in nuts, almonds, and others, in which the starch of the graminea is replaced by oil.

"The third nitrogenized constituent of the vegetable food of animals is VEGETABLE CASEINE. It is chiefly found in the seeds of peas, beans, len-

tils, and similar leguminous seeds. Like vegetable albumen, it is soluble
in water, but differs from it in this, that its solution is not coagulated by
heat. When the solution is heated or evaporated, a skin forms on its
surface, and the addition of an acid causes a coagulum, just as in animal
milk.

"These three nitrogenized compounds, vegetable fibrine, albumen, and
caseine, are the true nitrogenized constituents of the food of graminivorous animals; all other nitrogenized compounds, occurring in plants, are
either rejected by animals, as in the case of the characteristic principle
of poisonous and medicinal plants, or else they occur in the food in such
very small proportion, that they cannot possibly contribute to the increase of mass in the animal body.

"How beautifully and admirably simple, with the aid of these discoveries, appears the process of nutrition in animals, the formation of their
organs, in which vitality chiefly resides! Those vegetable principles,
which in animals are used to form blood, contain the chief constituents
of blood fibrine and albumen, ready formed, as far as regards their composition. All plants, besides, contain a certain quantity of iron, which
re-appears in the coloring matter of the blood. Vegetable fibrine and
animal fibrine, vegetable albumen and animal albumen, hardly differ
even in form; if these principles be wanting in the food, the nutrition
of the animal is arrested; and when they are present, the graminivorous
animal obtains in its food the very same principles on the presence of
which the nutrition of the carnivora entirely depends.

"Vegetables produce in their organism the blood of all animals, for
the carnivora, in consuming the blood and flesh of the graminivora, consume, strictly speaking, only the vegetable principles which have served
for the nutrition of the latter. Vegetable fibrine and albumen take the
same form in the stomach of the graminivorous animal as animal fibrine
and albumen do in that of the carnivorous animal."

58. — FACTS, AND THE EXPERIENCES OF THE AUTHOR AND OTHERS.

The Author's dietetic experience deserves insertion, partly as a
guide, but perhaps equally as a beacon. In March, 1835, on his
first opening in New York, Mrs. Nicholson, of vegetarian board-
ing-house notoriety, called for a phrenological consultation, and
indoctrinated him with her anti-flesh eating ideas; which he
adopted practically. The effect of bathing and no meat acted
like magic in improving his health. He was never as well before,
and but once since. Before, he was unmistakably in a consumptive decline, which must soon have terminated fatally, but for
this timely rescue. After two or three years he began gradually
to decline again, yet lived a rigid vegetarian for over twelve
years, when he was persuaded again to try a little meat; yet for
about eight years more he ate but very little meat. About 1855

he returned to an ordinary mixed diet with a most decided improvement in his health, and still continues to eat about as much meat as others usually eat.

He has meanwhile noted the effects of abstinence from meat on others, and come to these conclusions : —

1. That abstaining from meat, when one has been accustomed to it, will sometimes have a beneficial effect almost magical, but that after months or years of such abstinence, a *return* to a mixed diet will again also *re-improve* the health ; on the principle that horses, kept on oats, when turned out to grass, at first often grow poor and weak, but, on returning to oats, are decidedly better than if they had been kept on them all the time.

2. That all eat by far *too much* meat, else, abstaining from it would injure, not benefit.

3. That those who abstain from meat often fail to supply its place, and thus suffer. Certain it is, that as a general thing, vegetarians become extremely irritable, and often die suddenly. Where is Graham? Dead long ago, though just before his death, at fifty-six, he was as sprightly as a boy. And a post-mortem examination showed that no vital organ was diseased. Shame, that he should mortify his disciples and nullify his doctrine by his own premature death. He was always one of the most irascible and pugnacious of men, and forever at war with everybody, friends and foes equally. He alienated every one of his admirers ; told everybody how cordially he hated his wife, and she him ; and died one of the bitterest of misanthropists possible. Readers curious on this point will find its proofs in two of his poems, published in a Northampton paper about four months before he died ; which evinced a gloom, misanthropy, melancholy, morbidity, and consequently mental agony, rarely ever expressed to a like extent. Why? Because his system *lacked* and intensely *craved* some dietetic aliment his food had failed to supply ; on the principle that a craving child is always intolerably cross. If his anti-flesh diet was as beneficial as he declared, why should he both become so bitter with spleen, and then die in his prime? Why did he not live to be ninety, and live and die serene, genial, and jubilant?

Where are his disciples? Nearly all are dead, or backslidden. Drs. Shew, Burdell, and others who lived out his doctrines, died younger than their leader, and just when they became fully ma-

tured, and prepared for work.   Let their early death be the com-
mentary on their doctrines.

Dr. Trall, about the only public living advocate of this
doctrine, is reputed, with what truth deponent saith not, to be
extremely nervous and impatient, if not irritable.   Let his personal acquaintances attest.   And vegetarians generally, judging
from long observation, are a dyspeptic, moody, crotchety, dissatisfied set; at least neither genial nor companionable.   Facts
do not favor their doctrines.

Per contra, the Bible Christians in Philadelphia, many of whom
have tasted no meat for two, three, and four generations, are so
remarkably good, devout, and pleasant, that a given amount of
Destructiveness and Combativeness in them sufficient to render
meat-eaters violent tempered, only makes them forcible, yet
amiable.

"But you contradict yourself.   You argue one way theoretically,
and the opposite practically.   Thirty years ago you gave out in your
lectures and writings, that you were a thorough vegetarian, but now
'back down ' on yourself and disciples.   Be consistent, at least with
yourself, by sticking to your old landmarks."

Truth is infinitely above persons.   The Author has rather
added to former views than changed them ; but wrote then, writes
now, from *conviction*.   Let his right hand *perish* sooner than
knowingly mislead mankind.   Public men little realize what momentous responsibilities inhere in leadership.   They should first
make *very* sure that they are *right*, and then swear eternal fealty
to *truth*.   Let O. S. Fowler perish, if needs be, but let eternal
truth prevail ; as prevail it surely will.   To see and frankly admit
an error, is noble ; to knowingly *propagate* one, accursed.

59. — Summary of this flesh-eating Argument.

Previous reasonings seemingly contradict each other, while
truth is always self-consistent.   Yet they are reconcilable thus —
and to these conclusions all of the Author's experiments and
observations have brought him : —

1st.   That as the same person requires different kinds of food
at different periods of life — milk during infancy, more and
stronger food during growth, the heartiest during middle life,
but those less rich as life declines ; so that the race was originally

adapted to eat some meat throughout all its history; enough, though only enough, to use up what fish, flesh, fowl, eggs, milk, butter, cheese, &c., can be produced without curtailing the fullest supply of grains, vegetables, and fruit; yet most during its early meridian, while clearing off, draining and subduing the earth, and fitting it up for the future. Thus men must eat meat as long as they need to go to war; and they require war till all wrongs are righted and evils obviated, unless all concerned agree to submit to arbitration. Men need meat as long as they have much rough hard work to do, which will be some time yet; and while they require self-protection, which will be till all concede all natural rights to all; which will not be in our day. Yet the great body of human food should be mainly vegetable, with the less meat as man advances. Hence the structure of his teeth is mainly graminivorous, yet they allow of his eating cooked meats, but do not fit him to seize, tear, and swallow living animals.[52]

2d. That at all times he is adapted to eat much *less* meat than he now eats, and much more in winter than in summer; and very little if any in the tropics, but to subsist mainly on those juicy fruits which resupply the perspiration incident to high temperatures; while those of high latitudes should eat meat and fat, the growth of which fall promotes. Siberians and Kamtchatkaus would find it difficult to obtain from vegetables all the carbon they need.

3d. That those who would nurture their moral natures and subdue their animal, should forego meat; while all should partake the more of fruits and vegetables the warmer the weather.

4th. That those whose stomachs are sour, that is, who are troubled with wind, should not eat meat, because its fermentation, or, in plain terms, its *rotting* in the stomach, and the distribution of this putrid mass throughout the whole system, is really horrible, and much worse than that of vegetables. The stench of decaying meat *out* of the system is awful; then how much worse *within* it? No more meat nor of anything else should ever be eaten than can be digested before it ferments; yet souring vegetables are not as bad in the system as decaying meat.

5th. FINALLY, when the appetite is normal, and the taste well disciplined,[60] *natural relish*, in all persons, at all times, and during all ages, will render an infallible verdict as to whether, and •

what kinds of meats, vegetables and fruits, are for the time being best for each.

SOME KINDS of meat are better than others. Beef and mutton are much better than pork, ham, and bacon, at least in warm climates. Yet in Texas, where beef is so plenty and pork so scarce, all who can afford it eat "hog and hominy." Negroes there will not work on beef; while "up north" none will eat pork who can afford beef and mutton.

"PORK AND BEANS" is a favorite dish everywhere, and very hearty. Lumbermen live almost wholly on it, with hot saleratus bread, and strong coffee ; yet their hardy habits, exercise in the cold, &c., would make even invalids healthy. The Chinese live and work very hard mainly on pork and rice, probably for the same reason that Southerners like hog and hominy, namely, because the hominy furnishes muscle and organic materials, while the pork furnishes carbon to heat up.

BUFFALO meat should give strength, but has an unpleasant flavor.

GOATS, DEER, and all kinds of game, are better than veal, which is yet immature.

SECTION III.

THE PREPARATION OF FOOD BY COOKING, ETC.

60. — DESICCATION ABSOLUTELY NECESSARY.

ATOMS, the minutest possible, constitute all food. These particles often grow together very firmly, as in grain, which is hard when dry, and dry so as to "keep" during transportation and use. How could they possibly enter into the organic composition until they are separated? True, the stomach can accomplish this, but has quite enough to do without. Obviously this should be done as much as possible beforehand. Men have adopted grinding and cooking to effect this desiccation. Seeds swallowed whole often pass clear through the alimentary canal and are voided intact, thus yielding none of their nutrition. Hence grinding and cooking a given amount of grain makes it go further in feeding and fattening animals than if eaten whole. In fact, one end of mastication is this disintegration, which grinding and cooking greatly aid. Throughout all ages, nations, and families, mankind have adopted both the grinding of grains into flour and the cooking of their food, before eating it; obviously in order to disintegrate it.

Some let meat hang as long as it will hang without falling; that is, till its particles have been loosened from each other by incipient decay.

PULPY food, like most fruits, do not need cooking, unless they are so sour as to require to be sweetened, like cranberries, or else mixed with other food, as in making pies, dumplings, puddings, &c. Good fruit is injured in flavor and quality by being cooked; yet tough fruits, like some leathery kinds of apples, are improved by baking. Tomatoes are better raw than cooked, while cooking potatoes right makes them so mealy that the gastric juice can penetrate among and attack all the particles at once.

61. —FLOUR AND BREAD, THEIR MATERIALS, MANUFACTURE, &c.

BREAD is the veritable "*staff of life.*" From time immemorial, and throughout all nations and tribes, except the most degraded savages, some kind of bread has been the staple article of human diet, and will doubtless so continue while men eat; and therefore deserves primary consideration, especially since its chief materials are incorporated into most other kinds of food. Other edibles may be generally introduced, as potatoes have lately been, yet never to take the place of "flour victuals," but only to accompany them. With many kinds of food we do not eat meat, yet we eat bread with all kinds, and more bread usually than anything else.

GRAIN — wheat, rye, oats, barley, &c., crushed and ground into flour — constitutes the chief ingredient of bread. It consists simply of seeds, and all seeds contain nourishment, in order to feed the sprouting chit, till it can put forth its roots and draw sustenance from the earth. It is this nutritious principle, stored up for the purpose of nourishing the plant in its embryo, which sustains human and animal life; and the probable reason why the flour of grain forms the best species of nourishment for man is, that it is so highly organized, and so condensed. It can also be ground fine, and by proper management, preserved for years.

Chemically analyzed, wheat, the best of the entire cereal family, contains about four fifths of nutritious substances; rye, barley, and oats, about the same; rice nine tenths, and Indian corn

20

about seven tenths, while meat contains only about five and a half tenths.

We make flour, both fine and coarse, bolted and unbolted, into various forms of food, both with shortening and without, with and without sweetening, with various kinds single and mixed, as all wheat, all rye, all Indian, all barley, all oatmeal, all rice, or part wheat and part Indian, or "rye-and-Indian," or "wheat-and-rye." We also boil each of these kinds of flour into puddings, the main ingredients and dietetic uses of which are the same as bread; or sweeten, shorten, and fry in fat, making doughnuts; or shorten and add fruit, as in the manufacture of apple fritters, and also of pies of all kinds, pot and meat pies included; or thickened into soups of all kinds, or made into " dressings; " and thus work them into nearly all the food eaten. Even meat eaters live mainly upon them, and so do many species of animals. Undoubtedly after ages will discover and perfect many other kinds of grain now growing wild in our swamps, mountains, and forests, as a recent one has Indian corn, but cereal grains will always be a staple article of food.

FLOUR, being thus promotive of life and all its ends, its preparation, in the best and most nutritious form, is commensurately important. Two egregious errors are usually committed in grinding. The weight of the upper stone, and the rapidity of its motion, usually both grinds it so fine, and heats it so hot, as to more or less " kill " its life, and impair its nutritive properties. Coarse ground corn meal is much sweeter than fine ground — proof enough that fine grinding injures.

Grain is ground thus fine that it may be bolted the more closely, so as to make the whiter bread. Shall looks be allowed to impair quality? A good portion of the bran left in, greatly improves its nutritive capability; else Nature would have allowed its separation from the flour without grinding. Its presence also greatly promotes that intestinal action so essential to digestion.[71] Its absence facilitates that torpor of the bowels and consequent constipation, which paves the way for those stomachic complaints to be discussed hereafter.[122] Fine flour given to hens, cattle, horses, and all other animals, will soon disorder them effectually, and breed disease; and unless man were stronger constitutioned than they, it would break down and bury all who use it. Indeed,

it is now effectually consuming its consumers by hundreds of
thousands; not suddenly, but gradually, by impairing digestion,
and thus inducing other diseases to which their death is ascribed.
Those who eat coarse and unbolted flour bread, thereby obviate
half their sickness, by keeping the intestinal canal open, and thus
carrying off those causes of disease which fine flour bread, by inducing constipation, retains in the system to engender sickness.
Nothing but dire necessity should induce one to live habitually
on fine flour bread.   It immediately causes intestinal sluggishness,
stomachic disorder, and dyspeptic troubles.

BROWN bread also tastes better than white superfine, as all who
make trial can perceive.   This is another conclusive proof of its
superiority.[50]   New England's ancestry ate coarse bread, made of
rye and Indian, and lived longer, besides enjoying far better
health, than their fine-flour-fed descendants have any prospect of
living; and Scotch oat-cake and porridge eaters rarely know how
dyspepsia feels till they exchange them for "killed" flour bread.
Dyspeptics also find coarse bread indispensable; and what is thus
necessary to weak stomachs would of course go far towards keeping strong ones strong.   Even sailors cannot live on fine flour
bread; much less can the sedentary classes.

The nutriment of fine flour bread is also too condensed.   Sugar
is highly nutritious, yet eaten alone soon disorders digestion;
because there is too much of it in too small a compass.   A due
amount of bulk is as essential to perfect digestion as the nutrition
itself.   The bran helps to "fill up," and, besides restraining over-
eating, gently irritates the intestinal coating, and provokes action.
Lovers of fine flour are quite welcome to insipid and half "killed"
white bread; yet only partial starvation should induce one to
partake of it more than a few meals at a time.   Those whose
bowels are too tender and aperient, that is, who are inclined to
diarrhœa, may eat fine flour bread; but twenty-five years hence
very few will be ignorant or foolish enough to eat white bread.

62. — LEAVENED AND UNLEAVENED BREAD.

To RAISE the bread is the next process in its preparation.   This
consists in causing fermentation, by which a gas is generated
which insinuates itself throughout the doughy mass, and thus
raises it, or renders it porous.

This portion of the bread-making process is also greatly over-done. Fermentation is the first stage of decay. It creates the gas by souring the dough. To raise dough without proportionally souring it, is not possible; because, from the souring alone is this raising gas derived, though habit prevents our tasting it. But let it stand a little too long, and it tastes very sour. Or eat un-leavened bread a few months, long enough for your vitiated taste to become normalized, and it will utterly loathe and reject the best of yeast bread.

UNLEAVENED bread will also keep twice or thrice as long as what is raised. Of this, ship bread, Boston crackers, and wa-fers, are examples. This leavening is incipient decomposition, and from the gas evolved during the baking, alcohol in large quantities can be manufactured; and alcohol is the child of de-composition or rottenness. Yeast is obtained by excessive fer-mentation; and the world over the fermenting process is the de-caying process. This incipient decomposition is introduced by the yeast into the dough, and of course impairs its virtue. Hence, excessive fermentation is highly injurious.

Bakers' bread is fermented almost to death in order to make the greatest possible loaf out of the least flour. People love to be gulled. If two loaves, both containing the same quantity and quality of flour, but the one puffed up by excessive fermentation, while the other is not thus injured, though abundantly light for utility, were proffered for selection, nearly all would prefer the hollow bulk, though they knew it to be inferior to the smaller, though better loaf. This tempts bakers to contrive all sorts of devices to swell their loaves; and, to neutralize the souring, they put in alum to absorb more water, so as to weigh more, along with ammonia and other things, which leave the bread vitiated by dele-terious compounds. Eating bakers' bread is better than actual starvation, yet nothing but dire necessity should induce one to live habitually upon it.

SOUR MILK and saleratus bread is less objectionable, because the gas which raises it is created, not by decomposition, but by the chemical combination of the acid of the sour milk with the alkali of the saleratus, and raised too quickly to allow the dough to sour, and hence preferable to bread raised with turnpike, yeast, and the like. "Milk emptyings" bread, besides being

whiter and sweeter than that made with other emptyings, becomes
light before it sours much, and is universally used throughout
the West.

Let bread be made, then, of coarser flour, unbolted, or bolted
but little; be raised with saleratus or milk emptyings, and not
unduly bloated up; be thoroughly baked — and its crust is its
best portion — and never eaten warm; for then mastication rolls
it up into firm masses which the gastric juice penetrates with difficulty; and then be eaten more abundantly than any other article
of diet.

UNLEAVENED bread, is, however, immeasurably preferable to
leavened. All raised breads, milk emptyings rising included,
are soured in and by the *act and fact* of being raised, and,
deposited in the stomach *pre-soured*, of course turn the rest of
the contents of the stomach sour much sooner than unleavened
bread. Nature keeps the stomach very warm. This fermented
bread is what causes most of this modern dyspepsia, on the principle that putting sour milk in with sweet, turns the *whole* mass
sour sooner than putting in sweet.

THE BEST RECIPE for making bread, is: Take what flour
is required for a meal; add a little salt, though the less the
better, for salt is very irritating; superadd barely water enough
to make a thinish batter, only a little thicker than for ordinary
griddle cakes; beat and work it, the more the better; have your
oven and pan *sissing* hot; make a thin loaf, only about a quarter
of an inch thick; and when put into the oven, its strong heat
will instantly strike a *steam-tight crust* over bottom, top, and
sides, and then turn the water in the dough into steam, which
this crust *retains*, and which puffs up all parts of the dough, and
lightens the bread. A thick loaf would press out this steam, and
leave the bread heavy; whereas, the crust of a thin loaf confines it
where it is generated, namely, throughout every part of the dough,
and thus leavens the entire mass.

THIS bread will lie on even a sour stomach till Nature can
digest it, instead of passing off by fermentation. Crumb it into
one tumbler of warm water, and leavened bread into another, and
keep both equally warm, and two batches of the leavened bread
will ferment to one of the unleavened.

BAKING IRONS, in pairs, with cups in the lower one, opposite to like cups in the upper, the lower cups filled with dough, the upper put on, both pre-heated, and the steam will puff up the dough sufficiently to fill both halves.   This is better than a pan.

A MONTH'S or year's supply can thus be baked at once, but must be baked hard, like ship-bread, and ground in your coffee-mill, or softened by hot water, as wanted for use, or eaten crisp.   Bakers should prepare flour this way, instead of by fermentation.   It can thus be transported like ship-bread.

AERATED, or patent bread, is every way better than fermented, and made upon a right *principle*, yet not always made just right. As a general thing, it merits commendation and use.

FLANNEL CAKES, buckwheat cakes, and all cakes raised with yeast, or fermented, are liable to the same objection just urged against leavened bread, yet are usually worse, because still more sour.

"HOT SALERATUS BISCUITS" are about as bad as fermented bread ; because potash, in all its compounds, whenever it gets access to flesh, eats and keeps on eating, without diminution ; and most persons have some crack somewhere in their alimentary canal into which this saleratus will work, and eat on to their perpetual in- jury.   Hence it aggravates bronchial difficulties, and provokes a hacking cough.   It also wads up, while being eaten, into doughy masses, which sour before they can be digested from their outside.

RICE contains a greater proportion of nourishment than any other article of diet, and the virtue of oatmeal is attested by the powerful frames and strong constitutions of the Highland Picts. Fortunately it is coming into general use, and all should promote its introduction.   As a diet for children, when eaten with milk, it probably has no superior, if equal.

RYE is not generally appreciated.   Unbolted rye flour, made into hasty-pudding, is one of the most easily digested things which dyspeptics can eat. It is also exceedingly palatable.   Rye bread is nutritious, aperient, and, but for its color, would un- doubtedly rival wheat.   Try it as a change.

BARLEY bread was once a staple article of diet.   May it again become a general favorite.   The distillery should no longer be allowed to consume so wholesome, palatable, and excellent au article of food.

63. — PASTRY, EGGS, AND SPICES.

CAKES and pies are rarely eaten as food, but usually as a relish merely. They are generally deemed unwholesome, and justly so, because composed of flour and grease, or shortening sweetened — a compound exceedingly difficult of digestion. Flour sweetened is all right; but when shortened as well as sweetened, the stomach dissolves it with difficulty; and hence the unsuitableness of cake for children.

BAKERS' cake is still more injurious. Quantities of ammonia, of which hartshorn is made, are put in to render it light; and to all this is added colored coatings, composed of poisonous ingredients. Domestic cake is bad enough, but bakers' is utterly unfit even for adult stomachs, much more for juvenile.

If any doubts remain of the unwholesomeness even of domestic cake, the following receipts must effectually obviate them : —

POUND CAKE. — "A pound each of butter, sugar, and flour, and ten eggs." As ten eggs weigh a pound, of course half the cake is butter and eggs, and only one quarter flour, and that completely saturated with sweet, grease, and eggs, baked *an hour*. Now we know that eggs cook abundantly in three minutes, and become extremely tough and hard in six; and since hard-cooked eggs are universally conceded to be difficult of digestion, what must they be after being baked an hour, and in fat and flour?

SPONGE cake consists of only one fifth flour, two fifths eggs, baked to a crisp, and the balance sugar. Shrewsbury cake contains one third flour, above one third butter and eggs, and the balance brandy, sugar, and nutmeg. Jumbles are composed of about one third flour, one quarter sugar, and above one third of eggs, milk, and butter. Soft cakes contain nearly half melted butter. Butter and eggs make up above half of a cake called " wonders ; " and wondrously unhealthy it must be. Above half of even plain gingerbread consists of cream, butter, molasses, and ginger. Of composition cake, only one fourth is flour, and nearly three fourths eggs, butter, cream, and brandy ; a full quarter being melted cream and butter. Since melted butter, fat, and cream compose about half of most of our cakes, while about one quarter consists of eggs baked nearly or quite an hour, is not cake, of necessity, most unwholesome? Add to all this, that nearly a fifth of the frosting of bakers' cake is composed of oxides of lead, to impart color; who that eats cake but must thereby impair the stomach, engender disease, and hasten death? Our ancestors ate little cake, yet their descendants think they cannot live without it; and a mistaken kindness feeds it to children as freely as if it were the staff of life, and aggravates the evil by feeding it *between meals.*

PIES may be rendered wholesome or unwholesome, at the option of the maker. The union, however intimate, of bread and fruit, forms the best diet in the world; you may live wholly on it. An excellent crust can be made of flour, potatoes, and milk, or water, without shortening. Yet all pies should be eaten, not after a full meal, but as a *part* of it — and as the *first* part rather than the last; because we eat them mainly as a relish; and all know how much keener the appetite is at the beginning than close of the meal. If cakes must be eaten, let them be eaten when the Chinese eat their relishes — first, not last; and at breakfast instead of supper.

EGGS, properly cooked, are undoubtedly as wholesome and nutritious as palatable.[50] They contain quantities of carbon, and also gluten, fibrin, and the very compounds required by the animal economy, and are especially good for children. Yet very much depends on the mode of cooking them. Fried in grease, as "ham and eggs," or "pork and eggs," they are hard of digestion, as well on account of being generally over-done, as saturated with melted grease. Poached eggs are liable to a similar objection. But soft-boiled eggs, eaten with bread or other substantial food, are as useful as delicious. Use little butter or salt, because a little practice will render eggs better alone than seasoned. Butter, salt, pepper, everything mixed with them, takes from, or obscures the taste in eggs; yet it is this taste which makes us relish them.

SPICES and condiments are injurious. Their very nature is irritating, heating, and feverish. Like alcoholic liquors, they stimulate temporarily only to debilitate ultimately. They impart n) inherent, protracted vigor to the system, but only goad, lash up, and then prostrate. Especially do they irritate the stomach, besides blunting the taste, disordering the appetite, benumbing the nerves they touch, and of course deteriorating natural relish.[51] They induce us to eat too much, because we eat, and keep eating; vainly attempting to make up in quantity that gustatory pleasure lost by this blunting. They also weaken the salivary glands. Mustard, peppers, cloves, ginger, cinnamon, and the like, deteriorate relish and promote dyspepsia; except that red pepper, in some states of the stomach, provokes its action without exhaustion, and benefits.

VINEGAR, pickles, &c., are undoubtedly beneficial, their acid being just what the stomach needs; yet chow-chow gives dyspeptics more trouble than anything else they eat. Still, in these and all like cases normal appetite is an infallible guide.[50]

Finally, let the principle, that whatever detracts from or obscures the natural taste of food, thereby impairs the luxury of eating, be always borne in mind and put in practice. The deliciousness is in the *food*, not the spices; in the bread, not butter, or gravy, or sauce, or other things often eaten with it as relishes. When we cannot enjoy simple food simply prepared, we cannot enjoy it with all the "seasoning," improperly so called, with which it can be cooked or eaten. Whatever is fit for food, Nature has already seasoned for us infinitely better than art can season it.[60] And since condiments both obscure Nature's rich flavors, and also blunt our powers of perceiving them, to say nothing of their deleterious consequences, practical wisdom dictates that food should be eaten with as few spices and relishes as possible. Yet modern cookery is all seasoning, a total perversion of Nature's dietetic simplicity.

Confectionery is so closely allied to pastry as to deserve a passing remark. Ice creams are not objectionable, except when the stomach is overheated. Their being frozen is their greatest objection. They may be eaten at, or right after meals, with comparative impunity, provided they are allowed to melt first, or else are eaten *very slowly*, so that they warm *in the mouth*. But candies in all their forms are very detrimental, because so very rich; because colored with poisonous ingredients; because usually eaten between meals or late at night; and especially because they pervert the relish, so that natural food tastes insipid, and rich food is sought to fill the vacuum they create. They are exceedingly liable to sour on the stomach, which they always overload, and thus stupefy the brain, breed worms, and incite disease. Children

21

especially should never be indulged in them.   They also soon ruin the teeth.   This is a sure sign that they first impair the stomach.

64. — FRUIT.

GOOD FRUIT is one of the most delicious articles man can eat. Of this all are practical witnesses.   Its lusciousness warrants their utility, to which it is proportionate.   Honey and sugar are most delicious at first, but soon cloy, because their nutrition is so highly concentrated.   Not so with good fruit.   Let a person moderately hungry, sit down to a plate of honey, or butter, or sugar, and he loses his relish before he has taken a tithe of the real gustatory pleasure he can take in as many first-rate peaches, or pears, or apricots, or nectarines, or even apples or berries, as his stomach will bear.   Than delicious fruit, what greater dainty can be served up to man throughout Nature's ceaseless round of bounties?   For what other luxury will man pay as high a price?   Vergaloo pears often command one dollar per dozen.   Fifty cents apiece are often given for a peach or pear, more than treble the cost of ice cream, than which they are certainly more delicious. Yet there are still better fruits than these.   All love good fruit. See how fruit-crazy all children are, and what enormous quantities of pears, peaches, strawberries, apples, &c., are annually consumed in our cities.

Now, since that is best which tastes best,[50] and since fruit relishes better than anything eaten, therefore it is the most wholesome.   It prevents or removes constipation, and often acts like a charm upon both the body and mind.   Different constitutions require different kinds, yet ripe fruits of the right kind, are better even in sickness than medicine; and, eaten with good bread, nothing is equally palatable or wholesome.   They rarely cloy the appetite or clog the stomach, but tend to keep the bowels open, head clear, passions cool, and the entire man healthy and happy. Just try this experiment.   Sit down to a breakfast of first-rate fruit and unleavened bread, and say if it is not the best breakfast you can have.   Than peaches cut up and sweetened at supper, what is more delicious?   Or than strawberries and cream with bread?   Of choice pears this is still more true.   Berries with bread and milk are good eating.   When none of these can be obtained, good apples, baked or raw, relish well.

Nature provides a perpetual round of fruit. Apples keep the entire year, and pears of the very best varieties are kept till the appearance of strawberries the next year. A friend of the Author had Coe's golden drop plums the first of June, which he had kept perfectly sound all winter, and the frost damson keeps till November; while the amber primordium ripens early in July. Many other kinds ripen along through the winter and spring. Pears and plums can be kept the year round as easily as apples; and summer fruits, by canning, can be kept perfectly fresh for a year. And by the use of hot-houses, fruit can be picked from the trees in winter or spring. We can also preserve them or make them into jellies. Yet this process, besides deteriorating from their flavor, impairs their digestibility. Preserves are too rich. Their nutrition is too much concentrated. Yet the virtue of the juice can be extracted and then *dried*, so as to preserve its original flavor and dietetic utility. Or most kinds of fruit can be dried, and thus kept, though this process dries out much of its goodness as well as sweetness. Dried fruit, stewed, is far better than none.

Stewed apples sweetened, make an excellent relish with bread; yet applesauce should be made every few days, instead of being made so rich as to keep all winter. But, after all, nothing equals simple bread and choice fruit, if people only knew it, both for health and luxury.

In general, good fruit loses much of its flavor and virtue by being cooked. Poor fruit may be improved by being cooked and sweetened; but first-rate fruit and bread ought to be good enough for a prince, and is in fact the best pie, and cake, and dessert, in the world.

GREEN fruit, however, is most pernicious. None realize how many lose their lives directly or indirectly thereby. Where it does not kill immediately, it often deranges the stomach, breeds worms, and induces other diseases, which, sooner or later, complete the work of death it begins. Adults are really culpable for eating fruit before it is fully ripe. No children would ever eat it if supplied freely with ripe. Parents should see to it that their children have good ripe fruit as much as bread.

Most city fruits, especially peaches, are picked green, before they get their flavor, so that they may keep the longer. Those who would have good fruit, must *raise* and pick it from their *own* vines and trees.

Foreign fruits are good, but indigenous are better. Nature adapts the products of every clime to its dietetic requisitions; and hence has made those fruits to flourish best in every clime which its inhabitants require. Yet imported fruits augment variety, and those which will keep well may be eaten freely with profit. Of these, oranges, lemons, pine-apples, bananas, and nuts are as healthy as delicious, yet are picked too green.

PEARS contain iron, which has been shown to be one of the most important agencies for carrying forward the life process.[41] The most delicious of them, as the Seckle, Rostizer, Beurre Bosc, Beurre de'Anjou, and others, are among the most delicious morsels with which man can regale his appetite. They are thus luxurious because they are proportionably beneficial.[50] So raise and eat them in abundance. And they ripen off the tree.

GRAPES probably stand at the head of all fruits. The ancients celebrated their first ripening annually by their most hilarious feasts, and worshipped Bacchus because he worshipped wine. They at first used grape juice just pressed, but found that what was left over, and fermented, also relished, and made wine of it; the consumption of which has descended to us, and extended to most civilized countries and peoples.

Grapes thin the blood, and also enrich it, thus doubly improving it; and can be so eaten as to produce almost any physiological effect desired. Eaten with the skins, they relieve constipation, and promote evacuation, while rejecting the skins, after chewing them well, so as to extract the part immediately under the skin, causes astringency.

FEVERS are mitigated, and often broken up, by their use. *The grape cure* restores chronic invalids, whom other cures fail to benefit. In their season, which can be made to last the year round, they should constitute an important part of human diet.

THE WALTER grape, originated and propagated by A. J. Caywood, of Poughkeepsie, N. Y., is said to *dry on the stem*, that is, make raisins, by which they could be had everywhere, year in and year out, if extensively cultivated; to grow farther north and south, and on a greater variety of soils, than any other kind, besides ripening earlier, keeping longer, growing better, and being more prolific and luscious. It is a seedling of the Diana and Delaware, and is the *ne plus ultra* of all the modern varieties, besides being a first best wine grape. Rogers's hybrids are well worth a trial.

THE WHOLE of the grape was undoubtedly made to be eaten, as a general thing, and its parts only when special physiological results are required. When the Deity created it, he compounded all its ingredients with a view to their highest combined utility. .

65. — SWEETS, MILK, BUTTER, CHEESE, &c.

SWEETS are as healthy as palatable.[60] They contain starch and carbon in great abundance, which are two of the principal ingredients required in the nutritive process. Yet they should be commingled with food just as Nature has mixed them with all kinds of edibles. Sugar is extracted from sorghum, the cane, beet, and maple, and even from cornstalks, and can be made out of almost anything which will serve for food. It should therefore be duly diluted, and then rarely cloys, but greatly enhances the palatableness of almost everything eaten, especially of "flour victuals." Sweet apples and fruit are much more nutritious than sour, and greatly facilitate the fattening of stock.

MOLASSES is good, because, besides yielding a great amount of nourishment, it stimulates the intestinal canal, and thus helps to evacuate obstructions and waste matter. Eaten with Indian meal made into puddings or cakes, it becomes highly aperient, and thus carries off causes of disease. Let children be served with it at least once or twice a week, nor should adults eschew it. But that made every few days directly from good sugar, especially loaf, by adding water and boiling, is very much better than that made down South, and exposed, during transportation, to the hot sun, till it ferments or sours, when it has a like effect with fermented bread.[62]

Those who eat sweets while making sugar, and even stock included, are said to thrive remarkably well.

Honey is also most delicious, and, duly mixed with other things, may be eaten with profit, especially in winter, but not in summer;. because it is highly charged with carbon, little of which is required in summer, but much in winter. Indeed, sweets generally should be eaten more sparingly in warm weather and climates than in cold.

Yet, when honey and other sweets sour on the stomach, they should rarely be eaten.

MILK is highly nutritious. It contains casseine, and this fibrine and albumen, in a highly soluble state, so that they can be easily carried to all portions of the system, and also nitrogen, a super-abundance of which, so that it can be deposited and remain, is essential to growth. A milk diet is therefore peculiarly adapted to promote the growth of children and youth; and the fact that Nature has ordained it as the natural food of infants, is no mean guaranty of its utility. Its promotion of the growth of all young still further recommends it.

Milk also promotes sleep, and hence is the better for supper, especially that of children, and probably for the wakeful. Sour milk and buttermilk, sweetened, are probably both nutritious and healthy — more so than sweet milk, because milk must be curdled before it can be digested. The author attributes his recovery from a consumptive attack to the use of buttermilk, and relishes sour milk sweetened much better than sweet. The Germans strain all their sweet milk into sour, and thus curdle it. Some cannot eat milk unless it is previously curdled. Curdled by adding sweet cider, it becomes delicious and wholesome.

BUTTER, made from the oily properties of milk, contains a great amount of carbon. Its nutrition, like that of sugar and honey, is highly concentrated. But it soon becomes rancid when exposed to heat, as it always is in the stomach; and in this form is pecu-liarly obnoxious. It often causes cutaneous eruptions, boils, and the like; and eaten in warm weather, and in those quantities in which it is generally consumed, loads the system with corruption, renders many miserable for life, and hurries thousands into un-timely graves.

CREAM is better than butter, and certainly more palatable, and may be eaten with bread, or bread and fruit, with comparative impunity, at least in cold weather. Some stomachs cannot manage butter, except in small quantities; and it proves detrimental to dyspeptics generally. Sweetened cream is far more palatable, and less objectionable.

MELTED butter, as eaten on warm bread, or on hot, short, or buckwheat, or wheaten cakes, is pernicious, because melting em-bodies it into masses, so that the gastric juice can attack it only from their outside, so that the warm inside decays before it digests ; yet mixed with food, it digests before it turns. Buckwheat cakes, swimming in melted butter and molasses, can be borne only by few. Add milk or cream, with sugar, or molasses, or honey, and they are even more delightful to the palate than with butter, and doubt- less as wholesome as delicious. Meat fried in butter is injurious. When the system wants carbon, butter may be eaten with profit, yet cream is better ; but since carbon superabounds in almost all, so as to cause much disease,[119] butter only enhances both this su- perabundance and its diseased consequences.

CHEESE suits some stomachs, and aids digestion, but often troubles children, and should be administered to them sparingly, if at all. Yet pot cheese, made of sour milk, is nutritious, and probably harmless.

Custards may be eaten except in cholera seasons, and when the bowels are loose. Nothing induces cholera in its various forms equally with custard turned sour in the stomach. It is so offen- sive to the bowels that, in their haste to expel it, they often empty out the blood.

66. — PEAS, BEANS, POTATOES, ONIONS, BEETS, CARROTS, TUR- NIPS, SQUASHES, &c.

Vegetables generally may be eaten freely, with profit. Ripe beans and peas contain a great amount of nutrition, "stick to the ribs," make good blood, and should not be allowed to fall into disuse. Made into soups they relish well, and constitute a stand- ing article of the diet. Daniel of old fared well, and looked fair, on lentils.

POTATOES, a new but popular article of diet, deserve all the practical estimation in which they are held, and are one of the best articles of human food, probably because they grow in the ground, and are therefore highly electric, and hence feed and sus- tain excitability. Eaten or mashed when first boiled, or baked, or roasted, they become perfectly disintegrated, so that the gas- tric juice penetrates and solves the entire mass all at once; yet eaten after they become cold, solid, tough, and leathery, they are most injurious, because the gastric juice can attack them only from the outside of their unchewed pieces. Though not very nutritious, yet on this very account they "fill up," and thus prevent our taking excessive nutrition in other forms. They are very fine and palatable when well prepared, yet should be eaten with bread, or their bulk will be too great for their nutrition. Potato starch pudding is one of the most nutritious and easily digested articles of diet to be found.

ONIONS are both palatable and wholesome. The French consume them freely. They are especially good in colds. The ourang-outang, when suffering from colds, eats them raw in great quantities, and would eat nothing else. They are aperient, and their sirup, sweetened, relieves oppressed lungs, and restores suppressed perspiration. For incipient infantile colds, they are admirable. When eaten by those who have been bitten by venomous serpents, or applied, pounded, as a poultice to the bite, they give immediate relief by extracting the poison; and sometimes cure hydrophobia. They soon turn black when applied to the feet of fever patients, because they extract disease. In El Passo, Texas, they grow to an extraordinary size, are amazingly prolific, and remarkably sweet and delicious.

GROWING ABOVE ground, or below, makes this genuine difference in vegetables; that, whatever grows *below* ground is *positive*, and therefore grows *from* the sun; whereas, whatever is *negative* reaches *towards* the sun, and grows *above* ground. Those, therefore, who are *positively* charged electrically,[42] that is, are highly *nervous*, need positive food, or that which grows below ground, to support their excitability, which it also increases; hence the fondness of the Irish for potatoes; while those rather passive than positive, cool almost to tameness, prefer and require *negative* food, or that which grows above ground; though eating tuberous or positive food would tone them up, as eating above-ground or negative food quiets and soothes those who are too excitable.

BEETS, carrots, and turnips are good food. Every family should eat them often. Parsnips are excellent, yet rather hard to digest.

Cabbage and pork digest with difficulty. Only strong stomachs can master them; yet cold slaw digests easily and rapidly.

Greens are aperient, healthy, and palatable.

Squashes and pumpkins are good, either stewed and eaten as sauce, or with bread, or made into plain pies; yet should not be spiced to death, or till their taste is nearly obliterated, and utility impaired. To some constitutions, squash is especially serviceable.

IMMATURE esculents, such as green cucumbers, radishes, corn, &c., are at least doubtful as to utility. Wait till they get their growth and maturity. The mere fact that they are green, makes strongly against them. As a general thing, all edibles should be fully matured before eaten, partly because ripening so far disintegrates their particles that the gastric juice can penetrate them ; whereas, their greenness causes them to pass into the stomach in solid chunks, which the gastric juice can attack only from their surface, so that they ferment before they can be digested. Only those whose digestion is excellent should venture to eat them. To children and adults having weak bowels, they always prove injurious, and sometimes suddenly fatal. They often kill even cattle and horses. Why jeopardize *life* for a momentary indulgence?

Vegetables and fruit are far better when grown in rich soil than poor, in new than old, and quickly than slowly.

NUTS, as generally eaten, are unwholesome, because often eaten between meals, which is injurious, and when the stomach is already overloaded, and because they contain a great amount of carbon, the superabundance of which is one great cause of disease.[119] Yet eaten with, and as a part of food, they would undoubtedly prove highly beneficial, as they are eminently nutritious and palatable.[80] The inhabitants of the South of France, Savoy, and a part of Italy, live almost exclusively on chestnuts during fall and the early part of winter, making them into bread and puddings in place of flour. Nuts abound in vegetable oil, and of course in carbon, and also in glutine and fibrine, — three of the most important elements required for sustaining life, — yet should be dried or cooked.

SECTION IV.

HOW TO EAT; OR, MASTICATION, QUANTITY, TIME, ETC.

67. — THE MASTICATION AND SALIVATION OF FOOD.

How shall food, thus selected, be eaten? With the teeth always — with the stomach never. Nature forbids our throwing it in as with a shovel. By rendering its only passage-way small, she literally compels us to deposit it in small parcels. She has also furnished us with a mouth, set all around with two rows of

22

teeth, which fit exactly upon each other, and are every way
adapted to crushing it to atoms, as shown in engraving No. 5.
We cannot swallow our food without its being more or less chewed.
To persuade, as well as compel such mastication, Nature has
rendered it highly *pleasurable*. Instead of its being tasteless, she
has given it a far more delicious flavor than all the spices of India
could impart. Yet man does not know how to enjoy a tithe of
the gustatory pleasure she has appended to eating. Not one in
thousands knows how to eat! All know how to eat enough, yet
few know how to eat *little* enough.[68] All know how to eat fast
enough, but very few know how to eat slowly enough. And
strange as it may seem, few know how even to *chew*, simple, easy,
and natural as this process is! Nine hundred and ninety-nine in
every thousand eat mostly with their *stomachs* instead of with
their teeth. One would think that this poor slave had to perform
twice its proportionate task, simply to digest the enormous quantities of heterogeneous compounds forced upon it, instead of being
compelled, in addition, to do what the teeth should previously
have done. Yet this practice is universal. Is eating indeed so
very onerous that it should thus be hurried and slighted? Most
men pitch and shovel in their food in great mouthfuls following
mouthfuls, thick and fast, which they give a twist or two, hit a
crack or two, and poke down "in a jiffy;" eating in five minutes as
much as would take a full hour to eat well. Americans generally
treat eating as they treat impertinent customers, to be dismissed
without ceremony, for something appertaining to business. Than
the due feeding of the body, what is more important?[47] Of
course the time occupied in eating should correspond. Besides,
how can we expect to enjoy the gustatory pleasure Nature has
associated with eating, unless we take ample *time* for such enjoyment? Instead of despatching our meals to get to business, we
should despatch business, but eat at perfect leisure. We should
never sit down to the table in a hurry, nor till we have dismissed
all idea that we have anything else on hand, and should then eat
as leisurely as if time and tide waited for us. The ox and horse
eat as leisurely as though their food was their all. Only swine bolt
down their food; and well they may, for their tastes are so coarse
that they eat what is most loathsome, and derive their pleasure
from quantity mainly. Shall man imitate swine? Shall he bolt

his food and hurry off to business, and thus forego gustatory enjoyment, as well as shorten his days; thereby curtailing that very business he is so anxious to do? Take ample time to eat well, and you will live the longer, which will enable you to do the more business. Eating fast is the worst possible stroke of business policy you can adopt. Let business stand, while you eat with the utmost deliberation. Let *nothing* hurry you to, or at, or from the table. Make eating a *paramount* business, and the acquisition of wealth a trifling toy in comparison. No one should deposit an ordinary meal in less than an hour. How foolish to swallow it with swinish voracity in five minutes! Yet some make quick eating their *boast.*

THE LOSS of gustatory enjoyment consequent on eating fast, though great and irreparable, yet is one of its smallest and lightest evils. It breaks down the stomach, and thus unmans and diseases the entire system. No other cause, if even a combination of causes, is as prolific of dyspepsia and all its dire array of evils, as this and sour bread. We have not overrated the importance of a due selection of food, yet its proper mastication is as great. Eat slowly and masticate thoroughly, and the kind of food eaten, however noxious, will rarely break down the stomach; but eating the best selection of food fast will ruin almost any stomach. How can the gastric juice penetrate the food unless it is mashed fine? Food deposited in chunks defies its solvent power for a long time, meanwhile irritating and weakening its vigor; whereas, if it were well crushed before it entered the stomach, this juice could penetrate it, and digest it before fermentation occurs.

THE SALIVATION of food is effected by its mastication. Nature has stationed five glands about the mouth, two at the back part of the jaws called the parotid, two at the sides of the lower jaws called the sub-maxillary, and one under the tongue called the sublingual, always found at the root of boiled tongues, which secrete a half-watery, half-stringy viscid, called saliva, which they discharge into the mouth when food is presented. Chewing mingles this saliva thoroughly with what we eat. Taking food into the mouth provokes these glands to secrete and discharge great quantities of this saliva. Even the sight of food "makes the mouth water." Tantalize a hungry dog a few minutes with the sight of his dinner without giving it to him, and this saliva will run out at the corners of his mouth, and hang down in transparent gelatinous strings. That clear, tasteless spittle which lubricates every healthy mouth, especially while eating, is composed mainly of it.

It fulfils some *important* end in the nutritive economy, else it would not exist in such great abundance. Probably half its virtues are not yet known; but the following chemical analysis of it, and some of its effects on food, attest both its utility and absolute necessity : —

" M. Mialhe has recently made numerous researches with reference to. the physiology of digestion. The essential basis of the alimentation of animals, he states, is constituted by three distinct groups of bodies: albuminous, fatty, and saccharine matters. The labors of modern chemists have shown that albuminous substances become assimilable through the assistance of the gastric juice, which, by its acid, swells these azotized products, and by its *pepsin* liquefies them, a phenomenon analogous to that of diastasis on amidon. Fatty matter becomes assimilatable by the intervention of bile, but with regard to feculaceous and saccharine matter, says M. Mialhe, there is nothing positive known. This lacuna in science he has endeavored to fill.

" The new facts at which M. Mialhe has arrived, tend to show that all hydro-carbonaceous substances can only undergo the phenomenon of assimilation when they have been decomposed by the weak alkaline dissolutions contained in the vital humors; either immediately, as with glucose, dextrine, sugar of milk; or mediately, as with cane sugar and amidon, which have to be first transformed in the economy, the one (cane-sugar) into glucose, the other into dextrine of glucose. As to hydro-carbonaceous substances, which are neither susceptible of fermentation nor of decomposition by weak acids, or alkalies in solution, such as lignite or mannite, they escape, in man, the digestive and assimilating action. But by what chemical action is the amidon transformed into dextrine and glucose? Numerous experiments have proved to M. Mialhe that this transformation is produced by the saliva, through a principle which the humor contains, a principle comparable, in every respect, to *diastasis*. In order to isolate it, human saliva, first filtered, is treated by five or six times its weight of alcohol, alcohol being added until precipitation ceases. The *animal diastasis* is deposited in white flakes. It is gathered on a filter, from which it is taken still moist, and dried in layers on glass, by a current of warm air, at a temperature of from forty to fifty degrees (centigr.); it is preserved in a well-stoppered bottle. This active principle of the saliva is solid, white, or of a grayish white, amorphous, insoluble in alcohol, soluble in water and weak alcohol. The aqueous solution is insipid, neutral ; the sub-acetate of lead does not give rise to precipitate. Abandoned to itself, it soon becomes acid, and whether or not in contact with the air. This *animal diastasis*, studied comparatively with diastasis extracted from germinating barley, presents the same mode of action. It transforms amidon into dextrine and glucose; acting on starch, and elevating the temperature to seventy or eighty degrees, the liquefaction is nearly immediate. One part of this substance suffices to liquefy and convert two thousand parts of fecula. The agents, such as creosote, tannin, the powerful acids, the salts of mercury, of copper, of silver, &c., which destroy the properties of *diastasis*, act in the same manner with respect to the active principle of saliva. At an equal weight they both liquefy and transform the same quantity of hydrated-amidon. It appears, even, that the active principle of germinated barley is seldom as energetic as that of saliva, which is owing to the greater facility of obtaining the latter in a pure state. Finally, as a last resemblance, the *animal diastasis* existing in the saliva of man rarely exceeds two thousandths, and this is exactly the proportion of the diastasis contained in the germinating barley."— *Lancet.*

Its SOLVENT powers are wonderful, sufficient to convert *two thousand times* its own bulk of food into a paste-like mass prepared for the action of the gastric juice; besides facilitating deglutition, for without it food would be too dry to be swallowed easily. It also liquefies the starch of food, one of its important ingredients.

Unless we both masticate and salivate our food, we oblige the stomach to do both its *own* work and that of the teeth; whereas, especially weak stomachs are barely able to do their own work. No food can make good blood without good salivation. Please note this principle, as we shall found several important directions on it for the cure of disordered digestion.

Food is next swallowed, or passed down the œsophagus, or meat-pipe, a long duct connected with the back part of the mouth (see engraving, No. 16), and furnished with longitudinal and transverse fibres, which, contracting from above downwards, impel the food down into the stomach; but, contracting from below upwards, as in vomiting, expel it upwards, into and out at the mouth, often with great force.

68. — THE RIGHT QUANTITY OF FOOD DETERMINED BY APPETITE.

OUR CONSUMPTION of food for the time being should determine the amount we eat. The harder we work with head or hands, and the colder the weather, the more food we need, and *vice versa.* To eat just enough, but never too much, is most important.

NORMAL APPETITE is as perfect a guide touching *quantity* as kind;[60] and its loss or vitiation is most unfortunate.

INFLAMED appetite is the rule, and a normal one the exception. Mark its cause.

ALIMENTIVENESS is in rapport with the stomach, because it is its mental Faculty.[48] Both were made expressly for each other, and together subserve one end. Unless this reciprocity is perfect, how could the stomach's need of food awaken appetite, or too much food create nausea and vertigo? The perfect feeding of the body demands both this reciprocal sympathy, and that it be, as it certainly is, perfect.

ALL INFLAMMATION of the stomach, therefore, inflames appetite, which creates a morbid craving for food, akin to appetite, yet to hunger what fever is to health. Excess of food inflames the stomach, and this creates these morbid hankerings, which most mistake for hunger, yet they are caused by a *surfeit*. This renders their appetite morbid, and its cravings insatiable. And the more such eat, the more they crave. Let them eat and eat by the hour together, they still feel what they call hungry, though it is an insatiable morbid voracity. True, they feel weak, gone, faint, ravenous, and that they shall drop down, unless they can get something to eat soon; yet the more they eat the more they crave, because the more they inflame their stomachs, and of course Alimentiveness. Cannot they see that they eat twice as much as others, and four times more than many around them who enjoy uninterrupted health? How can they require so much when others get along so much better with so little? What could more conclusively prove that both their craving and diseases proceed from gluttony? Protracted abstemiousness will diminish these stomachic gnawings. A trial will surprisingly decrease them. And, in general, those who feel faint in the morning till they eat, ravenous before dinner, and hungry before supper, should attribute these cravings to an *overloaded* stomach instead of to an empty one. And those who suffer much from omitting a meal may rest assured that they overeat. Fasting gives little inconvenience to healthy stomachs; there is no more sure sign of a surfeit than these hankerings and this faintness, when a meal is omitted. Contradictory though it may seem, yet of all such cravings persevering abstemiousness is a perfect cure; because it allays that irritation of the stomach which causes them, and which full feeding enhances, and thereby reinflames appetite. Let those thus afflicted only *fast* instead of feast, and keep fasting till they, like those in health, can omit a meal with little inconvenience or prostration. Especially should such omit supper, and drink copiously of cold water before breakfast.[121]

OVER-EATING is one of the most prolific of all causes of disease. Unwholesome kinds of food engender far less disease, especially of the stomach, than excess in its *amount.* Gormandizing plain food injures many times more than unwholesome kinds. Health and disease depend far more upon how *much* we eat, than what. The majority of men make gluttons of themselves. How rapidly one platter full disappears after another from public and private tables? Note how fast and often plates are filled and emptied, and returned for more. Nearly all eat twice too much, or at least till they feel stupid, uncomfortable, and inert. Those eat too much who feel the lighter and livelier for omitting a meal. Dyspeptics eat as much again as others, while those in perfect health usually eat but little. The bully of the Erie Canal, in 1837, and of course the strongest, spryest, and toughest man on it, ate less by half than the average of his passengers. A man employed in a comb factory in Newbury, Mass., who has always enjoyed the very best of health, is surprisingly abstemious. Most who live to be aged, usually eat but very little, and hence their length of life. Men of great talents and virtues usually practise rigid abstinence. Wesley furnished a noted example. See what he did and endured, yet how little he ate, and how often he fasted! Bible recommendations and requisitions for fasting are undoubtedly founded on this fact.

FLESHY persons usually eat lightly, while spare, the world over, are generally great eaters; because, what the former do eat, they completely digest, extracting from it all its sustaining virtue, so that they need but little. Many gormands disorder their stomachs, so that the enormous quantities they consume are not converted into nourishment. A little food, well assimilated, yields far more nutrition and life than quantities crudely digested. In fact, gluttony doubly starves its subjects; first, by enfeebling and disordering digestion, so that it cannot extract the nourishment from food, and secondly, by a gnawing, hankering, craving state of the stomach, akin to starvation.

OLD PARR, who became a father after he was one hundred and twenty, and retained his health and all his faculties unimpaired, till he visited the royal court, aged one hundred and fifty-two, died about a year afterwards, from slightly letting down his extreme abstemiousness.

Louis Cornaro, who, by abandoning those excesses which broke his constitution and threatened him with death at thirty-six, baffled disease in its most aggravated form, by confining himself to less than twelve ounces of solid and exclusively vegetable food per day, was over-persuaded to increase this quantity only two ounces, the effects of which he describes as follows : —

"This increase, in eight days, had such an effect upon me that from being remarkably cheerful and brisk, I began to be peevish and melan-. choly, and was constantly so strangely disposed, that I neither knew what to say to others, nor what to do with myself. On the twelfth day I was attacked with a violent pain in my side, which held me twenty-two hours, and was followed by a violent fever, which continued thirty-five days, without giving me a moment's respite, my only sickness during *sixty-three years* of abstemiousness."

Richard Lloyd, "a strong, straight, upright man, wanting no teeth, having no gray hairs, fleshy and full-cheeked, and the calves of his legs not wasted or shrunk, his hearing, sight, and speech as good as ever," at one hundred and thirty years of age, being persuaded to substitute a meat and malt-liquor diet, for one consisting exclusively of bread, butter, cheese, whey, and buttermilk with water, "soon fell off and died."

Dr. Cheyne reduced his weight from four hundred and forty-eight to one hundred and forty pounds by abstinence, grew corpulent and sick on a more generous diet, and was restored by abstemiousness. His practical and theoretical maxim was, —

"The lightest and least of meat and drink a man can be tolerably easy under, is the shortest and most infallible means to preserve life, health and serenity."

Dr. James Johnson, one of the ablest of modern physiologists, who cured himself of an aggravated dyspeptic malady by rigid abstemiousness, and then wore out two armies, in two wars, and thought he could wear out another, says, —

"The quantity should never exceed half a pound in weight at dinner, even when that can be borne without a single unpleasant sensation succeeding. It is quite enough, and generally too much. The invalid will acquire a degree of strength and firmness, not fulness, of muscle, on this quantity, which will, in time, surprise his friends as well as himself." "Such will often derive more nourishment and strength from four ounces of gruel every six hours, than from half a pound of animal food and a pint of wine."

"Whenever our food is followed by inaptitude for mental or corporeal exertion, we are laying the foundation for disease by over-eating. Any discomfort of body, any irritability or despondency of mind, succeeding food and drink, at the distance of an hour a day, or even two or three days, may be regarded, other evident causes being absent, as a presumptive proof that the quantity has been too much, or the quality injurious. Those who, a few hours after dinner, feel a sense of distention in the stomach and bowels, or any of the symptoms of indigestion which have been pointed out; or a languor of body or a cloudiness of mind; or have a restless night; or experience a depression of spirits, or irritability of temper next morning, have eaten too much, or some improper kind, and must reduce and simplify till they come to that quantity and quality of food and drink for dinner which produce little or no alteration in the feelings, whether of exhilaration immediately after dinner, or of discomfort some time after this meal. This is the criterion by which the patient must judge for himself."

"I tell you honestly what I think is the cause of the complicated maladies of the human race. It is their gormandizing, and stimulating, and stuffing their digestive organs to excess; thereby producing nervous disorders and irritation." — *Dr. Abernethy.* "It is the opinion of the majority of the most distinguished physicians, that intemperance in diet destroys the bulk of mankind." "Most of all the chronic diseases, the infirmities of old age, and the short period of the lives of Englishmen, are owing to repletion." — *An eminent medical Writer.* "I firmly believe that scarcely any sedentary or literary man can exceed from twelve to sixteen ounces of solid food, and from fourteen to twenty-four of liquid per day, and keep within the bounds of temperance." — *President Hitchcock.* "Nothing is more supremely ridiculous than to see tender, hysterical, and vaporish people perpetually complaining, yet perpetually cramming; crying out that they are ready to sink into the ground and faint away, yet gobbling down the richest and strongest food and highest cordials." — *Dr. Cheyene.*

Agents and tourists among the Indians concur in declaring that they will eat from six to fifteen pounds of meat in the twenty-four hours, spending most of their time in eating food when they can get it.

"For a few days, after getting into camp, Indians will eat from eight to ten pounds each, and for the first day or two even exceed that quantity." — *Captain Duval.* "The Osages often eat from ten to fifteen pounds of fresh meat in the course of the twenty-four hours, particularly on returning from a fatiguing hunt, when, I have no doubt, they frequently consume from five to six pounds at a meal." — *Captain Rogers.* "They would consume from six to eight pounds per day. This is under instead of over the true estimate." — *Major Armstrong.* "I have seen a prairie Indian eat and destroy, upon his arrival in camp, fifteen pounds of beef in twenty-four hours. I am further of opinion that they will eat daily ten pounds throughout the year." — *Robert Cook.* "The Esquimaux consumption of food is enormous, and often incredible. They eat, perhaps, twenty pounds of flesh and oil daily. Sir W. E. Percy weighed

23

out to a half-grown Esquimaux boy eight pounds of sea-horse-flesh, one pound twelve ounces of bread, one pint and a quarter of rich gravy soup, a gallon of water, and six wine-glasses of spirits — a 'quantity no way extraordinary.'" — *John Ross.*

Admiral Saritcheff gave to a Siberian Yakut, who was said to have eaten, in twenty-four hours, "the hind quarter of a large ox, twenty pounds of fat, and a proportionate quantity of melted butter for his drink " — " a thick porridge of rice boiled down with three pounds of butter, weighing together twenty-eight pounds; and although the glutton had already breakfasted, yet did he sit down to it with great eagerness, and consume the whole without stirring from the spot." A good calf, weighing two hundred pounds, "may serve four or five good Yakuti for a single meal. I have seen three of these gluttons consume a reindeer at a single meal." — *Captain Cochran.*

"Ten of our Hottentots ate a middling-sized ox, all but the two hind legs, in three days; but they had very little sleep during the time, and had fasted the two preceding days. With them the word is eat or sleep. The three Bosgesmans who accompanied us to our wagons, had a sheep given to them about five in the evening, which they entirely consumed before noon the next day." — *Barrow.*

The Author's father once knew a glutton who ate two chickens, with the usual accompaniments of bread and sauce, and called for more. A dinner prepared for eight workmen was next brought on, which he despatched, and when he called for more still, bread and a whole cheese were set on. When the landlord reproved him for cutting the cheese in slices instead of in towards the centre, he replied that "it made no difference, since he calculated to eat the whole; " to avoid which the landlord started on a drove of cattle he was driving, and thus hurried him from his unfinished meal, though he took in his hand a large slice of bread and another of cheese.

The Author's experience fully confirms these converging testimonials. When so crowded professionally that he was obliged to postpone meals or dismiss customers, he occasionally chose the former, and soon found that it doubled and trebled his capability . to endure mental labor; and adopted the practice of fasting whenever he was pressed with business, and preparatory to lecturing, which a preceding supper always greatly mars and enfeebles in matter and manner. He always prepares himself for speaking by abstinence. To write on a full stomach is an utter impossibility. No one who has not frequently practised abstemiousness in quantity and quality, can appreciate the far greater flow of thoughts, words, and facts, and the enhanced clearness of mind and intensity of feeling produced by it. It may indeed be carried so far as to prostrate; yet a full meal is as lead tied to the soaring eagle. Shall we fetter the immortal *mind*, by indulging appetite? Shall propensity blight the godlike powers of the human soul? Gluttony is the great sand-bank of the mind. Abstinence would enhance the progress of our scholars, the mental and moral powers and consequent usefulness of ministers, and the intellectual acumen of all who require mental strength and activity, as well as the feelings, which even suffer most. Over-eating blunts and benumbs all our keener, finer, holier emotions, and curtails enjoyment more universally and effectually than almost any other cause; besides all the untold anguish of body and mind it induces. The extent and magnitude of the evils of intemperance in drinking, though they far exceed even the glowing descriptions of all its opponents combined, fall far below the evils of excessive eating. The former are limited to comparatively few; the latter is almost universal, and practised from the cradle to the grave. Mothers begin by nursing their infants every time they cry, though this very crossness is generally occasioned by excessive nursing; and still aggravate the evil by stuffing the young with pies, cakes, candies, nuts, apples, and the like, from morning till night, year in and year out; so that most children *grow* up gormands. And this soul-and-body destroying habit "grows with their growth."

Soldiers are more vigorous and healthy on scant than on full rations. Pugilists are fitted for the bloody ring, and horses for the race, by great abstemiousness combined with extreme exertion of muscle, which proves that abstinence facilitates labor. In short, all dietetic facts and principles go to establish these two conclusions, that all eat double the quantity of food necessary for the attainment of the highest state of mental and physical vigor and endurance, and that over-eating is the great cause of modern disease and depravity. *Try abstemiousness:* the well, that they may retain and enhance health; invalids, that they may banish feebleness and maladies, and again enjoy the blessings of health ; the literary, that they may augment mental efficiency ; laborers, that they may increase working ease and capability ; and, above all, the sedentary, that they may ward off the impending evils of confinement within doors. Eat not one mouthful too little, for Nature can cast off surplus food better than supply or endure its deficiency ; but the exact quantity most promotive of strength, talents, and happiness, is incalculably preferable to either too much or too little.

Whether homœopathy is potent or harmless, one thing is certain, that its dietetic prescriptions are most beneficial. Abstemiousness and water, rightly applied, will restore almost all to health, while frequent eating puts back almost all convalescents, and often induces a relapse, which hurries its victim, already renovated by sickness, and prepared for a return of health, into a re-opening grave. Even many convalescents, whom over-eating does not kill outright, are injured by it for life, and loaded anew with disease. Let all heed these warnings, thus frequent and palpable, and learn that to become an epicure one must first become a stoic.

The fact is, we may accustom ourselves to eat less or more, with this difference, that the former habit leaves the muscles and brain unoppressed and active ; the latter stupefies the whole man, by diverting the energies from all the other organs, and concentrating them in the stomach. The Germans eat heartily, the Spaniards lightly, yet they are as healthy as the Germans, and do not suffer from want of food, but eat all unperverted appetite requires. Those who crave great quantities should deny their appetites, and need not fear starvation, but should practise temporary self-denial. "Self-denial"? No; for eating just enough will increase *present* as well as future gustatory enjoyment. Gormands neither appreciate nor enjoy delicious flavors.

69. — How Appetite can be restrained.

MANY readers, conscious of excess, would give something to know how they can govern this incessant craving. Every little while they suffer from excess. They firmly resolve to eat less, and succeed at a single meal, only to eat the more afterwards. Indeed, few things are more difficult than governing a morbid appetite, whether for alcoholic liquors, or unhealthy viands, or excessive quantities of food. He who can do this, can march to the stake. To rule a kingdom is play compared with controlling a morbid appetite. Yet this is not so difficult to those who know *how*. Many try hard enough, but do not try *right*. Follow these directions, and this task will soon become easy.

First. Take upon your plate, in one or two parcels, all the food, except the dessert, you think best to eat at a meal, and leave off when that is finished, instead of "backing up" for another load. By this means alone can you fully realize how much you do eat.

When this is impracticable, notice how much you have previously taken, so as to bear in mind the sum total consumed. But if you take potato after potato, and slice after slice of meat, and bread, and the like, relying upon an already inflamed appetite for your guide to quantity, or till your stomach, stretched by a thousand surfeits, is pained by fulness, be assured you will over-eat. Weighing a few meals, till you have learned to estimate correctly by the eye, will aid you in curtailing appetite.

The Scotch custom of placing before each child all it is to have at that meal, every mother should apply to her children, and all adults to themselves. Never make them eat food to save it.

When pressed with business or writing, limit yourself to a pound of bread per day, exclusive of fruit.

Second. Eat only in *small mouthfuls*. Those who pile in great mouthfuls, and chew only till they can barely swallow, and then hurry in as much more as their mouths will hold, eat far more in a short time than they suppose. But taking a small quantity at a time, and chewing it well, makes a little go a great way, both in satisfying appetite, and in nourishing the body; meanwhile strengthening instead of impairing digestion. See children take a small bite, and laugh, play, and talk, perhaps even while chewing it, and then take a little more, and thus spin out their eating a long time. Do likewise, and you will find it easier to stop eating a small meal than now a large one. The stomach of those who eat fast, and in large mouthfuls, hardly realize how much food it has taken until it is almost crushed under its burden. Following these simple directions of parcelling out your meal at the commencement, and then eating in small mouthfuls at a time, and masticating thoroughly, will render government of appetite easy. But to govern a craving appetite with fast eating is next to impossible.

THIRD. *Eat seldom.* But this calls up for canvass frequency, —

70. — HOW OFTEN SHOULD WE EAT? LUNCHEONS, &c.

LET NATURE, not habit, answer. Her division of time into twenty-four hours plainly indicates that we should eat, sleep, exercise, study, &c., only once every twenty-four hours. If she required additional frequency, she would have divided time accordingly. By eating every two hours, we should soon become habitually hungry that often. We consume more food in winter than summer, yet live comfortably on two meals. Habit makes us desire two, three, or six meals and luncheons. A tribe of trapping Indians eats once daily, and that after hunting from daylight to dark. The English, from habit, think they must eat six times, while the Thracians thanked their gods publicly that Cyrus and his army ate but once, exclusive of a morning luncheon. Let all objecting laborers think how utterly puerile are their labors compared with the herculean exertions of ancient soldiers, whether marching, or building, or besieging, or fighting. Since they endured so much on one meal, cannot you so little on two? Your stomachs, like your muscles, must have about eight hours' rest diurnally. To digest and discharge each meal requires about six hours; so that two meals and resting would nearly fill in all the time, and allow a little extra to finish off digesting each meal.

"But why not eat less and oftener?"

Because we are much less liable to over-eat at two meals than at three; the food sours less; can be digested easier and more completely, and has ample time to rest.

INVALIDS should eat seldom and little, because their debility or disease prevents their consuming much food. A light diet is one of the best of cures, because most diseases come from overeating. Why take more food than can be digested, only to clog and irritate? Still, a sudden change from three meals and a lunch to one, or even two, is not advisable. Better begin with a light supper, then postpone dinner and omit supper, and after a year, or two, or three, eat only a light breakfast.

LUNCHEONS are objectionable. If two meals are sufficient, a lunch between them must be injurious. The stomach, on receiving its allowance, empties into itself a copious discharge of that gastric juice which dissolves the food, and does not secrete another supply till all that meal is disposed of, and another demanded. Hence, what we eat between meal times must lay in the stomach undigested, only to irritate and disease. Besides, to interfere with this process by introducing a fresh mass into one partly dissolved arrests its action, and causes that first received to lay until incipient fermentation takes place. Nuts, cakes, candies, oranges, fruits, &c., should be eaten *with* meals, not between them; and giving "pieces" to children will derange their stomachs, and breed worms. Dainties, ice-creams, &c., should be eaten at meal times only.

THE BEST TIMES for eating are probably eight or nine A. M., and three or four P. M. An early breakfast or dram is said to prevent fever and ague, &c. Let temperance men answer the dram part, and their answer will apply to the early breakfast. My own experience favors a late breakfast.

LATE SUPPERS are injurious, except in cases of genuine hunger. Those whose business precludes their eating till just before they must retire had better eat then than go to bed hungry; for the stomach can work while we sleep — indeed, works the best then; but those who can eat when they prefer, should eat at least three hours before retiring. An overloaded or inflamed stomach interferes with "Nature's great restorer," and often engenders bad dreams, which sometimes culminate in nightmare. Especially eschew apples, nuts, cakes, &c., at night. Eat no supper, or, if any, three or more hours before retiring, and you will feel far better the next day, because your night's sleep will be the sweeter and sounder.

IF THREE meals are eaten, about seven, one, and six are their best hours. But those literary and business men who can get along with from eight to ten hours' work, should do up their eating before they begin work, and after they have finished it, but not disturb their stomachs by either dinner or luncheons during their working hours. Even laborers, if once accustomed to it, could do more work, and easier, without than with stopping for dinner; that is, by doing their whole day's work at one time. So can horses. In Texas they never stop to feed at noon.

Section V.

THE DIGESTIVE PROCESS, AND ITS ORGANS, THE STOMACH, LIVER, PANCREAS, ETC.

71. — STRUCTURE AND OFFICE OF THE STOMACH.

DIGESTION is one of the most remarkable operations in Nature. Its results are indeed amazing. Behold your dinner, now an inert mass of meat, bread, and vegetables, yet good digestive organs, within an hour or two after it is eaten, send it coursing throughout your system, to strengthen and warm you, mounting to your brain, and working itself out throughout all your mental operations in thinking, or in public speaking, or in praising God, loving your family, doing good, &c.

NO. 14. — THE STOMACH, AND ITS ORIFICES, BLOOD-VESSELS, ETC.

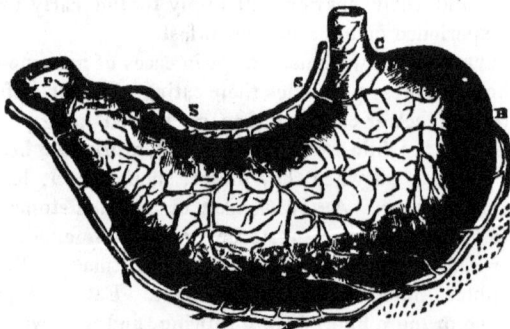

C. The cardiac orifice through which the food enters.
P. The pyloric orifice through which the chyme passes out.
S. S. The coronal artery of the stomach.
    Another artery is seen passing under the stomach, and those lines
    seen to pass in all directions are ramifications of blood-vessels.

Digestion accomplishes all this. We can hardly say which is the most important, breathing or digestion, for both are indispensable.

SOME RECEPTACLE must be pre-arranged for this digestion, able to hold fluids, and of course spherical or oblong. This food must be assorted, which requires considerable space and length; and therefore this receptacle must be tubular in form, so as to

contain its contents.   It must also have a great amount of SUR-
FACE.

THE STOMACH and intestines supply all these requirements, and
accomplish all these ends. The folding of the latter allows a
great amount of function to be executed in a small space, which
is increased by their being ruffled and shorter on one edge, and
thus convoluted, as seen in engraving No. 16.

How soon the horse drops dead when his maw, or second
stomach, is eaten through by the bot-worm! How suddenly cold
water on an over-heated stomach suspends life by palsying this
organ! How sudden and fearful are the ravages of the cholera,
which consist solely in disordered digestion! How rapidly children, taken down with bowel complaints, fall away and die! Yet
nothing but suspended digestion causes this leanness and death.
How effectually impaired digestion, in the form of dyspepsia,
frustrates both physical and mental energy. A vigorous stomach
is indispensable to energy in any and every other portion of the
system. Let us then examine this organ.

It consists of a sack capable of holding from a quart to several
gallons, according as it has been more or less distended by excess
or deficiency of food and drink. Its upper side is much shorter
than its lower, thus appearing like a bag held horizontally, and
ruffled on its upper edge. It has two openings, the one where
the food enters, located at its left superior side, and called the
cardiac orifice, from its proximity to the heart; and the other,
situated at the right superior side, named the pyloric orifice,
through which the food, after having undergone the chymifying
process, makes its egress into the duodenum, or second stomach.
The latter orifice is constructed with a valve, so arranged as to
close upon and send back whatever presents itself for egress not
completely dissolved; and it departs from this rule in extreme
cases only, and where things cannot be digested without remaining so long in the stomach as seriously to threaten its injury.
Hence the ejection of food either way, undigested or much as it
was eaten, is a sure index of a deranged stomach, because a
vigorous one would first dissolve whatever is soluble.

IN STRUCTURE, the stomach, like all the other internal organs,
is composed of three membranes; an outer, called the peritoneum,
or glossy coat, which lines and lubricates all, and allows them to

24

slide upon each other without friction, the absence of which causes adhesions; the middle, which is composed of muscles laid transversely, and crossing each other in all directions, which contract upon its contents, so as to give them a rotary motion; and the inner, or mucous membrane, which is extremely delicate, and when healthy, of a pale cream color. Nerves and blood-vessels also permeate all its parts, as seen in engraving No. 14, the latter imparting vitality, and the former creating pain when it is diseased and oppressed, and interlacing all the states of the stomach with the whole nervous system,[25] brain, and mind.

When a healthy stomach receives its food, this mucous membrane, or some glandular structure interwoven with it, empties into it a clear, slightly acid, but almost tasteless fluid, called the *gastric juice*, quite like saliva in appearance, previously secreted, so as to be in readiness.

THE GASTRIC JUICE is a most powerful solvent, capable of reducing to a milky homogeneous mass, called chyme, all those heterogeneous substances taken as food. It as it were sets free or extracts the carbon, fibrine, casseine, nitrogen, hydrogen, &c., electricity included, which compose food and support life. It even dissolves food *out* of the stomach, though not as quickly as in.

The solvent powers of a healthy stomach are most astonishing. An East India bird swallows and digests even wood. Man's solvent powers, by Nature, far exceed what we imagine possible. Some have swallowed knives, and digested their bone and horn handles. Felines, serpents, &c., eat and digest their prey, bones, fur, and all. How surprisingly some stomachs bear up, sometimes a century, under the continued abuse daily heaped upon them, even by the most temperate, much more by the intemperate? How often and how outrageously do all abuse it by eating too fast, or too much, or unwholesome kinds of food, or taking alcoholic or narcotic poisons, and yet retain most of its pristine vigor?

But all abuse proportionally weakens its solvent powers. This causes its contents to lay so long in the stomach that its heat induces souring or fermentation, which aids its dissolution, and helps to relieve the stomach of its load. Yet this is incipient decomposition, or, to call it by its true name, the commencement of the *rotting* process. To ferment is to *putrefy*. Nor is it possible for food to sour in the stomach without engendering corruption. Especially is this true of the fermentation of meat. All know how vast the amount of putrefaction eliminated by its decay out of the stomach. Fermentation engenders the same in it. Is it, then, any wonder that the rotting of meat in the stomach should cause its victims to feel so wretchedly? Is not here a powerful argument against meat eating, especially when the stomach is not *perfectly* good? Meat actually putrefying in the centre of the system, to be sent all through it, is literally frightful to contemplate! And yet this very process is perpetually going on, in a greater or less degree, within the stomachs of all in the least afflicted by dyspepsia; and this class embraces the mass of Americans. This chemical fact, that the souring process is incipient rotting, together with the fact that the food of the great mass of our nation does thus ferment, develops the prolific cause of most of those chronic, malignant, and all other diseases which bring suffering and premature death on the mass of mankind. Men cannot, therefore, guard too carefully against all injury of this important organ. Its healthy and vigorous condition is indispensable to life and happiness. Its abuse is suffering and death. As starvation, by withholding nutrition, soon destroys life, so imperfect digestion proportionally impairs it. Dyspepsia is partial starvation on the one hand, by withholding the materials of life, and death on the other, by engendering corruption. Hence, whatever dyspeptics do or leave undone, they should first restore the flagging energies of their stomachs. The scholar who is impairing digestion by study, instead of disciplining his mind, is undisciplining it in the most effectual manner possible, and by that very study which otherwise would strengthen it; because stomachic diseases effectually prostrate the brain.[25] Such should stop studying till they have effected a cure. Those whose stomachs are strong should keep them so, and, if weak or disordered, should give up or abstain from whatever impairs them.

This gastric juice acts mainly upon the OUTSIDE of the food eaten, thus evolving nourishment *gradually* — a provision of great practical utility. Otherwise we should be obliged to eat perpetually; which would be inconvenient, if not impossible.

THE MOTION of the stomach greatly facilitates digestion. Its muscular coating, by contracting from all points upon the food, as it were *churns* it till it is dissolved. As the muscles of the gizzard of fowls contract upon their food so powerfully as to grind it by friction against the gravel stones mixed up with it ; so the muscles of the human stomach keep perpetually squeezing and whirling the food over and over, always one way. This motion all must have observed within themselves. In cases of heartburn, which is caused by the souring process, this rolling of the food is particularly observable, in conjunction with the rising and burning caused by the inflammation of the stomach.

This motion is involuntary, else we should be obliged to *will* it continually, which would be exceedingly inconvenient, as it must be perpetual, so that we could do little else. Breathing also greatly facilitates it. Every inspiration hauls down the stomach to make room for the ingress of air,[43] and every expiration redoubles this motion by allowing it to return to its place ; and as breathing is perpetual, so is this stomachic motion. Unless it had been very important, Nature would never have devised so effectual a means of securing it ; and those who arrest it by tight lacing, do so at their peril.

NO. 16. THE DIGESTIVE TUBE, AFTER CLOQUET.

1. Œsophagus laid open.
2. Showing its cardiac orifice into the stomach.
3. Interior of the stomach, with its rugæ.
4. Duodenum, or second stomach, commencing at the pilorus.
5. Gall bladder, with the cystic duct, which passes downward to open into the duodenum.
6, 6, 6. Small intestines, terminating in the cæcum.
7, 8. Appendicula vermiformis.
9. Right ascending colon.
10. Transverse arch of the colon, seat of colicky pains.
11. Left descending colon.
12. Sigmoid flexure.
13. Rectum.
14. Anus.
The arrows point the way the food passes.

Nature still further facilitates this motion by those *abdominal muscles* which pass up and down across the stomach and bowels, so that we cannot well move the body backwards, forwards, sideways, any way, without using these muscles, and thus, as it were, kneading the stomach. Probably the stomach rolls its contents the same way all water turns when running out of a tunnel, namely, from left to right. Rivers roll the same way, as is proved by the fact that the mouths of all streams which empty from the right side are narrow, and have a hollow gouged out, because the water is *rolled under* the moment it strikes the main stream; while those streams which empty in on the left bank are always broad, but shallow, and usually have a bar at their mouth.

The earth rolls in passing around the sun, and the moon around the earth, the same way that water rolls in running — all doubtless in accordance with that great law that motion rotates. Probably the blood in both the arteries and veins rotates the same way.

MODERATE EXERCISE promotes digestion, by promoting this motion. While violent exercise robs digestion to help the muscles, exercising leisurely helps push the food along down the alimentary canal. Two dogs, fed alike, and killed two and a half hours after, in the one put upon the chase, digestion had hardly commenced, while in the other one, which was allowed to lie around, it was nearly completed. This proves only that *hard* work after eating retards digestion, but not leisurely. Children never take noonings, but are generally the most lively after eating — never more stupid. Lethargy and indolence are sure signs of over-eating. Those who cannot work, study, and do anything better after their meals than before, have over-eaten. Food, like sleep, invigorates from the first mouthful. Normal functions always promote, never obstruct each other.

72. — THE LIVER AND PANCREAS; THEIR STRUCTURE AND FUNCTIONS.

THAT LARGEST GLAND, situated mostly within the right side of the body proper, about half way between the shoulders and hips, is the liver. Its extreme length varies from nine to twelve inches, and its thickness from a thin edge to about six inches. It weighs about four pounds, yet its dimensions vary greatly in different persons. It has two lobes, the right being some four

times larger than the left, and two coats, its outer, called peritoneal, which invests most of it, and from which its five ligaments
are derived, and the inner or fibrous. It is reddish brown.

Its STRUCTURE is cellular, quite like that of the blood cells of
the lungs. Its arteries and veins are remarkable for their number and size; the arteries bifurcating, as in the lungs, till they
become infinitesimally minute, when they emerge into piles of
granules, having cells, in which its function, the extraction of a
yellowish biliary matter, is performed. These cells empty this
bile into ducts, larger and larger, till all become one duct, which
empties into the gall bladder, and this into the duodenum.

This bile is yellow, but becomes green by exposure. It acts
upon the fatty matter of the duodenum, which it renders soluble
and fluid, and helps convert chyme into chyle. A part of it also
enters the bowels, stimulates their evacuations, and relieves the
blood of its superfluous hydrocarbon, out of which bile is in part
formed. The gall is secreted from the dark and venous blood
while returning back to the heart, about eight pounds flowing
through the river per minute. This bile is composed mainly of
carbon, and this is one of the means by which the system relieves
itself of surplus carbon. Hence those whose livers are weak
should avoid fat, and eat substances less highly carbonized, so
that they may have less carbon to secrete, besides eating less.
Animal food taxes the liver somewhat less than vegetable.

Soda is also secreted from the venous blood, and contained in
the bile, and, being required in the vital process, is taken up by
the liver, and returned into the circulation, to take part in respiration — a most ingenious contrivance for supplying the system
with the soda it requires.

THE PANCREAS is glandular, flattened, about six inches long,
tapering, located nearly under the stomach, and formed of lobes,
lobules, granules, and sacs, which secrete a fluid almost identical with saliva, and empty it into small ducts forming one canal,
which empties into the duodenum.

These two fluids, the biliary and pancreatic, commingling with
the chyme, separates its nutritious from its innutritious portions,
somewhat as rennet separates the whey and curd of milk from
each other; forming chyle, a half-liquid grayish substance, closely
resembling milk in appearance, laden with fibrine, carbon, nitro-

gen, oil, and other substances required to support life. In fact, its composition is almost identical with that of blood, and requires only contact with air to impart that red color and oxygen which make it into blood proper. The importance of these two glandular secretions, shows how absolutely indispensable health of function in each is to human life, and the consequent evils of their abuse, and importance of their restoration.

This chyle, thus separated in the duodenum from the refuse portions of food, both are urged along together into and through the intestines by that muscular or middle coating which surrounds the entire alimentary canal, arranged circularly and transversely, so that its action rolls its contents along irresistibly. This canal is some six or eight times as long as its possessor is tall, and into it open a vast multitude of little mouths, or suckers, which, called lacteal vessels, or chyle-drinkers, pass through the three coatings, and open upon the mucous membrane of the intestines, these being in a great number of folds, by which the surface, and of course power of function, of this canal, is greatly increased. These lacteals suck up the chyle as it is thus urged along over them, and passing backward behind the intestines, and then through innumerable little glands called the mesenteries, empty themselves into larger, and these into still larger ducts, till they form one duct which passes up along inside the back-bone to near the neck, where it empties its contents ·into· the right subclavian vein, nearly under the right clavicle, or collar-bone ; while the residuum, or waste portions of the food, are expelled along through the small intestines into the ascending colon, pass up on the right side of the abdomen into the transverse colon, which runs along under the stomach, and thence into the descending colon, then down the left side into and out through the rectum. Intestinal inflammation, as in dysentery, cholera, &c., sometimes draws blood into the

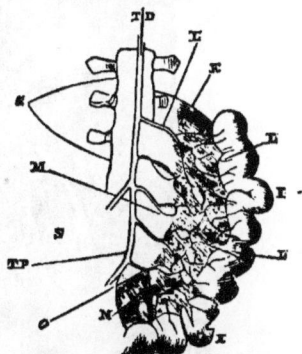

NO. 10.—INTESTINES, LACTEALS, AND MESENTARY GLANDS.

T. D, T. D.   The chyle duct.
L.   Lacteals.
M. G.   Mesentery glands.
S.   Spinal column.
F.   Folds of the intestines.

•

bowels through these lacteals, which often weakens or kills suddenly.

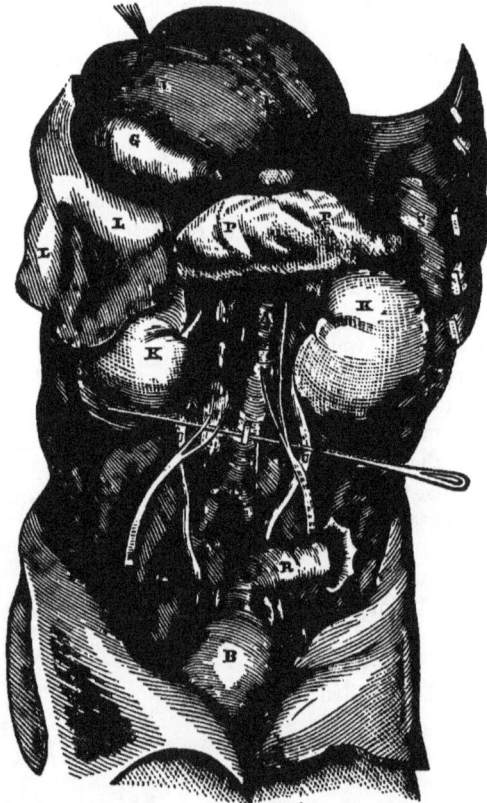

L. The liver turned up to show its under side.	A. The descending aorta.
G. Gall-bladder.	V. V. The ascending vena cava, which carries
P. The pancreas.	venous blood to the liver.
K. The kidneys.	R. The rectum.
S. The spleen.	B. The bladder.

THE SPLEEN is a large gland situated to the left of the pancreas, connected with the stomach, in structure resembling the liver, and contains lymph, yet its exact function is unknown. Behold these means for turning food into blood, and sustaining life!

CHAPTER IV.

FLUIDS; THEIR NECESSITY, OFFICE, AND SUPPLY.

SECTION I.

FLUIDS; THEIR NECESSITY, OFFICES, AND EXIT; CISTERNS, ETC.

73. — NECESSITY AND USES OF WATER IN CARRYING ON THE LIFE PROCESS.

ONLY A FLUID could *transport* all these life materials and excretions from and to all parts. And most of them, chyme, chyle, albumen, oxygen, carbon, &c., are either fluid or gaseous.

This fluid is continually passing off by perspiration, urination, expiration, &c. Much of it is turned into steam, and escapes by insensible perspiration.[93] Of course it must be re-supplied equally fast, or soon become exhausted. How is this re-supply furnished.

Water supplies this fluid. It covers the greater part of the earth's surface, often many hundred feet deep, and constitutes a large proportion of all that lives. Nothing can grow without it, nor, mosses excepted, any dry thing live. The ancients supposed it the parent of whatever is endowed with life; and experience teaches us that without it plants and animals parch up and die.

No man can live without it. Indeed, three fourths of us are composed of water, and so are four fifths of our blood. Whether this element is required on its own account, or as the great *porter* of the system, we will not now stop to inquire; but, be its use what it may, it is as essential to life even as solid food, or any thing but air.

"How, then, could Dr. Alcott live over a year without drinking a drop of liquid, and others a less time, yet experience no thirst?"

All we eat contains it. Meat consists of about three fourths water; carrots, beets, turnips, potatoes, and cabbages about nine tenths; eggs about seven tenths; milk nearly nine tenths; and thus of other kinds of food; so that we cannot eat without introducing it into the animal economy.

25

IMBIBITION is, however, the main source of supply. All that lives, drinks. Trees and vegetables drink through both their leaves and roots. Insects drink — mosquitos freely. All animals must have fluids to drink, or perish.

Probably water *consists* in part of aqueous animalcules, which supply some nutrition to drinkers. Nature fills all space with some form of life; then why not water? Phosphorescent animalcules abound in sea-water; then why not all water contain some kind of animalcules? They abound in the aqueous structure of the eyes, for we can often *see* them darting in all directions before our vision, and of course in other liquids. The fermentation of water probably kills off one kind, but creates another.

THIRST — probably created in much the same way with hunger [49] — results from a scarcity of liquids in the blood; and its ravenousness almost equals that for food. *Love* of drinks is one of the strong loves of all that lives. So imperious is this aqueous demand, that Nature has stationed a FACULTY *of the mind*, with its cerebral organ, called *Bativeness*, charged expressly with supplying the system with appropriate liquids. It is located adjoining Alimentiveness,[48] because it is a necessary part of the alimentary supply. During infantile life, it forms the chief agent for introducing food, as well as liquids, into the system, and is correspondingly active.

WATER, AND JUICES from fruits and vegetables, constitute the chief sources of this supply, which is abundant. The clouds pour it down copiously in showers, soaking rains, and pelting storms, which the earth imbibes, only to liquefy the sap or blood of vegetables and fruits, and thus promote their growth, and proffer it to man in gushing springs, beautiful streamlets, and great arterial rivers, white with floating palaces. All Nature cries for water, and is answered by its copious supply, which signifies its necessity. Let us "thank the Lord" for water, as well as for food.

THE BEST liquid is undoubtedly the juices of fruits. They were made most delicious, because "that is best which *tastes* best."[50] They contain nearly all the elements of food, fibrine, albumen, acids, and sweets, and constitute vegetable blood, which is quite like animal, in composite elements. They are soft, that is, contain no lime, and hence are especially adapted to those fully grown, and declining from age. The system needs bone material or lime, which it obtains from food, especially its rind, and probably can obtain enough from that source.

74. Soft Water vs. Hard.

Hard water is rendered so mainly by holding lime in solution, which impairs its washing and bathing properties. It also lodges along the capillary blood-vessels, which it finally fills up or emboncs, and thereby occasions natural death ; and this partial emboning also causes the sluggish circulation and feebleness incident to declining years. Of course this natural decline keeps even pace with this emboning, which hard water increases, and thus hastens death. Of course, therefore, soft water promotes longevity, because it leaves these blood-vessels open the longer. Use soft water if you would prolong life; but avoid hard, unless you are willing to accelerate its close. And it will creep along quite fast enough, without being hastened by drinking or cooking with hard water.

Calculus, which so often obstructs urination, besides rendering it extremely painful, is composed of lime, which has passed through the kidneys, lodged at the outlet of the bladder, and dammed up its contents within it. The catheter affords relief only temporary, besides being irritating.

Soft water retards this calculary formation, and thus promotes urinary, and sexual, and general health and improvement. In short, it is every way immeasurably better than hard. All owe its supply to themselves.

75. Spring vs. Well Water, and Country vs. City.

Well water is generally used the most, but ought to be the least; because it often contains foreign ingredients much less favorable to life than those of spring water. All justly prefer springs to wells when both are equally accessible. Why should not that water proffered directly to us by Nature be better than that obtained by digging? and flowing water than stagnant?

City well water is perfectly abominable ; because it reeks with city filth from all gutters, stables, cesspools, puddles, &c. All this corruption filters into the ground, and exudes into city wells. The earth would cleanse it but that there is so much filth as to completely saturate the entire ground, and thus impregnate all city well water, which renders it perfectly loathsome to the taste. City water-works are therefore one of the greatest of blessings to their inhabitants, and ought to be got up for all cities, small and large, except when rain water can be had.

RAIN water, next to the juices of fruit, is the best form of liquid for the system. Caught on tin, or slate, or hard composition-roofs, and kept in deep, underground cisterns, it constitutes by far the very best water man can use for drinking or cooking, is always cool, keeps perfectly sweet the year round, and costs but a trifle.

A FEW DOLLARS are sufficient to construct one large enough to supply a good-sized family the year round. It can be constructed very cheaply thus : —

76. HOW TO CONSTRUCT A RAIN-WATER CISTERN FOR FIFTEEN DOLLARS.

ONE LARGE enough for ordinary family use should be at least ten feet in depth and diameter, though twelve would be far better, and every inch in either diameter or height adds several barrels to its containing capacity. Every foot deeper and wider would about double the amount of water it will hold; and the deeper it is, the cooler and sweeter its water, and the less liable to ferment, and the easier the formation of its top. While about it, you may as well make it large *enough;* while being larger than really necessary will not hurt or add many cents to its cost. Our mode of structure has nothing to say respecting its size. Determine that by other circumstances. Let your hole be dug about four to twelve inches larger than you propose to have the inside of your cistern, and have a perpendicular trench sunk a few inches along up that side where you propose to draw up your water, in which your pipe can ascend from the bottom of the cistern to the pump. Level off your bottom so that the water will settle in a little basin somewhere in it, from which its rinsings.and dirt can be easily dipped up.

BEGIN the construction of your cistern by procuring a spruce board, one inch thick, about six to eight inches wide, and three times longer than the proposed diameter of your cistern — a thirty feet board for a cistern ten feet in diameter, thirty-six for one twelve, &c. If you cannot find one long enough, it can be easily spliced, by putting their ends together, and nailing a short piece across them so that it will lap from each on to the other. This piece should be about three feet long, and so nailed as to come on the *inside* of your cistern.

Before you nail the pieces together, *saw* this board *crosswise* on its *inner* side every three or four inches, and the oftener the smaller the cistern, *almost* through, but not quite, so as to allow of its being *bent round*, in order to form a *hoop*. This lapping piece must also be sawed. Bend it, and fasten the ends as just above described for lapping. The rounder it is bent the better, yet your cistern will hold water if it is not just so regular in shape. Brace this bent board by nailing a narrow piece or two, or three or four, across it, which will also enable you to handle it by standing in its middle. You will also need to work from its inside. We will call this round-bent board the *hoop*. Its object is to make a mould by which to form the inside of your cistern. It should be in size anywhere from three to six inches *smaller*, all around, than the hole for your cistern. The larger it is the thinner the walls of your cistern. It may as well be six inches from this hoop to the outside of your cistern hole. The farther it is, the more material will be required to fill it in forming your cistern. Four inches will do, and there is no need of over eight, while five or six are enough to give all needed body to your cistern wall.

Procure material for the outside wall of your cistern thus: Sand, coarse or fine, will do for the whole of it, except water lime. Sand and gravel, coarse or fine, will also do. There must be among it sufficient fine and coarse sand to give it the required "*tact*," as the masons say ; that is, enough to fill up all spaces, and make one solid mass. This is to fill in *between* the hoop and the outside of your cistern hole, taking the place of the *brick* now generally used.

Stones, larger or smaller, clinkers, any thing solid, can be imbedded in this mortar; but if any are too large to go in between the hoop and the ground, a place must be dug into the latter to allow the former to go in behind the hoop. Furnace dross, pounded oyster shells, slate stone gravel, full of all sized pebbles, from the size of the fist or even head, down to sand, almost any pebbles and stones taken from a shore or stream, chip-stones from a marble yard, brickbats, almost anything to which lime-mortar will adhere, will do for material. The main body of the cistern can be made wholly of brickbats, of any and all sizes and shapes, such as are thrown away at brick-yards, by pounding apart, to give sufficient firmness to form one compact mass, and letting the rest go in whole, or wholly of blacksmiths' clinkers, or foundry dross, similarly pounded, or anything hard.

THE BOTTOM of your cistern is to be formed by taking about two or three bushels, — the more the larger your cistern, — or enough to cover the bottom of your entire cistern hole about two inches thick, but with no stones larger than your bottom is to be thick, for you want a smooth bottom; which should descend to the middle, or else towards the side *opposite* to where the water is to be drawn out, so that all dirt will settle into this lowest spot, whence it can be easily dipped out when the cistern is emptied to be cleansed.

Add water lime at the rate of about one sixth or eighth of the whole bulk of this material, the less the coarser your materials, and the less economical you are, and costly your lime. One tenth water lime will probably do to nine tenths of gravel, yet if you prefer to be extra safe, one eighth to one sixth will make you so. Masons will tell you one third, but of this there is no need.

Mix the two well together dry, by shovelling. Then add sufficient water to make the mass about as thick as ordinary mortar, so that it will run and pack into one solid mass. Spread this evenly over this bottom, leaving a place to stand in at the hollow, as above suggested. Even it all down, and work down all projecting pebbles till it becomes smooth. This material should be used as soon as may be after it is wet, because its first set is the best; though a second wetting and setting will do by adding more lime. Your bottom is thus formed and about done. Let it stand untouched an hour or more, or over night, till it is well set; unless you are in haste; but if so, cover it over with sand, a few inches to a foot or two in the middle portion, but not around the edges. This sand will enable you to keep on working without injuring your bottom, but around the outside, where the wall comes, there must be no sand.

Now place your spruce board hoop, before described, so as to be about four to six or more inches from the outside of your hole all around. No matter whether it is more or less than four inches from your board to the earth.

Take half a bushel of the finer quality of your material, all sand will do better, and about six quarts water lime, mix well by shovelling, add water enough to make a mortar of it, and put it in the *inner* corner, at the bottom of your hoop, and work it well into this bottom to make a good *junction* between the bottom and the side of your cistern, run the point of your trowel around inside the bottom of the hoop to smooth down any projecting material, and consider your work fairly begun.

BEGIN YOUR PIPE for pumping out your water right here, by inserting a stick about an inch in diameter and a foot or two long, nearly perpendicular, so that its lower end shall be even with the bottom of the hoop, and between the hoop and ground. A lead pipe, bent, and laid under your hoop, one end opening into the bottom of your cistern, and the other behind the hoop, is better. Its object is to conduct the water from the cistern into a pipe, for the present, which we are about to show you how to make. If you prefer a lead pipe, and can get it, now is your time to place it. If you make a filter, it must open into it.

This hoop should have four auger holes, with ropes tied in each, by which to lift or draw it along up as you proceed.

Mix enough material and wet enough lime and material to fill up between this hoop and the earth, about one part lime to six or eight parts of material, and fill in behind the hoop, the better if not filled quite to its top, putting in any stones you can get in and have the mass solid.

THIS CEMENT PIPE can be made by setting this inch stick at the *end* of this lead pipe, between the hoop and dirt, or else one end against the outside of the lower edge of your hoop, but this would prevent your emptying the cistern below this hole. A short lead, say three or four inches, is the best. Place this stick at the end of the short lead pipe; have it perpendicular, put fine material all around it; let it be in the perpendicular trench described in making your cistern hole, and keep drawing this stick along up, thus leaving a cemented hole behind it.

This hoop must now be lifted, or pulled upwards to within an inch or so of the top of the material already placed — about four inches, if your board is six inches wide, and filled again to within an inch or so of its top.

This lifting must be even, or on all sides *at once*, so as not to break the material already placed. Still, if it becomes broken, your trowel, rubbed along over the cracks as soon as the board is hoisted, while the wall is green, will fix it all right again.

Your best plan probably is to let these four ropes in these four holes extend to the surface of the ground; put a pole through all four, with sufficient purchase to raise all at once; and at each rise shorten the ropes, or else raise the other end of the pole not lifted on. Repeat this last process of filling in behind the board, and lifting it till you have raised your cistern sufficiently to begin to form its top, or about four to six feet below the top of the ground.

After making the upper course richer with water lime than usual, so as to have a good foundation for its dome, the construction of which involves the only really difficult part of the whole process, proceed to make its dome as follows: —

Take another spruce board, one third longer than the diameter of your cistern; nail a short piece on each end to hold it up after it is placed; saw it almost through crosswise every three or four inches, as before described for the hoop, to allow bending, and tie the two ends, to keep it bent; set it on top of this round board hoop, the ends of the latter on the sides of the former, so that their outer edges shall be even. This short piece should be so nailed on as to lap from the horizontal hoop to the perpendicular one. Do the same with a second spruce board, thus forming four ribs for your dome, which must of course cross each other at their top where the mouth of your cistern is to be. Now knock in pieces one of your water lime barrels, and set its staves, one end on the horizontal hoop and the other lapping over on the upright ones; put thick-brown paper over any holes still left, thus forming a dome-shaped mould for the top of your cistern, all resting on this horizontal spruce board hoop, and about even with its outer edges. Now mix your material and lime, as already described, and build it up carefully around this dome, till the hole left becomes about two feet across on top. Make the material richer with lime than for the body of the cistern, say one fourth to one sixth, because this arch requires more strength, embedding brickbats, blacksmiths' cinders, stones (the thinner and flatter the better), so as to help strengthen this arch.

Now drive the hoops on one end of one of your lime barrels; nail them; knock out both heads; saw in two in the middle, — these short half staves will help in forming your dome, — and place one of the halves, with its smaller end down, on top of this dome, where the upright spruce boards cross, and build the same material right along up around this half barrel, the top of which should be about even with the top of the ground, which should be calculated beforehand, or else the ground rounded up to its top. Fill dirt all around over this dome, and keep pouring water daily over and around your cistern, outside, and let it stand a week, though a month is better. Your *cistern is built!*

Yet it must be finished off thus : —

Bore and saw through these upright spruce dome boards, where they cross ; knock them in to your cistern ; go down into it, and take out this dome and the spruce board ; sell them, hoop, dome, and all, to a neighbor, with which to build another cistern for himself ; for one cistern mould will answer for scores of cisterns, and can be so constructed as to be easily taken apart, without the sawing or boring above directed. Let the half barrel remain, and by nailing together the pieces which composed its head, you have a lower *cover* to the neck of your cistern, which will fit and set right down into this half barrel, and stop near its bottom, while another top cover, over all, will form an air-tight partition between these top and bottom covers, which will prevent the frost from penetrating into the cistern.

Of course an outlet must be left towards the top of this dome for the surplus water to pass off after the cistern is full.

FINISH OFF the inside of this cistern, and make it water-tight, as follows : As you keep drawing up this horizontal spruce hoop to make the cistern, and while the material is yet soft, rub your trowel along over it, to pack the material and fill up all its cracks and holes. After taking out your dome, beginning up by the half barrel, fill up all holes with a mortar of water lime and sand, all around and all the way down to the bottom, which finish out, and make tight with this mortar.

Make a thin wash about as thick as for whitewashing by putting

26

water lime into water, and wash your cistern over and over from top to bottom with a whitewash brush, and your cistern proper is all done; unless you choose to

MAKE A FILTER thus: Take soft or porous brick; set edge-wise, and end to end. Four or five long will make it large enough. Set in lime mortar, and one tier above the other for about six tiers, drawing in each tier, thus making a brick box around the mouth of your cistern, leaving a place for drawing the water large enough to hold two to four pails of water. The water thus let into the cistern proper will filter through the brick into the brick compartment about as fast as you draw it out.

CONDUCT your water to your cistern as to other cisterns, but you can make a cement pipe thus: Make the bottom of your trench, which runs from your spout to the cistern, rounding and narrow; have a round, smooth stick, say two feet long; throw this same cistern material into the bottom of this trench, into the top of which imbed the half of this round stick, to form a water trough; and repeat the process along the trench, which should descend into the cistern. Lay brick on top of this un-derground mortar trough, and cover them over with more cistern material.

DRAW THE WATER from this brick filter as you would from any other cistern. Lead pipe is objectionable, and can be dispensed with thus. We told you above how to place a short lead pipe leading from the bottom of your cistern to the end of the upright inch stick set perpendicularly in the cistern wall. Fill fine cistern material around this stick, and keep drawing it up after you whilst raising your wall, till it reaches the dome, thus leaving a hole after the stick in the cistern material. This pipe hole should be some two or more inches from the sides of your cistern. When you have reached the bottom of the dome, direct this pipe towards where your pump is to be. Insert your lead pipe into this hole. You can easily thus make a water-tight tube from the bottom of your cistern to the bottom of your pump, and connect pump and pipe as in other cases.

Your cistern is now in complete working order, just as good as if a mason had made it at a cost of nearly a hundred dollars, yet it has cost you somewhat as follows:—

Thirty feet of spruce boards, about	$0 60
Two barrels water lime (varying with the locality) . . .	6 to 8 00
Pebble and sand material, about	2 00
Digging cistern hole same as for others, about, ...	6 00
Amount of work, from	8 to 10 00
Total, ...	$26 60

But any intelligent man can do all the work, in which case it will cost only for the lime and boards, and less than ten dollars.

Tell masons and carpenters you do not need their services, and can all alone make a cistern for less than ten dollars as good as they would make at a cost of seventy-five dollars. Those who follow these directions will make no failures, and may justly be proud of the work of their own hands. Or, if you fail the first time, try again, avoiding the cause of the failure next time.

In clay soils, after the hole is dug, you can sometimes wet and pound the cistern hard, up to the dome, and it can be made tight by simply a coating of water-lime and sand, or even the wash above described, but the top must be upon a shoulder made by digging the cistern hole larger just here, and cast the top as above described.

Section II.

STIMULATING DRINKS. — ALCOHOLIC AND MALT LIQUORS; WINE, TEA, COFFEE, LEMONADE, ETC.

. 77. — Alcoholic and Malt Liquors.

Men differ, *toto cœlo*, as to whether alcoholic liquors benefit or injure mankind, mentally and physically, some waging war to the hilt against all forms and degrees of intoxicating drinks, while others, of equal intelligence and integrity, advocate their use in theory and practice. Even "doctors disagree" as to their use, many prescribing, others condemning them. Which class is right, and which wrong?

Scientific men owe it to themselves, and those they claim to serve, to lead people *right*, but not to mislead them, in a matter thus important. Truth is one, and those who are in the truth, will *agree*.

That scientific analysis required to settle this mooted problem is "out of our line," but a close, impartial observation of over half a century has given the Author something to say on this subject.

FIRST PRINCIPLES, not prejudice, should decide this matter. A flippant, elegant, eloquent, declamatory lecture is one thing, while *scientific* data and inferences are quite another. These we attempt.

WINE-MAKING destroys the integrity of the grape, already proved to be so beneficial, by excluding a large part of those materials its Maker saw fit to incorporate into it, besides injecting some elements into wine, alcohol for example, He saw fit to omit in grapes. This fact proves that grapes are better than their unfermented juice, and this than wine.

FERMENTATION SOURS it as that of dough sours bread.[62] Can its decay improve it? And a like principle applies to apple, and all other kinds of cider.

ACIDS, however, are demanded in the system; and, when not furnished from other sources, supplying them through wine and cider is better than none. On this principle they often cure dyspepsia, as also by their acid combining with and neutralizing some other acid, or some injurious or excessive acidity. Still, the real question is, whether all required acids can or cannot be supplied directly from fruits without their undergoing this decomposition. Probably they can, but when not thus supplied, that of wines and cider is better than none, and hence relatively beneficial.

In certain conditions of the system, pure wine certainly does promote circulation and perspiration, and thereby relieves congestion, with its consequent aches and pains.

FRUIT GROWERS thus become the best practical lecturers on temperance, as well as genuine philanthropists, by furnishing acids in fruits, and thus forestalling this craving for alcohol. Cheap fruits are the best and most effective temperance propagandists. We need *fifty times* more fruit than we now have; and we should then have less grog-shops by two to one.

78. — ALL INTOXICATION INJURES.

WHENEVER *wine or alcoholic stimulants of any kind benefit, they never intoxicate, and, as far as they intoxicate, they only injure.* The system *must keep warm.*[84]

This requires a large amount of carbon, which the stomach should furnish. But suppose it does not, death must ensue from cold, unless the needed carbon can be obtained from some outside source. Alcohol contains it, indeed, consists mainly of it, already eliminated, and ready to enter at once into combination with oxygen, in heating up the body. Alcoholic drinks, therefore, sometimes keep patients alive, by promoting animal warmth till the system can rally. Yet in all such cases the alcohol unites *at once* with the oxygen, *before it intoxicates.*

ALL intoxication injures, because it is consequent on *excess* of carbon, or more than the system can use.

THOSE POISONED by serpents, can drink a pint of strong whiskey, &c., without the slightest intoxication resulting from it, because its alcohol, that which would otherwise have intoxicated, is instantly seized and appropriated by the life force to neutralize this poison. Furnish it with whatever it demands, alcohol included, but whenever, and as far as, it is beneficial, it *never elates or stupefies.* This test is absolute and universal, and condemns all drinking for *hilarious* and social purposes, and all gratification of a morbid hankering after stimulants. Let the evils, vices, and woes consequent on intemperance, which Gough, with his thrilling eloquence, does not, cannot duly depict, warn all such that they "taste not, touch not, handle not, lest they" too "*perish* with the using."

ALCOHOL AS A MEDICINE, may sometimes supply needed carbon and stimulation, till reaction takes place; yet few sick persons need stimulants. They generally need rest instead. This is doubly true of chronic invalids. All stimulants, by *consuming* vitality without resupplying it, *draw on the constitution,*[28] which they generally exhaust instead of building up. The weaker persons are, the more they require quiet, not false excitements. Those who abound in vitality do not need them, while those who lack it can illy endure their draft on the life fund.[35] Physicians prescribe them too freely.

MALT LIQUORS, ale, porter, lager beer, &c., are open to a like objection with alcoholic, yet contain some nutrition, and their bitter often helps the liver. Still the liquor of stewed hops is better and cheaper. Observation and experience make against their habitual use, much more than for it. As generally drunk, between meals and irregularly, they injure much more than benefit. They create, and are generally drank to gratify a morbid appetite, which they never allay, but only enhance. Such an appetite should be denied when formed, but should not be formed. Like a morbid craving for food, alcoholic liquors, opium, &c., they cry " give " always, but never enough.

79. — TEA AND COFFEE.

TEA AND COFFEE are powerful tonics, too bracing for any nervous person to endure with impunity. They impede sleep for five or six hours after they are drank. All lovers of them strong, are nervous in the extreme. These drinks do indeed sometimes cure headache to-day, only to increase it for days afterwards. All inveterate tea and coffee drinkers suffer proportionally from headache, and usually sick-headache. If they will stop drinking them six months, their headache will stop. Is there no relationship between the amount of these narcotics now consumed and modern nervous irritability? The Author speaks only from observation, not experience, for in sixty-two years he has never drank a quart of either, all told; and could not be persuaded to take over a spoonful at a time, and not this once in months or years; nor ever, unless all jaded out, and as a temporary stimulant; when it improves and lengthens — naturally producing copiousness, but at a terrible subsequent sacrifice of energy.

COFFEE has a worse effect upon the nervous system than tea. Let inveterates in either discontinue their use six months, and they will barely begin to realize the damage they inflict by noting how much *better* they feel after they become once fairly weaned.

THE WARD BROTHERS, the champion oarsmen of this country, never drank tea and coffee.

"But we cannot drink cold water at our meals; for it, besides being unpleasant, cools the stomach so as to arrest digestion. What shall we drink? "

DRINKING NOTHING at meals is probably the best; the reasons for which will appear hereafter.

CHOCOLATE will do for those whose livers are in a first-rate condition; otherwise it produces an intense headache. Those who drink it should watch its effects.

CEREAL coffee, made by serving wheat, or rye, or corn, or

barley, or sweet potatoes just as Java is served — brown, grind, and steep, or crust coffee made by browning and steeping bread, is nutritious, and wholly unobjectionable, as well as palatable. Burn it the more the bitterer you wish it.

LEMONADE is an excellent drink for those on whose stomachs it does not sour. The system requires both sweets, which are analogous to alkalies, and sours or acids. The two probably correspond with those positive and negative electric forces by which life is carried on. They certainly have a strong mutual affinity, enter into that combination called effervescence, and leave a sediment analogous to charcoal. Lemonade embodies both, though not in their effervescent form, yet they probably combine in the system. At least the deliciousness of lemonade is Nature's warrant that it is proportionally beneficial.[50]

MORE LEMON, with less sugar than usual, is much better than more sugar with less lemon.[48]

TAMARIND water is, for a like reason, also beneficial.

SECTION III.

FLUID EXCRETIONS.

80.—THE KIDNEYS AND BLADDER; THEIR STRUCTURE, OFFICE, &c.

THE KIDNEYS, right and left, are composed of an exterior or cortical substance, from a sixth to a fourth of an inch thick, and a medullary, which consists of a series of about fifteen pyramidal bodies, their bases towards the surface, and their points turned inward, each being a distinct gland, formed of uriniferous tubes, which terminate in *papillæ* at their apex. These uriniferous canals in the cortical substance are *extremely convoluted*, but become straight on reaching the pyramidal structure. The renal artery ramifies throughout this structure, into veins, both being tortuous, and containing an inconceivable number of deep red granules or corpuscles, each of which has a tuft of capillary vessels, in which the renal arteries terminate and veins begin. Convoluted ducts, at first extremely tortuous, begin in these granules, and terminate in straight tubes on the inside surface of this cortical substance, in papillæ, which open into the pelvis of the kidney, and from which the urine they secrete empties into the pelvis of the kidney, a strong, white, fibrous, tough structure, having three compartments, one central, and one at each end.

EACH KIDNEY is about four inches long, and over two wide, shaped like a bean flattened, the right the lowest, the left under the spleen, and behind the stomach, their lower margin extending a little below the lowest ribs, and enclosed in a peritoneal tunic, easily separated from the gland, whitish in color, strong, elastic, and attached to the kidney by a very fine tissue.

No. 18.— LONGITUDINAL SECTION OF A KIDNEY.

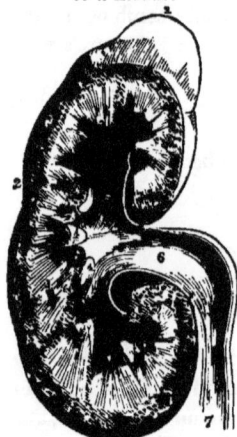

1. Renal capsule.
2. Cortical structure.
3, 3. Uriniferous tubes, each collected into its conical fasciculi.
4, 4. Papillæ.
5, 5, 5. The three centres.
6. The pelvis of the kidney.
7. Its ureter.

THEIR OFFICE is to secrete urine, which is composed mostly of water, urea, and animal matter, lithic acid, several inorganic salts, as ammonia, soda, phosphate and sulphate of lime, magnesia, silica, &c.

Its quantity increases in the aged, because its quality is deficient. That is, the kidneys must have a much greater amount of water to carry off the same amount of urea. Thus water increases with the amount of liquid in the blood, and in cold weather, but diminishes as perspiration and cold increase.

Unless the blood is freed from these substances noxious to life, its functions soon run down and die, but not till feelings, mental and physical, the most awfully distressing, supervene. Their dormancy, inflammation, and derangements, of which sexual errors are the chief cause,[582] create an incalculable amount of bodily and mental disease and suffering, not to say real agony.

TWO URETERS or ducts run from the kidneys, which empty this urine into them, to the bladder, into which they pour it as fast as it is delivered.

THE BLADDER is a temporary receptacle of this urine, to prevent its constant discharge as fast as it is made, which would be most loathsome and nauseating, for without this bladder urine must continue to discharge perpetually, awake and asleep, creating an intolerable stench, which all would be obliged to carry with them to church and party, wherever they went and whatever they did. All this the bladder now prevents by allowing its retention till it is full, when it is emptied, partly voluntary and partly involuntary. Its undue retention is most injurious and painful, and weakens the retaining muscles. This call should always receive immediate attention.

81. — THE GLANDS AND ABSORBENTS; THEIR STRUCTURE, AND SYMPATHY WITH THE MIND.

THE GLANDS of the system are formed somewhat like the lungs, with two sets of capillary vessels, the one for the ramification of blood, and the other for secreting their respective materials. The accompanying engraving furnishes a faint illustration of the arterial structure of a gland. Both the venous and secretory structures are similar, all their respective ramifications being almost infinitely minute.

The various secretions made in these glandular ramifications are emptied into ducts, and these into one another, till all are emptied into one common reservoir, and carried to their place of destination.

NO. 19.—STRUCTURE OF A GLAND.

Though all parts of the system reciprocate their several conditions with all the others,[25] yet this reciprocity seems to be more intimate between the glandular functions and the cerebral than between any of the others. Every change and phrase of mental action produces a corresponding change in the glandular action. Thus, thinking of food "makes the mouth water," that is, excites a copious secretion and discharge of the salivary glands; sadness retards, and pleasurable emotions augment, the action of the liver; the former accelerating and the latter preventing digestion; grief provokes a copious secretion of the lachrymal glands in the form of tears, and sudden joy sometimes has a similar effect; and thus of the others. But the most conspicuous illustration of this principle applies to that secretion which creates life. See "Sexual Science," Part VI. 27

The great practical lesson taught by this reciprocity, is the importance of keeping the mind in that calm and happy frame which promotes glandular secretion, and thereby health.

THE ABSORBENTS are stationed throughout the entire system, for the double purpose of taking up foreign-matters, such as biles and other tumors, which do not come to a head, and also depositing surplus fat, which is only its surplus carbon, stored up against its future want. When imperfect digestion or a deficiency of food renders the supply of carbon unequal, for the time being, to its demand, these absorbents take up this fat and empty it into the chyle ducts, and so into the circulation. Hence the falling away of the sick or starving. When this fat or store of carbon is exhausted by protracted hunger or stomachic disease, these absorbents take up even muscle and cellular tissue, and empty them also into the circulation, which causes the extreme emaciation of the starving, of consumptives, dyspeptics, and the sick generally. This provision against any deficiency of nutrition is inimitably beautiful and useful. But the fact that all animals fatten best in the fall, thus laying in a stock of this fatty fuel just before it is wanted, is equally so.

SECTION IV.

THE BLOOD, AND ITS CIRCULATION; THE HEART, AND ITS
STRUCTURE.

82. — OFFICE, INGREDIENTS, AND CIRCULATION OF THE BLOOD.

SOME PORTER, to bring and carry these life materials to and from all parts, receive and distribute all new material, and gather up and eject the waste and vitiated matter used up by the life process, is indispensable. THE BLOOD constitutes this "common carrier" of the system. With its looks all are familiar. It is composed chiefly of two parts, blood corpuscles, or red globules, about $\frac{1}{300}$ of a line in diameter, and one quarter as thick, which multiply or reproduce their kind, and naturally adhere to each other at their sides, and form columns, like coins placed above each other; and serum, that yellowish fluid which rises to the top of blood left to stand and coagulate.

SERUM is composed of about ninety parts water, eight of albumen, casein, and the rest salts, &c. Albumen abounds in female blood more than in male. It contains fibrine, the constant tendency of which is to assume organic shreds, which inflammation increases. Clots of fibrine are rudimentally organized. These globules imbibe the oxygen from the air in the lungs, and carry it to those tissues which expend it, and then absorb, or gather up the carbonic acid gas generated by the life process, and carry it to the lungs, from which it is extracted by the nitrogen of the air.

The average quantity of blood, in given persons, is about one fifth that of their bodies, those weighing one hundred and fifty pounds having about thirty pounds, or four gallons, one third of which is constantly in the arteries, and two thirds in the veins.

83. THE HEART; ITS STRUCTURE AND WORKINGS.

THE CIRCULATION of this blood, thus freighted by the stomach and lungs with the materials of life, must now be effected. It must be propelled, too and fro, throughout every minute part of the system, so that every shred of every muscle, nerve, tissue, and organ, bones included, may extract from it what materials each may require, and return to it for rejection all their used-up and vitiated materials.

While *breathing* creates most of the force which propels the blood,[42] yet the *heart* is its regulating organ and aide-de-camp. Breathing undoubtedly stimulates the heart itself to palpitate.

IN STRUCTURE the heart is a cavernous muscle, enveloped by the lungs,[39] oval-shaped, about five inches long, and four thick, largest relatively in robust, but smaller in delicate persons and females, weighing about eight ounces, encased, and kept in its place by a membrane called the pericardium, and resting upon the tendinous, or upper portion of the diaphragm, with its base upwards and backwards, and

No. 20. — ANTERIOR VIEW OF THE HEART, FROM BOURGERY.

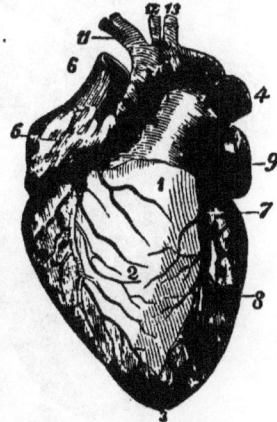

1. Base.
2. Body and right ventricle.
3. Apex.
4. Pulmonary artery.
5. Right auricle.
6. Vena cava superior.
7. Anterior coronary artery, running along the anterior fissure which separates the ventricles.
8. Left ventricle.
9. Auricle.
10. Aorta.
11. Arteria innominata.
12. Left primitive carotid.
13. Left subclavian.

its apex pointing towards the fifth rib, left side, at its junction with its cartilage.

Two AURICLES, or receiving chambers, and two *ventricles*, or expelling chambers, form its internal arrangement, and constitute in reality two hearts, bound and working together; the right auricle receiving the blood from the veins, and by its contraction propelling it into the lungs,[38] and the left auricle withdrawing it from the lungs, and speeding it throughout the body.

VALVES prevent the backward, and compel the forward flow of this blood through the heart and system. Their structure is illustrated in the accompanying engraving from Bourgery.

No. 21.—INTERIOR OF THE RIGHT AURICLE AND VENTRICLE.

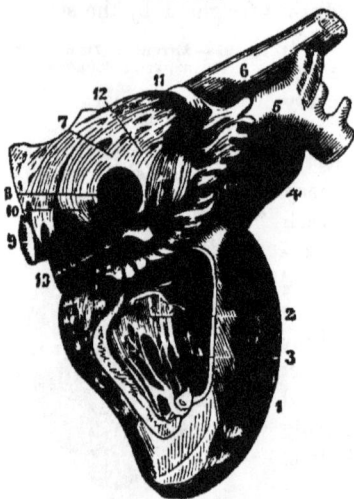

1. Right ventricle.
2. Tricuspid valve.
3. Chordæ tendinæ.
4. Pulmonary artery.
5. Aorta.
6. Descending vena cava.
7. Right auricle.
8. Orifice of the ascending vena cava.
9. Vena cava ascendens.
10. Valvula Eustachii.
11. Orifice of the descending vena cava.
12. Position of the tuberculum Loweri.
13. Valvula Thebesii, overhanging the orifice of the coronary vein.

FIBRES compose the main body of the heart. They are spiral and tortuous, crossing each other in all directions, twisting around its apex, and flex upwards towards its base. They contract at every pulsation.

ARTERIES receive the blood from the left ventricle, and conduct it to the head, arms, legs, every visceral organ, and every part and parcel of the system, and to the heart itself. They are firm, elastic, cylindrical tubes, formed of three coats, the external, composed of tissues, which connect them with surrounding parts, the middle of fibrous, which give its cylindrical form and firmness, yellowish color, elasticity, and a thin, delicate, smooth membrane, resembling mucous membrane.

These arteries are guarded from lesion by being deep.

seated, often open into each other, and branch into infinitesimal capillary blood-vessels, situated between the arteries and veins, in which the blood performs its chief function. These capillaries, too fine to be seen by the naked eye, form a network so closely woven together that the finest needle cannot puncture the flesh without drawing blood by piercing one or more of them. They empty into the veins, which carry the blood back to the heart, and running just under the skin. All the blood thus has to pass through two sets of this infinitesimal structure, one in the lungs,[37] in which it receives, and the other throughout the body, in which it gives off, its vital properties. The blood is red and brisk in the arteries, but dark blue and sluggish in the veins.

THE MUSCLES of both the heart and of the arteries aid the propulsion of the blood. "Aid," because the main propelling agent is electricity.[38] These muscles, acting involuntarily, must have some incentive to act. The electricity derived from breathing probably furnishes this stimulant. Will certainly does not. Then what does? Electricity both generates the main propulsive force which circulates the blood, and also provokes the muscles of the heart and arteries to push it forward. Backward it can never go, because of valves stationed all along the veins, which close the instant the blood begins to turn back, and holds it where it is, till it can again go forward. Tying a string tight around the base of your finger, and winding it towards the tip, would press the blood back into the arteries but that these valves prevent. They will oblige it to *burst through the flesh and skin* before they will allow it to go backward.

THE CONTRACTION of the heart, and of course arteries, transpires, on the average, in healthy adults, about seventy times per minute, varying from one hundred and forty pulsations in infants, to one hundred in children, and descending to sixty in old age, but averaging about seventy-two in middle life, besides being accelerated by all kinds of action, mental and physical, and by fevers, but being suspended in syncope, as in fainting turns.

TWO OUNCES of blood is the average amount propelled at each pulsation, or about ten pounds per minute, which is some *two hundred and fifty pounds* per hour, *three tons* every day and night, ten hundred and eighty tons per year, and *seventy-five thousand* tons in "three score years and ten." But this blood is handled

over *four times* in each pulsation, once in drawing it in from the
veins, again in pumping it into the lungs, a third time in withdrawing it from the lungs, and a fourth in passing into the
arteries, exceeding a thousand pounds every hour, twenty-four
thousand pounds every day and night, and nearly *nine million*
pounds annually.   Assuming that the average amount of blood
is twenty-five pounds, or four hundred ounces, the whole of the
blood passes through the heart once in about every three to four
minutes, fifteen to twenty times per hour, and over *six hundred
times* from each sunset to the next.

And at every round it is forced through two sets of gauze-like
strainers, the finest imaginable, of which one is several inches
long, besides forcing a part of it through the capillaries of the
liver, spleen, and kidneys; and all this with a force sufficient to
scud it throbbing and rushing throughout the entire body, and
into all those minute capillary vessels through which it passes !
How little we realize how wonderfully we are made !

To inspect still more closely its mode of action.   The two
upper chambers, or auricles, contract upon the blood they contain·
at the same instant, thereby bracing and balancing each other.
Their contraction produces a vacuum, into which blood is again
received from the veins.[42]   The two ventricles, or lower chambers, likewise contract together, thus also bracing each other, at
the same time forcing the blood, the right into the lungs, and the
left into the arteries.   By this means time for rest is allowed the
heart, the two auricles taking a short, though only a very short,
nap, while the ventricles contract, the latter going to sleep, and
waking up again, while the auricles contract — all its parts getting
tired, and taking rest as quickly and as often as the heart beats.
The heart must have rest as much as the muscles and nerves.
Yet if, like the muscles, it required six or seven hours of *succes-
sive* sleep, death would inevitably supervene.   Behold the simplicity yet efficiency of this arrangement for securing time to the
heart to rest without suspending life !

THE MUSCLES, or walls of the heart, are thick, large, and strong,
the ventricles being much stronger than the auricles, because they
have more to do.   The auricles only receive the blood from the
veins and lungs, or rather empty it out of themselves, so that it
may run in till it again fills them up and causes spontaneous con-

traction, while the office of the ventricles being much more laborious than that of the auricles are much the larger, and the left ventricle is by far the largest and strongest, because it has the most to do.

1. This circulatory process can be comprehended by remembering that the right side of the heart, auricle and ventricle, have to do wholly with the dark or venous blood, and the left with arterial or red blood.

2. The two auricles, or upper chambers, draw the blood into the heart and empty it into the two ventricles, or lower chambers, which propel it — the right into the lungs, and the left throughout the system. Or thus: —

3. The right *upper* chamber withdraws the blood from the veins, and empties it into the right *lower* chamber, which, contracting upon it, forces it into the lungs, while the *left* upper chamber, or auricle, withdraws it from the lungs and empties it into the left *lower* chamber, or ventricle, which propels it throughout the system.

How withdraws? As far as it promotes the circulation,[24] it does so on the same principle by which water is sucked up out of the well into the pump, and up that pump to that valve which carries it still higher. The heart is in every respect a self-acting force pump. As the working of the pump creates a vacuum into which the pressure of the atmosphere on the top of the well, which is sufficient to lift an unobstructed column thirty-two feet, forces the water till it is again full; so the contraction of the right auricle of the heart upon the blood it contains, forces out that blood into the right ventricle, and thus creates a vacuum into which the pressure of the atmosphere upon the surface of the body, and of course upon the veins, together with the contractile power of the veins, the pressure of the muscles upon them, and the electricity in the lungs, propel the blood along into these auricles. And just as the water in the pump above the valve is forced up and out, so the right ventricle pumps the blood into the lungs, to be withdrawn again from them by that same principle. But for this external pressure of the atmosphere upon the veins, they would burst, strong as they are, and but for this internal pressure, the external would be sufficient to press their walls together too closely to allow the blood to circulate.

SECTION V.

ANIMAL HEAT; ITS MANUFACTURE, DISTRIBUTION, AND EXIT.

84. — ITS NECESSITY AND AMOUNT.

WARMTH brings life to man, animal, reptile, insect, and vegetable, while cold brings death, except when the vital forces in
resisting it react, and generate warmth, and in cold-blooded
animals. Neither food nor breath are any more necessary to life
than is warmth. Life itself waxes and wanes with its amount
of animal heat. How soon death results from being in the cold
water of the upper lakes! How effectually it stupefies cold-
blooded animals, reptiles, alligators, and insects! Swallows,
chimney and all others, remain only during hot weather, because
insects, their food, abound only then, and are killed off by cold.

THE HUMAN SYSTEM must be kept up to about ninety-eight
degrees Fahrenheit, in order to work well, and can rarely rise
much above, or fall much below it, without serious injury, except
that children are over a hundred degrees, while old people sometimes fall to ninety-two degrees.

John Clark, a native of Connecticut, born more than a century ago,
was peculiarly affected by cold weather. In the cool mornings of nearly
every month in the year, his hands would become benumbed, and almost
entirely useless, his tongue stiffened so that he could scarcely articulate,
the muscles of his face contracted and stiffened, and one or both eyes
closed in a very peculiar manner. This infirmity was hereditary.

This was undoubtedly owing to defective lungs, and a consequent want of oxygen in his system. Or there might have been
some defect in his digestion, by which a due supply of carbon was
not extracted from his food. Many others are also troubled with
being habitually cold, even in summer. Consumptive parents,
and all predisposed to this disease, also feel cold or chilly, and
have cold hands and feet, and perhaps what is called goose-flesh
on the skin.

In short, warmth is one of the great agencies of Nature, of
which the sun is the chief source; hence the utility and agreeableness of sunshine, which is not duly appreciated.

HEAT ESCAPES perpetually from the human body, because it is
warmer than the air, except in extreme cases. If the atmosphere

were as hot as our bodies, it would be most relaxing, from want of oxygen. The air must generally be much colder than our bodies ; so that, since heat is diffusive, and tends to equalization, we lose heat all the time, and in right cold weather, *very fast.* Hence the coldness of corpses and of most surrounding objects. Our bodies would soon sink below the living point, unless supplied with heat from some *internal* fountain. Sufficient external heat to keep us warm enough would prevent the due oxygenization of our blood, and thus cause death. Whenever atmospheric heat approaches ninety-eight degrees, it creates that profuse perspiration which at once " cools us off." In short, the loss of heat, even during the hottest weather, is great, and in cold, enormous. Liebig estimates this loss as follows : —

"According to the experiments of Despretz, 1 oz. of carbon evolves, during its combustion, as much heat as would raise the temperature of 105 oz. of water at 32° to 167°, that is, by 135 degrees ; in all, therefore, 105 times 135°=14207 degrees of heat. Consequently, the 13.9 oz. of carbon which are daily converted into carbonic acid in the body of an adult, evolve 13.9×14207°=197477.3 degrees of heat. This amount of heat is sufficient to raise the temperature of 1 oz. of water by that number of degrees, or from 32° to 197509.3°; or to cause 136.8 lbs. of water at 32° to boil; or to heat 370 lbs. of water to 98.3° (the temperature of the human body); or to convert into vapor 24 lbs. of water at 98.3°.

"If we now assume that the quantity of water vaporized through the skin and lungs in 24 hours amounts to 48 oz. (3 lbs.), then there will remain, after deducting the necessary amount of heat, 146380.4 degrees of heat, which are dissipated by radiation by heating the expired air, and in the excrementitious matters.

"In this calculation, no account has been taken of the heat evolved by the hydrogen of the food, during its conversion into water by oxidation within the body. But if we consider that the specific heat of the bones, of fat, and of the organs generally, is far less than that of water, and that consequently they require, in order to be heated to 98.3°, much less heat than an equal weight of water, no doubt can be entertained, that when all the concomitant circumstances are included in the calculation, the heat evolved in the process of combustion, to which the food is subjected in the body, is amply sufficient to explain the constant temperature of the body, as well as the evaporation from the skin and lungs."

A rugged man, after eating a hearty breakfast, shoulders his axe on a cold winter morning, and works all day in the snow. Though the thermometer is many degrees below zero, while he is ninety-eight degrees above, with his coat and vest off, so that the transfer of heat from his body to the air is very rapid, yet he is all aglow from head to feet, inside and out, with animal heat. The Indian keeps warm in northern latitudes with only a blanket, his half-naked body being exposed most of the time to the cold air. The deer, moose, wolf, &c., keep warm without fire or clothes.

The preservation of this warmth, by its perpetual manufacture within the system, becomes a paramount life necessity. Though a snake may be so frozen that, when bent, it will snap like a pipe-stem, and yet come to life afterwards by warmth, yet man must be kept warm up to about the same temperature, summer and winter, in "Greenland's icy mountain, and on India's coral strand." How is this heating effected?

85. — How Breath and Food generate animal Warmth.

COMBUSTION is the only source of all artificial heat; and whatever burns, thereby produces heat, probably by setting free *latent* heat, rather than by its creation.

DECOMPOSITION results from all combustion. Burning consumes or disembodies what it burns, and therefore soon *burns up* its materials, unless they are re-supplied.

CARBON is the base of all that burns, and whatever burns, — coal, wood, charcoal, vegetables, sweets, gases, &c., — consists mainly of carbon.

OXYGEN is the burning agent, as carbon is the burnt, of all combustive processes. Carbon and oxygen, combining with each other, and ignited by the vital forces, create that "*animal warmth*" which maintains the equal temperature of the body.

BREATH AND FOOD generate this warmth. The stomach eliminates carbon from its food,[65] sets it free, and empties it into the blood, and the lungs furnish it with oxygen,[41] and the two, commingling, are carried *together* into the fine capillary blood-vessels, and then pressed into mutual contact, when vitality seizes both, ignites them, and generates heat by their combustion wherever and whenever the blood flows.[83] That is, the oxygen of the air inhaled is forced in the capillary blood-vessels into close contact with the carbon of the food eaten, and having mutually a strong chemical affinity for each other, they unite in combustion, and burn each other up, on precisely the same principle employed in warming rooms, generating steam, &c. Nothing will burn without oxygen. Hence, though cotton is extremely combustible when it can obtain oxygen from the air, yet it will not burn when compactly baled, because it cannot get oxygen to burn with. Nowhere in Nature is heat produced except by some form of combustion. Animal heat of course forms no exception. Chemistry shows that the affinity of oxygen for carbon is even greater than it has for iron; [41] so that, when all these are forced into close mutual contact within the capillary blood-vessels, the oxygen loves carbon better than it loves iron, leaves iron, and uniting with the carbon, creates animal heat. In producing fire, we must have fuel or carbon to start with, and then blow a current of air upon the fire, and the oxygen of the air combining with the carbon of the wood, produces combustion and evolves heat. But the carbon in the blood being unencumbered, free, and very abundant, and thus of the oxygen, there is no need of fire to start with. They burn without, and burn each other up *spontaneously,* thus engendering that immense amount of animal heat within the system which re-supplies that given off by the cooling process just explained and the body, together with all its parts, internal and external, is kept at that elevated temperature necessary for the maintenance of life.

86. — Carbonic Acid Gas ; its Formation, and Expulsion.

Smoke and ashes result from all combustion. Of course that of these two gases must and does eliminate both. And the ashes, or rather coals, of this internal combustion, analyzed, are almost identical in their chemical compounds with charcoal, both being composed mainly of carbonic acid. Combustion can never . take place, out of the system or in, without creating this acid ; and that combustion which heats the system, forms some ten or twelve ounces of carbonic acid per day. This substance is hostile to life, and exceedingly poisonous, as seen when inhaled in a tight room in which charcoal is consuming. Its superabundance is fatal to life. Hence, unless some means were devised for ejecting it from all parts of the system where this combustion creates it, those parts must die. How is the system cleared of this foe?

By the iron in the blood. That iron first made love, in the lungs, to the oxygen, also in the lungs, and wooed her to leave her husband, the nitrogen of the air, and run away with him,

which she, faithless one, gladly seconded.[41] But no sooner is she
brought into close proximity, in the capillary blood-vessels, with
the *carbon* in the blood, than she finds another paramour in this
carbon, which she loves still better. Carbon reciprocates this
love; when, jilting her iron paramour, she rushes into the arms
of this charcoal paramour so ardently, that they consume each
other, and die of excess of love, leaving only their burnt car-
casses in the form of carbonic acid.

The iron of the blood thus left desolate, — good enough for
him, — he ran away with oxygen, the wife of the nitrogen of the
air, and carbon served him just right to run away with his stolen
wife — by way of making the best of his desertion, proffers his
hand to this carbonic acid, is accepted, concludes a union, and,
being a great traveller, takes his new bride along back with him
by slow and leisurely movements to the lungs. Their union, not
being extra cordial, this carbonic acid finds in the nitrogen of the
air in the lungs a much more agreeable companion than in the
iron, and, quitting the iron, rushes through this gauze membrane
of the lungs,[39] combines with this nitrogen, and is brought out of
its pent-up enclosure into the wide world, again to enter into the
formation of vegetables and food.

Yet is the iron not sorry for this desertion, because he has
found a new supply of oxygen, which he likes far better than carbonic acid. Or thus : The nitrogen in the air, and the iron in the
blood, mutually agree to *swap wives*, each liking the other's wife
better than his own, and as these wives both love each other's husbands better than their own, they "jump at" the proposed exchange.
This series of faithless desertions on the one hand, and of runa-
way matches on the other, accomplishes that grand end of heating
up the system so comfortable in itself, and so indispensable to
life — a means as ingenious as the end attained is indispensable.
By these means the system guards itself against the otherwise
fatal consequences of those sudden and extreme changes of the
atmosphere from heat to cold, is prevented from freezing on the
one hand, and from burning on the other, and always kept at the
required temperature.

· This discloses another primary office of respiration — the generation of *animal heat*. It also shows that one of the principal
offices of digestion is the subserviency of this same heat-manufac-
turing end.

Philosophical readers, who love to trace out the relations of cause and effect, say whether these combinations, evolutions, and re-combinations are not beautiful in the highest possible degree. And do they not go far towards explaining the *instrumentalities* by which life takes place? This wonderful process, thus far an unfathomable mystery, the very attempt to solve which has been considered blasphemy, bids fair to be brought within the range of scientific investigation. That great philosopher, Liebig, has put us upon the track, and thus opened a new and most delightful field of philosophical research.

87. — The Regulation of Animal Heat by Food.

The atmospheric temperature is extremely changeable, sometimes one hundred degrees above, and anon forty below, zero. Some means must therefore be ordained to create the more heat the colder it is; and the less the warmer, so as to keep the bodily temperature even. This self-acting instrumentality, as simple as efficient, effects it, viz. : the colder the air the more dense it is, and therefore contains the more oxygen and nitrogen for its bulk. Hence the three pints of air inhaled at each breath, yields the more oxygen the colder it is, just when the more heat is needed. The colder the air the more heat it both requires and generates; so that healthy persons need little fire even in winter; because Nature increases the supply of heat in proportion to its demand.

Then since the fourteen hundred cubic inches of air breathed per hour yields much more oxygen in winter than summer, yet can combine with only its fixed equivalent of carbon, we need to eat the more food, and that the more highly carbonized the colder the weather. Hence appetite is the better the colder the weather, and relishes more highly carbonized food, such as fat, four fifths of which are carbon. This is equally true of butter, honey, various oils, nuts, and the like. Hence the Esquimaux can drink down gallons of train-oil, and eat twenty or more pounds of meat per day, and fourteen pounds of candles at a meal, without injury; indeed, cannot live without an immense consumption of carbon. The great condensation of the air consequent on extreme cold allows him to inhale proportionate quantities of oxygen, to burn up which he must have this great supply of carbon. We should, therefore, eat more in cold weather than in warm, and food richer in carbon.

Some argue from this that meat is necessary in winter; yet vegetable food contains more carbon than animal. The albumen of wheat is over half carbon, and four pounds of starch contain as much as thirteen of meat. Molasses and sugar are about all carbon, except their water. All vegetable oils contain about four fifths carbon, and hence nuts should be eaten in winter. Honey, butter, olive oil, &c., contain it in as great proportion as fat meat, which is made by an excess of food in fattening animals over breath, and liable to be diseased.

Graminivorous animals, reindeer, &c., can inhabit very cold regions, while most graminivori are confined to warm. If meat is so conducive to animal heat and life, why are lions, tigers, &c., confined to warm climates? As oats keep the horse abundantly warm, why not oatmeal keep man warm enough in winter? Ask the Highland Scotch, from time immemorial, if their oatmeal cakes and gruel have not kept them warm enough to camp out, even in winter, with snow for their pillow and blanket.

But the great trouble of civilized life is, not to get carbon enough, but to get *little* enough. This is especially true of the sedentary. They breathe but little, because they exercise little, and because they live mostly in heated rooms, where the air is both rarefied and vitiated. Hence they take in but little oxygen, and therefore require but little carbon to burn it up. Yet such eat, and keep eating, as heartily as out-door laborers, and often more so. That very cold which brings relief sharpens up appetite, and they take still more carbon, thus keeping up both its superabundance and their disease; whereas, if they would not increase such quantity, meanwhile breathing freely so as to burn up its surplus, they would obtain permanent health.

88. — REGULATION OF ANIMAL HEAT BY FIRE.

FIRE, indispensable in generating steam, smelting, &c., can also be made to regulate animal heat. Though vigorous exercise in perfect health would probably furnish all needed animal warmth, yet we often require to apply our minds while sitting, as in writing, reading, listening, and in sickness, exhaustion, infancy, &c., where there is too little action to keep warm by breathing alone, when fire becomes comfortable and indispensable. Fire is hardly less beneficial than water. If we do not keep sufficiently warm by air, we must supply the deficit by fire. Colds, those great disease breeders, come from being too cold. Yet even in sickness, when the circulation is low, it is better to provoke as much natural heat by friction and clothing, and rely as little on fire, as possible. Invalids, of all others, require oxygen, which artificial heat always and necessarily reduces. I pity those who are obliged to resort to fire for warmth. They may live along from hand to mouth as to health, yet can never know the real luxury of a comfortable temperature. Such should by all means practise those directions for enhancing the circulation, to be given hereafter.

Still, men rely far too much on external heat, and far too little on internal. Though we require fire, yet this alone can never keep us sufficiently warm. How hot, think you, must be the atmosphere to keep the body, inside as well as out, at the temperature of ninety-eight degrees? Hot enough to burn the skin to a crisp. Try the experiment on a corpse. Fire is utterly powerless to keep us duly warm. Most of our heat, indeed all of it, must be generated *within* us. The use of fire is to keep us warm by *retarding the escape* of internal heat, not to actually infuse external heat into us. Those who cannot keep themselves warm by breathing and food, can never keep warm at all, because in and by the very act of warming a room you prevent the manufacture of internal heat, by rarefying the air, and when the fire is in the room heated, by burning out much of its oxygen, so that the lungs cannot carry enough to the blood to support the required internal combustion.[41] External heat, therefore, so far from keeping us warm, actually prevents that warmth in the ratio of its intensity. That is, the warmer we keep our rooms, the colder we must keep ourselves. All this, besides the smoke and noxious gases necessarily consequent on burning fuel.

To put this matter on the reader's own experience. How many times in your lives, in weather so cold that you could not keep yourself warm in-doors, when compelled to drive out into the cold have you so accelerated circulation and perspiration as in a few minutes to be quite warm enough, though just before chilly by a hot fire? And this natural warmth is much more delightful than artificial. Out of doors is the place to keep thoroughly warm in cold weather.

Sedentaries know no more about the backwoodsman's table luxuries, than he about "city fixins;" and the way he can beat them keeping warm in cold weather, notwithstanding their hard coal and air-tight stoves, can be known only by trying.. Those having constitutions unimpaired, should remain where there is as little fire as possible, and never rely on it to warm feet or hands, but only on natural warmth.

Those who generally occupy WARM apartments cannot well imagine how much more brisk, lively, buoyant, intense, and happy the feelings are, and how much more clear and vigorous all the intellectual operations, while one is kept warm by exercise in a cold day, than by sitting in a hot room; nor how lax and listless, in comparison, are we rendered by artificial heat. Abundance of exercise, respiration, and good food are the great receipts for keeping comfortable in cold weather.

The evils consequent on staying perpetually within doors in cold weather, and in hot rooms, are exposed too forcibly by our subject to require enlargement. Housed victims can obtain only a small supply of oxygen; first, because the air they breathe is so rarefied by heat that a given bulk contains but little; secondly, because the fire has burnt out much of the vitality of that little; thirdly, because they have breathed what little air there is over and over again, and thus loaded it with carbonic acid gas; and because they exercise so little that they secure but little action in their lungs. Such live slowly, yet are incurring disease.

CARBONIC ACID GAS is generated by all combustion, which, besides always impeding its exit, sometimes actually infuses it. Hence the blue veins and languor of those who keep themselves housed in winter.

AIR-TIGHT stoves shut out oxygen by preventing the circulation of the atmosphere, and are a perfect abomination, except where a frequent opening of the door renews the air. Have a draught whenever you must have a fire. All close stoves paralyze life and hasten death. Open fireplaces are the best.

THE RUSSIAN stove, made wholly out of brick, can be made easily and cheaply, makes an even heat, and gives off an astonishing amount for the fuel consumed.

89. — Clothes as regulating Warmth; their Necessity, Quantity, Kinds, &c.

Apparel supplies one of man's natural wants; else he would have been created with a thick skin, covered with an abundance of hair or fur. He was obviously designed to inhabit both the frozen and the torrid zones of the equator and both poles, where, without some protection against the extremes of the heat and cold, he must freeze to death in one, and roast in the other. Clothes furnish this protection, besides enabling him, by varying its quantity, and quality, as the weather changes, greatly to promote the required uniformity of temperature. They do not generate heat, but they do retard its escape. Wrapping up ice keeps in its cold; while wrapping a hot iron keeps in its warmth.

All wear by far too much clothes. Habit is allowed to determine the amount more than Nature. The error begins in the cradle. Mothers, extra tender of infants, pile on so many clothes, night and day, as to weaken their skin.[641] From the first they are literally smothered with clothing. Besides keeping the nursery quite too warm, the babe must have on several thicknesses of clothes, and then be covered up most of the time under several thicknesses of bed-clothes, with only a small breathing-hole left. It is just as you habituate them; with this difference, that shutting in the animal heat relaxes the skin, and paves the way for those colds so injurious.[94] Extra clothing promotes, colds instead of preventing them. They should not take cold; yet of this there is little danger, because that same self-acting regulator of heat which exists in adults, exists also in them. Rely on this, and do not engender disease by extra clothing.

After they are three years old they generate animal heat very rapidly, if allowed to play. Give them the liberty of the yard, and risk their getting cold, unless they have previously been nursed to death. And this muffling up boys with comforts around their necks, in addition to neck wrappers, caps pulled down tight around their ears, warm mittens, warm over-clothes, a cart load of bed-clothes, and the like, is consummate folly. When running out and in, they will keep warm without all this fuss.

The Indian, even in colder latitudes, keeps more comfortable in the coldest weather, with only his blanket thrown loosely around his shoulders, and much of his body exposed directly to the cold, than we with a quarter of a score of thicknesses, and cotton batting to boot. We need clothing, yet should rely upon it only as a partial regulator of heat, not as our principal warming agent. Clothes, by retarding the escape of heat, cause us to require less food and breath, so that those who cannot get enough to eat, should dress extra warm, while those who can eat should dress lightly. Extra clothing also relaxes the skin, and prevents the generation of animal heat, which leaves the system colder instead of warmer. The young and robust should habituate themselves to but little clothing, even in winter, relying for warmth more on Nature and less on art; yet we should not change too suddenly. Too much is better than too little. Keep warm we must; but should augment internal heat by increased exercise and breathing.

As clothing is worn to regulate the temperature, its quantity, of course, requires to be greater in cold weather than warm; yet varying its quantity with every variation of the weather is unnecessary, for the internal heat is in the exact ratio of the external cold. This alone shows that we should rely on Nature's provision for warmth, instead of on art — should breathe and eat more as the weather becomes colder, instead of dressing warmer.

Yet invalids, and those whose circulation is defective, require such variation. As most of us now are, these changes would benefit; yet we should diminish its necessity by enhancing the internal heat.

CLEANLINESS demands a frequent change of raiment. Since perspiration brings out a great amount of corrupt and poisonous matter through the skin,[93] most of which is absorbed by the under clothes, of course they should be changed and cleansed frequently. The necessity of this will be rendered apparent by the following experiment: Taking off and rolling up your under garment, wash your body, and the unpleasant sensations consequent on putting it on again show how much corruption it has imbibed, and how repugnant it is to a clean skin. The same sensations are experienced when you return to bed, after having been up a few minutes. This also shows the importance of airing, and frequently changing the bed-clothes. None should sleep in the under garments worn day times.

FLANNEL AND SILK under clothes in cold weather are rendered advisable by the weakness of the skins of most city, and many country people; yet those who can keep warm without them should put them on later and take them off the earlier, and wear them till they can remove them without taking cold. Silk is highly extolled for comfort; yet, like flannel, retains the perspiration and effluvia. Cotton furnishes the best material for under and summer clothing.

90. — ATTIRE FOR THE HEAD, NECK, HANDS, AND FEET.

SOMETHING should obviously be worn on the head, if only to keep the hair in place, yet hardly for warmth, which the hair secures. Hats and caps keep it too warm, unless well ventilated, while chignons outrage good taste, and blunt the mind by palsying its cerebral organ, the brain,[25] but the turban is unobjectionable.

A TIGHT NECK dress is most injurious, because it retards the flow of blood to and from the head. Stocks do this, and by choking cause bronchial troubles. A tight necked dress also confines in the clothes and around the body that nauseating effluvia generated, which an open neck allows to rise and pass off. The Byronic mode of dressing the neck is preferable to all others, and advisable in those ladies who can keep warm with it, and in *all girls*.

THE BEARD of men, when allowed to grow, protects the throat, permits the escape of perspiration and effluvia, looks masculine, was not created for nought, and cannot be cut off with impunity.

THE HANDS can be kept warmer without mittens than with, for they obstruct natural warmth. Put them on late, and only in extreme cases, and warm your hands by rubbing, whipping, &c., and they will rarely ever suffer from cold.

GLOVES in summer, worn for looks, are supremely ridiculous. What! Human hands so homely that gloves must cover their deformity? and human fabrics than divine? and rat skin than human? Gloves hide the bewitching beauty of the female hand. Natural beauty surpasses artificial. Hands unadorned are adorned the more.

BARE ARMS promote health and comfort, especially while at

work, by allowing the free escape of waste matter. Children who go with bare arms will be the healthier, and feel the more comfortable.

WARM FEET are most desirable, as cold ones are most injurious. Warm feet guard the system against the ingress of disease, while more diseases enter the system through cold feet than through all other channels put together.

That old saw, "Keep the head cool and feet warm," is full of practical wisdom. In fact cold feet induce headache by a partial congestion of the brain; nor is there a greater cure for headache than rubbing, washing, soaking, and toasting the feet, because they draw off that extra rush of blood to the head which caused it to ache.

To secure due warmth in the feet, *wash and rub them often.* Few things are more promotive of health than the daily ablution of the feet. It will nearly double the health of every reader who will practise it, as well as unspeakably enhance his serenity of mind. Jefferson attributed his uniform health, even in advanced life, more to this one practice than to any other. Running in the water in summer does children good. Let all children be brought up to wash their feet every night, on retiring, in cold water. Than the prevailing idea that cold water applied to the feet is injurious, nothing is more erroneous or foolish. Is it poisonous? Warm wet feet are not the precursors of the winding-sheet, though cold wet feet often breed disease. Keep up the circulation in them, and they may be wet half the time without injury. The great evil is not in wet, but COLD feet, of which the judicious application of cold water is the greatest known preventive.

The proper dressing of the feet so as to secure the required warmth, then, becomes a matter of great importance. Reliance for keeping them warm should not be placed on shoes, stockings, and fires. The principles of fire and dress, already applied to the body,[87] apply equally to the feet. Almost exclusive reliance should be placed on vigorous *circulation*, as secured by exercise and washing, not on stockings, boots, and over-shoes. In fact, the latter generally *impair* the circulation, and thus induce coldness of the feet instead of warmth. In general, the lighter dressed the warmer, provided they have sufficient *exercise.*

Stockings are decidedly injurious, because they retain the perspiration, which invites cold. Experiment will satisfy all who try it, that feet keep warmer without than with them. Those who try it will be surprised at the result. A friend was awakened early one cold winter morning, to take some travelling conveyance which could not wait, and unable to find both his stockings, started off with but one, intending to get a pair at the first stopping-place. But finding the unstockinged foot the warmest, he postponed several days, when still finding it the warmest, he discontinued the use of the other, and has done so ever since, and says his feet are much warmer for it. All similar trials that have come to the Author's knowledge have resulted similarly. Yet it is recommended that the experiment be commenced in midsummer, and that the feet be washed daily. These views may seem strange, because contrary to custom; but try them before condemning.

Heating the feet with brick, stones, and the like, is also injurious. Warm them by walking, stamping, and the like, instead. And in riding, by far the best plan of warming them is to get out and walk or run.

GOING BAREFOOT in summer is most beneficial to children. All love it dearly, and this is Nature's warrant for its utility. The soles of their feet are furnished from birth with a thick epidermis,[91] which going barefoot renders very thick and tough, and abundantly protects them from injury, of which all poor and barefoot subjects are examples. It will not give them cold, but will prevent sickness by promoting health and circulation in the feet all through their after life.

"But how they look barefoot!" exclaims fastidious mothers. What just said of covering the hands applies equally to dressing the feet. If bare feet were fashionable, they would look no worse than bare faces or hands. The Persians esteem uncovered faces as ugly looking as we do uncovered feet; whereas, feet are quite ornamental as well as useful, and children look almost as bad with them muffled up in summer as ladies do with covered ears. Still "every one to his liking."

"But unconfined feet grow large, broad, and homely," it is further objected. Then go to China and done with it. As though cramping the feet, and preventing their natural development, increased their beauty! As though you could improve on Nature, and correct her deformities by art! Let Nature "have her per-

feet work," yet you who choose may warp and cramp your feet
to your liking.

LARGE SHOES, and "broad across the soles," are most desirable
during growth, as narrow soles and cramped feet are most injurious. Tight shoes and boots interrupt pedal circulation for
the after life, and thus induce other and more aggravated ailments. Give feet "the largest liberty."

CORNS, always consequent on wearing too tight boots or shoes,
should warn all to wear those which neither pinch nor pain. To
cure them, wash them often in cold water, keep them well pared
down with a sharp razor, put a wet cloth on them at night,
burn up all pinching boots and shoes, and wear a piece of deer-
skin over them, with a hole cut in it, just where the corn comes.

SECTION VI.

THE SKIN, PERSPIRATION, ETC.

91. — THE STRUCTURE AND OFFICES OF THE SKIN.

PROTECTION against all prospective evils and dangers, is one of
Nature's first laws. The body must be guarded at all points.
Its extremely delicate organs and functions must not be interrupted or interfered with, on pain of death. Some envelope, hard
to break through, some fender to resist all aggressions, must en-
case its entire surface. Yet it must be so flexible as to allow
perfect freedom of action.

FOREWARNING of transpiring injury is also a necessity.[20] We
must be made to *shrink back* from whatever is impairing our
organism, besides learning to avoid it ever afterwards.

EXCRETION must be amply prearranged. The waste and
poisonous ingredients generated by this life process must be
allowed to escape.

THE SKIN effects all these, and several other like ends. It
consists of a tough, yet exceedingly thin membrane, enveloping
the entire surface of the body, in structure quite like the mucous
membrane which lines the inside of the alimentary canal. It is
composed of three coatings — the cuticle, or epidermis, a horny,
insensible over coat, such as we see often rubbed up by bruises,
and raised in blisters. This outside skin is thin over the joints,

so as not to obstruct their motion, but thick in the palms of the hands and soles of the feet, even from birth — a wise provision indeed. The middle coating, called rete mucosum, contains that coloring matter which paints the various races their various colors — the African, black, for example. The cutis, dermis, or true skin, is the great instrumentality of sensation, absorption, and exhalation.

Its MODE of producing sensation and touch is illustrated in the engraving of one of the papillæ, or extremities of the nerves, which originate in the brain, and after traversing and ramifying throughout the entire body, finally terminate in an infinitesimal network of nerves at the skin.

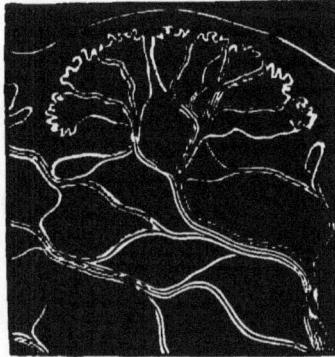

No. 22. — PAPILLA OF THE SKIN. AFTER GERBER.

LITTLE PORES fill this cutis perfectly full, about three thousand being contained in every square inch. It is also filled with two sets of capillary nerves and blood-vessels, the latter being especially numerous here so as to support the former, and thus create sensation. Indeed, it is probably composed mainly by these tissues, and its innumerable pores are doubtless formed by their interweaving. Through these pores the waste water, and much of the excrementitious matter engendered during the vital process, escapes; causing the perspiration to be sensible or insensible, according as it is more or less copious.

SENSIBLE perspiration causes sweat to ooze out and stand in drops, or run down in streams, from all parts of the body, as when we take violent exercise in hot weather, drink copiously of warm water, and the like.

INSENSIBLE PERSPIRATION is perpetually escaping from all parts of the skin, and rendered plainly perceptible by inserting the hand in a glass tumbler turned bottom upwards, or by laying the hand on glass, or even drawing the finger slowly across it.

THE REGULATION of animal heat is also effected in part by this perspiration. In hot weather our internal heat is sometimes so excessive that, unless dissipated somehow, it would melt the fat, and cause death. This surplus is carried off by perspiration thus. All bodies absorb heat when passing from a dense medium to one more rare. Hence water, in passing into steam, takes up a great amount of heat, which it again gives off in returning back to water, on the well-known chemical principle that all bodies give off heat when passing from a rarer medium to a denser. Here, again, water becomes a porter. An excess of heat aids the conversion of water into steam, which then takes up. this surplus heat, carries it out of the system, and gives it off again while condensing back to water — a self-acting and most efficacious arrangement for effecting an indispensable end.

This explains why it is that men can remain in ovens heated hot enough to cook meat, and long enough to bake it, without destroying life. They *sweat out* the surplus heat, or else their own flesh would also bake. .

PERSPIRATION must needs, and does perform some most important end in the animal economy. These forty ounces of water do not steam forth perpetually from the system alone, but bring along out with them much of the waste matter engendered by the vital process. This process is one of perpetual *waste*. It is estimated that all the matter in the system, at any given time, becomes useless, because its vitality is "used up," is carried off, and its place re-supplied by foreign substances every seven years. Probably half that time would be nearer the fact. Of course, if this matter were allowed to remain just where it is created, the system would soon become as filthy as the Augean stables. To prevent this, it is carried off as fast as it is manufactured.

How? By that same aqueous porter which brought it. As the blood brings a load of oxygen, and, as soon as it is unloaded, takes on the carbonic acid created by the combustion of that oxygen; [86] so after the water in the blood has carried out and deposited its freight of fresh muscle, nerve, &c., it takes on another freight of waste matter, and issues forth out of the system in the form of steam.

But for some such expulsive principle, this water would lay inert in the system. Force is necessary to expel it, and doubly so to expel its accompanying corruption. Now does not this conversion of water into steam, which necessarily manufactures force, create the force required to expel both the water and its freight?

• At all events, out it comes, and drags along out with it *more than half* of the refuse of all we eat, drink, and take into the system. Though the kidneys, bowels, and lungs help to evacuate this waste matter; yet the skin is the great sluice-way for this excrementitious egress — that scavenger of life which collects up all the leavings and filth out of the highways and byways of the city of life, and empties them on through this gateway. Hence the

92. — IMPORTANCE OF KEEPING THE PORES OF THE SKIN OPEN.

When these pores are closed, this waste matter is shut within the system, to clog the organs of life on the one hand, and breed disease on the other; for, be it remembered, that most of this waste matter, like carbonic acid, is both *poisonous*[86] and in the way. It *must* escape, or extinguish life. Woe to that system which retains it within its borders!

Combe ably enforces this point as follows: —

"In tracing the connection between suppressed perspiration and the production of individual diseases, we shall find that those organs which possess some similarity of function sympathize most closely with each other. Thus the skin, the bowels, the lungs, the liver, and the kidneys sympathize readily, because they have all the common office of throwing waste matter out of the system, each in a way peculiar to its own structure; so that, if the exhalation from the skin, for example, be stopped by long exposure to cold, the large quantity of waste matter which it was charged to excrete, and which in itself is hurtful to the system, will most probably be thrown upon one or other of the above-named organs, whose function will consequently become excited; and if any of them, from constitutional or accidental causes, be already weaker than the rest, as often happens, its health will naturally be the first to suffer. In this way, the bowels become irritated in one individual, and occasion bowel complaint; while in another, it is the lungs which become affected, giving rise to catarrh or common cold, or perhaps even to inflammation. When, on the other hand, all these organs are in a state of vigorous health, a temporary increase of function takes place in them, and relieves the system, without leading to any local disorder; and the skin itself speedily resumes its activity, and restores the balance among them.

"One of the most obvious illustrations of this reciprocity of action is afforded by any convivial company, seated in a warm room in a cold evening. The heat of the room, the food and wine, and the excitement of the moment, stimulate the skin, cause an afflux of blood to the surface, and increase in a high degree the flow of the insensible perspiration; which thus, while the heat continues, carries off an undue share of the fluids of the body, and leaves the kidneys almost at rest. But the moment the company goes into the cold external air, a sudden reversal of operations takes place, the cold chills the surface, stops the perspiration, and directs the current of the blood towards the internal organs, which presently become excited — and, under this excitation, the kidneys, for example, will in a few minutes secrete as much of their peculiar fluid, as they did in as many of the preceding hours. The reverse of this again, is common in diseases obstructing the secretion from the kidneys; for the perspiration from the skin is then altered in quantity and quality, and acquires much of the peculiar smell of the urinary fluid.

"When the lungs are weak, and their lining membrane is habitually relaxed, and secretes an unusual amount of mucus from its surface, the mass thrown inwards upon the lungs by cold applied to the skin, increases that secretion to a high degree. Were this secretion to accumulate, it would soon fill up the air-cells of the lungs, and cause suffocation; but to obviate this danger, the Creator has so constituted the lungs, that accumulated mucus, or any foreign body coming in contact with them, excites the convulsive effort called coughing, by which a violent and rapid expiration takes place, with a force sufficient to hurry the mucus or other foreign body along with it; just as peas are discharged by boys with much force through short tubes by a sudden effort of blowing. Thus, a check given to perspiration, by diminishing the quantity of blood previously circulating on the surface, naturally leads very often to increased expectoration and cough, or, in other words, to common cold.

"The lungs excrete, as already noticed, and as we shall afterwards more fully see, a large proportion of waste materials from the system; and the kidneys, the liver, and the bowels, have in so far a similar office. In consequence of this alliance with the skin, these parts are more intimately connected with each other in healthy and diseased action than with other organs. But it is a general law, that whenever an organ is unusually delicate, it will be affected by any cause of disease more easily than those which are sound: so that, if the nervous system, for example, be weaker than other parts, a chill will be more likely to disturb its health than that of the lungs, which are supposed, in this instance, to be constitutionally stronger; or, if the muscular and fibrous organizations be unusually susceptible of disturbance, either from previous illness or from natural predisposition, they will be the first to suffer, and rheumatism may ensue; and so on. And hence the utility to the physician of an intimate acquaintance with the previous habits and constitutions of his patients, and the advantage of adapting the remedies to the nature of the cause, when it can be discovered, as well as to the disease itself. A bowel complaint, for instance, may arise from overeating as well as from a check to perspiration; but although the thing to be cured is the same, the MEANS of cure ought obviously to be different. In the one instance, an emetic or laxative to carry off the offending cause, and in the other a diaphoretic to open the skin, will be the most rational and efficacious remedies. Facts like these expose well the glaring ignorance and effrontery of the quack, who affirms that his one remedy will cure every form of disease. Were the public not equally ignorant with himself, their credulity would cease to afford to his presumption the rich field in which it now revels.

"The close sympathy between the skin and the stomach and bowels has often been noticed, and it is now well understood that most of the obstinate eruptions which appear on the face and rest of the surface, owe their origin to disorders of the digestive organs, and are most successfully cured by treatment directed to the internal disease. Even among the lower animals, the sympathy between the two is so marked as to have arrested attention. Thus, in speaking of the horse, Delabere Blaine says, 'By a well-known consent of parts between the skin and alimentary canal in general, but between the first passages and the stomach in particular, it follows, in almost every instance, that when one of these becomes affected, the other takes on a sympathetic derangement also, and the condition is then morbid throughout. From close observation and the accumulation of numerous facts, I am disposed to think, that so perfect is this sympathetic consent between these two distant parts or organs, that they change the order of attack as circumstances occur. Thus, when the skin is primarily affected, the stomach becomes secondarily so, and vice versa,' so that 'a sudden check to the natural or acquired heat of the body, particularly if aggravated by the evaporation of a perspiring state,' as often brings on disease of some internal organ, as if the cause were applied to the organ itself.

"In noticing this connection between the suppression of perspiration and the appearance of internal disease, I do not mean to affirm that the effect is produced by the physical transference of the suppressed exhalation to the internal organ. In many instances the chief impression seems to be made on the nervous system; and the manner in which it gives rise to the resulting disease is often extremely obscure. Our knowledge of the animal functions is, indeed, still so imperfect, that we daily meet with many occurrences of which no explanation can be given. But it is nevertheless of high utility to make known the fact, that a connection does exist between two orders of phenomena, as it calls attention to their more accurate observation, and leads to the adoption of useful practical rules, even when their mode of operation is not understood. Nothing, indeed, can be more delusive than the rash application of merely physical laws to the explanation of the phenomena of living beings. Vitality is a principle superior to, and in continual warfare with, the laws which regulate the actions of inanimate bodies; and it is only after life has become extinct that these laws regain the mastery, and lead to the rapid decomposition of the animal machine. In studying the functions of the human body, therefore, we must be careful not to hurry to conclusions, before taking time to examine the influence of the vital principle in modifying the expected results.

" It is in consequence of the sympathy and reciprocity of action existing between the skin and the internal organs that burns and even scalds of no very great extent prove fatal, by inducing internal, generally intestinal, inflammation. By disordering or disorganizing a large nervous and exhaling surface, an extensive burn causes not only a violent nervous commotion, but a continued partial suspension of an important excretion ; and, when death ensues at some distance of time, it is almost always in consequence of inflammation being excited in the bowels or sympathizing organs. So intimate, indeed, is this connection, that some surgeons of great experience, such as the late Baron Dupuytren, of the

Hotel Dieu, while they point to internal inflammation as in such cases the general cause of death, doubt if recovery ever takes place, when more than one eighth of the surface of the body is severely burnt. And whether this estimate be correct or not, the facts from which it is drawn clearly demonstrate the importance of the relation subsisting betwixt the skin and the other excreting organs.

"In some constitutions, a singularly enough sympathy exists between the skin and the bowels. Dr. A. T. Thomson, in his work on Materia Medica (p. 42), mentions that he is acquainted with a clergyman who cannot bear the skin to be sponged with vinegar and water, or any diluted acid, without suffering spasm and violent griping of the bowels. The reverse operation of this sympathy is exemplified in the frequent production of nettle-rash and other eruptions on the skin, by shell-fish and other substances taken into the stomach. Dr. Thomson tells us that the late Dr. Gregory could not eat the smallest portion of the white of an egg, without experiencing an attack of an eruption like nettle-rash. According to the same author, even strawberries have been known to cause fainting, followed by a petechial efflorescence of the skin.

" We have seen that the insensible perspiration removes from the system, without trouble and without consciousness, a large quantity of useless materials, and at the same time keeps the skin soft and moist, and thereby fits it for the performance of its functions as the organ of an external sense. In addition to these purposes, the Creator has, in his omniscience and foresight, and with that regard to simplicity of means which betokens a profoundness of thought inconceivable to us, superadded another, scarcely less important, and which is in some degree implied in the former; I mean the proper regulation of the bodily heat. It is well known that, in the polar regions and in the torrid zone, under every variety of circumstances, the human body retains nearly the same temperature, however different may be that of the air by which it is surrounded. This is a property peculiar to life, and, in consequence of it, even vegetables have a power of modifying their own temperature, though in a much more limited degree. Without this power of adaptation, it is obvious that man must have been chained for life to the climate which gave him birth, and even then have suffered constantly from the change of seasons; whereas, by possessing it, he can retain life in a temperature sufficiently cold to freeze mercury, and is able for a time to sustain, unharmed, a heat more than sufficient to boil water, or even to bake meat. Witness the wintering of Captain Parry and his companions in the Polar Regions; and the experiments of Blagden, Sir Joseph Banks, and others, who remained for many minutes in a room heated to 260°, or about 50° above the temperature of boiling water. The chief agents in this wonderful adaptation of man to his external situation are undoubtedly the skin and the lungs, in both of which the power is intimately connected with the condition of their respective exhalations. But it is of the skin alone, as an agent in reducing animal heat, that we are at present to speak.

"The sources of animal heat are not yet demonstrably ascertained; but that it is constantly generated and constantly expended has been long known ; and if any considerable disproportion occurs between these processes, it is at the immediate risk of health. During repose or passive exercise, such as riding in a carriage or sailing, the surplus heat is readily carried off by the insensible perspiration from the lungs and skin, and by the contact of the colder air; but when the amount of heat generated is increased, as during active exercise, an increased expenditure becomes immediately necessary."

93.— COLDS CAUSE MOST DISEASES.

COLDS consist in *suppressed perspiration;* nothing else, and are occasioned thus: Cold always contracts. This is an established law of things. Hence a sudden change of the temperature of the skin from heat to cold causes its pores to contract; many of them to close. This shows why we perspire so little in obdurate colds and fevers. The injury they inflict arises mainly from their shutting up this waste matter in the system. And the reason why, during colds, the lungs, nose, &c., discharge copiously a thick, yellow phlegm, is, that this corruption, shut in by the closing of these pores, yet being hostile to life, is carried to the lungs, and converted into phlegm, to the kidneys, bowels, and even to the brain, and discharged through the nose and all the other outlets; and hence that increase of all these excretions as mentioned by Combe.

Many of us know, by experience, that these cold customers are exceedingly troublesome. How dull, feverish, restless, and miserable they render us, and how full of aches and pains? They are the principal cause of teeth-aches. If you have a bad tooth, it rarely troubles you except after you have taken a cold; and the way to cure this painful malady is, to cure that cold which caused it.

FEVERS, too, are mainly the results of colds. That sand bar of health, the fever and ague, always supervenes on colds. Avoid them, and you escape it. And those neighborhood epidemics which sweep over city and country, affecting nearly all, prostrating many, and cutting off more or less in the midst of life, are generally only colds, and prevail only because certain states of the atmosphere have conspired to occasion colds, and these the choleras, influenzas, or other distempers. Avoid these colds, and these plagues will pass you by as those of Egypt did the Israelites. None can have a cold without having a fever, for colds cause fevers. Though fevers may be caused by other violations of the laws of health, yet colds are always their usher. Hence the adage, "Stuff a cold and starve a fever," is erroneous.

Bilious, and kindred attacks always supervene on colds, generally commencing with chills, just as colds do; and though the stomach is also disabled, yet, but for the cold, it would not have given out. It may have been previously foul, and have thus generated a great amount of corruption, which, however, open pores would have continued to carry off; whereas, this outlet closed, it is retained, accumulates, obstructs, poisons, and at length prostrates, perhaps destroys, life. *Colds cause more than half the diseases of all climates*, except those created by impaired digestion. Indeed, even when the latter breeds disease perpetually, open pores carry it off as continually, so that little damage is done. But shut these pores, and beside the waste matter retained, all that corruption engendered by imperfection in any of the vital organs, is also shut in to poison and destroy. Keep clear of colds and you will escape diseases, because other causes will rarely be sufficient to induce them. As five-eighths of the waste matter of the vital process escapes through the skin, why should not the closing of this avenue occasion that proportion of the diseases prevalent? Let those who think this attributes more diseases to colds than really belong to them, note the universal fact, that they always precede and induce consumption, — that great mower of human life. Did you ever know a consumptive patient whose attack did not set in after a terrible cold? Consumption is only a cold protracted and aggravated. No matter how predisposed, hereditarily or practically, persons may be to consumption, they will never have it till they take a "heavy cold." Keep clear of these precursors and ushers of this disease, and your life is insured against the disease itself. And those thus predisposed should, in a special manner, guard against contracting colds, and when taken, break them up as *quickly as possible*, for their *life* depends upon the issue.

CHILDREN rarely, if ever, sicken till they get *cold*. Of the correctness of this assertion, let observation be the test. All colds do not make them down sick, yet they never become sick till they have taken cold. Keeping them from the latter guarantees them against sickness. Even when their disease appears to be seated in the stomach, or head, or other organs, its origin will generally be found in suppressed perspiration, as shown in the extract from Combe. All cramps and lung difficulties are, of course, the direct products of colds. So are most bowel complaints, and brain fevers, influenzas, and almost all complaints incident to childhood. Keep the young from taking colds, or break up all colds as soon as contracted, and they will never be sick, nor die, except of old age.

RHEUMATIC affections also prove and illustrate our doctrine. It is submitted to all thus afflicted, be it more or less, whether these pains in their joints, muscles, and bones, are not doubled and re-doubled every time you take cold. The same holds true of the headache — generally a rheumatic affection of the brain.

A PROMISING YOUTH, in East Bradford, Mass., took a most violent cold, which induced a correspondingly violent fever, and hurried him into his grave. Another brother, while attending the funeral of this one, also took a terrible cold, which in a few days swept him also into eternity. A sister, exhaused by watching this brother, also took a very severe cold while attending his funeral, and, in consequence, was soon bereft of reason, and then attacked with a scorching fever, of which she died in about a week. All three deaths were distinctly traceable to colds. Three or four other members of this self-afflicted family were also sick simultaneously, of colds, the weather at the time of these funerals being particularly unfavorable.

Reader, trace the sickness around you back and up to its cause, and you will be surprised to find colds the author of nine cases in every ten. Recall your own ailings, and see if this principle does not explain their origin.

But why particularize further? Do not the experiences of most, and the observations of all, prove that colds are the chief causes of disease? And the distinctions made by physicians between different forms of fever, and other diseases, are not founded in the *nature* of such diseases, but are only different modes of attack and manifestation of the same disease — the closing of the pores.

THEIR PREVENTION, therefore, becomes as important as they are injurious. To consumptive subjects it is life, as these colds are death. How, then, can they be prevented?

BY KEEPING THE SKIN ACTIVE. Animal heat abounds at the surface so as to fortify it against those changes of temperature which affect the skin mainly. Hence the great accumulation of blood-vessels at the surface. Probably no part, the head possibly excepted, is as abundantly supplied with them as the skin. Hence its warmth. Now vigorous surface circulation will keep these pores so warm as to resist the closing action of the external cold. In such cases these atmospheric changes do no evil. They close the pores only where the surface circulation has become impaired. Keep that vigorous, and it will ward off all colds, extreme cases of exposure possibly excepted. Whatever, therefore, tends to promote the activity of the skin, thereby fortifies the system against colds. The two means of promoting such action, are the promotion of circulation in general, and the external application of friction and water.

94. — BATHS, AND THEIR MODES OF APPLICATION.

FREQUENT ABLUTION of the entire person effectually fortifies the system against colds. How surprising an amount of scurf and dried skin are taken off by an occasional hot bath and friction! Right bathing will stave off consumption, no matter how great the hereditary predisposition. Astor's wealth would not compensate for a discontinuance of this practice, because colds, with all their evils, would soon follow. And any reader not accustomed to frequent bathing, would actually find a greater prize in its judicious application than if he should inherit the fortune of all the Rothschilds; because, by removing diseases and their causes — obstructions — as well as prolonging life, it will promote general enjoyment more than all the wealth of the world! Its habitual use renders one *cold proof*, and keeps both hereditary and acquired predispositions to disease at bay, as well as doubles and trebles ability to endure both physical and mental exertion. Even as a luxury, it is equalled only by food and sleep. Its pleasure is the greater the colder the weather, because of the greater the reaction and subsequent delightful glow. Still, it must be rightly managed, else it results in evil proportionate to its good, and should never be taken except where there is sufficient energy in the system to produce a delightful *reaction and subsequent glow* — these sure signs and concomitants of its utility. A. Combe remarks on this point as follows : —

"For GENERAL use, the tepid or warm bath seems to me much more suitable than the cold bath, especially in winter, and for those who are not robust and full of animal heat. Where the constitution is not sufficiently vigorous to secure reaction after the cold bath, as indicated by a warm glow over the surface,'its use inevitably does harm. A vast number of persons are in this condition; while, on the contrary, there are few indeed who did not derive evident advantage from the regular use of the tepid bath, and still fewer who are hurt by it.

"Where the health is good, and the bodily powers are sufficiently vigorous, the cold bath during summer, and the shower bath in winter, may serve every purpose required from them. But it should never be forgotten, that they are too powerful in their agency to be used by EVERY ONE, especially in cold weather. In proportion as cold bathing is influential in the restoration of health when judiciously used, it is hurtful when resorted to without discrimination; and invalids, therefore, ought never to have recourse to it without the sanction of their professional advisers.

"Even where cold bathing is likely to be of service, when judiciously employed, much mischief often results from prolonging the immersion too long, or from resorting to it when the vital powers are too languid to admit of the necessary reaction — before breakfast, for example, or after fatigue. For this reason, many persons derive much benefit from bathing early in the forenoon, who, when they bathe in the morning before taking any sustenance, do not speedily recover their natural heat and elasticity of feeling.

"For those who are not robust, daily sponging of the body with cold water and vinegar, or with salt water, is the best substitute for the cold bath, and may be resorted to with safety and advantage in most states of the system; especially when care is taken to excite in the surface, by subsequent friction with the flesh-brush or hair-glove, the healthy glow of reaction. It then becomes an excellent preservative from the effects of changeable weather. When, however, a continued sensation of coldness or chill is perceptible over the body, sponging ought not to be persisted in: dry friction, aided by the tepid bath, is then greatly preferable, and often proves highly serviceable in keeping up the due action of the skin.

"For habitual use, the tepid or warm bath is certainly the safest and most valuable, especially during the autumn, winter, and spring, and for invalids. A temperature ranging from 85° to 98°, according to the state of the individual, is the most suitable; and the duration of the immersion may vary from fifteen minutes to an hour or more, according to circumstances. As a general rule, the water ought to be warm enough to feel pleasant without giving a positive sensation of heat; the degree at which this happens varies considerably, according to the constitution and to the state of health at the time. Sometimes, when the generation of animal heat is great, a bath at 95° will be felt disagreeably warm and relaxing; while, at another time, when the animal heat is produced in deficient quantity, the same temperature will cause a chilly sensation. The rule, then, is to avoid equally the positive impressions of heat and cold, and to seek the agreeable medium. A bath of the latter description is the reverse of relaxing; it gives a cheerful tone and activity to all the functions, and may be used every day, or on alternate days, for fifteen or twenty minutes, with much advantage.

"A person of sound health and strength may take a bath at any time, except immediately after meals. But the BEST time for valetudinarians is in the forenoon or evening, two or three hours after a moderate meal, when the system is invigorated by food, but not oppressed by the labor of digestion. When the bath is delayed till five or six hours after eating, delicate people sometimes become faint under its operation, and, from the absence of reaction, are rather weakened by the relaxation it then induces. As a general rule, active exertion ought to be avoided for an hour or two after using the warm or tepid bath; and, unless we wish to induce perspiration, it ought not to be taken immediately before going to bed; or if it is, it ought to be merely tepid, and not of too long duration.

"These rules apply of course only to persons in an ordinary state of health. If organic disease, headache, feverishness, constipation, or other ailment exist, bathing ought never to be employed without medical advice. When the stomach is disordered by bile, it also generally disagrees. But that it is a safe and valuable preservative of health in ordinary circumstances, and an active remedy in disease, is most certain. Instead of being dangerous by causing liability to cold, it is, when well managed, so much the reverse, that the author of these pages has used it much and successfully for the express purpose of diminishing such liability, both in himself and in others in whom the chest is delicate. In his own instance, in particular, he is conscious of having derived much advantage from its regular employment, especially in the colder months of the year, during which he has uniformly found himself most effectually strengthened against the impression of cold, by repeating the bath at shorter intervals than usual.

"In many manufactories, where warm water is always obtainable, it would be of very great advantage to have a few baths erected for the use of the operatives. Not only would these be useful in promoting health and cleanliness, but they would, by their refreshing and soothing influence, diminish the craving for stimulus which leads so many to the gin-shop; and, at the same time, calm the irritability of mind so apt to be induced by excessive labor. Where the trade is dirty, as many trades necessarily are, it is needless to say how conducive to health and comfort a tepid bath would be on quitting it for the day.

"On the Continent, the vapor and hot-air bath are had recourse to both as a means of health and in the cure of disease, to a vastly greater extent than they are in this country. Their use is attended by the very best effects, particularly in chronic ailments, and where the water-bath is felt to be oppressive by its weight; and there can be no question that their action is chiefly on the skin, and through its medium on the nervous system. As a means of determining the blood to the surface, promoting cutaneous exhalation, and equalizing the circulation, they are second to no remedy now in use; and consequently, in a variety of affections which the encouragement of these processes is calculated to relieve, they may be employed with every prospect of advantage. The prevalent fear of catching cold, which deters many from using the vapor-bath, even more than from warm bathing, is founded on a false analogy between its effects and those of profuse perspiration from exercise or illness. The latter weakens the body, and by diminishing the power of reaction, renders it susceptible of injury from sudden changes of temperature. But the effect of the vapor-bath properly administered is very different. When not too warm or too long continued, it increases instead of exhausting the strength, and, by exciting the vital action of the skin, gives rise to a power of reaction which enables it to resist cold better than before. This I have heard many patients remark; and the fact is well exemplified in Russia and the North of Europe, where, in the depth of winter, it is not uncommon for the natives to rush out of a vapor-bath and roll themselves in the snow, and be refreshed by doing so; whereas, were they to attempt such a practice after severe perspiration from exercise, they would inevitably suffer. It is the previous stimulus given to the skin by the vapor-bath which is the real safeguard against the coldness of the snow.

"Common experience affords another illustration of the same principle. If, in a cold winter day, we chance to sit for some time in a room imperfectly warmed, and feel in consequence a sensation of chilliness over the body, we are much more likely to catch cold on going out, than if we had been sitting in a room comfortably warm. In the latter case, the cutaneous circulation and nervous action go on vigorously; heat is freely generated, and the vital action of the skin is in its full force. The change to a lower temperature, if accompanied with exercise to keep up vitality, is then felt to be bracing and stimulating rather than disagreeable. But it is widely different when the surface is already chilled before going out. The vitality of the skin being diminished, reaction cannot follow additional exposure; the circulation leaves the surface and becomes still more internal; and if weakness exist in the throat or chest, cold is the almost certain result. Many suffer from ignorance of this principle.

"The vapor-bath is thus calculated to be extensively useful, both as a preservative and as a remedial agent. Many a cold and many a rheumatic attack, arising from checked perspiration or long exposure to the weather, might be nipped in the bud by its timely use. In chronic affections, not only of the skin itself, but of the internal organs with which the skin most closely sympathizes, as the stomach and intestines, the judicious application of the vapor-bath is productive of great relief. Even in chronic pulmonary complaints, it is, according to the continental physicians, not only safe, but very serviceable; particularly in those affections of the mucous membrane which resemble consumption in so many of their symptoms. Like all powerful remedies, however, the vapor-bath must be administered with proper regard to the condition and circumstances of the individual; and care must be taken to have the feet sufficiently warm during its use. If, from an irregular distribution of the steam, the feet be left cold, headache and flushing are almost sure to follow."

THE HAND bath is preferable to all others, because it is more easily applied; requires much bodily exertion, which facilitates the required reaction; and can be discontinued the instant a

chilly sensation begins to supervene, beyond which no bath should
ever be continued a single moment. Salt, vinegar, and other
stimulants added to the water, facilitate this reaction, by exciting
the skin, as does also sea-bathing, which, under certain circumstances, is most excellent.

95. — THE CURE OF COLDS BY PERSPIRATION ; GLASS-BLOWERS.

OPENING THE PORES, in the closing of which colds consist, can
be effected in part by washing and rubbing, but *perspiration*
forces them open more effectually than probably any other means
whatever.   Indeed it is the great antidote of colds and their
dread array of consequences.   It is immaterial what induces this
perspiration so that it is copious, and does not eventuate in another cold.   Where the patient is able to exercise sufficiently to
burst open these pores, whether he takes this exercise out of
doors or in a warm or cold atmosphere, is not material so that he
induces it.   In short, get into a dripping SWEAT, and then cool
off without contracting more cold, and you will drive it off, as
well as feel many fold better.

Where colds are taken in their incipient stages, before they
have prostrated the system, the best means of breaking them up
is to drink copiously of water, warm or cold, or of warm lemonade, or of currant jelly and warm water, or warm composition tea,
which is excellent to start perspiration, and then work right hard,
almost violently, meanwhile pouring down one or another of these
drinks by the quart.   Do not overdo so as completely to exhaust,
but so as to secure profuse perspiration.   This, together with the
water, which, if taken in quantities, *must* have some exit, will re-
open these closed pores, and destroy the disease.   Warm herb
teas will fill the place of water, yet are no better in their effects,
and less liable to be taken, on account of their bitterness.

SOAKING THE FEET in hot water, and then toasting them on retiring, meanwhile drinking copiously as above directed, and then
covering up extra warm ; or even the extra drinking and covering
will answer the same purpose ; yet care must be taken to keep the
extra clothes on, so as not to contract a new cold — the principal
evil attendant on this simple and effectual cure.   How many of
us, while young, cured our cold thus?   But day time is best.   Eat
little or no breakfast, but drink copiously of cold water for an

hour or two after rising, and provided you can endure it, exercise vigorously, and then return to bed, cover up warm, and sweat till your hands begin to shrivel. Sleep if you can. On rising, wash all over in warm saleratus water, rub dry and briskly, and keep in a gentle perspiration all day by exercise. Or eat little breakfast, and begin to drink and exercise about eleven in the forenoon, or even later, and pursue the same course, omitting dinner, and eat only a light supper, or at least a light dinner and very light supper, and retire early, or as soon after you have done exercise as possible, so as not to renew your cold.

THE WARM BATH, followed by friction and exercise, is also most excellent, and will generally prove efficacious. Yet here, too, care must be taken to guard against renewed colds — not by staying in the house, or muffling up, but by *exercise* — the very best means of inducing perspiration in the world, because the most natural.

THE WET SHEET is another excellent method, especially for those who are not able to exercise sufficiently to get up the required perspiration. Whatever secures copious perspiration breaks up cold, besides unloading the system of its obstructions and poisons. Evacuating the bowels, especially by injections, will facilitate, yet is not indispensable. Vomiting, especially by drinking warm water, just at the lukewarm, sickening temperature, will render essential service. Hot bricks wrapped in wet cloths, and laid at the feet; sitting in a tub of right hot water, covered over with a bed-quilt to keep in the heat and steam; a rum sweat, produced by burning alcohol under a chair on which the patient sits, covered around the neck by a quilt; anything, everything which induces a profuse perspiration will rout these disease-breeders.

THE TURKISH BATH, rightly administered, is one of the best of all the baths, and will break up colds, chronic rheumatism, &c., and make one feel like a new being. It should be much more generally patronized than it is. For ladies, it is unrivalled, relieving their obstructions, nervousness, &c., remarkably.

GLASS-BLOWERS furnish an excellent illustration of routing colds by inducing perspiration. Obliged to labor excessively hard, and around a furnace so extremely hot as to keep the material at a white heat, they of course sweat profusely, all their clothes being often wringing wet.   Yet the sides of the building must be open to the wind, else they could not endure the heat an hour.   And they go from their furnaces to their houses while thus perspiring, and hence often take severe colds one day, which, however, they generally sweat out the next, so that these repeated colds make but a short stay, and do but little damage; simply because they expel them by inducing copious perspiration. This simple fact furnishes a practical illustration of the true method of curing colds, of great value.

SPONTANEOUS perspiration is by far the best.   Children often sweat freely while asleep, awaking only to call for water.   This is a most favorable symptom; and the desired water should be freely administered till they wake up, when they should be washed off in saleratus water under bed-clothes, followed by friction and brisk play, so as to keep it up.   Yet care should be taken not to contract additional cold.

In fine, to break up colds, *start the sweat*, by what means it matters little, so that it is copious, protracted, and not followed by more cold.

SECTION VII.

SLEEP; ITS NECESSITY, OFFICE, AMOUNT, TIME, PROMOTION, ETC.

96. — INDISPENSABILITY, UNIVERSALITY, AND OFFICE OF SLEEP.

ALL THAT LIVES, sleeps.   All animals, from snail to man, all fish, fowls, and insects, sleep.   Even all vegetables and trees sleep profoundly during winter, only to awaken with spring to renew their two great works, growth and reproduction; though the sleep of annuals is death.   Dormancy is one of the attendants and even functions of life.

A SLEEPING INSTINCT accompanies all life, which, at about equidistant intervals, *compels* not rest merely, but a suspension of consciousness in sleep proper.   Rest is good, but insufficient without sleep.   It precedes and accompanies sleep, but rest is one thing, and sleep quite another; sleep being more than rest.

A Scotchman in Boston, in 1843, claimed, no doubt sincerely, to have slept but once in seven years, yet was seen to assume an easy posture, close his eyes, nod, and appear, for all the world, just as others do when they doze.

LOVE of sleep is quite as strong an instinct as love of food.[43] Those denied both a given length of time will starve rather than keep awake any longer in further search of food. This proves that sleeping is quite as important as eating.[40] Soldiers, wearied with long marches, *will have* sleep, though they know that, in stopping to take it, they will be taken prisoners, and *put to death*. In battle, with balls flying all around them, they must still sleep, despite the danger thereby incurred.

DORMITORIES occupy as much, and constitute as necessary, a part of our houses as both kitchen and parlor. Men provide for sleeping quite as much as for eating; that is, all make absolute provision for both, and accordingly, by common consent, suspend work to obtain it.

THE OFFICE of sleep must therefore be as absolutely necessary as this demand for it is both imperious and universal. *Precisely* what it accomplishes science has not yet declared, yet it probably both reoxygenates the blood, and accomplishes that *assimilation* and appropriation of food which renews the organism, ready for another effort. It is to life what re-loading a discharged gun is to its next discharge, — its *sine qua non*. This view is supported by these two facts, that we *breathe* more and deeper while asleep than ordinarily while awake, and that we *grow* during sleep, being nearly half an inch *taller* after than before a sound night's sleep, and everywhere plumper and larger, as well as by the fact that growing children and youth sleep the most and most soundly, while old people sleep the less, and less soundly; their sleep being more like an insane stupor than sweet sleep proper. All can observe that, just as they begin to go to sleep, they fill their lungs fuller, and empty them farther than before; which snoring also illustrates. .

CORRUPT MATTER is cast off the most rapidly during sleep, as is evinced by the fetid, nauseating smell of bed-rooms and bed-clothes in the morning, and of all dark bed-rooms. It is awful, and re-enforces their complete ventilation most effectually.[45]

THE LUXURY of sound sleep is also one of the greatest proffered by their Good Father to man and beast. Though unconscious, yet we really *enjoy* a good sleep much more than "a square meal." None should allow business, or anything, to curtail this luxury, and parents should promote it in children, instead of "drumming them out of bed early." Indeed, the best way to do the greatest day's work possible, is to get a complete sleep the night before.

The RESTORATIVE and invigorating effects of sleep are indeed a perpetual marvel. How refreshed it renders us in the morning, after being so tired the night before? How wonderfully a five minutes' nap sometimes enlivens and strengthens the system, at least equalling a hearty meal in resupplying vitality. Work away with the head, or hands, or both, if you will, just as long as you can sleep well, but stop working as soon as your sleep departs, or you will break down, or else become insane. Keeping well slept out and rested up, will add incalculably to your capacity to enjoy, endure, and accomplish ; while promoting sleep, promotes all the other life functions. It completes the supply of vitality, probably by *appropriating* all its material to their respective uses.

97. — Its Amount, Duration, Best Time, Promotion, &c.

GREAT WORKERS are always correspondingly great *sleepers.* Not that they always sleep very long, but always very *soundly.* To cut short the full time required for sleep, is to cut short one's *capacity* to work, and of course the work itself; while promoting sleep promotes power to work. Sleeping abundantly *saves* time. Wasting time in needed sleep is a misnomer. Yet we can oversleep as well as over-eat and exercise. The due medium is the great desideratum. Physiologists differ as to the length of time required, and well they may, because different persons require different lengths, according to circumstances. Yet there is a right length, easily determined.

THE TIME spent in sleep furnishes no criterion of its amount, because some sleep more in an hour than others in a night. Some may doze away half their time, yet be starved for sleep, while others sleep abundantly in five or six hours, depending on its soundness and previous fatigue.

While the constitution remains unimpaired, the sleep is sound and refreshing, so that seven to eight hours in the twenty-four are probably sufficient, yet broken constitutions require eight, or more. Over-eating also demands additional sleep, as does excessive toil of any kind, of which all are experimental witnesses. All disorders of the stomach and nervous system also require additional time for sleep, because it is then less refreshing. Hence different persons require to sleep different lengths of time, and even the same persons different lengths under different circumstances. Exceedingly active persons, who, when awake, are wide awake, require to sleep longer than those who are half asleep when awake. Convalescents also require to sleep more than usual. Each must, therefore, judge for himself, and while all should sleep enough, none should sleep too much. Over-sleeping is as injurious as gluttony. How stupid, palsied, and good-for-nothing it renders us, as all can doubtless testify. Our own appetite for sleep, as for food, unperverted, furnishes us with an infallible guide.⁶⁰ Nature will rouse us to consciousness when our sleep is out; and, when thus aroused, all should spring at once from their couch. To hug the pillow, half asleep and half awake, is most pernicious, and, like over-eating, only craves the more, besides too often inducing, or at least facilitating, impure feelings.⁴⁶⁶ ⁻ ⁴⁷⁴. Would that the importance of rising immediately on waking could be duly impressed, especially on youth.

NIGHT is too obviously Nature's appointed time for sleep to require proof. All animals, fowls, and insects, except those expressly constituted to find their food by night, retire with the sun, but awaken with the first "peep of day." Not that all should sleep from evening to morning twilight, but what time we do sleep, should be in the night, except in special cases. This sitting up half the night and sleeping half the next day, reverses the order of Nature, and must therefore prove injurious. Extraordinaries excepted, all should rise with the break of day, especially children, who should retire soon after the hens do. Better sleep mornings than too little; yet either retire the earlier, so as to have your sleep out at least before sunrise, or else take a short nap in the middle of the day. Those whose previously formed habits prevent their going to sleep early, even though they go to bed, should break up such habits. "Early to bed and early to rise," is the motto for health. The customs of society may sometimes require morning sleep by preventing a due degree of night sleep. Thus often a public speaker finds his nerves so excited that, though he retires, the blood courses through his throbbing brain so as utterly to defy sleep, to compensate for which, he needs to sleep mornings.

32

NERVOUS persons, and especially excitable children, however, constitute an exception to this general rule. That such should retire and rise late is proved by this law: That the earth is charged with more positive electricity in the after part of the day than during any other part of its diurnal revolution, is apparent, as is also its reason. This charges excitable persons positively; which makes them "work the best when the sun is in the west;" and their excitability continues into the earlier part of the night, which precludes early sleep. Hence the custom of sitting up late nights. Hence also most writers write best between two and eleven, P. M. Yet towards morning, when the earth has lost these stimulating sun rays, such become calmer, and sleep best in the later part of the night, and in the morning. Excitable children should therefore on no account be roused from sleep to prepare for school, but left to sleep till noon if they like. Sleep whenever you can sleep best, but sleep abundantly.

To PROMOTE sleep, then, is sometimes most important. Many cannot obtain enough. Any preternatural excitements of the brain and nervous system prevent its due supply, as do mental troubles, over-exertion, disordered stomachs, and disease of any kind. In all these, and kindred cases, sleep should be promoted.

PREVIOUS PREPARATION is the starting point. As to enjoy our meals, we must first become hungry, and also prepare them, so we should sharpen up our sleeping appetite, and also prepare ourselves, mentally and physically, for this delightful repast and grand restorer of exhausted energy. This can be facilitated by a due degree of action, especially muscular. To overdo causes wakefulness, yet a due quantity of daily employment promotes refreshing sleep at night. Those who would enjoy sleep must exercise, especially those whose wakefulness is caused by nervous or cerebral excitability. They should also avoid excitement, and seek quiet in the evening before retiring, and reduce that cerebral action which keeps them awake. Becoming comfortably tired prepares for refreshing sleep.   .

The wakeful should especially go to bed soon after becoming drowsy, else they become wide awake, and remain so perhaps much of the night. This direction is particularly important. · Yet going to bed only to lay awake, or before we are prepared for sleep, is also bad. We should try to go to sleep as soon as possible after going to bed.

AMUSEMENTS, if of a pleasing, soothing kind, also promote sleep, especially domestic, as playing with children, conversing with friends, and the like.[649] But exhilarating, exciting amusements intercept sleep. Especially promotive of sleep is a quiet, happy frame of mind, while unpleasant feelings, especially anger, retard it, so that the former should always be cultivated, and the latter avoided, both in ourselves and children. "Let not the sun go down upon your wrath," is doubtless founded in this physiological law. Hence induce children to have a good play or frolic just before going to bed.

RELIGIOUS contemplations and devotional exercises are especially promotive of sleep. They diffuse over the soul a delightful quiet, a heavenly calmness, which invite sleep. A physician once directed a wakeful patient to THINK ON GOD, when he would, but could not sleep; and the patient said that for forty years, whenever wakefulness returned, following this prescription soon lulled him to sleep. Family devotion induces a similar preparation.

MODERATE FASTING promotes sleep, while a full stomach retards it. The English think differently, and eat on retiring; but if a full stomach facilitates sleep, we should become hungry when we became sleepy, whereas sleep diminishes appetite. In fact we eat less when we sleep abundantly, and the more, the less we sleep.

INVALIDS, and the sick in particular, require to sleep much. As a restorative, medicines bear no comparison with sleep. Hence wakening the sick to give drugs is consummate folly. There is no better sign of a favorable turn of disease than a disposition to sleep, provided it be natural. A state of mere stupidity is a bad omen; but this differs materially from natural sleep.

BEING DISTURBED when once asleep, till fully rested, causes subsequent wakefulness. Many weakly mothers have ruined their health and lost their lives by crying children. Yet they can so train them as to sleep soundly all night, from infancy to maturity.[640]

DAY NAPS are also most excellent for invalids, children, and all who do not or cannot obtain sleep enough during the night. A mere doze is to such most refreshing. If you cannot get to sleep the first few times, keep trying till you can, and you will soon form the habit. Even if you do not lose yourself, the rest will benefit.

The best posture for promoting sleep is doubtless recumbent on the back, because it facilitates respiration. Laying wholly on either side often causes the internal organs and even brain to sag and remain more on that side, which is evidently injurious. Habituate children to sleep on the back, and if on either side, also on both sides.

A slight elevation of the head may be beneficial, yet habit aside, the horizontal posture for both head and body is probably the best.

99 — BEDS AND BEDDING.

ON WHAT shall we sleep? Something HARD. Mattresses are preferable to feathers, because not hard enough to give pain, nor soft enough to enervate. Straw beds are none too hard. Feather beds are decidedly unwholesome, especially in summer. Being animal matter, they are subject to decay, and hence their unpleasant odor, which of course vitiates the air and breeds disease. They also relax and weaken. Sunk into a pile of feathers, perspiration cannot escape, sleep is disturbed and does not refresh, and we awaken with a headache, feel prostrate, and unfitted for pleasure or business. Not so with mattresses. Of these, those made with cotton are excellent. Ellsworth, in his patent report, says they are " the cheapest, most comfortable, and most healthy material for bedding known to the civilized world. Vermin will not abide in them : unlike hair and wool they contain no grease, do not become stale or acquire an unpleasant odor like feathers, besides being in many cases medicinal — raw cotton worn on parts affected with rheumatism being known to be one of the best and most effectual cures." [640] He also considers them as cheap again as any other kind, as seen in his following estimate : —

Cost of Hair Mattress, at 50 c. pr. lb., 30 a 40 lbs., from 15 to $20
"   Wool   "   30 c. " "   cost   " 11 to 12
"   Feathers "   30 c. " " 40 lbs.,   12
"   Moss   "   —   " "   "   12
"   Cotton "   30 " 8 c., with cost of ticking at 12½ cts.
per yard, labor, thread, &c. $6 65

WOVEN WIRE mattresses are still better than cotton, and the best of all mattresses. They are manufactured by the Woven Wire Mattress Company, of Hartford, Conn., are remarkably

elastic; yield to the least pressure, yet return to their original form
the instant pressure is removed; need no shaking up; retain
none of the fetid matter imbibed by all other mattresses; furnish no lodgment for vermin; never sag, or wear out, or get out
of order, or need repair; cannot burn; are absolutely noiseless,
beautiful, and cheap; need no slats or springs below, and only
a quilt above; are easily transported; allow a light and heavy
person to sleep together without inconvenience; and form a mattress *in every respect* ABSOLUTELY PERFECT. We say all this *experimentally*, and most unqualifiedly recommend them above all
other kinds for use in families, hotels, vessels, hospitals, and everywhere. Those long bed-ridden could never become sore on them.
All this holds equally true of the wire pillows made on this
principle.

The habit of sleeping under a stack of bed-clothes is also equally
as pernicious as a superabundance of clothes by day. They prevent sleep, and retain about the body all the corrupt effluvia it
throws off, which should be allowed to escape. None should sleep
cold, yet all should habituate themselves to as little as possible
and keep comfortable. And during the day, these clothes should
be thrown upon the backs of chairs, and thoroughly aired in a
draught till towards evening.

The practice of covering up the head under the bed-clothes is
most pernicious. One may almost as well not breathe at all as
to breathe over and over again the same fetid air.[46]

PILLOWS are usually made so thick as to make a bend in the
neck, and thus retard the free passage of the air during sleep.
This greatly increases the snoring. All Eastern nations use a
small block, having a hollow place in it fitted to the back of the
head, raising it sufficiently to make it horizontal with the body.
All sleep on their back. All pillows should be thin, or else one
should be laid *lengthwise* of the body, so as to avoid a short bend
in the neck. Let head, neck, and body be parallel to each other,
in sleeping as in standing.

CHAPTER V.

THE MOTIVE AND MENTAL APPARATUS, AND FUNCTIONS.

Section I.

THE OSSEOUS AND MUSCULAR SYSTEMS.

100. — The Human Skeleton.

VITALITY thus supplied, would have been useless but for some means for effecting its expenditure. It may be considered the raw material of life, the stock in trade of the mechanic, which next requires to be *worked up* into the various ends of life, or it will avail nothing. For this expenditure Nature has made provisions quite as ample as for its supply, in two ways, motion and the mentality, sensation included. To subserve these two ends, the entire human structure, the inimitably beautiful vital apparatus included, was created.

WITHOUT motion, man must always have remained in one place, like the oyster, and been incapable of speaking, eating, or doing a single thing, and without mind and sensation he would have been incapable of experiencing one single emotion of 'pleasure or pain. But behold and admire the number and variety of functions effected through their united instrumentality! In fact they embody all the ends of his being.

To effect these great ends, organs adapted thereto are necessary. These organs consist of the osseous, muscular, nervous, and cerebral systems, to the discussion of which our subject now brings us.

BONES form the timbers of the human superstructure. But for some framework within the body, both to keep the various organs in place, and to form, as it were, timbers or fulcrums for the attachment of the muscles, motion would be impossible. The first provision of a motive apparatus consists in devising these supporting timbers.

BONES constitute such a provision. With their general appearance all must be familiar. They are composed principally of two substances, animal and earthy, into the latter of which lime and phosphorus enter — the former imparting life, and the latter firmness. In youth the animal predominates, and hence the greater flexibility of young bones. This also prevents fractures, aids to break the falls of children, and facilitates growth; it being the first part of the bone formed, as seen in the tender cartilage, of chicken bones. But as age advances, the earthy materials of bones predominate over the animal, because the muscles, having become stronger, require augmented stiffness to prevent their bending, and because experience enables us to guard against falls. As the earthy predominates the bones become more and more brittle, and hence the greater frangibility of the bones of the aged, till, in a certain disease which consumes their animal matter, they break from slight strains; whereas, in another disease which consumes their earthy matter, but leaves their gelatinous, they can be bent any way, and even tied up in knots without breaking; yet in this case motion is impossible. These bones are also ramified with blood-vessels and nerves, the former to supply growth and vitality, and the latter to impart sensation.

They are not formed into one solid, continuous stick, but number about two hundred and fifty-two, united by joints, and held together by powerful ligaments. At these joints, the bones enlarge, and become spongy, though the weight of their ends is not greater than that of their middle portions, which, together with an elastic plating between them, serves to deaden the blows of a fall or jump upon the feet, so that, before it reaches the brain, it is comparatively obviated, and that delicate structure saved from contusion. Throw two hundred pounds down ten feet, a distance we often jump, and how hard it strikes. Not so with man. A membrane is also stationed at all the joints to secrete an oleaginous substance more slippery than oil, to lubricate them, and prevent their wearing out by the powerful and almost perpetual friction occasioned by muscular contraction and the weight of the body, and to render easy motion.

POWERFUL CORDS tie the bones together at their joints, so as to resist their tendency, when the muscles contract powerfully upon them, to slip past each other, and prevent sprains and dislocations, the evils of which many experience. They are fitted into one another by *hinges*, a ridge in one exactly fitting to a corresponding depression in the other, and the *ball and socket* joints, as in those of the hips and shoulders, where a ball in one fits exactly into a socket in the other, so as to allow motion in all directions.

SIMILAR bones not scattered about at random, are always found in similar positions, exactly fitted to subserve their respective ends.   Thus attached they constitute the human SKELETON, or framework of the body, as represented in the accompanying engraving, which, with the description, is copied from A. Combe.

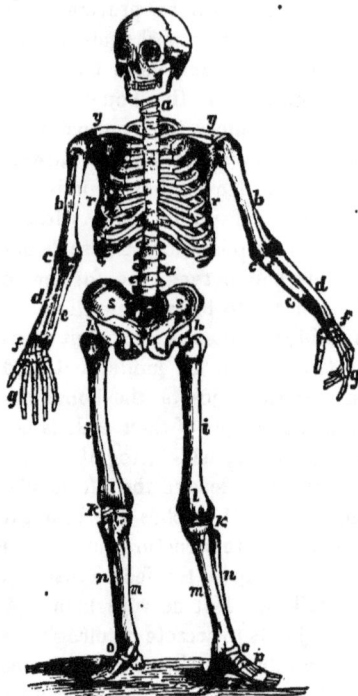

NO. 23.—THE SKELETON.

"The TRUNK, as will be seen from the annexed engraving, consists of the SPINE *a a*, the RIBS *r r*, the STERNUM *x*, and the PELVIS *s s*.   The spine vertebral column, or backbone *a a*, which supports all the upper parts, is a very remarkable piece of mechanism.   It is composed in all of twenty-four separate bones, called VERTEBRÆ, from the Latin VERTERE, to turn, as the body turns upon them as on a pivot.   Of these, seven, called CERVICAL VERTEBRÆ, belong to the neck; twelve connected with the ribs, and called DORSAL, to the back; and, five, called LUMBAR, to the loins.   The base of the column rests on the SACRUM *w*, which is closely compacted between the bones of the pelvis *s s*.   The vertebræ are firmly bound to each other in such a way as to admit of flexion and extension and a certain degree of rotation, while, by their solidity and firm attachment to each other, great strength is secured.   Some conception of this strength may be formed, when we consider the enormous loads which some athletic men are able to carry on their shoulders, or raise in their hands; the whole weight of which is necessarily borne by the vertebræ of the loins.   As the space occupied by the abdomen gives large outward dimensions to this region of the body, it is only upon reflection that we perceive that the whole force exerted by the human frame in its most strenuous efforts centres in the bony column we are now examining.

"While the smooth or rounded forepart, or BODY of the vertebræ, affords support to the superincumbent parts, the projecting ridge behind, and rugged processes at the sides, combine with it to form a large tube or canal, extending from the top to the bottom of the column, and in which the spinal marrow is contained and protected. Between each of the vertebræ a thick compressible cushion of cartilage and ligament is interposed, which serves the triple purpose of uniting the bones to each other, of diminishing and diffusing shocks received in walking or leaping, and of admitting a greater extent of motion than if the bones were in more immediate contact.

"The ribs *r r*, twelve in number on each side, are attached by their heads to the spine, and by their other (cartilaginous) extremeties to the STERNUM, or breast bone *x*. The seven uppermost are called true ribs, because each of them is connected directly with the sternum, by means of a separate cartilage. The five lower ribs are called FALSE, because one or two of them are loose at one end, and the cartilages of the rest run into each other, instead of being separately prolonged to the breast bone. The use of the ribs is to form the cavity of the chest for the reception and protection of the lungs, heart, and great blood-vessels, and to assist in respiration, by their alternate rising and falling. This action enlarges and diminishes by turns the size of the chest and the capacity of the lungs.

"The PELVIS *s s*, is formed by the broad, flat bones which support the bowels, and serve for the articulation of the thigh. A general notion of their appearance and uses may be obtained from inspection of the engraving, which, however, does not represent with perfect accuracy the minuter structure.

"The bones of the UPPER EXTREMITIES are, the SCAPULA or shoulder blade; the CLAVICLE, or collar-bone *y*; the HUMERUS, or arm-bone *b*; the RADIUS *d*, and ULNA *e*, or bones of the forearm; and the small CARPAL and METACARPAL bones *f*, and PHALANGES *g*, forming the wrist, hand, and fingers.

"The SCAPULA is the broad flat bone lying at the upper part of the back, familiarly known as the shoulder-blade, and so troublesome to many young ladies by its unseemly projection. It serves to connect the arm with the trunk of the body, and gives origin to many of the muscles by which the former is put in motion. The COLLAR-BONE *y*, extends from the breast-bone outwards to the scapula. Its chief use is to prevent the arms from falling forward in front of the body; and hence it is wanting in the lower animals, whose superior extremities are much closer to each other than those of man.

"The HUMERUS, or arm-bone *b*, is adapted by a kind of ball and socket joint to a corresponding surface in the scapula, and hence enjoys great latitude of motion, and, from the shallowness of the receptacle, is somewhat liable to dislocation. The RADIUS and ULNA *d e*, constituting the forearm, are connected with the humerus by a hinge-like joint, which admits readily of flexion and extension, but not of rotation; and as the articulation is of a peculiar construction, it is rarely dislocated. The movements of pronation and supination, or turning round the hand, are effected, not by the elbow joint, but by the radius *d* moving upon the ulna *e*, by means of joints formed for this purpose. The wrist and finger-joints are too complicated to admit of explanation here.

33

"The lower extremities consist of the os FEMORIS, or thigh-bone *i*; the PATELLA, or knee-pan *l*; the TIBIA *m*, and FIBULA *n*, or leg-bones; and the TARSAL and METATARSAL bones *o*, and PHALANGES *p*, composing the ankle, foot, and toes.

"The thigh-bone *i*, is articulated by means of a large round head, deeply sunk into a corresponding hollow in the pelvis, at *h*; freedom of motion being thus combined with great security. The thigh may be moved backwards and forwards as in walking, and also outwards and inwards, as when sitting on horseback, or with the legs crossed. The socket being much deeper than that of the shoulder-joint, the thigh-bone has not the same range of motion as the humerus, but it has proportionally greater security.

"The PATELLA, or knee-pan *l*, is well known. It is a small bone, constituting the projection of the knee. It increases the power of the muscles which extend the leg, and protects the front of the knee-joint. The TIBIA *m* is the principal bone of the leg, and is the only one articulated with that of the thigh. Its lower end forms the projection at the inner ankle. The FIBULA *n* is the long slender bone at the outer side of the leg, the lower end of which forms the outer ankle. The TIBIA and FIBULA both contribute to the formation of the ankle-joint, which, like that of the knee, is almost limited to flexion and extension."

101. — THE MUSCLES, THEIR NECESSITY, STRUCTURE, AND MODE OF ACTION.

ROPES AND PULLEYS, or their muscular equivalents, now become necessary in order to put these bones in motion. Without them this beautiful structure of bones and joints, every way so perfectly adapted to serve as a foundation for the motive apparatus, would be as inert as so many sticks. The MUSCLES supply this want. They lie beneath the skin, upon and around the bones, and constitute the red meat of animals and man. Every human being is endowed with some five hundred and twenty-seven, of all required shapes and sizes, exactly adapted to produce all those innumerable and most powerful motions of which man is capable. They overlap, underlie, and interweave each other in all conceivable ways, and are enclosed in a smooth peritoneal membrane, which allows them to slide upon each other without friction, else their powerful contraction would soon wear them into shreds. They are composed of innumerable strings or fibres, bound together into one common bundle, the contracting or shortening of which results in motion. Indeed, this contractile power constitutes their sole function, and is effected by an expenditure of vital force, thus: As one end of these several muscles is attached to one bone, and the other to another across a joint, their contraction moves one or the other of these bones, and of course produces motion. This is illustrated more fully in the accompanying engraving and description.

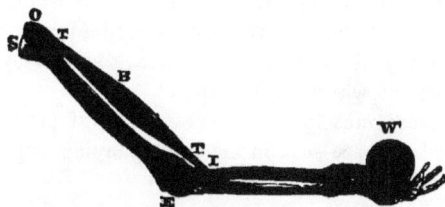

/ No. 24. — THE MUSCLES OF THE ARM.

The figure represents the bones of the arm and hand, having all the soft parts dissected off, except one muscle O B I, of which the function is to bend the arm. O the origin of the muscle; B the belly; I the insertion; T T the tendons; S the shoulder-joint; E the elbow. When the belly contracts, the lower extremity of the muscle I, is brought nearer to the origin, or fixed point O, and by thus bending the arm at the elbow-joint, raises up the weight W, placed in the hand. A motion of an inch at I, causes a motion of fifteen to twenty inches at W.

MUSCLES are largest in their middle, that part which contracts, and taper off into tendons — those strong cords seen in the wrists, backs of the hands, insteps, and above the heels, so that many muscles may be attached to a single bone, else the size of the bones must have been bunglingly large. The strength of these cords is tested by hanging slaughtered animals up on sticks thrust under these tendons, and also by the tenacity with which they adhere to the bones, as well as by our ability to stand on'one foot and toss the body about by one of these tendons — that of Achilles, at the heel. Their attachment is formed on processes or ridges in the bones, or on their heads near joints, which processes are the larger the more powerful the muscles.

Single motions are generally effected by the contraction of individual muscles. But most of our motions are compounds of several, effected by many bones, joints, and muscles acting in concert. Thus the simple lifting of the hand to the head, is effected by the combined motions of the wrist, elbow, and shoulder; and in walking, apparently so easy, nearly all the muscles and bones of the body are brought into requisition; so much so, that even tying the hands greatly impedes it.

Many of the motions of the body, as climbing, leaping, lifting, &c., require the CONCERTED as well as powerful action of every muscle of the body. This concert is effected by means of a cerebral organ of motion, located in the cerebellum, in the middle line of the head at the nape of the neck. Indeed, all the internal organs, — heart, lungs, liver, &c., — undoubtedly have each their cerebral organs, just as the stomach operates by means of Alimentiveness, of which see Volume II.

Some of these muscles and their manner of producing their respective motions, are seen in the accompanying engraving and description, copied from Combe.

NO. 25.—THE MUSCLES.

"To understand the uses of the various muscles, the reader has only to bear in mind that the object of muscular contraction is simply to bring the two ends of the muscle, and the parts to which they are attached, nearer to each other, — the more movable being always carried towards the more fixed point. Thus when the STERNO-MASTOID muscle f g contracts, its extremities approximate, and the head, being the movable point, is pulled down and turned to one side. This may be easily seen in the living subject, the muscle being not less conspicuous than beautiful in its outline. Again, when the powerful RECTUS or straight muscle b, on the front of the thigh, contracts with force, as in the act of kicking, its lower end attached to the knee-pan and leg, tends to approximate to the upper, or more fixed point, and pulls the leg strongly forwards. This occurs also in walking. But when the SARTORIUS, or tailors' muscle c is put in action, its course being oblique, the movement of the leg is no longer in a cross direction, like that in which tailors sit; and hence the name SARTORIUS.

"Another variety of effect occurs, when, as in the RECTUS or straight muscle of the belly i i, sometimes one end and sometimes both are the fixed points. When the lower end is fixed, the muscle bends the body forward, and pulls down the bones of the chest. When, as more rarely happens, the lower end is the movable point, the effect is to bring forward and raise the pelvis and inferior extremities; and, when both ends are rendered immovable, the contraction of the muscle tends to compress and diminish the size of the cavity of the belly, and thus not only assists the natural evacuations, but co-operates in the function of respiration.

"In contemplating this arrangement, it is impossible not to be struck with the consummate skill with which every act of every organ is turned to account. When the chest is expanded by a full inspiration, the bowels are pushed downwards and forwards to make way for the lungs; when the air is again expelled, and the cavity of the chest diminished, the very muscles *i i i*, which effect this by pulling down the ribs, contract upon the bowels also, — pushing them upwards and inwards, as can be plainly perceived by any one who attends to his own breathing. By this contrivance, a gentle and constant impulse is given to the stomach and bowels, which is of great importance to the min contributing to digestion and in propelling their contents; and one cause of the costiveness, with which sedentary people are so habitually annoyed, is the diminution of this natural motion in consequence of bodily inactivity."

102. — THE POWER OF THE MUSCULAR SYSTEM.

THE NUMBER, variety, and power of the motions capable of being produced by these muscles are indeed most wonderful, as all have seen and experienced. They enable us to climb the lofty tree, and even the smooth pole of liberty; to mount the towering mast, and not only support ourselves in the rigging of the ship, but to put forth great muscular exertion while she is tossing and rolling, and that in the midst of the hurricane. Standing upon our feet, we can toss our bodies, weighing from one hundred to two hundred pounds, several feet upward and forwards, and in all directions, for many hours in succession, as in dancing and the circus. We can transport it fifty or sixty miles between sun and sun, and even carry many pounds weight upon our backs. We can chase down the fleetest animal that runs. We can labor briskly every day, for scores of years. We can lift and carry several times our own weight. We can accomplish a multiplicity of powerful and protracted bodily exertions, and do a variety and amount of things almost without end.

"The muscular power of the human body is indeed wonderful. A Turkish porter will trot at a rapid pace, carrying a weight of six hundred pounds. Milo, a celebrated athlete from Crotona, accustomed himself to carry the greatest burdens, and by degrees became a monster in strength. It is said that he carried on his shoulder an ox, four years old, weighing upwards of one thousand pounds, for above forty yards, and afterwards killed it with one blow of his fist. He was seven times crowned at the Pythian games, and six at the Olympian. He presented himself the seventh time, but no one had the courage to enter the lists against him. He was one of the disciples of Pythagoras, and to his uncommon strength the learned preceptor and his pupils owe their lives. The pillar which supported the roof of the school suddenly gave way, but Milo supported the whole weight of the building, and gave the philosopher time to escape. In his old age, Milo attempted to pull up a tree by its roots and break it. He partly effected it, but his strength being gradually exhausted, the tree, when cleft, re-united, and left his hand pinched in the body of it. He was then alone, and, being unable to disengage himself, died in that position.

"Haller mentioned that he saw a man, whose finger being caught in a chain at the bottom of a mine, by keeping it forcibly bent, supported by that means the weight of his whole body, one hundred and fifty pounds, until he was drawn up to the surface, a height of six hundred feet.

"Augustus XI., King of Poland, could roll up a silver plate like a sheet of paper, and twist the strongest horseshoe asunder.

"A Frenchman who was attached to Rockwell & Stone's circus resisted the united strength of four horses, as was witnessed by thousands.

"A lion left the impression of his teeth upon a piece of solid iron.

"The most prodigious power of muscle is exhibited by fish. The whale moves through the dense medium of water with a velocity sufficient to carry him, if continued at the same rate, round the world in little less than a fortnight; and a sword-fish often strikes his weapon quite through the oak planks of a ship." — *Western Literary Messenger.*

The Stuart family were most remarkable for great physical strength, which harmonizes with the principle that all distinguished men are both from strong-constitutioned and long-lived families.

"THE LAST OF THE STUARTS is one hundred and fifteen years old. Hundreds of persons can bear testimony to his amazing strength, from which circumstance he got the by-name of 'Jemmy Strength.' Among other feats he could carry a twenty-four pounder cannon, and has been known to lift a cart-load of hay, weighing a ton and a half, upon his back. Many a time has he taken up a jackass, and walked through the toll-bar, carrying it on his shoulders. It will be long before we can look upon his like again, to hear of his stories of 1745, and his glowing descriptions of the young Chevalier." — *A Scotch Paper.*

Jonathan Fowler, of Guilford, Conn., walked out knee deep through the mud, oyster-shells, and filth of a sea-shore at low tide, to a shark left by the retiring tide in a pool, captured it while yet alive, though it was weakened by having but a scanty supply of water, shouldered it, and brought it alive on his back to the shore, which weighed five hundred pounds! — quite a load, considering that it was not the most portable of articles, nor the best of roads. The feats of the Ravel family, Bedouin Arabs, and circus performers, astonish us.

Yet these and kindred exhibitions of strength are by no means the ultimatum of man's muscular capability? A due degree of *training* would enable him to accomplish much more. We are but Lilliputians in comparison with what mankind will yet become. Most exalted are man's muscular powers. He might vie with the lion himself as to absolute strength, and carry heavier burdens than horses. Indeed, Turkish porters now transport six and eight hundred pounds at a time on their backs with ease, and the Belgian giant could stand up under *two tons*. The Chinese have no horses, and carry their teas and silks between two men, hundreds of miles, on their backs! If man can effect all he now does without either muscular discipline or the application of the laws of hereditary descent, how much more with? The human race is yet in its teens in everything,[516] muscular capability included. We little realize the extent to which it can be carried *in our own selves*, if properly disciplined.[36]

Section II.

EXERCISE; ITS VALUE, BEST MODES, AND THE LIFTING CURE.

103. — It promotes all the other Functions.

THIS MOTIVE APPARATUS, so perfect, so powerful, was not created to lie dormant, but to be USED. Almost innumerable arrangements in nature *compel* such exercise. Man is ordained to exercise his muscles in tilling the soil, in order to procure food; in changing his position, and moving from place to place; in making and working machinery, using tools, building, printing, making that vast variety and quantity of articles of clothing, furniture, ornament, and all the innumerable things used by mankind; and even in reading, writing, eating, walking, talking, looking, breathing, and all those millions of ends, great, little, and almost infinitely diversified, requiring locomotion, which every member of the human family is compelled to put forth continually through life.

We have already seen how important is digestion,[47] circulation,[83] respiration,[38] perspiration,[92] and sleep,[97] all of which exercise promotes. Who has not seen his veins become prominent and hardened during vigorous exercise on account of the increased passage of blood through them; whereas, this swelling appearance is never found in the indolent, except in fevers. Who does

not know that a smart lift, or work, or run, or vigorous exercise
of any kind, increases the frequency and power of the pulse, as
well as the rapidity and volume of the inspirations? That it
equally accelerates the perspiration, all are witnesses. Who has
not seen the sweat run down in streams from all parts of the body
during hard labor? And who does not know how much more
heartily we eat, and sweetly and soundly we sleep, with than
without work? Nor is there an important function of our nature
which muscular exercise does not promote, and inaction intercept.
By enhancing respiration, it augments the amount of oxygen,[41]
carbon,[47] fibrine, glutine, and caseine consumed, indeed of all
the materials derived from food and breath, and also greatly increases the expulsion of all noxious matter from the system in
the form of phlegm, perspiration, and respiration. Besides hurrying the circulation by increasing the introduction of oxygen,[42]
it still further increases the flow of blood, by urging it along
through the veins, for the contraction of the muscles upon the
veins urges their contents forward — backward it cannot go [83] —
towards the heart. Exercise also quickens the action of the bowels
and of the digestive process generally. All these functions, constituting no small portion of life itself, labor enhances, and thus
augments life and all its pleasures and powers. In short, muscular action promotes every function and power, mental and
physical, of our entire nature, besides being indispensable to all.
He who does not work can therefore enjoy only a lower degree
of life and its pleasures; muscular inaction deteriorating, diseas-
ing, and vitiating the entire man and woman. Nature still further recommends muscular action by

104. — THE PLEASURES OF EXERCISE AND LABOR.

Since obedience to her laws occasions pleasure,[18] and since
muscular exercise is thus undoubtedly one of her laws, we might
expect it to be freighted with a great variety and amount of *enjoyment*, as experience proves it to be. Confine yourselves, or
even sit or lie, in one position all day, and you will find inaction to
be exceeding painful. See how animals, on breaking away from
close confinement, run, and skip, and hop, and frisk, as though
they did not know how to contain themselves. How many times,
after having remained inactive for some time, on going out you

have been filled with an amount of pleasure by action better felt than described. Only after our muscles have been drilled long and severely, and even become enfeebled, if not diseased, by inaction, can we keep still without pain. Idleness is unnatural. Action is natural and pleasurable in its very constitution. See how much real pleasure children take in playing and running — so much that they race from morning to night, and cannot be kept still by any means whatever.[644] How much pleasure a smart walk, or ride, or dance, and the like afford. The sedentary little realize how much pleasure can be taken in *manual labor* — it being excelled only by that taken in eating, breathing, and sleeping. Indeed, those who do not work or take vigorous exercise in some way, can experience but little pleasure in life; for they can neither eat, nor sleep, nor breathe, nor think, nor feel, with that real *relish* so essential to enjoyment. "He that will not work, neither shall he eat," is written quite as legibly on the physiological constitution of man as in the Bible; labor being indispensable to appetite, and this to the enjoyment of food, besides the far greater amount of food which Nature allows him who works to eat with impunity. Nor should the laborer envy the rich their ease or their dainties; for he has "meat to eat which they know not of," luxuries of which they can never partake till they create a relish for them by laboring like him. We should as soon forego the pleasures of appetite or rest as of manual labor, because, though walking, riding, hunting, bowling, dancing, and other kinds of exercise are better than none, yet none of them compare with *work* as a means of promoting health. No form of play, no other kind of exercise, at all compares with *labor*, especially *agricultural*, for expanding and strengthening the chest, developing all the organs, and thoroughly exercising every muscle and organ in the body. We had better ride, or walk, or dance, or play ball and the like, than do nothing; but had better work than do either or all. To derive the pleasure from muscular action it is capable of imparting, we must *do* something — must effect some useful *end*. Exercise for its own sake is comparatively insipid; but achieving some useful results, redoubles both its utility and its pleasures. You may play, but let me *work*. Give me an axe, or saw, or hoe, or scythe, or rake, or shovel, or some kind of tool, and a place to use it, and you may enjoy the pleasures of even

34

the dance and hunt. Let me plough, plant, and raise food for the table, set out and tend trees, and enjoy their fruit, and add to the products of the earth, and thereby to the aggregate of human happiness. God has told. man *practically* to "till the earth and keep it," and that he must eat his bread by the sweat of his brow. Not, by any means, as generally interpreted, that such toil is a curse. So far therefrom, it is a *blessing*, and one of the greatest pleasures of earth. No labor is ever a curse, nor other than one of Nature's greatest LUXURIES, except when excessive in amount, or ill-timed. Words cannot portray the evils consequent on the false notion that labor is a curse. Indeed, if our world produced all we require spontaneously, without any requisition for human labor, it would hardly have been worth living in. These views of the utility of labor confirm the fact that

105. — MOST GREAT MEN LABORED HARD IN YOUTH.

WHAT DISTINGUISHED man in this country or age, or any other, but took a great amount of exercise while young? And most of the world's geniuses were brought up to *hard* work. Adam Clarke was noted, when at school, for his great physical strength in rolling stones. Shakespeare, while composing his immortal plays, carried brick and mortar to build places for their performance. John Wesley rode and walked a great many thousand miles, and it was this habitual exercise which prepared his gigantic intellect to put forth those mighty efforts which enabled him to do so much good, and immortalize his name. Clay was a poor boy, and actually worked for a living. Henry Bascom, the great western orator, travelled west *on foot*, with his axe on his shoulders. The old Roman and Grecian orators took a great amount of exercise in order to prepare themselves for public speaking, and they put in practice one fundamental principle, of which we moderns, with all our boasted light and inventions, have lost sight — that of strengthening the voice by gymnastic exercises. No one can have a good voice without having a good muscular system ; and hence, to improve the tone of the latter, will augment the power of the former — an additional reason why public speakers should labor. Sir Walter Scott, after confining himself to his desk for several days, till the energies of his brain had become exhausted, would mount his horse, call out his dogs, and follow the chase for days in succession, till he had restored his prostrated energies, and then returned to his study. When Byron entered college, fearing that his tendency to corpulency would injure his personal beauty, of which he was very proud, he took extremely severe exercise daily in order to reduce it, besides leading a very abstemious life. Webster, in his Saratoga speech in 1844, said that he was a backwoodsman, born in a "log cabin," on the borders of the unbroken forest, and inured to hard labor. And often, breaking away from public life, and shouldering his gun, he ranged the forests for days in search of game, besides taking much exercise daily. Franklin, the beaconstar of his profession, a practical printer, was a hard worker. Patrick Henry, that unrivalled star of genius and eloquence, labored on the farm while young, and was passionately fond of music, dancing, and the chase; the latter of which he often followed for weeks together, camping out in true hunter's style.

"After his removal to Louisa, he has been known to hunt deer, frequently for several days together, carrying his provision with him, and at night encamping in the woods. After the hunt was over, he would go from the ground to Louisa court, clad in a coarse cloth coat, stained with all the trophies of the chase, greasy leather breeches, ornamented in the same way, leggings for boots, and a pair of saddle-bags on his arm. Thus accoutred, he would enter the court-house, take up the first of his causes that chanced to be called; and if there was any scope for his peculiar talent, throw his adversary into the background, and astonish both court and jury by the powerful effusions of his natural eloquence." — *Wirt's Life of Patrick Henry.*

Need we mention the father of our country, its pride and pattern? Washington, when not employed by his country, labored assiduously upon his farm; and was actually driving his plough when he received the news of his election as president. Harrison, "the *farmer* of North Bend," led a life of great physical exertion and exposure. Burns, the Scottish bard, actually composed much of his poetry when at work on a farm. President Dwight, the great theologian and scholar, attributed much of his mental vigor to daily labor in his garden. John Quincy Adams, one of the most learned men of his age, said he found much daily exercise indispensable. It is a uniform fact, that those students who have been brought up without having labored, seldom take a high intellectual stand, except in parrot-like scholarship. They always show a want of mental vim and pith, and the powers of close, hard thinking. After they enter upon the business of life, their case is still worse. They rarely rise to eminence. Thank God if you were obliged to *work* hard and constantly till sixteen. The Author, leaving home with only four dollars in the world, with his all upon his back, travelled four hundred miles, *worked* his way to college, and through college, and, instead of earning his money by teaching school, supported himself by sawing, splitting, and carrying up the wood of his fellow-students, *three and four flights of stairs*, improving in this way every hour, except study hours, and often portions of the night. His fellow-students laughed at him then, but now the scales are turned. He thought it a hard row to hoe, but a rich harvest has it yielded; and you, reader, owe to this same cause no small portion of whatever delight or benefit his lectures, writings, and examinations afford. And one means of writing thus much — how well let others judge — is interspersing composition with labor. Rising early and engaging briskly in some sort of labor, usually agricultural, till the circulation reaches a high pitch, and sends the blood rushing around the system, which gives more pleasure than even breakfast, and then putting on paper the ideas which this bodily exercise creates as a means of promoting authorship alone, excels all others. Nothing will aid composition as much as purchasing a small plot of ground on which to work. Nor has his health ever sustained as much injury from exposure, or excessive professional application, or any other cause, as from that deficiency of work which some twenty years study and severe professional labor have partially prevented. Nor has anything done more to restore the health thus impaired than a return to work. Pardon this personal allusion, but profit by the lesson it teaches. Reader, be your occupation what it may, pleasure or business, mental discipline or professional attainments, take this advice, *work hard and daily from two to six hours*, and you will accomplish more study, despatch more business, and perform and enjoy more in whatever you engage, ten to one, than by perpetual application. As the bow always bent loses its elasticity; so continued application either exhausts or disorders the brain and impedes mental energy and discipline, which daily labor will wonderfully promote. Ye who aspire after renown, *work*. Ye who would do good, *work*. Ye who would fulfil man's great terrestrial destiny of being happy, *labor daily.* And ye who arc too proud or too lazy to work, be content to suffer. Good enough for you, because you violate a cardinal law of your being. This arraigns for condemnation

106. — This Anti-working Doctrine and Practice.

In view of these two. fundamental laws of our being, — the great demand of nature for muscular action, and its subserving all the great ends of life, — what of those who are *above* work? Above? Rather *below* it; for he who thinks himself too good to work, is in reality too *bad.* No man or woman can ever be above labor, without being above his nature and his God. Shall the Almighty Maker of all things not only work the six days of the creation, but "from everlasting to everlasting," and shall man, "the work of his hands," be above his Maker? That human being is no man, no woman, only some paltry thing, who is too proud to engage in manual labor. "To till the earth and to keep it," is an honor, not a disgrace — is to become "co-workers with God," not menials. And he or she who is too proud to labor, ought, in all consistency, to be too proud to breathe and eat; because the former is quite as much a constitutional function and demand of Nature as the latter. Ashamed to be seen at work? As well be ashamed to look, or talk l Away with this dogma that labor degrades. It elevates and ennobles. Its influence upon the mind is most beneficial. It begets a resolution and energy of character, which infuses into all our feelings and conduct that indispensable element of success, *power.* It requires that perpetual grappling with difficulties and overcoming of obstacles which inspire and cultivate a firmness and determination imparted by nothing else. Hence tho' youth brought up to do no work while young, fails to cope with difficulties, but yields to them through life, and of course accomplishes little. This shows why rich youths make such poor scholars. Boys had better be street scavengers, and girls kitchen drudges, than brought up not to labor at all; for no kind or amount of work is as bad as either idleness or no labor. Excessive toil injures, but *some* sort of work benefits. Play is good for children, but not enough. They must learn, by toiling through those opposing obstacles the removal of which constitutes labor, to grapple in with all kinds of difficulties with that determined resolution which says in action,

"I can and I will;" "Get out of my way or I'll get you out." The greatest curse now impending over our land is this anti-working fashion. Parents seem to vie with each other who shall support their children at the greatest remove from doing anything. And one of the greatest errors of the day is, that labor is the business of drudges, and degrades; the wrong inflicted on workers, great as it often is, being trifling compared with the depravity and suffering which this anti-working tendency does so much to rivet upon the elite.

Yet all anti-workers have their reward. Those thus brought up turn out to be inefficient, and often vicious. This explains the prevalence of vice among the rich, the fact of which is palpable. Those who have the wealth of Astor should make their children work; not by forcing them, for this might make them hate it, but persuading them to it, and enamouring them of it, so that they labor from choice.

Dear, delicate, fashionable city ladies, generally homely, because indolent and sickly, and therefore "ugly looking;" so extra exquisite that they must never soil their soft hands by doing the least thing about house; too nice, and delicate, and refined, and genteel, and senseless, besides much more, to be so vulgar, may possibly endure a fashionable promenade once in a while, and an occasional "airing" in the easiest riding carriage that can be made, are so very genteel that they must ride to church, though only two or three blocks off! Such should have a patent machine, by which their servants could chew their food and pump breath into them without any effort of their own, so as to place them at a still greater remove from labor! And their extra delicate and helpless children should lay down, and lie there all their lives, and save the trouble even of eating by letting pap drop into their open mouths, and run down their tiny throats of itself!

Many poor but proud pretenders to gentility, who have scarcely enough to eat, yet would fain make a genteel appearance — starving the kitchen to feed the parlor — if accidentally caught in kitchen habiliments, must blush, and apologize, and falsify outright ·by pretending that their servant has just left, and they had to prepare dinner. Out upon that proud nothingness which has to work, yet lies to hide it! This anti-working pride is contemptible in the rich, but in such, intolerable! What! Begging pardon for obeying the laws of your being, ha! What greater sign of littleness! Away, toadstool grandees, into merited insignificance and infamy! Come, ye laborers, inherit the blessings conferred by toil. Such perverters of their natures should have a short paralysis of their muscles, so as to enforce their practical value. Indeed, partial paralysis always follows protracted inaction. Muscles used but little decline till they become so weak that exertion, otherwise a source of exquisite delight, becomes' irksome, and fatigue follows trifling exercise. Such are most heartily to be pitied, yet their punishment is just, and self-induced.

LABOR IS DIGNIFIED. The honorables of the earth are its laborers. Nothing is mean which Nature requires, but worthy of universal commendation. What she has anointed and crowned let not man despise. This idea that labor is degrading, had its origin in kingly and feudal times and institutions, of lordlings and serfs. Would that it had never been imported to our republican shores. Is it not in the teeth and eyes of every principle of republicanism? Yet our cardinal doctrine of equality is fast erasing it, and elevating labor to that post of honor assigned it by Nature. True REPUBLICANS will never think the less of those who labor, and those who do should emigrate. Our country, our institutions are not congenial with their doctrines or practices. The old world is already consecrated to aristocracy and caste, this to equality. Go to Turkey, or India, ye purse-proud, labor-despisers; here you are strangers in a foreign land, for our institutions conflict with your practices. Go where you can find congeniality, and leave us who love equality to the peaceable possession of this our home. Here you are eyesores, and stand in the light of those to whom this land of right belongs.

"Let any woman who esteems herself in the higher classes of society put the case as her own, and imagine that her son, or brother, is about to marry a young lady, whose character and education are every way lovely and unexceptionable, but who, it appears, is a seamstress, or a nurse, or a domestic, and how few are there who will not be conscious of the opposing principle of caste. But suppose the young lady to be one who has been earning her livelihood by writing poetry and love stories, or who has lived all her days in utter idleness, and how suddenly the feelings are changed! Now, all the comfort and happiness of society depend upon having that work properly performed, which is done by nurses, seamstresses, chambermaids, and cooks; and so long as this kind of work is held to be degrading, and those who perform it allowed to grow up ignorant and vulgar, and then are held down by the prejudices of caste, every woman will use the greatest efforts, and undergo the greatest privations, to escape from the degraded and discreditable position. And this state of society is now, by the natural course of things, bringing a just retribution on the classes who cherish it. Domestics are forsaking the kitchen, and thronging to the workshop and manufactory, and mainly under the influence of the principles of caste; while the family state suffers keenly from the loss. Meantime the daughters of wealth have their faculties and their sensibilities developed, while all the household labor, which would equally develop their physical powers, and save from ill health, is turned off to hired domestics or a slaving mother. The only remedy for this evil is, securing a proper education for all classes, and making productive labor honorable by having all classes engage in it." — *Miss Catherine E. Beecher.*

One probable reason why labor is despised, is, that it is generally required in such excess as to be extremely onerous. Such excess is injurious, and should never be required or yielded. On the other hand, we should render it as delightful in fact as nature has rendered it by constitution,[103] thus seconding her evident intention. Laborers should not be required to strike another blow after becoming just comfortably tired. We should work for *play*, and only when labor is pleasure !

107. — EXERCISE DOUBLY REQUISITE FOR THE YOUNG.

HOW BRISKLY and almost incessantly lambs frisk, calves run, colts prance, kittens play, and the young of all animals exert their muscles? Do children form an exception to this law? What mother or nurse has not been surprised, if not provoked by their incessant activity and noise from morning till night, year after year, from the cradle till they take leave of the parental roof? Try your best to keep them still, you will fail. To prevent their action is as impossible as to prevent their breathing; and as injurious as impossible. This restless activity is interwoven throughout their whole natures, and for the best of reasons. Their growth being rapid, the materials for which are deposited by the blood, of course their digestion, respiration, circulation, and perspiration must be proportionate. Exercise promotes all these functions,[103] and thereby augments growth — is indeed indispensable to it. Swing up an arm or foot so as to prevent its action, and see how it shrinks, and becomes enfeebled and diseased; but restoring its action, enlarges, restores, and strengthens it. So of the system as a whole. To prevent their spontaneous activity, besides being the worst purgatory which can be inflicted upon those dear sufferers who are shut up and required to keep still, prevents the development of bone, muscle, nerve, and brain, and thereby weakens every one of their powers, mental and physical, and thus becomes the worse curse which can be forced upon them.[104] Rejoice in the gambolings of children, noisy though they be, because augmented health and mentality are the products. Sacrifice temporary convenience on the altar of so great a good to them. Do not interdict what their highest good requires. Did Nature implant this perpetual restlessness to be suppressed? We fight against her requirements at our and their peril. Many a mother has followed her children to their graves because she broke down their constitutions by interdicting their play. Rather promote than retard this natural demand. Nor fear, much as they will play if allowed, that they will run too much. After they have been unduly kept in for a long time, they may perhaps play beyond their strength at first, but not long. It is hardly possible for them to overdo. Not one in scores of thousands ever does this, but nearly every child in civilized life is more or less enfeebled and diseased by playing too little, together with overconfinement. Parents should make provision for such play as much as for their meals.

" But I cannot possibly stand their perpetual uproar."

Then turn them out of doors. Mind neither cold nor wet. Wash them all over, mornings, or even their feet, nights, in cold water,[95] and neither will hurt, but only benefit them. Their racing will convert both into instrumentalities of health.[103] Do not be too tender of them. Confinement kills scores where exposure kills one, and even then the exposure would be harmless but for previous confinement. There are weathers not suitable for them to be out, yet then they will want to stay in.

" And what shall we do with them then?"

Have a play-room under cover set apart expressly for them, filled with facilities for play. It need not be warmed; they will keep themselves duly warm by exercise. No house should be without its children's play-room any more than without a kitchen, or bed-room. And such rooms should be large and airy, and lighted, if possible, from the top, so as to save window glass, or

35

else furnished with inside shutters. Whole flocks of children, of different ages, should be turned out to roam over hill and dale unrestrained, the elder succoring the younger; or rather, all under the care of teachers, who, from every flower, and mineral, and production of nature met in their rambles, shall teach them Nature, her operations, and her laws. Whatever you do for children, or what leave undone, *give them their perpetual fill of exercise.*

Children and youth should labor, but not to excess. One of the reasons for this has already been given.[105] It inures them to overcoming obstacles. It also furnishes an exercise of muscle more severe than play, and trains them to habits of work, so essential to their health and happiness through life. They should also practise rendering themselves serviceable to others while young. And then there is something in labor which hardens the whole system, brain included, rendering it compact and firm, and capable of enduring what those not inured to work can never sustain. Especially should labor be rendered *inviting* to them, never repulsive. If possible, induce them to work from choice, not compulsion. This can be easily effected in a variety of ways. One is by giving boys a parcel of land, and letting them plant, tend, and harvest on shares, and have the avails. This will also teach them the value of money, by showing them how much labor it requires to earn it. Another way is, by giving them tools and a workshop, and encouraging them to make sleds, wagons, kites, boxes, and what playthings they want, as well as tinkering up other things required. By a variety of kindred devices they can be induced to labor from love of it.

Yet this subjecting young children to excessive and perpetual toil is ruinous. As soon as or before they enter their teens, parents say to them in actions, if not in words, "I have toiled hard and long for you, and now you must pay me off, principal and interest, by working still harder for me." But let such remember that children have much more than paid their own way, all along from birth, in the pleasures they have occasioned, and instead of owing, have actually brought their parents in debt; or rather, both are indebted to their common Parent for the mutual pleasure they have occasioned each other.

Children are also put to trades too early, and bound out to

severe taskmasters, obliged to work hard early and late for six or seven years, and often poorly fed and lodged at that; thus expending in the services of their "boss" those energies required for the development of their own bodies and brains. Many mechanics make it a point of economy — though it is the worst kind of robbery — to get much of their work done by apprentices. The present apprentice system is abominable, utterly unjust, and often wickedly cruel, as many readers know by sad experience. Its object should be to teach the trade, not to enrich the employer. That well learned, — and by this time the trouble of teaching and keeping will be amply recompensed by the labor of the apprentice, — they should be allowed the full avails of their labor, instead of being compelled to work hard for several years for nothing but their food and clothing, and then thrown empty upon the world at twenty-one; whereas, if they had been paid all, or even half, the net profits of their labor, they might have had a home of their own, and capital with which to commence business, and more than all, *good constitutions*, now well nigh ruined by over-working while growing. Many children and youth, while growing rapidly, are lazy, especially those who mature late, because they require all their vitality for growth, and to give them strong constitutions. Such should not be compelled to labor much beyond what they themselves prefer, lest they should expend in labor those vital energies required for growth. Have no fear that they will be lazy after they have attained their stature and maturity, after their reservoir of vitality is full and overflowing, for their very indolence now will contribute to their efficiency then, by increasing their health and strengthening their constitutions; thus giving them the greater surplus for muscular and mental labor. Yet we would have all children work every day after they are ten years old.

. These principles apply equally to putting youth into stores and offices too young. And the smarter they are, the worse. Slim, spare, flabby, their morning sun passes into an early cloud, or sets in the darkness of premature death! Without abundant *exercise*, they cannot possibly have strong muscles or vigorous health, and without these can never do, or become, or enjoy much.[24] Many readers can testify that their apprenticeship broke down their constitution, and impaired all their capabilities, all their enjoyments for life.

But worst of all is this compelling young children and youth to work steadily in the factory ten, twelve, or more hours daily, year after year, without vacation, or any time to play, or recreate, or enough even to eat and sleep. See how pale, slim, haggard, and jaded out they all look. Give them a six months' play day, and see how it will improve their health, and looks, and minds. Sigh' for our country in view of the multitudes of our youth now subjected to this deteriorating practice, and mourn instead of rejoicing over our mechanical prosperity. The farm is the place for children. What if factory labor is light, it is confining, and prevents muscular exercise. Even excessive labor is less hurtful. After the growth is completed, and the constitution every way consolidated, factory labor is less injurious; but you should work desperately yourself rather than let your children be confined to the factory.

Thus far our remarks have been applied to boys. Yet to girls such application is even more important. They should never be confined either to the chair in sewing, or the factory-room, for reasons given in "Maternity."[603] Women may sit and sew, or knit, after they are thirty, and the more the older they grow; but no girl should learn any female trade requiring her to sit, as in sewing, folding books, coloring prints, or observe any other fixed posture, or confine herself in the factory, till after thirty, on pain of a broken constitution and shortened life; yet elderly women may sew, tend machinery, and the like, with comparative impunity. Nor should young, growing girls be confined to lugging and tending infants.

If asked at what age children and youth may be put down to hard labor without much injury — excessive labor is injurious at any period of life — the following dialogue contains the answer. While riding in a stage with its proprietor, who keeps several hundred horses in constant employ, all of which he buys himself, he was asked: —

"What kinds of horses do you prefer to purchase?"

"Balky ones!"

"Why?"

"Because their fractiousness prevented their being used much till fully grown and hardened."

"At what age can horses be put down to hard work without injury?"

"Not till eight years old; they ought never to be broken earlier, and then they will wear like iron till they are thirty; you can hardly wear them out."

He would thus have one quarter of their lives spent simply in *growing and maturing*, as they will much more than make up this lost time by extra endurance afterwards. Only a few days previous we rode after an extra smart horse, twenty-three years old, whose skittishness prevented her being used till about eight.

These facts, palpable to all who will open their eyes upon them, illustrate a universal law, which requires that nearly or quite one fourth of the life of man should be spent in the formation and development of the physical powers. Youth should work only for play, besides having all the vitality requisite for growth, till they become full and run over with surplus animal life, so that they almost ache for something to do in order to expend it. When this period arrives, be it earlier or later, just give them a chance to do something for *themselves*, and they will not be lazy. Instead, they will take hold of the affairs of life " with an appetite," and accomplish wonders; whereas, compelling them to labor too young is the way of all others to make them hate work, and turn idlers as soon as out of their time. To put children to hard work at eight or nine, is to wear them out at thirty or forty; but if you would have them live to be a hundred, give them the reins till they are twenty or upwards, and allow them to be boys and girls, instead of making them young ladies and gentlemen.

SECTION III.

POSITION, FUNCTION, AND STRUCTURE OF THE BRAIN AND NERVES.

108. — ITS LOCATION AND STRUCTURE.

All those beautiful and perfect contrivances of stomach, liver, intestines, heart, lungs, skin, bones, and muscles, the entire man, if complete and in perfect order, would be utterly useless but for some means of *manifesting mentality*. The mind is the man,[27] and its measure is his measure. This alone crowns man with immortality, alone allies him to angels and to God, and alone endows humanity with its only wreath of glory, its only instrumentality of enjoyment. Mind alone enjoys; and since happiness is the great object of existence,[28] of course our enjoyments are proportionate to its amount and right exercise. To subserve its function, all other organs and functions were erected; and hence the, one end of life should be to promote its action.

But this mentality must have its *organ*. Nature's universal motto is an organ for every function.[23] As digestion, circulation, motion, hearing, and each of the other physical functions are performed by means of organs, shall not this crowning function of all have its organ also? It has; and that organ is the brain — an apparatus every way perfectly adapted to execute the mental functions.

"This dome of thought, this palace of the soul," occupies the cavity formed by the skull, and of course constitutes much of that crown of humanity — the head.   Being extremely delicate, it is protected by the skull, the spherical form of which is admirably calculated to guard it against injury, break the force of contusions, and prevent fractures.   Beneath this skull is a tough, hard membrane, called the dura mater, which envelopes the brain, and dipping down lengthwise through its middle portion, partially separates it into two halves, called hemispheres.   Under this is a thin lubricating film called the arachnoid, or spider's web membrane, and below it again is still another fine-textured vascular membrane, which dips down into all the folds of the brain, and is perfectly full of blood-vessels and nerves, being to the brain, probably, what the skin is to the body, the arachnoid membrane corresponding to the rete-mucosum of the skin, as the dura mater does to the epidermis.[92]   The same treble structure belongs to the heart, lungs, stomach, intestines, &c.[71]

The accompanying engraving (No. 26) represents the general structure of this organ.   Those crooked foldings, called convolutions, not unlike the folded structure of the intestines and lungs, doubtless subserve a similar purpose, namely, of allowing a far greater amount of surface to be folded up in a small compass,[71] so as to produce a corresponding increase of power without much increase of bulk; else the brain must have been enormous.   And this conclusion is strengthened by the fact, that in inferior animals these convolutions are barely perceptible, while, as we rise in the scale of mental capability, they become larger and deeper till we reach man.   And even in the human brain, those who are the most talented have the largest, deepest, finest, and most numerous convolutions.   Said that celebrated surgeon, George McLellan, of Philadelphia, —

"Called some years ago to make a post-mortem examination of the brain of one of the most distinguished public men of Delaware, I was perfectly astonished at the size and depth of its convolutions; I never saw anything like it in all my life."

This was doubtless because those subjects which had come before him in the dissecting-room had been those of inferior mental endowments, and consequently of smaller convolutions.

These folds, and of course the substance of the brain, are composed of two widely differing substances — the outer, called cincritious, from its pale ash color, and also cortical, from its surrounding the other, while the inner is white in color, and made up of converging and diverging fibres, and called medullary. These two substances, as well as its convolutions, are well represented in the following engraving. Its dark folds, designated by figures 1 to 14, show these convolutions.

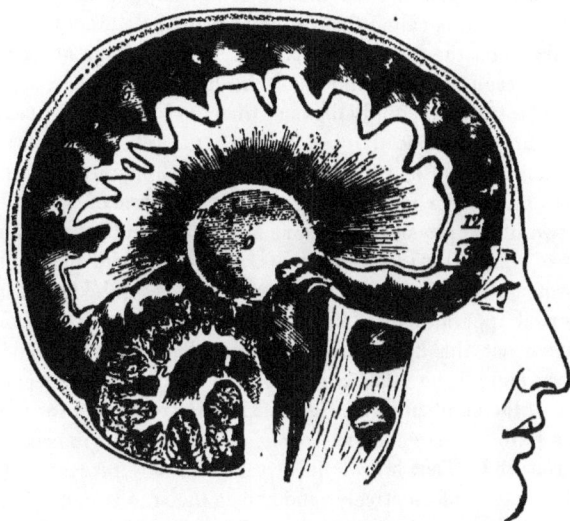

No. 26. — A PERPENDICULAR SECTION OF THE BRAIN AND SKULL.

The outer rim represents the skull, and those dots in it indicate its diploe — cells stationed to break the force of blows and prevent fracture. Those waves or lobes containing the figures represent the cincritious substance, and below it the medullary, the fine diverging lines of which represent the thread-like or fibrous structure of the brain.

These folds are here seen to appertain to the cineritious or outer portion of the brain, and this is undoubtedly that portion, the action of which produces mind. Those convolutions on the two sides of the falx, just where the above section of the brain is made, numbered from 2 to 14, are probably phrenological organs.

The brain is about the consistency of jelly, and its inner or medullary portion is composed of two sets of nerves, one of which converges from its centre to its surface, and the other from its surface to its centre. These nervous fibres are filled with a semi-fluid; indeed, four fifths of the substance of the brain and nerves are water,[73] called neurine, and probably exercises and transmits sensation and mental action by means of undulations or motions.

THE CEREBELLUM is a thick membrane resembling the dura mater, called the tentorium, stretched across horizontally just at 2, in engraving No. 26, separating the brain into two divisions, the upper and larger of which is called the cerebrum, or brain proper, which performs the mental functions, and the lower and smaller of which is called the cerebellum, or little brain, and probably carries on the physical functions. Severing the nerve which passes between the brain and stomach, destroys hunger and digestion. The stomach simply digests, whereas hunger and gustatory pleasure are experienced by ALIMENTIVENESS.[43] In like manner, the sexual emotion is experienced not in its apparatus, but in the cerebellum, by the cerebral organ AMATIVENESS of 329. Now, since two of the physical functions are known to be performed by means of cerebral organs acting in conjunction with the physical, the former stimulated by the latter — that is, since the stomach and sexual apparatus have their cerebral organs in the cerebellum, why have not the heart, lungs, muscles, liver, bowels, pancreas, kidneys, and all the other organs of the body, also their cerebral organs in the cerebellum? By what law have the two former and not the latter? Are such variations and exceptions in accordance with Nature? That law of universality already presented,[13] settles this matter affirmatively, and shows that the true office of the cerebellum is to perform the physical functions.

This conclusion is admirably fortified by the fact, that all the nerves which connect the brain with the body proceed from the cerebellum, none from the cerebrum. This establishes the most perfectly reciprocal inter-relation between the body and cerebellum, and the near relationship of the cerebellum and cerebrum renders their states also reciprocal, and thus is proved and explained that perfect reciprocity between all the states of the body and mind already pointed out.[25, 26]

These facts and deductions establish the conclusion that the brain does something besides think and feel; that it generates and sends forth that "vis animæ," or vital spirit, which animates all parts of the body, infuses life and action into them, and sets and keeps the entire human machinery in motion; so that its healthy state is essential to that of the body, and the disease of the one also causes that of the other.

109. — STRUCTURE AND FUNCTIONS OF THE NERVOUS SYSTEM.

THE NERVES are but a continuation or extension of the substance of the brain throughout the system. This is effected by means of the spinal cord *d*, fig. 23, which is enclosed in the spinal column or back bone. The substance of this cord and of the nerves closely resembles that of the brain, except that the cineritious is inside and the medullary on the outside — a reversion having taken place.

THE SPINAL CORD gives off nerves at each spinal joint to the heart, lungs, stomach, liver, viscera, and all the other internal organs. When these organs become chronically irritated, inflamed, or diseased, their nerves become similarly affected, so that, since each of these nerves unite with the spinal cord at its own particular joint and no other, by pressing on the joint which receives the nerve of the heart, a soreness, perhaps sharp pain, will be experienced by the patient, and thus of all the other internal organs. This test of disease is *infallible*, and tells at once and with certainty whether any of the vital organs are affected, and if so, which — five minutes being sufficient to decide the matter without mistake.

Nerves also go off through these joints to the hands, feet, muscles, bones, and every portion of the body. Another nervous track is called the great sympathetic nerve, which traverses the cavity of the chest from thorax to abdomen. Thus a double nervous inter-communion of all the organs of the body is maintained, both with each other and with their common centre — the brain. These nerves are always found in close proximity with

36

blood-vessels, both arteries and nerves; the three always accompanying each other throughout the system. And not only is every principal nerve thus supplied with blood-vessels, but even every shred of every nerve, and not only every muscle, but even every fibre of every muscle, is similarly supplied with both blood-vessels and nerves. Wherever there is life, there also will nerves be found, and the more life in any animated thing or part, there the more nerve.

THE FUNCTIONS of these nerves are of three kinds — those of sensation, voluntary motion, and involuntary motion. The nerves of sensation proceed from the back half of the spinal cord, and those of motion from the anterior half, and soon after they issue through the joints they unite, are encased in one common sheath, and cannot be distinguished from each other. Yet on cutting that nerve, say that which goes to the hand or issues from the anterior half of the spinal cord, all sensation is destroyed in it, so that it may be cut, burnt, anything, without feeling it, while on cutting that from the posterior half, all power of motion is destroyed. The involuntary nerves go to the heart, lungs, stomach, and other internal organs, so as to carry on their several functions irrespective of the will, while asleep, and when attending to the affairs of life — an arrangement absolutely indispensable.

THE NERVES OF VOLUNTARY MOTION are distributed mainly to the muscles, and enable us to govern them at will — to move the hands, feet, and body, in accordance with the determinations of the will, of which all of us are perpetually conscious; while those of sensation are ramified mostly upon the *surface* of the body, stationed as sentinels upon the outer walls to warn against the approach of all enemies to life and health — to tell us when we are too warm, or too cold, or in contact with anything injurious.[20] They are so minutely ramified that the finest needle cannot be thrust through any part of it without lacerating and paining some of them. The minuteness of this ramification is absolutely inconceivable.[39, 80, 98] Nature is as infinite in her littleness as in her greatness. Our huge earth, compared with which a mountain is as a grain of sand, is but an atom compared with her planetary sisters, Saturn and Jupiter; and even the whole solar system itself is a molehill compared with its grand centre, the sun, so massive as to baffle all known attempts at comprehension, while sun and planets, if rolled together into one mighty pile, are the merest hillock compared with that vast belt of suns and worlds perceptible to human vision.   And even all this' probably only a speck of this boundless universe !   O God, how vast is thy greatness !

Yet this same Infinite Architect of the universe descends as far below us in littleness as he rises above us in vastness.   Infinite magnitude, infinite capillary ramifications, are both alike to him. Words utterly fail to describe, and the human mind to conceive, the fineness of these capillary formations, as in the structure of his lungs,[39] blood-vessels,[83] pores, and nerves.   Verily, "Thy ways, O God, are infinite."   In this infinite littleness of nervous ramification in the skin, sensation takes place.   These nerves ultimately end in an infinitude of little papillæ, or feelers, which cover the entire surface of the body, and create that sensation of which we are all conscious.[92]

· THIS CAPILLARY nervous structure, as also the general arrangement of the nervous system, is well illustrated in the annexed engraving.

Those nerves are much more abundant at the surface of the body than internally; and hence in amputations, and all cuttings and bruises, boils and sores, the greatest pain is nearest the skin — it being comparatively slight after the cut or hurt has fairly passed below it.   Yet when a bone has become inflamed it is also exceedingly painful, yet here also the pain is mainly at its surface.   Since the inner portions are protected by the outer, as great a supply internally as externally would be a useless expenditure of vitality.

Yet a still greater sentry of nerves is stationed at some points

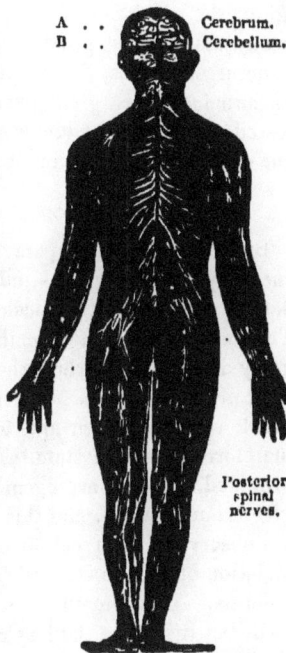

A . .   Cerebrum.
B . .   Cerebellum.

Posterior spinal nerves.

NO. 27. — THE NERVOUS SYSTEM.

than at others — about the eyes, hands, and especially ends of the fingers, the utility of which is beyond all computation, as all know by perpetual experience.

THE IMPORTANCE of the sensation thus effected is incalculable. Without it we could never know when we were too cold, or too warm; when our flesh was burning, or freezing, or bruised, or mangled, or experiencing any sort of injury or destruction, unless we chanced to see it. But now, contact with whatever injures them or the system, pain, which causes a spontaneous shrinking from the noxious body, and saves from further damage. The suddenness with which this warning and shrinking occur, as when we touch fire, or are cut, or pricked with any sharp instrument, is astonishing. The very instant we touch fire, we jerk the part burned from it, yet, instantaneous as it is, the nerves feel pain, telegraph that pain to the brain, muster the will, which gives the muscles a mandate to remove the part affected, and they obey, — all in the twinkling of an eye. The importance of this instantaneousness is very great, because the injury in cases of burns, punctures, bruises, &c., is extremely rapid; so that, but for this instantaneousness, great havoc would occur before it could be arrested, which this suddenness now prevents. Pain thus becomes one of the most useful institutions of our nature.[20]

110. — IMPORTANCE OF HEALTHY NERVES.

But this function of pain is by no means the only one experienced by these nerves, — indeed, is not their chief, or even their natural one. Strictly speaking, it is their abnormal function.[20] They never take on this painful action unless the body is abnormally affected, and when they do, do so from necessity, not as their natural function. Their normal function is to yield a pleasurable sensation when and because the body is in a natural, and, therefore, agreeable state.[16] For such a state Nature has amply provided. Every arrangement of external nature is adapted to give them pleasure, and this is their sole product when their laws are observed; such painful action being consequent only on the violation of such laws. We little realize how much pleasure they yield us. Like breathing, it is so perpetual as not to be appreciated, yet it is none the less real. And it might be doubled many times over if we but kept them in a perfectly healthy and highly active state. Take some examples. Your face, before it is washed in the morning, does not feel half that pleasurable glow experienced after washing it, because the ablution cleanses and quickens these nerves. Wash, say one limb, hand, or arm, or half of the body, or a part of a limb, and not the balance, and the washed portions will feel as much more clean, susceptible, and comfortable as can well be imagined. The experiment is well worth trying, and powerfully enforces the importance of those ablutions of the whole body already recommended.[95] Those who have not tried the experiment do not know how much more lively, brisk, buoyant, and happy bathing renders those who practise it, not at the time, merely, but for hours, and even days afterwards.

So also colds, which impair the sensitiveness of these nerves, either benumb them so that they feel but little, or fever them, and cause a kind of restless, crawling, burning sensation, which makes us almost desire to "jump out of our skin." What we call the creevels consist in a crawling, feverish, painful state of these nerves, and can be obviated by restoring them to healthy action. None realize how much of our suffering comes directly and indirectly from the disordered, and therefore painful condition of these nerves; nor how superlatively happy we could render ourselves by keeping these feelers in a vigorous and perfectly healthy state. But the entire drift of our habits tends to deaden and disorder them, and thus to convert the pleasures they were created to confer into pain.[26] We begin to vitiate these nerves in the cradle, by extra dressing and a confined and over-heated atmosphere,[45] and go on to weaken and disorder them more and more through life. Every cold we take, they are the chief sufferers. This we never need to do, and ought by all means to avoid. Have you never felt, while suffering from cold, an indescribable sensation of nervous crawling uneasiness, amounting to intense pain, so that you could neither sit, nor stand, nor walk, nor lie still, but seek a perpetual change of place, yet without finding relief? You feel as though you would fain spring right away from yourself, or shed your skin, if you could only relieve yourself from this wretched feeling. This state is particularly apparent when we have taken cold, — its warnings heeded would prevent all colds, — and in the incipient

stages of fever, 'while the chills of ague and fever are on, and
generally when we are unwell. What are called nervous, hyster-
icky people, are particularly liable to its attack; and their condition is indeed pitiable. Yet they should not have brought on this
nervous disorder.

111. — EFFECTS OF DISEASED NERVES UPON THE MIND.

THE EVILS of diseased nerves do not stop here. They extend
also to the mind, and render the entire being more and still more
wretched the more they are disordered. They not only inflict
the creevles and the fidgets upon the body, but still more upon
the mind. That connection of the nerves of the skin with all the
nerves of the body,[25] and of the latter with the cerebellum,[109] and
through it with the cerebrum, engenders the same condition in the
brain which exists in the nerves. It is not possible for the nerves
of the skin to be affected, without similarly affecting both the
brain and mind. If the former are in a feverish, unhappy, or
painful state, they diffuse that state throughout all we think, say,
do, desire, and feel. Nervous people — by these are meant those
whose nerves are disordered, though all have nerves — are always
fretful. They feel wretchedly in body and mind; and if they do not
worry, stew, and find fault with everybody and everything, it is
not because they do not feel irritable. Disordered nerves would
render an angel as cross as a fury.[26] However amiable a woman
may be by nature, just as surely as her nerves become disordered,
just so surely she becomes peevish and fretful, if not ill-natured
and bad-dispositioned. She would find fault in paradise, if there,
thus disordered. But restore her nerves to their normal, and
therefore happy, state, and you restore her to her original serenity
of mind and sweetness of temper. What worried her before now
gives her pleasure. She laughs now at what she scolded then.
Those mental troubles which then preyed upon her mind, have
now taken their flight. Indeed, she was troubled in mind only
because disordered in body. The troubles of such are imaginary,
not real; or, if real, are magnified in the exact ratio of the disease
of their nerves. If such have no real cause of trouble, they will
make it out of whole cloth. As every motion and touch in
the gathering bile give pain, which, if well, would give pleasure,
so with their minds. The irritation of their nerves irritates the

brain, and this renders them inordinately irritable about trifles, even in spite of everything calculated to promote a cheerful and happy frame of mind. Trifles excite them more than should the cares of kingdoms. A great load presses perpetually upon them. They feel as though some terrible calamity, what, they know not, impended over them, ready to fall upon and crush them. Their excited imaginations magnify molehills till they become mountains. They are rendered wretched from morning till night by a perpetual fever of excitement; tossed back and forth by currents and counter-currents of feeling, which they find it impossible to control. At one time they are elated beyond measure, and full of ecstasy. Some trifling thing, too insignificant to affect a healthy brain, casts them into the very depths of despair. Their sensibilities are morbidly alive to everything. They retire to their couch, but not to sleep. The boiling blood courses through their veins, while the laboring pulsations of their hearts shake their whole frame. Their thoughts wander to the ends of the earth, but to no purpose. They think and feel upon everything, only to increase their disease, and aggravate their mental sufferings. If Cautiousness is large, they are afraid of their own shadows, and see their path filled with lions and tigers. If Approbativeness predominates, they thirst for fame, but see the cup of praise dashed from their lips by merely imaginary neglects, or reproofs which are so construed as to induce the deepest chagrin and mortification. They seek sleep, but find it not. Hour after hour they turn upon their damask couches, exhausted by mental action, even to prostration, but unable to compose their excited, erratic feelings. Their brightest thoughts flit like meteors across their mental horizon, only to vanish in midnight darkness. And if tardy sleep at last folds them in his arms, frightful dreams disturb their shallow slumbers, and they awake enshrouded in deep, impenetrable melancholy. They feel most keenly, only to feel most wretchedly. Now and then a sigh, or groan, or "O, dear me!" escapes them, and they internally feel, "O, wretched man that I am." They seem burdened with, they know not what, but this only oppresses them the more. Things, otherwise their joy, are now their misery, and everything sweet is rendered bitter. Their nervous energies are wrought up to the highest pitch of inflamed action; yet they have no strength to endure this excitement. Days and weeks roll on only to augment their miseries, and increase their exhaustion. Their excited minds thirst for books, but mental application only enhances both their malady and its miseries. Do what they will, be they in what circumstances they may, their disordered nerves turn all they touch into occasions of wretchedness. The difference between the talents, character, and happiness of the same person when his nerves are healthy and when diseased, is heaven wide. None can ever know but those who know by experience. The way is thus prepared for showing how to keep the nervous system healthy ; becomes as important as happiness is desirable and pain dreadful. Do nothing to derange them, and they will never disorder themselves. Exercise is as requisite to them as to the muscles, or lungs, or any other portion of the body. Yet who ever thinks of providing exercise for them? One means of securing their action is by studying, and the other by exercising them direct.

Nature undoubtedly abounds with herbs and things, which, applied externally, in the form of ointments or decoctions, will secure a most delightful glow of nervous feeling, and consequently of comfort, bordering on ecstasy. Yet this is only inferential.

Do not overtax them by highly stimulating meats and drinks, such as alcoholic and fermented drinks; narcotics, as tea, coffee, tobacco, and opium, or mustards, spices, and condiments generally, which usually begin their work of derangement in the cradle. No kinds of stimulants should ever be administered to children or youth. They are sufficiently excitable and active already. Opium, in any and all of its forms, is most detrimental to infants.[637]

But mental excitement, anxiety, and trouble more effectually derange the nervous system than any other cause, and should therefore be avoided. The fact is, all should arrange their houses, lands, business, domestic affairs, and everything around them, little and great, so as to render themselves as happy as possible, and by all means avoid occasions of sad feelings and vexations. And if trouble does overtake them, as the loss of friends, domestic difficulties, failure in business, or anything of the kind, banish it as far as possible from the mind, and try to think on what gives pleasure. Children, also, should be crossed and provoked, and especially flogged, as little as possible; because the painful excitement thus occasioned is directly calculated to disorder the nervous system.[647]

To show how to restore disordered nerves would now be in point, yet can be more effectually presented presently.

Having expounded the principal organs and functions of the human body, and shown how to preserve them in a healthy and vigorous state of action, we are thus brought to consider the general subject of diseases and their remedy, which, next to the preservation of health, becomes an all-absorbing subject of human inquiry.

37

CHAPTER VI.

RESTORATION FROM DISEASES.

SECTION I.

HYGIENE BETTER THAN MEDICINES.

112. — MEDICINAL FOOD, VS. MINERAL MEDICINES; CALOMEL.

MOST CIVILIZED persons are more or less ailing or diseased. To say how many and how much, is utterly impossible; for no language can depict either the number or the aggravation of human maladies. Those who are *down* sick constitute only a very small proportion of those who are more or less enfeebled, or disabled, or have this weakness and that ailment, and yet keep about. They work on, indeed, but in perpetual pain. Even those called perfectly well fall far below the standard of physical vigor possible to them.[30]

DISEASE IS CURABLE, and health restorable; and to a degree far exceeding our most sanguine anticipations.[33] He who shows mankind how to *keep* well will be the greatest benefactor of the race, while he who shows all how to *get* well is next. Of course this chapter is the most important of this book, because it sums up and applies all its doctrines. Diseases teach us the value and laws of health, and Nature then teaches us how to cure them. All are most deeply interested practically in that problem we now propound, — How can diseases be cured, and health restored?

NOT BY MEDICINES mainly. Men generally think them their only curative reliance, especially in extreme cases. All run at once to the doctor and to the apothecary shop, as if their very life depended on their speed. Do such ever stop to consider just *how* medicines act? They may empty the alimentary canal, and infiltrate themselves throughout the body by means of the blood; but do they mend muscles, nerves, and organs, scrape up and reject disease, or change the organic particles? All this, and much more, is the *exclusive* work of Nature. Work thus delicate sho alone can execute. Medicines may neutralize poisons and acids, and supply nature with required materials, but this is all.

MINERAL medicines are especially noxious to life. What! actually *poison* the system in order to cure it? Shall we destroy life to enhance it? Does that which is constitutionally hostile to life promote it? This is perfect nonsense, and in the teeth of every principle of Nature. Besides, her entire economy is *pleasure,* never pain,[16] while poisons are always painful in their operation, besides being nauseous to the taste, which of itself is sufficient to condemn them. As those kinds of food which the system requires relish best,[50] so we shall *crave* what medicines we require. The curative process is constitutionally pleasurable, never painful. So treat a wound as to heal it in the best manner possible, and it will feel good and comfortable. Only what interferes with its restoration occasions pain. And this law holds true of all forms of convalesence. This new view of the restorative process is true, theoretically and practically. Shall obeyed law give us pleasure, and a return from transgression to obedience necessarily occasion pain? Does anything but violated law cause suffering?[20] Of course, then, medicines bitter to the taste or painful in their operation, Nature condemns in and by the very pain they occasion. Since obedience to law is followed by pleasure, therefore whatever the system requires will give only pleasure. What medicines it requires it will *crave and love.* Not that bitter medicines should never be taken, but that, when required, their very bitterness will be sweet. Otherwise Nature inflicts pain to secure pleasure; which she never does. Her motto is, *all* good, no evil. Any other view of her misrepresents and belies her; or, rather exposes him who makes it. Though she often brings good out of evil, and makes even the wrath of man serve her, yet she brings still greater good out of all good. Our shortest and surest road from sickness to health, therefore, never conducts us through what is repulsive or painful, but only through what is pleasurable. This fully established principle unequivocally condemns

POISONS, CALOMEL, AND DEPLETIONS. The very principle upon which they act, is their destruction of life. Taken in health, they induce sickness; then how much more aggravate it? And their reputation for curing diseases is due mainly to abstinence from food, perspiration, and emptying the stomach, all of which can be effected by processes entirely harmless. Their effect upon the teeth alone brands them with unequivocal condemnation; for whatever injures them, first disorders the stomach. Their decay foretokens incipient dyspepsia. Hence, since they are always impaired by these medicines, of which all who take poison are living witnesses, they of course always enfeeble the stomach.

CALOMEL powerfully stimulates the liver, but stimulates by *poisoning* it. Hence liver affections almost always follow its administration — always, except when both stomach and liver are extra powerful. Dyspepsia follows its use almost as surely as sunrise daylight, because induced thereby. Let observation, the more extensive the better, pronounce the verdict. Language can never adequately portray its ravages on health and life.

"GENTLEMEN: If you could see what I almost daily see in my private practice in this city, persons from the South, in the very last stages of wretched existence, emaciated to a skeleton, with both tables of the skull almost completely perforated in many places, the nose half gone, with rotten jaws, ulcerated throats, breaths most pestiferous, more intolerable than poisonous upas, limbs racked with the pains of the Inquisition, minds as imbecile as the puling babe, a grievous burden to themselves, and a disgusting spectacle to others, you would exclaim, as I have often done, 'O, the lamentable want of science that dictates the abuse of that noxious drug, calomel, in the Southern States!' Gentlemen, it is a disgraceful reproach to the profession of medicine, it is quackery, horrid, unwarranted, murderous quackery. What merit do gentlemen of the South flatter themselves they possess by being able to salivate a patient? Cannot the veriest fool in Christendom salivate — give calomel? But I will ask another question. Who can stop its career at will, after it has taken the reins in its own *destructive and ungovernable hands?* He who, for an ordinary cause, resigns the fate of his patient to mercury, is a vile enemy to the sick; and if he is tolerably popular, will, in one successful season, have paved the way for the business of life; for he has enough to do ever afterwards to stop the mercurial breach of the constitutions of his dilapidated patients. He has thrown himself in fearful proximity to death, and has now to fight him at arm's length as long as the patient maintains a miserable existence." — *Professor Chapman.*

"They affect the human constitution in a peculiar manner, taking, so to speak, an iron grasp of all its systems, and penetrating even to the bones, by which they not only change the healthy action of its vessels, and general structure, but greatly impair and destroy its energies; so that their abuse is rarely overcome. When the tone of the stomach, intestines, or nervous systems generally, has been once injured by this mineral, according to my experience (and I have paid considerable attention to the subject), it could seldom afterwards be restored. I have seen many persons to whom it has been largely given for the removal of different complaints, who before they took it, knew not what indigestion and nervous depression meant only by the description of others; but they have since become experimentally acquainted with both, for they now constantly complain of weakness and irritability of the digestive organs, of frequent lowness of spirits and impaired strength; all of which, it appears to me, they will ever be sensible. Instances of this description abound. Many of the victims of this practice,. are aware of this origin of their permanent indisposition, and many more who are at present unconscious of it, might here find, upon investigation, a sufficient cause for their sleepless nights and miserable days. We have often had every benevolent feeling called into painful exercise, upon viewing patients already exhausted by protracted illness, groaning under the accumulated miseries of an active course of mercury, and by this forever deprived of perfect restoration. A barbarous practice, the inconsistency, folly, and injury of which no words can sufficiently describe." — *Dr. Graham, of Edinburgh.*

This is the testimony of its *friends* — of distinguished members of the medical *faculty* — and is true of the *principle* on which calomel and all mineral poisons act. And the more virulent the poison, the worse. Those who take them may recover, yet it will be in *spite* of both disease and medicine; but their recovery will be slow, and constitutions impaired.

MANDRAKE root, made into pills, or steeped, and the decoction drank, touches the liver as effectually as calomel, yet leaves no poisonous after-claps. Tomatoes also promote liver action, as do quassia, hops, columbo root, ginseng, &c. Then why not provoke liver action by these innocuous vegetables, which do not, like calomel, expose, by taking cold, to life-long suffering, and various aches to which they were before strangers? All are quite welcome to swallow all of them, if they please; but had better do without them.

BLEEDING is scarcely less detrimental. It does not extract the disease, or at least only in proportion as it withdraws life itself, and, if repeated, diverts the vital energies from brain and muscle to the *extra* manufacture of blood.

Rely far less on medicines, even vegetable, as restorative agents, than on physiological prescriptions. Obeying the laws of health will prevent our being sick, and when sick, a return to this obedience is the most direct road to health. Still the existence of medicines shows that they should be taken. Yet why in the present highly-condensed form? Why not in that diluted form in which we find them in nature? In short, why not take them along with our food? That certain kinds are eminently medicinal, is a matter of universal experience. Thus, many kinds act as powerful cathartics. Then why not follow Nature, and always move the bowels by diet instead of by concentrated medicines? The *principle* that Nature has furnished us with all the medicines we require in food, and that medicines thus administered are always efficacious, and "leave no sting behind,"[49] was clearly an ordinance of Nature. What the system requires, it *relishes;* what is either repulsive to the taste or painful in its operation, is therefore injurious. Whenever the system requires any particular kind of medicine, appetite will crave those kinds of food which will effect a cure. Every medicinal law of Nature centres in this focus. Granted that mankind has not yet ascertained a tithe of the different kinds of food adapted to remedy given diseases, yet the fact that *some* kinds are "good for some complaints," shows that *all* diseases have their specific cure in particular kinds and commixtures of diet.

"But when we are sick we have no appetite for any kind of food."

Then fast. This is what your system then demands. Let it not be supposed that we rely mainly on medicines, nor even on medicinal food, to cure diseases, but on a general observance of the laws of health, and medicines, in food and out of it, as secondary aids. Nature is our great physician. Those patients who put themselves under her treatment may rest assured of a speedy and effectual cure.

113. — ALL SICKNESS, PAINS, FEVERS, BOILS, EXPECTORATIONS, COLDS, &C., ARE REMEDIAL.

"THIS FEVER must be broken at once, or it will wear you out." "This boil must be scattered." "This nervousness must be subdued by opiates, so that you can sleep nights."

FEVERS ARE FRIENDS. They *burn up* the waste, poisonous matters of the system, and clean out the Augean stables of physical corruption. They would not have been instituted unless they had been beneficial; for an All-wise God ordains nothing for torture, and nothing in vain. They consume that surplus carbon which is the chief cause of disease.[86] They always generate heat. How? By this very consumption.[85] They increase respiration. They make all their suffering victims *pant for breath.* This fact is apparent. Why? Solely to obtain that surplus oxygen requisite

for consuming this surplus carbon, and their combination generates the heat incident to all fevers.[84] Surplus carbon is clogging
and crippling all the functions.[120] Nature must unload it, or suc-
cumb to it. She cannot reject it, because it is all through the
body. She must set up a fire to *burn it up where it is*. She can
do this only by supplying its "fixed equivalent" of oxygen, which
she can augment only by augmenting the breathing; hence this
panting for breath in all feverish patients — breathing deep, fast,
and as if they were half crazy for more breath. This extra craving for breath means something. Means *what?* Means that extra *oxygen* is wanted. Wanted for what? To burn up surplus
carbon. Reader, think out this problem.

"FEVERS EXHAUST." And why shouldn't they, after so herculean a labor of rejecting all this filth and corruption?

FEVERS SIGNIFY LIFE, and remedial action, and therefore prospects of recovery. When the system is so far gone that it cannot
be restored, it yields to disease; whereas fevers are but its strugglings to get rid of it. Blisters illustrate this principle, by acting
only where there is sufficient life to resist them. As they cannot
be raised on patients about to die, so patients far gone have not
vitality enough to set up a fever.

FEVERS AUGMENT PERSPIRATION. The surplus heat thus generated by this extra consumption of carbon must escape somehow;
for the system needs only a tithe of it. It creates thirst, and'
then seizes the water thus supplied, turns it into steam in quantities, forcing it out in great drops everywhere trickling down, and
with it out go quantities of disease, of which that bad odor, that
fetid exhalation from the breath and whole surface of fever patients is demonstrative evidence. Else whence and why this awful stench? Put these four *facts* together, and learn from them
that as there is a water cure, and a motion cure; so there is also
a *fever cure*.

LET FEVERS RUN. Encourage, but on no account try to break
them. They come to relieve you. Give them what materials
they want, and *let them alone*. Yet be *just as careful as possible*
not to catch cold after their paroxysms. They exhaust, and also
sweat the skin, so that it becomes doubly exposed to colds, while
the system is yet exhausted with its rejective restorative effort.

CHILLS usually precede them. This is probably due to the vi-

tal force retiring to the centre of life, preparatory to making that
desperate purgatory effort it is now beginning. By all means
supply artificial warmth by keeping your room warm, going to
bed, and "*piling* on" the clothes, or, what is still better, going
into a bath just as *hot* as can be well borne; but on no account
try to break up fever and ague, or any other remittent, intermittent, or periodical fever by calomel, &c., because this leaves that
corruption they are rejecting still within the system.

All this class of fevers can be easily and effectually cured thus :
As soon as you become chilly, go into a bath just as hot as you
can well endure, and remain in it till the *fever* stage is well established; then jump instantly into bed, without getting chilly by
wiping, cover up warmly, go to breathing deeply,[43] drink all you
like, lay a cold wet cloth on your stomach, and *sweat away*, but
lay till long after perspiration subsides, and if possible go to
sleep, and keep well bundled up till you retire for the night.
Follow this recipe at every return of your chills, and curse me
if it does not soon cure you, provided you bless me if it does.

QUININE kills fevers by killing· the patient just that much, but
leaving all that poisonous carbon which created it still there.

DRINK to your heart's content. Soft water is the best. Lemonade, if quite sour, may do, yet sweet consists mainly of carbon,
the excess of which causes your fever. Cider may do, it furnishing an acid to combine with and neutralize the acids of the system.
But soft water is probably the best drinking material. Take it
cold or warm, as you prefer, but pour it down by the quart.

CATNIP TEA is good, for it starts the perspiration ; so does sage,
motherwort, &c. The Indians use catnip tea for causing perspiration.

FORMERLY doctors absolutely interdicted water in all febrile
cases ; but the life and death *instincts* of many patients, as indicated by their intolerable thirst, led some who had been given up
to die, and therefore were allowed what they wanted, to drink
quart after quart of water or cider, immediately after which they
broke out into a drenching perspiration, and began at once to
convalesce. Water should not be drank after calomel ; but the
evil lies in the *calomel*, not in the water.

BOILS confirm this theory, that sickness is a recuperative process. Do they not improve the health, in every single instance?

EXPECTORATION furnishes another illustration, by unloading the system through the lungs. Many years ago the Author had overworked his brain so long that, for months, his forehead ached terribly and incessantly — almost refused to do duty. Taking the cars after exhausting labor, in a severe storm and blow from the lake, in the spring, he sat a while by an open window, till a little hoarseness warned him that he had taken a slight cold.

This throat inflammation crept along down to his lungs, and ended in expectoration so copious, as seriously to interfere with his lectures. But it *cleared his head.* For the first time, in over twenty years, he had no aching forehead; and was at once enabled to resume writing, which this cephalic pain had obliged him to suspend for years. It was worth thousands of dollars in dollars, by giving additional strength to earn them, and many more thousands by promoting personal comforts.

COLDS, like sickness, clear the body of morbid matter. True, diseases originate in them,[94] but, if rightly managed, they would *unload* the system of disease, instead of prostrating it. The colds themselves do not generate sickness, but latent disease generates them.

The system works on under a load of disease it is barely able to carry, the blood so thick that it does not flow freely to the surface, and hence the colds which now stop up this cutaneous outlet of disease. It could barely stand up under this load before; after, it breaks down; yet, but for this load, it would have resisted this cold-taking *condition.*

It now summons all its energies to cast out this disease, sets up a fever to burn it up within the body, nauseates the stomach to prevent its introducing any more carbon for the present, perhaps unloads it through the mouth by vomiting, perhaps through the bowels by expurgation, perhaps also from head and lungs by discharges from both of thick purulent matter, and a foul breath; all perhaps aided by the kidneys. Now, if you will be very careful not to take any *additional* cold, or do anything else to oppress your life force, the first you know you will not only be well again, but feel *better* than before for years; whereas, if you allow these open sores to be suddenly checked, and your exhausted system to be again any way injured, expect to be sicker than if you had not had a cold, and have your constitution broken

38

besides; all depending on how it is *managed*. Colds often do, but never need to, end in sickness. Take them in the start, and they can be cured soon and easily; but let them run, with additions, and they will soon prostrate you; and sooner they are taken in hand the sooner they can be broken up. Those an hour, or a day, or a week old, will take an hour, a day, and a week to cure — the longer the older they are.

The Author respectfully commends these *original* views of sickness, fevers, and colds, &c., to both the profession and the public; and challenges their investigation in the light of both the facts, and the first principles of life and disease. Their scrutiny will enforce their truth.

Section II.

THE VARIOUS PATHIES; ALLOPATHY, HYDROPATHY, ELECTRO-PATHY, BREATHING-PATHY, BATHING-PATHY, FOOD-PATHY, TERRA-PATHY, SOLAR-PATHY, AND AN "UNKNOWN"-PATHY.

114. — Allopathy vs. Homœopathy; Hydropathy and Cold-pathy.

The victims laid low in death by allopathy, despite the curative powers of Nature, and those walking wrecks whose constitutions it has ruined, should warn the well to keep well, and the sick to try some other, *any* other mode of cure, in preference to this, as well as make its practitioners pause and tremble at its many fatal results.[112] How can they hold up their heads as honest, straightforward men? And the facts that so many of them are turning homœopathists, hydropathists, electropathists, &c., and also giving so little medicine now, when they once gave so much, prove that their *own* faith in its virtues is waning. Patients had better let Nature alone, than incur all this life and death *risk*. Doing nothing cannot be worse.

Homœopathy is based in the known law of inoculation, and has made inroads upon the old practice of which it may justly be proud. If its pellets do not cure, there is at least but little danger that they will kill, and that is something; yet this cannot be said of allopathy.

Its hygienic prescriptions are certainly most beneficial, and do much to obviate the disease — in fact would often cure it without any other means.

FOR CHILDREN, especially, it is preferable to allopathy, which is quite too "heroic" for these dear little ones. Yet herb tea is far the best for them, and "granny" the best practitioner, provided she does not overdo the thing.

ELECTROPATHY is a great improvement on its allopathic paternity, especially since it gives but *little* medicines, and looks all around for all aids other than medicinal; and relies much on *Nature*, that great restorer.

HYDROPATHY has certainly achieved curative wonders. Its power and efficacy probably exceed all other medicinal means now known. Of its wonderful healing virtues, its oxygen — of which it contains a large proportion — is probaby one great instrumentality; the various organs imbibing from it through the skin this great promoter of universal life. Scarcely less powerful for good is its efficiency and unequalled capability for removing obstructions — for taking up and carrying out of the system those noxious matters which clog the functions of life, breed disease, and hasten death. For reducing inflammations, and consequent pain, too, it has no equal. It is also an efficient promoter of normal action and of universal life. For reviving debilitated, withered organs, for rebuilding broken constitutions, for cleansing the stomach, bracing the system, and infusing new life throughout all its borders, water excels all medicinal agents combined. It is destined to lay medicines and the lancet on the shelf of the past, and to substitute throughout the whole earth the blessings of health for the miseries of disease, and to double the average span of human life. No family, no individual, should be without a knowledge of the best modes of its application in all sorts and stages of debility and disorder.

IT SOMETIMES injures, on the well known principle that "too much of a good thing is worse than nothing," but it should be proud of that great army of former invalids it has snatched from the jaws of death, and made happy in health. All honor to Preisnitz and his followers.

THE PRINCIPLES on which water cures, probably are, that it opens the pores of the skin,[93] and starts that great means of health into endoubled activity, increasing perspiration, circulation, excre-

tion, and digestion. Its "pack," which consists in wringing a
sheet out of cold water, spreading it on top of several bedquilts,
having the patient lie down in its middle while it and other bed-
clothes are wrapped and tucked in tight all around so as to ex-
clude air, and cause perspiration, and there letting him lie and
sweat for a couple of hours, then wash off and dress. It opens
the pores most effectually, and sometimes acts as if by magic.

Its COMPRESSES are also most beneficial. Those who have any
chronic aches or pains, will find a towel wrung out of cold water,
and placed over the stomach or liver, or any ailing part, every
night on retiring, and kept there till morning, will take out a vast
amount of fever, heat, and pain. Before you know it, your ache
is gone for good. It cures thus: That heat which causes the
pain [113] is all night turning the water in the towel into steam,
which takes up this heat, casts out the disease through this perspiration, and then retains this heat by this sweat passing back
into water. Note how hot this wet towel becomes after half an
hour. This heat *means* something — means that a vast amount
of *fever* is thus allayed, because its cause is removed.

To SWEAT the parts, cover up with an outer woollen cloth, so as
to retain the heat; yet it will probably be best to let it pass off
through the wet cloth. Try both methods, and choose the one
liked the best.

COLD is undoubtedly one of its means of cure. As a remedial
agent it is most efficacious, yet not at all duly appreciated. Why
are almost all men, women, and children so much better every
way in fall than summer? Because it is colder, and this because
cold braces and tones up the whole system. Why, after your
feet or hands have been growing cold, by riding in the cold, do
they suddenly become warm and glowing without much more
moving them? Because a latent property in cold begets reaction.[84] All know that exercising them in the cold warms them;
yet they sometimes get warm without exercise, and solely by the
simple effects on them of cold alone. Its bracing and tonic
effects are marvellous. Please note them.

A COLD-PATHY, well conducted, will be found one of the best
of all the cures, and materials for applying it abound out of
doors from October to April. It must be judiciously conducted,
so as every time to secure the required reaction, or it will injure
terribly.[95]

THAT GLOW which accompanies bathing is doubtless due to the reaction caused by this cold; for lukewarm baths do not produce it, but only those so much hotter than the person is as to produce reaction from the converse principle — *too* much heat. The colder and the hotter any bath, the greater this reaction, provided the system has vitality enough to react, or rise above it.

REACTION is indispensable to all baths. Without it they do irreparable damage. That bath which leaves you chilly and clammy damages most seriously; so do anything, but *something*, to induce it after each bath. And what are all fevers but reaction from preceding chills?

TOO MUCH water — more than the system has the strength to resist — is awful, and will soon finish off its patients. This is true of all baths, all water treatment, and in fact all treatment. Invalids, please take note and warning.

A SMALL SURFACE, when wet, readily reacts; because the rest of the system supplies reacting energy. Hence, those who cannot endure a complete bath, can take a partial one, say of one limb in the morning, another at night, and so on till the whole body is bathed.

THE BED BATH, for cold-blooded, weakly persons, is the best of all baths, for it cannot possibly injure. Try this: After being in bed long enough to get comfortably warm, pass a wet towel, previously wrung out of cold water and laid within reach, yet wrung lightly, over your whole body *under bed-clothes*, if you are able to bear it, over a part of it if you are not; and the heat of your body will turn this water into steam, which now envelopes you, softens your skin, takes out fever in obtaining the heat to convert this water into steam, and promotes sleep. Many are too much run down to endure the *combined* action of air *and* water, who would be benefited by either separately. Yet both together are best where sufficient vitality remains to react.

Let this wet towel lie all night over any spot where you habitually feel any pain. Note how hot it soon becomes, and thus learn how much good it is doing you. And in general, whenever you feel any pain, apply a wet cloth, instead of consulting a doctor.

WATER EMETICS are as efficacious as any other, and leave the stomach emptied, but unparalyzed by its ejecting effort. Mark on what different *principles* ipecac and lukewarm water act. The former is so utterly offensive and repulsive to the system, that it summons all its energies to expel it; making you so mortally sick as to compel a wrenching vomit; whereas, lukewarm water acts solely by virtue of its *temperature*. Both empty the stomach; but the nauseating drug has left more or less of its loathed grains to irritate the intestines and impair the blood, while water leaves you well. Choose between them.

LOBELIA is a much better emetic than ipecac. A Thompsonian course, consisting of a steam bath, a hot capsicum and bayberry-bark tea, with porridge, followed by a lobelia emetic, certainly does bring up an astonishing quantity of ropy slime, which is much better out of the stomach than in; besides leaving you as bright as a lark, and able to renew labor at once. The disuse of what is so useful is unusual.

115. — THE BREATHING CURE.

THE BREATHING PATHY is by far the most efficacious of all the cures. The Author hit upon it thus. When he first established, in his Philadelphia office, in January, 1838, he opened courses of lectures in several places at once, thus lecturing every evening. They brought such crowds for examinations, as finally to so completely exhaust him as to compel him, with all his hardihood, to dismiss callers, crawl up stairs by the banisters, and throw himself upon the lounge; when he involuntarily fell to panting, or breathing deep and fast, as if perishing for more breath, as one sometimes will when all beat out.

This extra breathing soon made him dizzy, by thinning a part, but only a part, of his blood. Presently this extra breathing caused reaction, and sent the blood bounding and rushing throughout his system, producing a prickling sensation all through those parts most exercised.

LECTURE TIME arrived, after about half an hour's breathing. He arose, and walking on to find a cab to take him to his lecture-room, was surprised to find himself so much stronger than he had supposed possible, that he walked on and on, two and a half miles, to Northern Liberty Hall, gave altogether the best lecture of the course, and walking home, set down to his desk and wrote *with all his might*, seemingly as by inspiration, *until after sunrise* the next morning, without food or sleep, just on the extra strength he had derived from that extra breathing. And thousands of times since, when "all beat out" by the office labors of the day — and it *takes* something to tire *him* — he has thrown himself on his back, first opening doors and windows, and by thus breathing deeply and fast, he establishes this reaction and consequent glow, rises in from five to fifteen, sometimes in two, minutes, completely rested and re-invigorated, and then holds his audience for hours.

He considers, as all who know him consider, his ability to endure labor, not merely astonishing, but seemingly in defiance of all the known laws of physiology.

GENERAL LYON incidentally confirmed and illustrated this breathing cure thus. At dinner, in Detroit, in 1849, he said, —

"PROFESSOR FOWLER, I have to ask scientific men hard questions, and want you to explain this physiological anomaly. Almost ever since you examined my phrenology in Washington, ten years ago, I have been the surveyor-general of three new States, and spent most of my time in the woods surveying; have taken corps after corps of men from behind the desk of the lawyer and counter of the merchant, many of them city reared and white livered, right out into the woods in mid-winter, with one buffalo robe spread upon the snow under, and another over us, perhaps soon snowed under, without even a tent, and perhaps wet up to their waist besides in traversing swamps and marshes, and yet never knew one of these city pampered men to catch cold on *going into* the woods; but I never brought a corps of young men *into* a city but in three days every one of them was barking with a cold. Why should none take cold on going *into* the woods, but none escape it on coming *out?*"

"Your puzzle, general, is easily solved by this physiological fact, that since breathing thins the blood, their extra breathing of fresh cold air in the woods sends their blood bounding to their skin so thinned by oxygen that it circulates freely at the surface, thus both protecting it against changes of temperature, and converting external cold into internal warmth; whereas, on coming into the city, they breathe the spent air of a stirred up seven by nine bed-room, which leaves their blood too thick to flow to and protect their skins, and thus predisposed them to colds."

ARMY experiences also illustrate the efficacy of this breathing cure on a large scale. Soldiers by the hundred thousand find themselves immeasurably better, notwithstanding all their exposures, than when at home; because, breathing copiously of fresh air promotes every other function, and expels disease with marvellous efficacy. But for its dysentery, consequent on its poor and changed water, army life would be healthier than city.

TEXANS, when asked why they lived in houses with openings large enough to crawl through, replied, —

"Because they are more healthy than tight ones."

Northern houses take too much pains to keep out their best doctor, cool air. No medicines are equally efficacious to prevent or cure any and all ailments. And this doctor charges as much *less than nothing* as it costs to shut him out.

TWENTY-ONE years ago, in his phrenological journal, the Author propounded this breathing-cure tonic and restorative, which is often quoted in common with others having a like origin, minus its origin. Still the ideas are just as good *without* credit as with. Thanks for their dissemination.

ALL cures will be aided by this breathing cure. Whether you take "calomel and jalap," or little pills, or all sorts of pills, or the water cure, or any other cure, just superadd this *deep and fast breathing* cure, and you will recover as if by magic, yet probably attribute your cure to other sources. It is at least both *cheap* and *handy*.

116. — AMOUNT AND KIND OF EXERCISE — WALKING, DANCING, ROWING, LIFTING, PLAYING, &c.

HOW MUCH exercise each requires for the time being can be determined only by the feelings of each at that time. As normal appetite constitutes an infallible guide to the required quantity of food,[48] so muscular appetite, unless rendered abnormal by inaction, will say when and how much exercise each requires at that time, and when they are taking too much, or at improper times. To determine whether we need it, is just as easy as to determine whether we require food, and by a similar index — an *appetite* for it. Those require it who are benefited by it, feel better after taking it, sleep more sweetly, experience an increase of appetite, or additional clearness of mind, or agreeableness of disposition, as indeed all whose business confines them much within doors, and also those who feel a craving for motion.

Sedentaries, convinced of their need of it, often take it in excess, or unseasonably, or too violently. That same appetite which demands it, closely watched, will admonish the instant this occurs, when the patient should desist *at once*. A kind of trembling, hurried, excited, and yet weakened state of the muscles, so that instead of playing easily and voluntarily, they must be *forced*, indicates excess, which always injures. Stop exercise the instant such trembling commences.

Excessive, and also fitful or violent exercise, especially for the sedentary, is injurious. Such should exercise *deliberately* as well as eat slowly, else exhaustion supervenes before a due degree of exercise is obtained.

It should be taken when the system is prepared to sustain it, and is often beneficial after severe mental application. Before meals, especially before breakfast, is generally a good season. Just before retiring is a good time, when it has not been taken during the day, and by those who resort to indoor exercise. "Better late than never."

Yet some work too hard, so that their muscles rob their brains, and thus become stupid in mind, averse to study, drowsy over books, and blunted in their finer sensibilities. Such should work less — should perhaps restrain their craving for action, just as those who overeat should restrain appetite.

From four to six hours of vigorous muscular exercise is the least compatible with first-rate health. Excellent constitutions may endure close confinement for years, yet must run down finally. A lower degree of health may be preserved on less exercise, but as the order of nature is to spend from six to ten hours daily in the open air, so the perfection of health requires a great amount of muscular action, and the more, generally speaking, the better, provided it is of the right kind. About four hours brisk labor per day will both suffice for exercise, and, well expended by each person on something productive, would just about supply the human family with comforts, luxuries of life, artificial wants, and extravagances, excepted. How admirable is this adaptation of the amount of labor requisite for health to that required to provide man with the necessaries of life. Since so much exercise is necessary for health, what shall we say of those merchants, clerks, lawyers, students, and the sedentary classes generally, who confine themselves to their offices, desks, and books, from morning till night, year in and year out, scarcely going out of doors, except to and from their business, and then *taking cars?*

39

If these principles of exercise were put in practice, very few city conveyances would be required or patronized, One would think that our sedentaries, starved almost to death for exercise, would embrace every opportunity to take it, walking at least to and from their business, sawing their own wood, and the like. Yet fashion requires that they hire horses to do the former and servants to do the latter.

DANCING can be made as beneficial as it is delightful. Though dancing but seldom, and then all night in hot and illy-ventilated rooms, and then going out exhausted and exposed to colds, together with most of the associations of the ball-room, are most pernicious; yet for sedentaries to select their company, and meet at each other's houses in the afternoon or evening, always avoiding over-exertion, and retiring by nine or ten o'clock, if practised often, would supply in part that deficiency of muscular action which causes so many to sicken and die, and restore many an invalid now perishing by inches with pure inanition, and preserve and even reinvigorate the health of many now going into a decline. Dancing *might* be, yet rarely is, so conducted as to prove eminently beneficial, without occasioning any evil. In fact it is founded in the nature of man, and can therefore be turned to a most excellent practical account in a great variety of ways. To sedentary young women, this form of exercise is particularly recommended. Yet all should dance to their own music, vocal or instrumental, or both, and also in company with their parents and elders. Young people should never dance exclusively by themselves. Yet our present purpose being to point out to the sedentary a feasible mode of taking exercise, to guard against evils too often associated with it is digressive.

Besides the sedentary, those laborers who sit or stand much in one posture, will find that change and diversity of manual action secured by dancing to dispel fatigue and promote health, and perhaps even render unhealthy occupations healthy. Seamstresses, goldsmiths, shoemakers, and many artisans of like occupations, who have no substitute, should dance daily as much as cat; and students will find it promotive alike of health and of the mental action, and therefore discipline they seek.[440]

WALKING is one of the very best kinds of exercise, easily taken, cheap, and every way adapted to the existing states of all.

When brisk, it taxes every muscle and all the functions, but when leisurely, it is adapted to invalids. In taking it, walk erect, allow the arms to swing as they list, keep the shoulders well set back, and, when convenient, walk with a friend. All the better if of the opposite sex, and a wife, husband, daughter, son, or lover, so as to impart to it that mental zest and luxury which greatly improve its utility. Yet walking alone and *musing* over some pleasant subject or reminiscences, or meditating, will benefit both mind and body together. To be useful, it must at least be *delightful*, and the more parts it brings into co-operative exercise the better, so that adding conversations improves it.

FARMING AND GARDENING, to those who like to see things grow, furnish one of the best forms of exercise. Man was made to raise his own food and fruits, and hence loves to see and make things *grow*. Spading, planting, hoeing, weeding, ploughing, and nursing and gathering vegetables, fruits, and flowers, develop the muscles, and promote every life function. Man was made to enjoy *raising* as well as eating good things. Working the ground, which is highly electric, restores and regulates those magnetic currents which manifest life.

AN ORTHODOX MINISTER, who preached near Boston, consulted me in March, 1860, as to what business he could engage in with success; his health having been completely broken down by preaching; was told that he only needed exercise, and that cultivating a garden would enable him to regain his health, yet retain his pastorate. He leased a garden, worked daily till comfortably tired, called again early in May, said his health was rapidly recovering, yet that he preached without difficulty, and his parishioners said *much better* sermons than before.

WORK of any and all kinds, by a law of things, becomes excellent exercise, proving it is inviting.[107] All kinds of exercise, taken as a task or drudgery, therefore injure. We should take some kind we *love*, and try to love whatever kind we do take.

GYMNASTICS are excellent, when not carried to excess, as they usually are. Each emulous to outdo all, often strain these muscles, yet leave those comparatively inert.

DIO LEWIS's light gymnastics are excellent, yet often fatigue without even yet giving the muscle-developing exercise demanded. They use up the vitality without taxing the muscles. They

are immeasurably better than none, and often effect remarkable
cures; yet there are better kinds.   Their company, mingling of
the sexes, gayety, laughter, and many like things, entitle them to
right hearty commendation, especially for sedentary ladies; but
as exercise they are completely distanced by

BUTLER'S LIFTING CURE.[36]   It brings the *entire* muscular system into *co-operative* action.   The strain of exercise should come
upon *all* the muscles, not on a few only.   This Butler effects by
elastic springs, which, by yielding, call one set of muscles after
another into *combined* action.   Lifting on what does not give,
throws too much strain upon *one* set, while a yielding weight
draws first one set, then another, into action, until finally *all*
unite, and then all relax together.

A SUDDEN strain or jerk is injurious.   The lift should increase
and decrease *gradually.*   All this, and much more, Butler's mode
of lifting effects.

A SUBSTITUTE for his perfect apparatus, which should be in
every family, may be made thus : Take about thirty feet of cod-
line, or any cord made of cotton, or that *stretches,* twist and
double, then twist and double again, tie the ends, and attach two
sections of a broom-handle, or any round stick adapted to lift by,
one to each end, each about a foot long, and, adjusting its length
to your height, stand on one stick while you lift on the other,
slowly but gradually increasing till you have put forth about
as much strength as you can with comfort, hold on two or three
seconds, and ease off gradually.   Now rest a few minutes, and
repeat, lifting still more, and rest again, then lift and rest again,
about four times in all.

ERECTNESS of posture in lifting is desirable, while to lift in
a stooping posture is injurious.   To obtain this posture, straddle
your stick, that is, let it pass up between the thighs, so as to keep
the spine straight and shoulders well thrown back.

ALL WEAK spots will be found and fortified by this mode of
lifting.   Those who are dyspeptic will flinch at the stomach,
while those who have weak lungs will hack after lifting; showing
that it searches out to strengthen those soft places, on that principle of balance already expounded.[34]

FIVE MINUTES can thus be made to yield more and better exercise than an hour in any other form.   This saving of time is

certainly something to those whose time is precious. It can also
be practised in your room, on rising and retiring, thus consuming
only scraps of time.

THE INDIAN DANCE, which consists in hopping up and down on
one foot after the other, or tossing the body back and forth from
right to left, meanwhile allowing the arms and visceral organs to
shake around as they may, is also one of the best kinds of exercise,
because it as it were *churns* the bowels. The Indians take it at
their feasts, to enable them to eat still more, because it is specifically adapted to cure dyspepsia, and promote digestion.

THE INDIAN LOPE, or run, is quite like the Indian dance, and
quite as beneficial. It consists in an easy, loping run, in which all
the visceral organs are allowed perfect liberty to shake around at
pleasure, and is really most excellent as exercise.

SWINGING THE ARMS, with or without dumb-bells, thrusting them
rapidly back and forwards, kicking the feet, but not against anything, and any and all such bodily exercises, are beneficial.

THE BEST TIME for taking exercise is in the morning, before
work begins, or just before retiring, but it should be *regular*.
Those who use their brains mainly, whether in business or professional pursuits, will find a right good lift to rest them amazingly, by equalizing the circulation, and diverting it from the parts
oppressed. Its recuperative effects are indeed wonderful. Taken
at night, or after the day's mental labors are closed, it distributes
the blood from congested centres, sends it to parts robbed by
your business, and especially equalizes the circulation before retiring, so that the system can at once begin to recuperate in sleep.
An evening's pull will redouble both your night's sleep and next
day's work, as well as your personal luxury of living. Adapt
your time to your circumstances, but take *some* time.

Will the reader be persuaded to rig up some apparatus, and
make vigorous trial for at least a month, sufficient to realize
experimentally some of the advantages to be derived from it.
Those really remarkable cures it has effected within the Author's
personal knowledge, should encourage all to at least give it a
fair *trial*, if no more. It is really working wonders.

That the special *reason* of this efficacy lies in its restoring *balance* of action, is proved by its working its greatest cures upon
sedentary, literary, and business men. Excessive brain action,

without proportionate muscular, caused the particular ailment of each,[34] and this exercise restores this lost balance, by calling an unused system of organs into action.

Many a man, now so run down that he thinks he absolutely must quit business or die, by simply spending fifteen minutes daily or tri-weekly in lifting, might work on, and work himself both well and *rich*. As a cure for dyspepsia it has no peer.

117. — The Sleeping, Laughing, Play-spell, and Electric Cures.

The sleeping cure has already been noted.[97] For wakeful, nervous persons, it is often "hard to take," but very curative. When a sick child or adult falls into a sound, sweet sleep, rest assured the patient is convalescing, and let all who are sick sleep all they can, and whenever they can. Yet that stupor produced by opiates or morphine is not sleep, has none of its beneficial effects, is a stupid counterfeit, and enhances the ailment.

The laugh cure is a new pathy, just introduced, but most efficacious. It can be taken in a daily play-spell, as tartar-emetic is taken in molasses. Whatever amuses and diverts supplies the medicine. If the sick patients love music, or company, or concerts, or any kind of games, such as billiards, or dominoes, or euchre, or anything else not hurtful, give them all they will take, and in the form each may prefer. Lively company in the sick chamber is better than cathartics or anodynes; but moody, plaintive, sad, mournful company ought never to go in, and should be kicked out unceremoniously.

A May gay party of ladies and gentlemen mutually agreed to throw off all restraints, doff their prim proprieties for the day, and just "go in" for a right jolly good time. In clambering up the side of a hill, some one espied a crow's nest high up, when all hands set up a "whorah for the crow's nest," each striving to be "in first." In their scrambling haste some lost their handholds, and footholds, and slid, or rolled down hill; at which the others set up a rousing shout of hilarious laughter, by which many of the laughers also lost their holds, and slid and rolled on down with them; when all laughed, and roared, and shouted, and screeched, till their sides ached, so that they really could not laugh any longer; and ever after the mention of the crow's nest was the key-note for a hearty ha, ha!

A YOUNG LADY, member of the party, many years afterwards, falls sick, grows weaker, is given up to die by her physicians and acquaintances, becomes too far gone to recognize her friends by name, and about to die; when one of the crow's nest party, determined to make one last desperate effort to save her, calls to see her; but finds her too far gone to recognize him, till he mentions the crow's nest story, at which she smiled. This smile gave her strength to smile more a few moments after, and this enough to giggle once or twice, and this to laugh right heartily soon after, till she laughed herself tired. This induced that sleep which strengthened her for another laughing spell; and sleep and laughing snatched her from the very jaws of death, restored her to life and friends, and she "still lives," a monument to the laugh cure; and married her saviour.

LAUGHING matches act like magic in restoring invalids, and are easily gotten up, thus: Set up or hold up a chip, a stick, a piece of paper, anything, and go to ha-ha-ing mechanically over it, and this "forced laugh" will soon bring on a genuine one, and this others still more hearty, which should be kept up till all hands are tired. Very little things will suffice for laughing timber. Laugh, if only at your own folly for laughing at such silly nonsense; whereas, nothing is silly which promotes health.

DAILY PLAY-SPELLS, say at night, will make you sleep the better, and this gives you strength to work the harder the next day, and ever after. And old admiring patron said, —

"Professor, don't ever fail to weave into every course of lectures your idea of a diurnal play-spell. I heard you tell your audience thirty years ago, once every day to dismiss all business cares, and give up to some recreation or amusement for an hour, have habitually followed that advice ever since, and cannot tell the good it has done me."

AMUSEMENTS of course come under this general head, but will be found discussed, *per se*, in Vol V., and in connection with family amusements in Sexual Science. This idea cannot well be broached too often, nor overdone.

ELECTROPATHY and animal magnetism often effect remarkable cures. Undoubtedly life is carried on chiefly by electricity. Sickness consists mainly in the derangement of the magnetic forces. Electricity or galvanism can be, and often is, applied so as to cure, by restoring these magnetic currents.

A MOTHER incidentally remarked that she expected any minute to be summoned to see her sons die of consumption in a neighboring city; was advised to try electricity to dissolve his tubercles, by putting the positive pole at the nape of his neck, and the negative over his lungs. This so dissolved the pus in his lungs, that it literally almost choked him by running so fast out of his mouth, took out their inflammation, and he recovered, went to work, took a terrible cold eighteen months afterwards, by standing around in the rain and slush to hear an out of door speaker in December, and when coming down the *second* time, cursed the galvanic battery because, by restoring him, it obliged him to endure the agony of dying twice, the first being virtually at an end before the battery restored him.

Its APPLICATION should be governed by this general principle. Sending the electric current *down*, the nerves relax, and take on the inflammation; while sending it *up*, tones them up; that is, for inflammations, place the positive pole at the *head* of the nerve affected, and the negative at its end; but for paralysis or inaction, place the *negative* pole at the extremity, and positive at the origin of an organ.

DR. BOWLES, of Philadelphia, is the best practitioner on this system within the Author's knowledge.

118. — THE SUN-CURE, EARTH-CURE, WILL-CURE, AND LET-ALONE-CURE.

BASKING IN THE SUN is often resorted to by animals, especially in the spring. Alligators, as soon as they are thawed out enough to crawl, mount some log, and sun themselves into warmth and life. Probably electropathy[117] and the sun-cure are virtually the same, and cure on the same principle, namely, by charging the system with electricity, and regulating and restoring its currents.

To APPLY it, sit or lie nearly or quite naked in the sun, or remain in a hot-house nearly nude, or sit or stand or lie in the sunshine from a window, a bay window being the best, or bask yourself any way you like in the sun's rays. Hence, being out of doors when the sun shines is beneficial, but not enough to "raise a blister."

SHADED HOUSES are very unhealthy, because rendered damp by their shade. Many a family loses one after another of their darlings from this cause and that, besides having some invalid member always on hand, because their houses are damp, and therefore mouldy, and therefore pestilential. You might mortally hate to cut down those grand old trees your father planted, but had better let in sunshine by turning them into firewood, than to inflict on the female members of your family, who suffer most, because always indoors, all the misery those trees cause them. Looking over those families living in shaded houses, see how much more sickly such are than those which occupy sunny ones, and learn the lesson they practically inculcate. Those who build among trees may expect to patronize doctors, apothecaries, nurses, and undertakers. Still, trees on the north, north-east, and northwest sides of houses do no damage.

OPEN SHUTTERS and windows for a like reason drive out moisture by letting in the sun. Do you think to keep your houses *cool* by keeping out the air? Simpletons! don't you know that the air is always *cooler* than you are? Is the air ever ninety-eight degrees? Does it not *feel* cool when it blows on you? Since the air is *never* ninety-seven degrees, of course shutting it out shuts *out* the cold, but shuts the heat *in*. A recent French writer advises housewives to keep houses cool by keeping the windows and blinds shut. The thermometer will tell him, and all others who choose to consult it, that any and all close rooms are hotter in very hot weather than open ones; because open ones allow the cooling air to sweep through and carry off the heat. Everybody's own *feelings* tell them that *all* draughts of air are *cooling* always, heating never.

HOT WEATHER also creates perspiration, which renders a draught of air still more cooling. Ladies, keep your doors, windows, and blinds open in hot weather, and, fathers, cut down all trees which shade your houses much.

THE EARTH or clay-cure is about equally efficacious. That is, the ground is highly electric, as "the magnet" proves. Contact with soil is marvellously restorative. A mud poultice applied to the stings of bees, wasps, and hornets, kills their venom almost instantly. This fact is full of meaning. Applying it to the bite of a venomous snake or mad dog will at once take down the swelling and ease the pain. Wet with water, spittle, spirits, any liquid, and apply at once.

40

For ANY pain, permanent or sharp, wear a dirt poultice; dry is good, but wet better; that is, every night lay on it a bag of earth or clay equal in size to the sore spot, and the first you know your pain is *non inventus est*. Try it for dyspepsia, liver and kidney difficulties, even consumption, catarrh, &c., and charge and credit the results to the Author. Though this application is *dirt*-y, yet it will make a *"clean* sweep" of your aches and pains. Try it for consumption, and you will snap your fingers at doctors' nostrums.

LYING and sleeping on the bare ground, say in a bunk of dirt indoors, will work wonders by way of drawing out disease, and toning up and restoring you. Soldiers and others who camp out generally lose their aches and grow rugged.

GOING BAREFOOT is excellent for children, so is playing in mud puddles.[641]

THE WILL-CURE is, however, by far the best and most efficacious of all the cures. It is God's own specific invention for this identical purpose. He "foreknew" that men would so outrage his health laws as to become sick, and hence need a remedial agent both always "on call," and the best restorative He could devise, and "invented" this. Its curative *principle* is based in the magic power wielded by the mind over the body, and each of its parts. This great truth has come up twice before,[25] but cannot be cited too often or forcibly. Those who *think* they are sick, *are* sick, although perfectly well, while those who *think* they are well, are well, even though sick. *Imagination* makes sick and makes well, *ad infinitum*.

VITATIVENESS [14] puts forth this *will to live*, and contributes essentially to the preservation of life by creating a resistance to disease. Thus two persons, A and B, exactly alike in constitutions, kind of sickness, and all other respects, except that A has Vitativeness large, and B small, are brought near the grave. A loves life so dearly, and clings to it with such tenacity, as to struggle with might and main against the disease, and he lives through it; while B, scarcely caring whether he lives or dies, does not stem the downward current, does not brace himself up against it, but yields to its sway, is borne downward and swallowed up in death. An illustrative anecdote: —

A RICH MAIDEN, who had already lived twenty years longer

than her impatient heirs desired, finally fell sick, and was evidently breathing her last. But overhearing one of her bystanding heirs congratulate another that she was now dying, so that they could enjoy her fortune, and feeling indignant, replied, "I won't die; I'll live to spite you;" meanwhile putting forth a powerful mental struggle for life, she recovered and lived many years, evidently in consequence of that powerful determination to live thus called forth.

MRS. RUNKLE, struck with consumption, kept trying to persuade her husband to promise her, in the event of her death, not to marry again; to which he kept replying, evasively, that they were trying to cure her, and hoped to succeed, but evaded a direct reply. When almost dead, determined with her last breath to extort from him a *categorical* answer, he finally frankly replied, —

"Well, Mrs. Runkle, if I should make a promise to a dying wife, which I consider you are, not to marry again, I should feel bound to fulfil it. Since you oblige me to say yes or no, I had rather not promise."

"Well, Mr. Runkle, if you *don't* promise me not to marry again, then *I won't die.*"

And she didn't — didn't, because she wouldn't; and is alive and well to-day, just because she *wouldn't* die. (Hadn't he better have *promised* her?)

MRS. GUNN, of Painsville, Ohio, struck with consumption, a most devoted mother, tried to induce her husband, in case she died, to keep the family together, not put the children out; but he would not absolutely promise. At last, though actually struck with death, her extremities already dying and sight failing, replied to his "don't know" answer, "Well, if *you* won't keep this family together then *I will;*" and suiting the action to the word, by a powerful effort of will, drove the retiring blood back through her system, got well because she willed to, lived to keep her family together till all were married, and procuring a manikin, lectured many years to the ladies on health.

The world is *full* of kindred facts. All must know of wonderful analogous cures. This vitative faculty causes and explains them, and even when medicines benefit, this Will-cure is the main cure. Without it other cures are useless, and with it, unnecessary. Nature can beat doctors. What she undertakes to do she does *well*. Vitativeness is her doctor and materia medica. Then put yourself under *her* sole care, just as you would under any other medical practitioner, and not insult her by mixing up her restoratives with doctors' drugs.

THE LET-ALONE Cure is but the outgrowth of this Will-cure. How many millions have grown worse by doctoring till they had no more means or hope, given up, did nothing, waited to die, kept on living to their wonderment, and finally *got well*. What a pity! not their getting well, but keeping themselves sick so long by so expensive a practice.

FAITH is only another form of this Will-cure and the Let-alone-cure combined. A calm, serene *trust* in the recuperative powers of Nature is both the best of all cures, and only another expression for faith in God and trust in Providence. This "faith" was the essential and curative ingredient in Christ's miracles. But for this faith would the man at the pool have been able or disposed to "take up his bed and walk"?

NOYES, the leader of the Oneida Community, heard these views from the Author's lips, while in Brooklyn, before he formed his Community, and has made this "Let-alone" "faith" cure its only remedial agent. The Mormons also make it theirs. They do indeed work miraculous cures, by making their patients *believe* they can cure, which belief revives and inspires Vitativeness to that action which cures.

LAYING-ON-OF-HANDS doctors all cure by this same will-power principle. See how applicants crowd their rooms, entries, and even adjacent sidewalks, awaiting their "turn!" Behold the cords of crutches and canes of those who could hardly walk there with them, but "arise and walk" home, and go to work without them! Their cures are amazing, in both number and efficacy. Effected on what *principle?* By inspiring *desire* and *hope* of life. If these patients, if all patients, will get and nurture this same desire and hope without these "laying on" mummeries, they will get well just as soon without as with them. But, God bless them; for without them patients would not get up this faith and hope, and hence must remain sick.

TRUST in the doctor amounts to the same thing. His medicines act like a charm, because the patient *thinks* he knows precisely what to give; whereas, that same medicine, taken without hope or confidence, would be useless, and the same hope and faith without any medicine, would cure just as well as with.

READERS are respectfully invited to *scan* this Will-power-faith-let-alone pathy, and if well, apply it to keeping well, but if sick, to your restoration, by a quiet *mental* resisting and stemming of the current of disease, and by a firm, resolute, mental clasp, hold on life; by resolving that you *will* get well, and fight off disease any how; by sending life-force to your stomach, bowels, lungs, head, hand, foot, even little-finger nail, or any other part affected. This will wonderfully promote all other pathies, yet interfere with none.

SECTION III.

CURES FOR SPECIAL AILMENTS.

119. — ASCERTAIN AND OBVIATE THE CAUSE.

ALL sickness is caused; [18] none is incidental, or providential. [14] Each twinge of pain has its *specific* cause, and must needs continue till that cause, and no other, is removed. This is proved by the general law of causation. [18]

THE FIRST restorative step, therefore, consists in obviating this *cause*, and the first step in this obviation consists in *knowing* just what that cause is.

Those pains and aches which accompany and indicate disease, reveal this individual cause. This is their specific mission. One cause inflicts one kind of pain, and another cause another pain. [21] This enables all to trace all their individual pains and aches to their own *exact* cause. Then trace up every ache to its *source*. Ask yourself what made this twinge, and from what that dull, heavy pain originated. This may take time, but *give* that time. Do nothing till you first know precisely *what to* do. The *diagnosis* of disease is the most essential means of its obviation.

THE NAMES given to this disease and that are of little account. Whether your fever is called bilious, or typhus, or typhoid, or intermittent, or remittent, &c., is of little account. [113] What concerns you chiefly is, whether it originates from a foul stomach, or from over-worked muscles, or brain, or chronic mental unhappi-

ness, or what its precise cause is. Look around sharply to see
what health law you are perpetually violating. It is palpable, for
otherwise you would not suffer. It may be the last thing you
would suspect. May not that tea or coffee you are so particular
to have every meal, and just so strong, cause that nervous headache, or rheumatism, or neuralgia, or terrible sick-headache you
are compelled to endure? Perhaps tobacco "had a hand" in it.
Rest assured that the more severe your pain, the more egregious
that outrage of the health laws which caused it.

"That cold caused it." Yes, but what caused that cold?
"That slow fever caused it." But what caused that slow fever?
"O, *my* disease is nervousness." Then what caused your ner-
vousness?

SEVERAL violations of the health laws probably produced it.
One violation will rarely prostrate the system, because it can conquer one enemy singly, but not several collectively. Perhaps the
very things you are now doing to cure it aggravates it.

EXCESS OF CARBON is a prolific cause of disease. The number
and aggravation of those diseases engendered by its excess in the
system is great. Why do Northerners sicken at the South? Because they continue to eat as freely as before ; yet, since a given
quantity of oxygen can combine with no more than its fixed equivalent of carbon, and since a warmer and therefore more rarified
atmosphere prevents their inhaling as much oxygen as at the
North, they of course evacuate less carbon from the system by
respiration than they take into it by eating and drinking. A surfeit of carbon is the necessary consequence, and this exposes them
to those malignant fevers which prevail in tropical climates.
Southern emigrants, who eat less and bathe much, escape, because
they occasion no such glut of carbon, and all who "move South,"
besides eating less, should eat food less highly carbonized, for the
same reasons that we should eat less, and *less* highly carbonized
food, in the summer than winter.[57]

That the summer complaints of children are caused by this
same excess of carbon, is rendered evident by the fact that they
prevail most in hot weather, and diminish as the cold season
approaches ; because they then inhale more oxygen, and hence
consume more carbon, thus partially restoring the proportion between the two. And if parents would serve less food, and that

less carbonated, to children during the summer months, many who now sicken and die would keep well. Hence, give little butter, fat, or sweets, because they all contain a great proportion of already superabundant carbon.

DYSPEPSIA consists mainly in this same carbonic surplus. This is also established by its improvement generally consequent on the approach of cold weather. And all whose health is better in the fall and winter than spring and summer, may know that their maladies are occasioned by surplus carbon, or over-eating.

CONSUMPTION consists in an excess of carbon over oxygen. As the lungs waste away, they afford a less surface for oxygenating the blood. Of course less carbon is burnt up, the body is cold, and the system decays. Let such be doubly particular to reduce their eating and enhance their breathing. Of what use is any more carbon than can be burnt up by respiration? And as their stomachs are more vigorous than their lungs, of course they should eat less than they crave.

These views are still further sustained by the chemical analysis of the putrid matter of boils, fever-sores, ulcers, diseased lungs, and the like, by its containing about fifty-four per cent. of carbon. Indeed, most obstructions, irritations, inflammations, and the like, will be found to consist mainly in its surplus. These abscesses may therefore fairly be considered as the outlets of that surplus carbon which occasioned them. Hence their beneficial influence. Hence, also, butter, fat, sweets, and other highly carbonated substances, provoke boils and cutaneous eruptions. So do high-living and over-eating.

Perhaps your system has been thrown out of balance by your vocation taxing only one set of organs. Perhaps something you eat or drink, or do, or don't eat and do, caused it.

At all events, hunt all around, and keep on hunting, till accumulated evidence assures you that you have finally ascertained; spotted the identical cause, or causes, for there are probably several causes. Of course their abbreviation is next in order. If they are consequent on over-work, of course work less; if in over-eating, eat but little; if in drinks, stop them; if in over-working only one set of organs, as the brain or muscles, change the action; or if in any extreme, go to its opposite. Probably one or another of the following cures will restore you, gradually if not rapidly.

119. — DYSPEPSIA, ITS EVILS, AND CAUSES, AND SIGNS.

INDIGESTION probably creates more disease than any other cause. Though it itself rarely terminates fatally, yet it is the parent of many ailments which do. It generates, by fermentation, that corrupt matter which clogs, irritates, and fevers the whole body. The amount of corruption it engenders is almost incredible, as is evinced in the foul breath of dyspeptics, which is as obnoxious to life as it is loathsome. How soon breathing it all would sicken you; yet you would inspire only what they expire. How vast the amount they expire every hour; yet this is by no means all they manufacture. All the evacuations put together cannot unload it as fast as it is engendered, and hence it gathers on the lungs and brain in the form of phlegm, which oppresses and irritates both, and engenders consumption, fevers, and all sorts of complaints. Dyspeptics expectorate most while suffering from indigestion, because the salivary glands are closely interrelated with the stomach, and hence the mucus consequent on indigestion. All bad-tasting phlegm should therefore always be *spit out*, never swallowed; yet sweet-tasted spittle should be swallowed.

MENTAL WORRYMENT is the main cause of indigestion. An overworked or worried *mind* has exhausted the energies of the brain, which has gone out on a foraging expedition in quest of vital force. It finds it in the stomach, and remorselessly appropriates to brain sustainment those vital forces needed for digestion. This robbery leaves the food so long undigested that it sours. Of course, eating fast, irregularly, wrong kinds of food, &c., aggravates it, as do all other wrong habits.

You are a business man, and have launched out so freely that debts and debtors, credits and creditors, all give you a world of trouble. You lie awake nights thinking how you shall work through your dilemma. You snatch meals and lunches, work early and late, rush here, there, everywhere, are more snappish than the snapping-turtle, grasp at this and that, and read the papers, eat, sleep, do business, do everything by *steam*.

SHUTTING OFF this steam is your first means of cure. Do anything, everything, without this, and it gripes on still. *Stop short*, and sober down. Get out of this eternal stew. Take a daily dose of the play-spell cure. Give yourself plenty of time to eat, sleep, and rest out. Do the best you can without worrying, but fret not thyself for anybody or anything. This removes its cause, and will soon remove itself.

You are a broken-spirited woman, confined by family cares. You lost your darling child, or husband, or mother, and keep nursing your grief; or your marriage has completely disappointed you. Where you expected so much, you find a great deal worse than nothing. You sip on patiently of your embittered cup till Nature gives out. Your bad, sad, disappointed feelings kill appetite, kill your interest in life,[118] and everything but that child, which is one causeless round of worriment. Your brain and nerves naturally become fevered, and *must* have vital force, rob your stomach, and breed dyspepsia.

But it is on the nervous system and brain that dyspepsia exerts its most deleterious influences. The corruption and rank poison it engenders cannot but lash up both nerves and brain to abnormal, and therefore painful action. Dyspeptics always feel irresolute, gloomy, and wretched, in proportion as their disease is aggravated, however favorable for enjoyment all their external circumstances. Disdain the fortune of an ASTOR if indigestion accompanies its reception. However wealthy, or respected, or beloved, or otherwise capacitated for enjoyment, they are poor, miserable creatures — poor, because they cannot enjoy, however much they may possess of the bounties of Nature; and miserable, because this disease turns even their facilities for happiness into occasions of pain. They would go mourning even in paradise.

THESE SIGNS show whether your complaints are caused by indigestion. It generally emaciates. Those who are perpetually growing more and more thin-favored, and specially sinking in at the abdomen and cheeks, may know that this disease is approaching; as may also all who feel a gnawing, sunken, fainting, "gone" sensation at the stomach, or are unable to postpone their meals without inconvenience, or who feel a ravenous appetite, and still continue to crave after they have eaten freely; or who feel prostrated, inefficient, listless, misanthropic, or irritable; hating, hateful, and fretful; or who belch up wind frequently — it being a gas formed on the stomach by the souring of their food.[62, 63] Dyspeptics are perpetually cramming, yet virtually starving, because their stomachs do not extract from food its nutrition, and paradoxical as it may seem, the more they eat the more they starve.

Besides being hollow-cheeked, and lank in the abdomen, they are generally costive. This is occasioned by the sluggishness of the stomach and bowels; so that the removal of this single symptom, or effect of this disease, will generally obviate this disease itself.

Acidity of the stomach, caused by souring of the food, generally accompanies dyspepsia. This acidity can and should be removed. One means is by taking those kinds of food and chemical agents which will neutralize it. Alkalies will sometimes do this. Oyster shells, baked and powdered, often neutralize the acids of the stomach, as is evinced by the wind they bring up, and often do at least temporary good. Weak ley, made from clean wood ashes, has a kindred effect.

Some acids decompose other acids, and hence some stomachic acidities may be cured by taking the right kinds of acids. Yet those found in fruits are far preferable for this purpose. Hence lemons often improve the tone of the stomach; and when they do, should be eaten freely before meals, or in food. Hence, also, very sour lemonade is often highly beneficial for dyspeptics, and should be drank, not in gills, but by the pint, when it produces a comfortable feeling in the stomach. Chemistry will yet discover a means of detecting the kind of acid in the stomach, and, of course, some kind of food or medicine which will effectually neutralize it — an application of animal chemistry of great practical importance, and which some of us will undoubtedly live to see made. There are effectual antidotes in Nature, and especially in food, exactly adapted to remove every species of stomachic disorder, by neutralizing or carrying off the noxious compound. In fact, science will yet discover particular kinds of food which will effectually counteract every and all disordered states of the whole body. Thus that rank poison, corrosive sublimate, can be at once neutralized by eating soap freely, or swallowing any alkali in large quantities. The poisonous virus infused into the system by the bites of mad dogs and poisonous snakes, can be effectually neutralized by taking certain chemical agents, of which vinegar is one. Mankind will yet discover some such antidote for every sort of morbid matter, obstruction, and disease incident to the body. Excess of carbon has already been shown to be one prolific cause of disease; and all diseases thus caused are easily obviated by taking little carbon into the system in the form of food, meanwhile introducing much oxygen in the form of breath to burn it out. Thus, suppose you have a boil or abscess, or fever-sore, as the corrupt matter consists mainly of carbon,[119] of course by eating little, and those kinds of food which abound in fibrine, tissue, &c., yet contain little carbon; you reduce the supply of carbon; meanwhile, breathe copiously, so as to burn it up fast, and you, of course, soon evacuate this surplus carbon, heal the abscess, and restore the healthy action of the system. Undoubtedly this principle might be applied effectually to the cure of consumption, as it has been to that of the gravel in eating water-melons. This principle of neutralization will soon be applied so as immediately and effectually to cure all sorts of disease, and prolong life to twice and thrice its present period. This point is earnestly commended to the scientific researches of chemists, and to the practical experiment of all.

Stomachic inflammation also accompanies indigestion, and causes those pains incident to dyspepsia. This can be easily reduced, and along with it those cravings of the appetite already shown to accompany dyspepsia. You eagerly ask how?

121. — The Drink of Dyspeptics — its Kind, Time, and Quantity.

COLD WATER is undoubtedly man's natural beverage.[73] Besides promoting health, its medicinal properties are also great. It is one of those powerful neutralizers of the corrupt matter in the stomach, the virtues of which have already been shown. Have dyspeptics not often noticed copious eructations of gas soon after having drank freely? The mineral substances of the water combined with and neutralized some of the obnoxious matter in the stomach, and hence the gas. Probably nothing equals water for reducing inflammation. Dip a burn into cold water, and keep it there half an hour, and its inflammation and consequent smarting will subside. Immersing a cut, or bruise, or sprain, or fracture, or rheumatic joint, or any other form of inflammation, into water, and both inflammation and pain will be diminished. The virtues of water, as an antidote of inflammation in all its forms, are fully

established by the water-cure. But this fact admitted, its application to the cure of stomachic irritation follows. No medicine,
no diet, nothing equals its judicious application, external and internal, to the stomach of dyspeptics. Its external application, in
the form of wet cloths laid on the stomach, and covered with several thicknesses of flannel to keep in the heat — and for this,
night is by far the best time — is most beneficial.[114] Injections two
or three times per day are even more so. But *drinking* cold
water is the medicine for dyspeptics after all, not by stint, but
by copious draughts.

Yet the best *time* for drinking is also important. This should
not be at meals, because it reduces the temperature of the stomach
below 98° Farenheit, requisite for digestion, which it arrests till that
temperature is again attained. In fact, dyspeptics should drink
nothing with their meals, even though their mouths are dry while
eating, because this very dryness will provoke that salivary secretion so essential to prepare the food for digestion,[71] whereas drinking, by rinsing down the food, obviates this dryness, and leaves
these glands to slumber. Dyspeptics should eat *dry* food, as
dry bread, crusts, Graham wafers, crackers, and the like, so as
to increase the *demand* for saliva to moisten the food, and thus
call the salivary glands into action. To discontinue these drinks
may be quite a trial at first, but only for a few days.

Dyspeptics should not drink till some hours after their meals,
or within an hour or two of the next meal, when they should drink
freely till within half an hour of meal time, and then discontinue,
so that the stomach may regain its temperature.

DRINKING BEFORE BREAKFAST copiously of water fresh from the
well or spring, accompanied by as vigorous exercise as the patient can bear, will be found especially serviceable. Drink freely
again an hour before dinner, and an hour before supper, if you
take any, which dyspeptics should omit, — or rather be contented
to drink instead of eating, — and again on retiring. If lemonade
agrees with you, drink of that occasionally in place of water, but
drink at these times and not at meals, and one month will greatly
improve the tone of your stomach.

Add to this all the exercise you can well endure, business relaxation, a light diet, thorough mastication, and slow eating, and
you will in one year — probably in a far less time — be well. Eat

in the main those kinds of food which agree best with you, and live much on coarse unbolted flour bread and fruit.

EAT LITTLE. Without this there is no salvation. Full feeding will effectually counteract all these and other remedial prescriptions — will even re-induce dyspepsia after it is cured, and of course aggravate it and prevent its cure. Make up your minds to *starve it out*, or else to suffer all its miseries, and soon end your days. Abstinence is the great panacea. All else only aids, but does not reach its ROOT. *Eating less and breathing more* will soon discharge that surplus carbon in which their disease consists. Nothing equals them as a cure-all. Fresh air, in large and perpetual doses, is by far the most effectual specific for dyspeptics and consumptives that exists. In short, let them follow the prescriptions of this work as to the selection, mastication, quantity, and digestion of food, and touching circulation, respiration, perspiration, sleep, exercise, &c., in addition to the specific prescriptions of, and they will soon be cured.

THIS ABSTINENCE cure, however, has this important qualification. Inflammation of the stomach is the first stage of dyspepsia, and creates this ravenous hankering which abstemiousness counteracts.[69] But years of inflammation and hankering often partially paralyze the stomach, which of course deadens the appetite in proportion, so that it becomes extremely dainty, and even loathes food. Or it is inflamed and paralyzed, and the appetite greedy or dainty, *by turns*, now one, then the other. And this inflamed state is by far the best, for it signifies more-remaining life. Nausea is much worse and harder to cure than greed, and requires the opposite treatment, namely, pampering and indulging. The dietetic rule for dyspeptics is this : *Pamper* appetite when it is dainty, by coaxing it up, and trying to get up a relish, but deny a ravenous.

122. — CONSTIPATION, ITS EVILS AND REMEDIES.

BOWEL DORMANCY is worse even than is generally supposed, and impedes all the mental and physical functions; so that to obviate it should be a paramount object of all it afflicts. It usually accompanies, and indeed causes most chronic complaints, which its obviation will generally cure. It especially impedes brain action, besides greatly aggravating melancholy.

LADIES suffer oftenest, and the most seriously from it; whereas they more especially require peristaltic regularity. They justly set a high value on good looks; yet none who are constipated can possibly look well, however elegant their toilet. It often induces other visceral ailments, which every woman should by all means avoid.[660] Bowel freedom also carries off other diseases, which would otherwise cause sickness; for Nature often uses them to unload the system of waste and poisonous matter which would otherwise clog it, and even endanger life. As long as they remain "all right," your chances for life and health continue good, which their constipation often forebodes gathering ailments really portentous of evil. Those who are constipated should inquire what physiological laws they are habitually breaking to cause it.

MENTAL MISERY of all kinds, especially affectional, as the death of friends, love troubles, conjugal discords, &c., often occasion it; so that those suffering from any affectional, pecuniary, or other disappointments, should rise above their troubles, besides taking extra care of this function.

No MEDICINES can cure constipation. Cathartics may move the bowels for the time being, only to constipate them still worse afterwards; and the more one takes the worse he is. All experiences of all will confirm this. None can afford to purchase relief to-day by redoubling the same difficulty ever afterwards. What you require is *permanent* relief, not temporary.

CURE BY FOOD. Some kinds of food are naturally aperient, while other kinds bind. Eat the former, but avoid the latter. Most kinds of fruits, and particularly grapes, eaten with their skins, open the bowels, while the bran part of most grains produces a like effect. Wheat, boiled or cracked, or coarse ground, but *unbolted*, and made into puddings, bread, &c., is one of the best of aperients. Rye, in its various forms, has a like effect. Rhubarb, both root and stem, are noted for producing this effect; so are peaches, figs, plums, green corn, onions, &c. A pudding made by stirring unbolted rye flour into boiling water, eaten with molasses, sugar, milk, or fruit sauce, will be found most excellent. So will Indian and oatmeal pudding, eaten with molasses. In short, all will know of some kinds of diet which open their bowels, of which they should partake when constipated. And the special advantages of these kinds of food are that they tend to *keep up* this action for days afterwards. Beyond all question, the true loosening means is *food*, not medicines. Teas, the decoction of herbs, of course belong to this class, of which thoroughwort, wormwood, catnip, smartweed, &c., furnish examples. Probably requiring "bitter herbs" to be eaten with "the passover," was based on this law, especially since it was appointed in the spring, when the bowels most need relaxing.

THEIR DAILY EVACUATION is another sure means of obtaining permanent relief. Periodicity is important in *all* the physical functions, this included. They are naturally constituted to move once per day.[70] None should allow any day to pass without attending to this function. Mothers should early train their children to be regular, and especially see that their growing daughters on no account neglect it. Shame sometimes dictates its suppression; yet as well be ashamed to breathe. An extra squeamish young lady once induced "St. Vitus' dance" by suppressing this intense desire during a party sleighride and supper of young people. Any involuntary suppression of involuntary desires rouses St. Vitus' dance. Neglect of this function often induces prolapsus of the bowels and viscerals, which this daily attention would avert.

A SET TIME each day should be selected. As when we habituate ourselves to eat or retire at a given time, we feel hungry or sleepy when that hour comes, however intent on the thing in hand; so, waiting on this function at a specified time daily, will soon create this monition at the time, though too busy to think of it without. If you effect no passage to-day, try again to-morrow at the same hour, and again the next, and every day, till your body falls into this habit. If this takes time, give time, for you are accomplishing a great *life work*. And the more difficult its establishment, the more you need it.

RUBBING AND KNEADING THE BOWELS is another aperient, and cure of dyspepsia.

The stomach often solves its food, and the bowels discharge it, without its nutrition being *absorbed*, or emptied into the blood. The system is thus exhausted by its digestion, without being nourished by it. This first part of digestion without this last, is nugatory, both being equally important. Weak lacteals weaken equally with a weak stomach or liver. Medicines affect them

but little, and only injuriously. If you are thin in flesh, this is
the probable cause.   How can these lacteals be quickened?

By BOWEL MANIPULATION.   This MECHANICAL bowel motion will
naturally promote their functional action.   In 1833, while in college, a previous graduate came around to cure dyspepsia, the
chief college ailment, swore his patients to secrecy, charged five
dollars, and cured them all, solely by this bowel manipulation ;
probably copied from the French custom of women, who make it
their " profession " to visit ladies at their houses for this purpose,
just as hairdressers do to dress their heads.   Pardon a personal
illustration.

After having preached this manipulating cure over twenty
years, a friend insisted on button-holing me to his clairvoyant
physician, who said my stomach *digested* its food well enough,
but that many of the lacteals are closed, and the others sluggish,
so that but little chyle, though abundant and good, reached the
blood.   I saw that this manipulation was precisely what my system then required, and applied it briskly on retiring and rising,
for a week or so ; when I found myself just as antic as a colt,
light-footed, able and disposed to walk off a dozen miles "just
for fun," light-hearted, clear-headed, warm-blooded, and ecstat-
ically happy.   What had mysteriously caused this marked change
for good ?   This manipulation, which can rarely ever be practised
without like results.   It always warms the hands and feet, obviously by introducing more carbon into the system, and produces
buoyancy by giving it more materials to work with. For a like
reason it redoubles all the other physical, and also all the mental,
operations.

OLD-TIME physicians frequently prescribed rubbing the feet,
spine, and other parts for various ailments, with marked benefit.
Then why is not friction of the bowels as much more useful as
their action is the more essential?

It may be performed by the invalid, or by another person.   If
the former, double up the fists and strike the abdomen in quick
succession, or else pat them successively with the open palms of
both hands ; or, bending the hands and fingers forward, strike it
with the ends of the fingers made rigid ; or, placing the thumbs on
the hips, reach the fingers forward towards the middle of the
bowels, and knead or work them with their extremities, or rub

them upward while pressing on strongly, and down lightly, by punching, pushing, and working them in all ways and directions quite briskly, but much more with the upward motion than downward; for they should always be raised or pressed upwards, but never downwards, for reasons soon to be advanced.

The more healthy the manipulator, the greater the benefit received, which opposite sexes redoubles.

123. — Bowel Prolapsus, Abdominal Supporters, Diarrhœa Opiates, &c.

The bowels often fall into a heap at the bottom of the pelvis basin, or unduly sink in above, but protrude below the navel, whereas they should round up from all sides to it, so that it will point straight forward; whereas, when they fall, it points *obliquely* upwards.

This sinking lets the stomach and lungs settle, because their support has settled; which leaves them *hanging* from their fastenings at the throat. This irritates them, and this produces a cough, which reinflames the bronchial tubes; and finally the lungs, and this often causes consumption; the doctors meanwhile doctoring away at their *lungs*, while the seat of the disease is in the bowels, which must be cured before this consumption can be cured; for, if arrested to-day, it would return to-morrow, because that hanging which causes it continues.

They must be *held up.* Then how?

Not by trusses, abdominal supporters, and all that, because they necessarily impede that *circulation* which alone imparts health and vigor. Few who use them ever think they are beneficial. They irritate and injure almost always, and necessarily.

A suspending sash can, however, be made in and by means of the drawers, so as to *hold them up*, and rest their weight on the *hips*, by a band passing over the points of the hips, and tying or buttoning behind. And, in general, the pants, drawers, skirts, &c., should depend from the hips instead of by suspenders over the shoulders, but on no account by any band around the waist; because this bears *down* on the bowels, and displaces, and therefore inflames them; whereas, this sash, passing down *under* them, then raising them up and carrying their weight upon the hips, has an effect the converse of that produced by a band *above* them.

42

This sash should be adjusted to the bowels of each by strings
or buttons, before or behind, — before, probably the best, — so as
to stow them away in it when it is fastened on. Those whose
bowels are large, or protrude, will find such a sash to afford a
surprising relief and immediate benefit.

· EXTRA FAT bowels are often consequent on a good stomach with
poor lacteals. They digest enough, but the lacteals fail to absorb
it from the intestines, and Nature, to get partly rid of it, turns it
into fat. Females will find a· kindred cause, especially applicable
to them, in "Sexual Science." [683, 684]

DIARRHŒA has its ·causes, uses, and cure. It often casts out
humors, and unloads the system. Thus, suppose a sour stomach or
closed pores, or other suppressions, are perpetually filling it with
disease, loose bowels cast it out sometimes as fast as it accumulates, thus allowing it to work better with them loose than close.
Their freedom *benefits* whenever it does not prostrate. When
you have caught a cold, or feel bad from any cause, and are constipated, expect relief soon after they begin to move; and, in
general, hail this aperient state as your savior when it does not
extend to prostration. This is doubly true of some females.[683]

LOOSENESS of the intestines, however, when it goes so far as
to prostrate, is most injurious. Summer complaints carry off
more children than all other diseases combined. It urges the
nutrition along too fast to allow its absorption, and is often ac-.
companied with griping pains as severe as often afflict mankind.
Cholera is but its most aggravated form. Instead of the nutrition
being taken up and emptied into the blood, *reversed* bowel action
casts the blood through the lacteals into the intestines, and then
out. This reversal makes short work of life itself, and all excessive looseness causes a most painful sinking, prostration, and
goneness.

· OPIATES are usually prescribed in such cases, but with only
evil. They may deaden the pain by stupefying the bowels; but
they leave the original difficulty worse than they found it; because
they paralyze that vital force which is struggling against it. To
do nothing is better than to prostrate. Vital force and disease
are in mortal combat, and opiates strike down the vital force
without at all arresting the disease. Their popularity is unwar-
rantable.

THE TRUE CURE is water, applied externally, as in the sitz bath and wet bandage, and internally by enemas. To the latter wheat flour may sometimes be added, partly as one of the best of emollients, and because the bowels will sometimes digest and appropriate its nutrition. Cayenne pepper will often prove highly beneficial by stimulating normal action and turning their current.

For chronic diarrhœa, wear a wet bandage night and day over the whole visceral region, wrung from hot water when they are cold, but from cold when they are hot. Whatever temperature *feels* most agreeable to the patient is the best.

The same kind of diet already prescribed for constipation, reversed by eating what binds, applies here also, and for a like reason.[120] Yet it is as singular as true that unbolted flour bread often regulates the bowels *both ways*, constipating when too loose, but opening when too tight. At all events, those who suffer from chronic diarrhœa should be especially careful not to eat anything injurious, or do anything to impair the general health. Grapes eaten with the skins chewed, but not swallowed, will help close the bowels.

BLACKBERRIES and black raspberries naturally check bowel action; so let those who are constipated avoid, but loose, eat them. A tea made by steeping their leaves has a like effect. So have the bark of the wild cherry, and the cherries themselves, which, covered with water two parts, and New England rum one part, can be preserved indefinitely. All the better if their pits are cracked, when a very little must suffice. Other bitters, as quassia, columbo-root, ginseng, wormwood, camomile, &c., often remove both constipation and looseness by promoting normal action.

BURNT FLOUR, a teaspoonful taken at a time and quite often, is very binding. A good deal will not injure.

VIRGIN MULLEN root tea, the first year's growth, that which has not yet seeded, has a like effect. Steep in milk.

These prescriptions put the reader on the track of analogous ones; but be especially careful not to check it *too soon or too much*.

OYSTERS, cooked in milk, sometimes sour on the stomach, and when they do, make short, sharp work. Those liable to bowel troubles, and all in cholera epidemics, should by all means avoid oysters when thus cooked. Ten chances to one they would give you no trouble; but at such seasons that one chance should not be run. Yet the oysters themselves are all right. The milk, probably, does the damage, just as in custards.[65]

VIOLENT EXERCISE, when the bowels are thus reversed, whether from custards, oysters and milk, vegetables, or anything else, that is, in all cases of cholera morbus, is probably good; but not in cholera, and only in robust persons. When cattle have gorged themselves with green corn, we drive and run them to the top of their speed till evacuation is produced.

124. — PALPITATION OF THE HEART, RHEUMATISM, NEURALGIA, CATARRH, AND ASTHMA, AND THEIR CURES.

A RAPID, POWERFUL BEATING of the heart, called palpitation, is rarely a primary disease, but usually only the effect of some other disease. It has two chief causes, dyspepsia and nervousness, and is a twin sister of both; so that the cures prescribed for these diseases will often cure, and always mitigate this ailment.

INTENSE MENTAL activity, both intellectual, and consequent on excessive study or brain action, or else passional or emotional, as in unhappy love, amatory excitement, especially personal,[470] are its chief procuring causes.

GENERAL diseases usually cause local ailments. One often breaks down his constitution, and fills his system with disease, which of course attacks the weak organs first. If his heart is weakly, though not diseased, it suffers the pain, not because it is especially disordered, but because it is less rugged, and therefore less able to resist, than the others. The load of disease breaks down the weaker organs first, just as too heavy a load breaks down the weakest wheel or part first; whereas, the real trouble lies in the excessive *load*, but for which the weak wheel would work on passably well. The cure for the oppressed organs, like that of the weak wheel, is to *take off* the general load of disease.

COLDNESS of the extremities and skin, along with headache, usually accompanies it, because the blood does not flow freely enough to the former to keep them warm, while an excessive accumulation of blood in the head causes a dull, heavy pain in it. The heart often suffers the pain, not at all because it is itself diseased, but because a thickening of the blood causes it to dam up as it passes through this door; that is, the blood is too thick and turgid, and hence lodges about the heart. Surplus carbon, consequent on eating more than breathing, is its great cause.

ITS CURE, therefore, consists in eating less and breathing more. The oxygen of breath thins it,[41] so that it flows the more freely. All thus afflicted have noticed that just as they inspire air its beat is quickened and strengthened, but slackens as they expire — proof conclusive that more copious breathing will obviate their difficulty. Such will also generally find their veins too blue, owing to a surplus of carbonic acid.[119] Respiration alone can remove this from the system, and thus still further thin the blood. Iron filings may aid. Whatever promotes circulation will relieve the heart, by leaving less blood collected in the veins, and remove the headache by withdrawing that surplus blood which occasions the congestion and consequent pain. This, friction and the bath will do much to effect. The foot-bath will be especially serviceable. Magnetism can also be successfully applied to relieve the heart and head.

RHEUMATISM, more painful than dangerous, proves that its victim has outraged some natural law — perhaps that of temperature. It generally results from colds. Gout does not differ much from it; while neuralgia is at least its first cousin. Try all the pathics in each form of this disease, especially hydropathy, by keeping a wet cloth laid upon the paining spot. A light diet is indispensable. The Turkish bath will sometimes rout it when other agencies utterly fail. Perspiration is its great cure. It can be applied directly to the spot affected, thus : —

WRAP OILED SILK or India-rubber cloth around the aching part over night. This will keep in the perspiration, and *steam out* the rheumatism.

NEURALGIA is consequent mainly on past or present nervous excitement, usually a nervous prostration, caused by an unhappy frame of mind. Of course the great cure must consist in obviating this cause. Then build up the general health, and apply water, cold or warm, whichever feels best, to the aching part. Usually cold water is best; yet it sometimes causes so *much* reaction as temporarily to increase the pain. Keep a wet cloth on it nightly.

CATARRH is an awful disease, but, alas, how common! Few wholly escape it. To say nothing of having a breath perfectly sickening, how noxious to the whole system is it to keep perpetually sweeping this foul fetid breath into the lungs at every inspiration, to infect the whole system with its loathsome pestiferousness !

It IMPAIRS THE BRAIN, and therefore the mind, memory, senses, power to study and think, and intellect generally. This is its greatest evil, and really awful.

COLDS, settling on the brain, cause it; and every cold makes it worse : so use all the means prescribed to prevent, and also to cure them.[96, 119] Its victims may well pay almost anything to get cured, yet need pay nothing. Either of these two remedies applied separately, much more both together, will cure it sooner or later, according as it has run longer or shorter. First :

A WET TOWEL, wrung from cold water, tied over the face, extending from the nostrils and lower parts of the ears up on to the middle of the head, during sleep, and pressed down snugly around the nose and eyes. The feverish heat consequent on this catarrh will all night keep turning this water into steam, which will keep carrying off this fever, night after night, and the first you know you will be well. If the disease has become chronic, it will hold on the longer, but the cure will be effectual. Next :

PASS SALT WATER up one nostril and down and out at the other. The "fountain syringe" has a nasal pipe just adapted to this passage. Snuffing up salt water, and also gurgling it in the throat, will do good, but the syringe is best.

ASTHMA is often a most distressing, though rarely fatal affection. It consists in the bronchial and air tubes of the lungs being too *small* for the lungs themselves. All thus troubled should habituate themselves to breathing *deep*, take *long* breaths, breathe with their *diaphragms*,[40] because their habitually practising this will tend to enlarge these tubes.[34]

CATCHING COLD generally increases all asthmatic difficulties, so forestall taking them, and break up those taken right speedily.[114]

A HEAVY ATMOSPHERE, by pressing heavily on the lungs, greatly promotes their inflation. One breathes with difficulty on high mountains, and inland localities, as also in balloon ascensions; and because the higher one is above the level of the sea, the lighter is the atmospheric pressure and the less forcibly it pushes the air into the lungs.[40] In Virginia City, Nevada, persons breathe with difficulty, because they are over six thousand feet above the sea level, that is, that much up in the air.

Tall and short chimneys illustrate the reason of this fact. A tall chimney produces a proportionate draught, because the taller it is the greater the atmospheric pressure at its bottom than top, so that the denser air at its mouth presses that nearest to it along up and out into the rarer and lighter atmosphere at its top.

Near the sea, or else in valleys, that is, as low down as possible, is the best place for such to reside, because this atmospheric pressure is the greatest there.

A hot, wet sheet, as hot as can well be borne, wound on the chest, and changed every few minutes for hotter ones, with an occasional cold one, is the best cure.

Section IV.

CONSUMPTION; ITS CAUSES, PREVENTION, AND CURE.

125. — How to stave off a Tendency to Consumption.

Suppuration of the lungs, and their consequent destruction, is called consumption; though sometimes other organs are similarly consumed.

A tendency to consumption is sometimes *inherited*,[512] that is, often attacks the children and relatives of those who die with it; yet, strictly speaking, Nature never transmits diseased organs, but only weakly ones. No matter how consumptive your parents and relatives may have been, you can escape it altogether by giving Nature a chance to counteract this tendency. She will not begin what she cannot consummate. "Possibly good, or none; nothing rather than bad," is her motto. All endowed with strength enough to be born alive, can, by proper regimen, attain a full human life, and grow stronger and stronger up to a good age; for Nature interdicts parentage to those either too young, or too old, or too debilitated, or diseased, or deformed, or depraved, to impart sufficient vigor to offspring for them to live a good life; thereby forestalling whatever imperfections would otherwise spoil her children.

Growth also counteracts even this entailed lung weakness, as it does all others, by causing all weak organs to grow relatively the fastest, and then compelling all strong ones to succor all the weak ones; on the well-known principle of balance already demonstrated.[34, 36] How often do weakly children grow stronger with age, and make healthy adults? No matter how consumptive you are by nature, observing the health laws and cultivating your lungs will enable you to surmount all such consumptive tendencies.

THOSE WHO INHERIT this consumptive taint absolutely must do these two things — keep up a good supply of vitality[28] by nurturing all their recuperative functions, and break up colds as soon as they contract.[96] But if they work themselves clear down, which they are apt to do, because this consumptive taint *consists* in more activity than vitality, and then allow colds to set in and redouble on them, they endanger consumption. They *must not* become permanently tired out, nor worn down, nor used up; but must keep well rested up and slept out.[97]

LUNG EXERCISE is another great preventive. Those thus predisposed should read loud daily, sing, and very loudly hallo, talk much and loudly, speak in public, breathe deeply, anything demanding lung action; yet be careful not to tax them beyond their strength.

WARM EXTREMITIES are to such most important, as cold hands and feet accompany, if they do not even constitute the first stage of this malady, by signifying a susceptibility to colds, because the surface circulation has become impaired. Such should promote circulation, and *keep warm* at any cost; as well as

BREAK UP COLDS as soon as possible after their contraction.[96] As long as those, however consumptively preinclined, keep their pores open, they may snap their fingers at consumption and the doctors.

A foul stomach often causes expectoration. Good lungs expel the foul matter generated by food decaying in the stomach, or by alcoholic drinks, &c., occasioning consumptive symptoms simply because the lungs are strong enough to expel this corruption, not because they are consumptive.

THE SIGNS of consumptive tendencies are, that those thus preinclined are generally tall, slim, long-fingered and limbed, spindling, small and narrow-chested, inclined to sit and walk stooping, with their shoulders thrown forwards and inwards, because their small lungs and stomachs cause a pectoral caving in, sink in where the arms join the body; have a long neck, sunken cheeks, long faces, sharp features, a palid countenance, light complexion, a thin, soft, and delicate skin, light and fine hair, rather a hollow, exhausted, ghastly aspect, long and rounding finger nails, cold hands and feet, with general chilliness and wakefulness at night, great excitability, very active minds, clear thoughts, excellent natural abilities, intense feelings, rapidity of motion, and a hurried manner; are easily startled and inspired, have a decided predominance of the mental temperament over the vital — of head over body.

The accompanying engraving of Grenville Mellen, the poet, who died of this disease, gives a good general idea of the form of the face and person of consumptives; yet those of full, fleshy habits may be predisposed to pneumonia or quick consumption, though equally so to all other local inflammations and diseases, because their systems are exceedingly excitable.

THE SMALL LUNGS and hearts of those predisposed

NO. 28. — GRENVILLE MELLEN.

to this disease render their circulation imperfect. To promote this should then be the first end sought by them. Whatever, therefore, tends to retard the flow of blood, especially at the surface, such as sedentary pursuits, confinement within doors, and particularly in heated rooms, habitual sewing, a cramped and forward posture, severe mental application, impure skin, sudden atmospheric changes, colds, and the like, should be sedulously avoided; whereas, a light diet, fresh air, out-of-door pursuits, abundant sleep, vigorous exercise, warm climate, and free circulation tend to prevent it. Keep the SKIN clean and active, directions for which have already been given, and you are safe.[95]

TIGHT-LACING is most pernicious to those thus predisposed, because it cramps the lungs, prevents their inflation, inflames them, shuts out oxygen, the deficiency of which is the great cause

43

of this disease, curtails the action of the whole vital apparatus, and consequent supply of vitality, occasions adhesions, and in many other ways induces this disease. No language can tell the number of premature deaths, of both mothers and their offspring, occasioned by this accursed practice. To girt up the vital organs is to commit virtual suicide.[006]

HOT DRINKS, especially tea and coffee, are also injurious, because they increase the liability to take colds, and fever the nervous system, already far too excitable. Drink warm drinks only when you wish to induce perspiration.

EXERCISE in the open air is also especially beneficial. Yet be very careful not to *overdo* — the great fault of consumptives, because their nerves are too active for their strength. *Alternate* rest and exercise, with abundance of fresh air, are your best remedial agents. Compared with them medicines are powerless. Doctor little, but *invigorate your general* health.

THE CHEST should be rubbed often, with the hand of a healthy and robust friend. Especially let mothers and nurses rub narrow-chested children much.

The FULL AND FREQUENT *inflation of the lungs* is especially advantageous. In this alone consists the virtues of Rammage's tube. Yet it can be effected better without than with any kind of tube. Sit or stand straight, throw the arms back and chest forward, and then draw in slowly as full a breath as possible, and hold it for some seconds, perhaps meanwhile gently striking the chest, so as to force the air down into the extremities of all the air-cells of the lungs, as well as enlarge the lungs, and keep up this practice habitually, and consumption will pass you by. Few practices contribute more to general health. An erect posture is especially important, and warping forward and inward — which consumptives are apt to do — very detrimental, because it cramps and impairs the vital apparatus, especially the lungs.

SEA VOYAGES are much recommended, and also southern climates. Both, by promoting *surface* circulation and perspiration, are eminently beneficial. Yet if the same ends can be obtained at home the effect will be the same, and all the evils incident to voyages, absence from home, exposures, &c., be avoided. Southern climates are even less favorable to consumptives than a northern, because of the rarefied state of the atmosphere, and consequent deficiency of oxygen — one of the main elements required by consumptives. Inhaling oxygen gas, perhaps, some-what diluted, will prove eminently serviceable. Whatever will cure this disease will prevent it, and the reverse.

126. — The Cure of Consumption.

COLDS BEGIN, and consummate this terrible business; hence, to prevent it, *they* absolutely must be prevented somehow. Any-thing, in fact, everything to prevent, and after they are taken, to break them up. Unless you do prevent them, expect to be over-taken by the consumption.

To prevent them, a *uniform temperature* is of the first and last importance, while sudden changes in the weather are most detri-mental. One uniformly warm is the best. Probably Santa Fé is the best place in the world for consumptive patients, for its temperature is about 75° the year round, and nearly the same night and day. This is substantially the case with the city of Mexico and Lower California. Florida is also even in tempera-ture, but damp, while the base of the Rocky Mountains is dry, yet changeable. But those who must stay where they are, should house themselves when it is cold, keep their room about so warm, and use clothing enough not to take any more cold; varying it according as the weather is warmer or colder.

A CHANGE of climate will often effect a radical cure. Thousands who cannot live at the north, on account of these changes and colds, live and are healthy at the south, or south-west, north-west, or California. But many

WAIT TOO LONG before they emigrate. One must never go to the north-west unless they have sufficient vitality to withstand its bracing cold, or it will hurry them right off; and those struck with a consumptive attack generally would live longer at home, and better.

HOP SYRUP, made by boiling hops in water, straining, boil-ing down, adding molasses, simmering down, then superadding lemon, and taking enough to keep the bowels' free. Its pro-portions, whether more sweet or more bitter, are immaterial. Taken on retiring, it will promote sleep, the hops quieting, be-sides unloading disease through the bowels. It must be made fresh every three or four days, or preserved by adding spirits, or boiling down till it will keep.

SPIRITUOUS LIQUORS will benefit those whose stomachs do not furnish sufficient carbon, but injure those in whom carbon superabounds, as it generally does. But when the stomach supplies too little carbon, they furnish it, help warm, and prolong life, and even restore it.

BUTTERMILK AND BONNYCLABBER, sweetened, will sometimes effect a cure, and at all times will benefit. The Author, at sixteen, induced a very severe consumptive attack; took only bread and sweetened buttermilk, prescribed by a neighbor, an elderly lady; was benefited by it from the first day of its use, and every day, and recovered in about three months. It soon becomes palatable.

THE GREAT PRINCIPLE of the cure centres just here. As the lungs waste away, they furnish the less oxygen. A given amount of carbon can combine with only its " friend equivalent " of oxygen. Therefore, since feeble lungs introduce but little oxygen, of course the stomach must introduce only a proportionate amount of carbon. · All must eat the more or the less, accordingly as they breathe the more or the less. Since consumptives can breathe but little, they must eat but little. Yet many of them have a ravenous appetite, consequent on an inflamed stomach,[60] which loads down their systems with surplus carbon, only to compel their small and inflamed lungs to *cast it out* in *addition* to supporting them. Starvation is bad, so is surplus aliment. If, and as far as, this yellow matter comes from surplus carbon, the more food the more carbon and expectoration. Abstemiousness is the remedy for such.

THIS EXPERIMENT will furnish a decisive test. Eat very little for several days, and if you feel lighter, calmer, pleasanter, and better, know that you are eating too much relatively for your breathing. The patient can determine this important matter better than the doctor.

COPIOUS NIGHT SWEATS probably consists in an effort of Nature to carry off disease through the skin, which they leave peculiarly susceptible to colds; so be doubly careful to keep warm by tucking in your bed-clothes till after they have subsided.

DON'T COUGH any more than you really must, and then only to raise. To cough because you feel a tickling irritation, only increases it. Breathe on as long as possible without coughing, raise all you can while coughing, and stop coughing as soon as possible.

TAKE NO OPIATES. If you cannot get sleep without them, go without it. The stupor they cause deadens not the disease, but the system's *power to resist* it. Unless Nature can cure you, you cannot be cured..

A RAVENOUS APPETITE must be denied. A light diet will give more strength than a generous.

COD-LIVER OIL is the standing prescription for consumption, and it often helps to cure by supplying carbon; yet any other oil will supply just as much, and be less expensive and nauseating. Butter, cream, fat pork fried to a crisp, suets, olive oil, &c., cost less, but do better; and those predisposed to this disease will find animal and vegetable oils anti-consumptive.

BATHING AND RUBBING will prove most beneficial, especially rubbing the feet, abdomen, and back, by a robust hand. Washing all over, under bed-clothes, by piecemeal, in saleratus water, made by putting a lump of saleratus, or else bicarbonate of soda, the size of a chestnut, into a pint or so of water, will neutralize the acid which causes the fever.

THE CHILDREN of consumptives absolutely must be kept from school till well grown; be allowed to run and play during growth, so as to give their lungs full action; be provoked and denied as little as possible; kept back mentally, but brought forward physically; not allowed to stay in bathing over two or three minutes at a time, and bathe mostly inside; live much on bread and cream; allowed nuts, and not required to sew, or begin business early, but vegetate *till twenty.*

SECTION V.

NERVOUSNESS, INSANITY, ETC.; THEIR CAUSES AND CURES.

127. — THE AMOUNT AND CAUSES, EVILS AND SIGNS, OF NERVOUS IRRITABILITY.

DISORDERED NERVES, commonly called nervousness, probably creates more disease and suffering among men, and especially women, than all other ailments combined; and much more in America than anywhere else on earth; and more and still more every year. We have already shown that dyspepsia is only another form of nervousness,[120] as are also rheumatism, neuralgia, &c.[121] Consumptives always have too much nervous excitabil-

ity,[125] besides being usually extremely excitable for a long time
before this disease strikes them. In fact, disordered nerves build
all other disorders and diseases; because nerve and brain are the
ultimate and centre of all else. These are to all the other organs
just what the head is to the body. Every other organ and parcel
of the body was created to subserve the nervous function; because it is the primal function and the ultimate end of life. All
else is vassal to the nervous system, while it leads it imperiously
over the body as a whole, and all its parts. Please duly consider
why the nerves are thus supreme, and learn therefrom why all
nervous disorders must similarly affect all the other functions.

THE SUFFERINGS consequent on nervous diseases are far greater
than on any and all others. The reason for this has been explained in the preceding paragraphs, namely, their relative importance.

THE MIND is affected by them more than by all others; because
these nerves are in such sympathetic interrelation with the brain,
that special organ of the mind, of life, and of all its functions,
as well as of all enjoyment. An angel in heaven with disordered
nerves could not be happy, and must needs feel wretched. Much
more a mortal on earth. Neither rich nor learned, wise nor good,
need ever hope to be happy any farther than their nerves are in a
healthy state.[24, 26]

SINFULNESS is aggravated and caused by these nervous disorders. Thus, a really good, pure, amiable woman, by over devotion to family, becomes nervous, and therefore so cross-grained
and hateful, so sour and malignant, that she scolds husband and
children, servants and guests, right and left, and for things which
deserve unqualified praise, solely because of the abnormal *mood*
into which they throw her. And if all hands are nervous, then
all hands scold and quarrel, accuse and slander, back and forth,
with depraved unction and earnestness; making their home a
Bedlam, and engendering both animosities and infidelities *ad infinitum*, solely because all are suffering from nervousness; nor
can their sinful *spirit* be cured till their nerves are restored to
normal action. If ministers would preach this doctrine, millions
of well-meaning, but now cross-grained, women would at once
set about that *physical* regeneration which would restore them to
purity and goodness; whereas, preaching ordinary sermons to

them till doomsday would leave them still as bad and wicked in *action* — they are now all right at *heart* — as ever. Abnormal *physical* conditions have generated those depraved mental states which must continue to defile their feelings and actions till their nervous *cause* is removed.

HUSBANDS, suffering perpetual detraction and reproaches from your nervous and therefore maligning wives, have you no "interest" in both relieving yourself of these slanderous and groundless accusations, which originated in your wives' embittered *state* of feeling, and this solely in her nervousness? and good, sweet wives, virtually fretted perpetually by a cross, because a nervous, husband, and this because he is overworked, called hard names by the thousand, unable to do any one thing to please him, though you try your *very* best, should you not "take stock" in restoring him to himself, yourself, and your children, by getting him out of this fussing, snarling, crabbed, rabid *mood?* How many wives live, crushed and heart-broken while they live, and die many years sooner than they otherwise would, solely in consequence of that utterly hateful and repellent *spirit* of their husbands, which is due solely to their nervous disorders? and how many husbands, finding no domestic peace, no cosey, loving feelings in the female they are obliged grudgingly to support, seek relief in gambling, or billiards, or carousing and dissipation with other women, who would be pattern husbands but for their wives' gangrene temper, due solely to her nervousness. Why do so many wives and husbands, amiable, affectionate, and everything desirable at marriage, become mutually disappointed with each other, say they wish they never married, and anon become perfectly fiendish towards each other, not from any natural ugliness, but because their noble, even heroic struggles for mutual interests have deranged their nerves, infuriated their tempers and all their passions, and spoil the tempers and destroy the lives of both, and their children to boot?

DRUNKENNESS depraves. This all concede, and all drunkards illustrate. Why? Solely by deranging and abnormalizing the nerves.[28]

TEA AND COFFEE derange the nerves,[79] and thus generate a cross-grained, ugly-tempered feeling, which vents itself on husband, children, and servants, however good. Tea and coffee drinkers, how many spiteful sentences think you are lodged in that cup of tea or coffee you are consuming? It irritates your *spirit* principle, and the feelings and actions it begets must affect you *forever*. So beware how you drink what, when drank, will prompt you to feel and say what you *should* regret as long as you exist.

TOBACCO chewers, and smokers, and dippers, this means you, too. Let that hankering, fidgety, rampant, snappish feeling you experience mornings, before you get your tobacco, convince you that it is disordering your nerves, and thereby creating depraved feelings of one kind or another. Only sole-leather persons should chew, or smoke, or drink tea, or coffee, or alcoholic liquors.

"Do you really consider, Professor, what serious and sweeping charges you are thus hurling by wholesale at your fellow-men? You accuse our ministers and their wives, our "mothers in Israel" and our virgin daughters, our savans, judges, senators, and presidents, as well as common people by *millions*, of sins and depravities numberless in variety, and most henious in kind. Are you prepared to *prove* all these* wholesale accusations? for if not, you are a most wicked slanderer, on the principle that to accuse an innocent person of theft is quite as bad as stealing itself."

Does drunkenness create depravity? Rather, does it *not?*[26] How? By deranging the nerves. Some things affect one part of the system and others another. Alcohol affects the brain and nerves. It makes the drunken debauchee fight in frenzied rage one minute, and seek her house "whose steps take hold on hell" in frenzied passion of another kind, the next. Bacchus was wild with fierce, surging, false excitements; so are all his votaries. What is "delirium tremens" but wild frenzied excitement? Then does not *all* intoxication induce it in that proportion? Are the swearings, fightings, murderings, &c., of inebriates depravities? Then does not intemperance create depravity? But *how?* Solely by abnormalizing the action of the nerves.[26] Therefore whatever *else* demoralizes the nerves, depraves in that proportion. Tobacco, smoked or chewed, produces a "tremens" analogous to that caused by alcohol, as all accustomed to it experience when they quit it suddenly. That awful feeling tobacco consumers experience mornings before they get it, and when deprived of it, is a tobacco delirium tremens, consequent on abnormal nervous action, which begets a depraved state. No higher proof of this is required than the feelings consequent on its abstinence. And the more wretched you feel when deprived of your pipe, quid, or cigar, the more it has already impaired your nerves, and will increase its ravages. Tea and coffee create a like tremens for a like reason. Opiates have a similar effect. Whatever irritates, therefore, abnormalizes, and all abnormal action is sinful; that is, contrary to Nature.[26]

READER, please duly consider whether [26] does or does not state a fundamental natural truth; and since it absolutely does, learn from it that *whatever* causes abnormal nervous action, creates depravity of *spirit* along with sinfulness of *soul*. Then do tea, coffee, and tobacco cause abnormal nervous action? Let the "tremens" they cause, in proportion to their amount, together with the nervous susceptibility of their consumers, answer; and let that answer be *heeded*. Both propositions are true, and, taken together, prove that tea, coffee, tobacco, and alcoholics deprave.

Yet these are by no means man's *only* nervous depravers. Whatever impairs the nerves depraves the spirit. Excessive devotion to business, financial embarrassment, affectional troubles, waiting on the sick, reading novels, the passions, in the intense excitements they create, excessive study, &c., create and augment sinfulness. Let us see how.

A SWEET ANGEL MOTHER, all devotion to her family, has a sick child or parent, caring for whom worries her by day, and keeps her awake nights, till her nerves become disordered, which makes her cross and ugly to husband, arbitrary and dogmatical towards children, scolding this, blaming that, and chastising the others, without any cause, except in her nervousness; but for which she would have remained angelic and self-sacrificing.

They die. Of course grief still further deranges her nerves, which renders her still more violent-tempered and abusive; that is, depraved. And yet, but for their sickness and death, she would have remained an angel still.

A TENDER-HEARTED MAIDEN is courted, till she loves with her whole being, and then discarded. She feels most wretched, how wretched only those can tell who "know by sad *experience*." All day she pores, sad and heart-broken, over her fatal bereavement, and all night she rolls and tumbles in genuine mental agony over the wrong she suffers. Of course her strained nerves give way,

44

gradually but effectually. A slow fever sets in. This, of course, makes her cross and irritable. She is no longer that sweet, patient, innocent, angel maiden she was before; but is impatient, impertinent, cross-grained, spiteful, and hateful, on that very principle which makes the sick child cross.

Suppose, instead, her love affairs had run smoothly, and she had married and lived in perfect affection, this would have kept her nerves healthy, and this her temper angelic. There is no telling how much affectional disappointments affect the moral virtues.[443, 450] See this whole range of truth unfolded in "Sexual Science." The effect is given there, the cause here.

In FINE, let all bear ever in mind that deranged nerves create depraved feelings and actions; so that whatever causes nervous disorders, thereby engenders depravity. Where have been the eyes of ministers of religion not to have seen this range of truth, and used it to promote that moral excellency they are hired to promote? Ministers, church-members, and outsiders, refute these doctrines, or else accept them. They challenge you.

THE CAUSES of all this modern nervousness, and therefore depravity, are many and aggravated, and enter into all the usages of civilized society. It begins in the cradle — *in* the cradle? No; but long before it, in parental nervousness; is augmented by maternal scoldings and chastisements from infancy;[643] is redoubled by early schooling and precocity; is brought to a head by novel and magazine reading, false, fashionable excitements, and juvenile "love spats," and breaks in marital disappointments, alienations, and infidelities, and resultant vices and wickedness. What wonder that her strained nerves finally give out, and that her girlish sweetness is thereby soured, only to be supplanted by fretfulness of mind and disease of body? What a pity! How great the loss to herself and family! When will men and women learn that all violations of the physical laws induce sinfulness.

MAKE ALLOWANCES, then, for nervous wives, husbands, children, and acquaintances, especially for your *own nervous selves*, by remembering that nervousness distorts and depraves all it touches; and also learn the infinite practical importance of keeping or putting your nerves in a healthy state.

THE SIGNS of nervous derangement much deserve special consideration.

A TENDERNESS on the top of the head, amounting perhaps to soreness, is one of its surest signs, because the nerves centre at this point, so that irritated nerves create pain on the top of the head.

UNHAPPY FEELINGS, a morbid, dissatisfied, churlish, ill-natured state of mind is one of its surest signs. Morbid nerves sour all the mental operations.

TWO STATES, as of appetite in dyspepsia, characterize nervous disorders, in common with all others — an irritable, craving, fiery state, and a benumbed, deadened, lethargic, stupid, and partially paralyzed state; the former characterizing the earlier, the latter the more advanced stages of this disease. Sometimes they alternate, like appetite in dyspepsia, now fiery, then stupid and moody. A wild, excitable, firm, rampant state signifies the former, and a murky, forlorn cast of emotion the latter. Your *state of feeling* should tell you whether or not you are nervous.

128. — THE CURE FOR NERVOUSNESS.

ASCERTAINING ITS PROCURING CAUSE or causes, is the first and most important step.[119] Nothing light, or trivial, or temporary could effect results so painful and serious. Look all around and see what fundamental life law you have long been violating.[21] This disease may be sympathetic. Since the nervous system ramifies throughout all the organs, their ailments, of course, similarly affect it. Dyspepsia always fevers it.[120] What is gout but a chronic, nervous inflammation? and are not its victims extremely testy and irritable? Perhaps it results from that old love disappointment you have seemingly forgotten, yet which begets an occasional sigh. Or it may be a married disappointment, or that death which struck to your very heart, or that terrible fright you once had, or some business disaster.

A MERCHANT in New York, in 1857, who had always made it a special point of honor to meet every engagement promptly, on going, perfectly well, to his business in the morning, found some of his customers' notes protested. Having done his best, and the deficit only trifling, he relied on the leniency of his bank, in which he had always had large reserves, to help him through; but it refused him one dollar. A note he indorsed for another was protested, and his name published in an evening paper in the bankrupt list; he went home, stupefied by the day's excitement, struck dumb and insane, lingered, and died! How many wives die instantly, or in a day or two, in consequence of the sudden death of some one dearly beloved! A lady died instantly because her lap-dog fell from her carriage and was run over. Analogous cases are transpiring perpetually, all teaching this great practical truth, that *all painful mental states disorder the nerves.*

"But how can they be *helped?* Can a mother forget her sucking child, just laid away in death? Should she? What family, what heart, but has its skeleton?"

"Sexual Science" gives "directions touching mourning for the dead and absent,[460] and " broken hearts, and how to mend them,"[456] and then remember that much of your trouble, if not wholly imaginary, is at least magnified many fold by your own morbid feelings; that you are in trouble chiefly because you *think* you are; that if you *thought* the converse, it would *be* the converse; that the least said the soonest mended; that "evil is to him who evil *thinks;*" that *crying* over " spilt milk" makes you spill more, but never gathers up that already spilt; that your *grief* over a thing hurts your *self*-hood a hundred fold more than the thing itself; that it may be bad enough, but *feeling* badly makes it ten times worse, yet does nothing whatever towards obviating it; that if you can obviate the evil you should; but if you cannot, self-interest requires that you patiently "*endure* what you cannot cure," and "make the best" of what is; but *never* on *any* account *hurt yourself* by grief. At least you must not expect to recover while this cause remains, any more than that a sore will heal while its proud flesh remains.

Having thus ascertained and obviated the *cause* of this nervousness, your cure consists, —

NOT IN OPIATES, or morphine, or nervines, or valerian, or any or all those nostrums usually administered, for if they give relief by paralyzing the nervous system, they do it only damage; but if by stimulating it, they injure it; because the very trouble is this very stimulation. It needs no tonic, for it is toned up to the disease pitch already. Opiates, morphine, &c., stupefy, palsy, and benumb for the time being, only to make them far more excitable ever afterwards. If they have strength enough to react, they are still more irritable the next day; but if they have not, they are permanently paralyzed. If you can get no sleep without them, sleep produced by them does you no good; for it is stupor, not sleep. They kill time and your constitution together. Away with them all. Don't tamper with your precious nervous system, but bear present pain rather than inflict future injury.

STOP WORRYING. Every bad feeling makes you and them worse, yet does no good. Make the best of what is.

AVOID STUDY and mental action generally. Do let your over-worked brain rest till it recuperates. Its feverish, fitful action is of little account. And remember, action now discounts future action at a fearful discount. STOP thinking and studying.

SLEEP, sleep, sleep, all you can, day and night.[97] To this end dismiss cares and troubles, and quiet down. Let the world jog on, and things take their course, while you stop a bit to rest. No cure for nervousness at all equals sleep; yet to obtain it is most difficult. Though perpetually worn out for want of rest, you can compose yourself to sleep only with difficulty, sleep lightly, are restless, disturbed by dreams, easily wakened, and find great difficulty in again getting to sleep. Nine hours per diem are none too much, for you sleep slowly when asleep, yet exhaust yourself rapidly while awake, and hence should devote the more time to this all-important function.

SUCH AMUSEMENT enjoy whatever you can enjoy — operas, con-certs, visits, riding, gardening, flowers, travelling, anything pleas-urable; for pleasure is medicinal. Make fun your business for the present.

YOUR SKIN, not your stomach, furnishes your readiest mode of reaching and relieving your nerves. See how forcibly engrav-ings Nos. 22 and 27, and contex, illustrate and enforce this great truth.

WILL AND WATER are your chief remedies. The skin absorbs medicines. This is proved by their appearing in the urine of those who have bathed in water impregnated with them. But Nature is jealous of all interference. Give her all needed facili-ties, and leave events to her; for what can be done she will do.

TAKE EXERCISE, as much as you can bear; but be especially careful not to overdo. Nervousness renders you loath to begin, but when begun, extremely liable to overdo. Not to do too much absolutely, but do too *fast*, so as to make you tremble.

Exercising moderately will enable you to do much more without overdoing. Remember your nervousness throws you into a hurried, flurried, worried, rushing mood, so that you are apt to exercise too violently at first. Cultivate deliberation in exercise, in everything. Try moderately all the pathics but allopathy [115] to [119]; take the best of care of your general health, and wait patiently on nature, and every day will find you better than its predecessor. Following these directions will restore the most aggravated cases of this disease, and make new men and women of many now miserable thousands.

129. — PREVENTIVES AND CURES OF INSANITY.

A DISEASED MIND, of all the diseases incident to human nature, is the most grievous, crushing, and absolutely insupportable. To have limb after limb cut from the writhing body, most excruciating though it be, bears no comparison to that horror of horrors experienced " when mind's diseased." Those thus afflicted have been known to hold their hands in the fire, cut and bite their flesh, or to submit to amputation, and then remark that these things were diversions compared with the indescribable mental anguish they endure. Well may the heart of every philanthropist beat with its fullest and strongest pulsations of sympathy in view of the anguish experienced by the raging, bewildered maniac; and well may government attempt the amelioration of those thus afflicted, by erecting asylums for their comfort and cure. What practice is as barbarous, as absolutely horrible, as that of confining the maniac, perhaps in a dungeon, in chains, or the strait jacket, treating him as if he were criminal, and perhaps scourging him at that! He is sick, not criminal. To punish one who is dying of fever, or consumption, is truly horrible; but to chastise a maniac is as much more so, as his disease is more painful than all others. Ordinary sickness can be endured; but let reason be dethroned, let self-possession be swayed from its moorings, let imaginary demons torment, and all the passions be thrown into tumultuous uproar, the whole man no longer himself. Of all objects of commiseration, such are the most deserving.

To PREVENT this disease is far better than to cure it. The following prescriptions, faithfully adhered to, while they will greatly mitigate this disease, after it is once seated, will, in most cases, if not in all, where it is hereditary, prevent its developing itself in actual insanity.

Both to prevent and also to cure this disease, it is first necessary that we understand its CAUSE, so as to counteract or obviate it. The cause of insanity, or rather insanity itself, consists in the excessive *excitability* and *over-action* of the brain and nervous system. Its prevention, therefore, can be effected only by reducing this over-action. And the remark is too obvious to require more than its mere presentation, that precisely the same remedial agents should be employed to reduce this morbid inflammation of the brain which are now employed to reduce other cases of inflammation, and the same means by which tendencies to other forms of inflammation may be prevented, will prevent the inflammation of the brain, and its consequent derangement of mind. Let it never be forgotten that insanity is a purely physical disease — as much so as consumption or cancerous affections, or any other bodily indisposition; and both preventives and cures, to be effectual, must be calculated to prevent or reduce this inflammation.

SUPERIOR NATURAL ABILITIES INVARIABLY accompany a tendency to insanity, including the most intense emotions. Both consist in that same exalted cerebral action which causes insanity. Only the very flower of humanity need ever fear becoming insane. In fact, this affliction is only the very excess of talent and sensibility. Do superior talents depend upon the powerful action of the brain? So does insanity, only the cerebral action is still greater. As but a narrow line separates the sublime and the ridiculous, so but a step divides the highest order of talents from madness. It requires a prodigiously smart man to become crazy. Whoever is subject to insanity is nobody's fool.

Hence, then, to prevent hereditary tendencies to insanity from developing themselves, it is necessary only to prevent this constitutional excitability of the brain from progressing beyond the point of healthy action. And to do this, it is only requisite to divert the action from the brain to some other part, to remove exciting causes of cerebral action, and to keep the brain as quiescent as possible.

A CHILD'S hereditarily predisposition to insanity will show itself in his ecstasy of feeling when pleased, and in the overwhelming depth of his anguish when crossed; in the power and intensity of his desires, in his haste and eagerness about everything, and in his being precociously smart and acute. In this lies the danger. Parents generally try to increase this action, by plying them with study, keeping them confined at school, and seeing how very smart they can make them. But to prevent this tendency, pursue directly the opposite course. This highly wrought cerebral action requires to be diminished, not enhanced. Study increases it; so does confinement; but physical exercise diverts it from the brain to the muscles. All children thus predisposed should be kept from school till well grown, and allowed to run, play, and be happy; but never crossed or tantalized, nor enter upon the cares and business of life till fully matured, and then check that boiling energy which courses through their veins.

Of all occupations, farming is the most suitable for them, as the labor it requires diverts the energies from the brain, and works off that excitement, the excess of which constitutes this malady. With nothing to do, this energy accumulates, and gathers upon the most susceptible part, the brain, and ends in derangement; but open the valves of labor for its escape, and health and sanity are preserved.

LET THEM SLEEP. Put them in bed early, and keep them from being excited evenings. Young people thus predisposed should not attend balls or parties, or any exciting scenes, in the evening, nor read novels, play cards, or any other exciting games of chance, nor take alcoholic stimulants of any kind or degree, not even wine, or cider, or beer, and scrupulously avoid even tea and coffee, because all these tend to augment and develop that excessive cerebral action from which they are in danger. They should take laxatives, not tonics — what will diminish their excitability, not increase it. Alcoholic drinks often induce derangement, even where there is no hereditary predisposition to it; much more, then, will they develop a latent susceptibility already existing.

STIMULATING meats and drinks are most efficient agents in developing latent insanity. The simplest diet is the best. Milk, by being productive of dulness, is decidedly beneficial. Bread-stuffs will be found far preferable to meats. Indeed, meat should be eaten sparingly, because it is a powerful stimulant. It heats and fevers the blood, oppresses the brain, and increases the very tendency to be avoided. Bread, milk, Indian and rye puddings, vegetables, rice, fruit, and the like, should constitute the chief diet of those thus predisposed. LETTUCE eaten with lemons is excellent, because quieting. Of course from spices, mustards, peppers, and condiments, they should wholly abstain. Excepting alcoholic drinks, nothing is equally pernicious. Only those things should be taken which open the system, and keep it cool. Fruit may be eaten in almost any quantity with advantage, and so may jellies. But, unfortunately, sweet things are relished by such less than things that are sour and hot, such as pickles, peppers, &c. Eat them, but they will hurt you.

COLD WATER, especially the shower-bath, is certainly cooling, and pre-eminently calculated to carry off the superabundant heat of the system, and obviate that feverish tendency which constitutes the predisposition to be avoided. Nothing will be found more beneficial to the insane than cold water applied externally, especially to the head, and taken internally in copious and frequent draughts. This prescription must commend itself too forcibly to the common sense of every reader to require comment or defence.

AVOID THOSE SUBJECTS on which relatives or ancestors were deranged. Thus, one of the topics of derangement appertaining to the family of a young man who hung himself in 1842, on account of his having been disappointed in a love matter, was the social affections. He should have known this, and therefore have nipped his affections in the bud, unless he was sure of their being reciprocated, and consummated by marriage. In short, he should never have allowed his affections to become engaged till he was sure of marriage — a direction suitable for most young people, but doubly so for those thus predisposed, because love is a very exciting thing anyhow, whereas they require peace and quiet. Still, unless such are able to govern their love, they should locate their affections, though they need not therefore be in haste to marry. A partner having a cool, soothing temperament, should alone be chosen.[615]

THE MOST EFFICACIOUS prevention, after all, is to place intellect on the throne, and to bear in mind that this hereditary tendency exists, and when your feelings become powerfully awake to any particular subject, remember that they are constitutionally too active, and therefore magnify everything; and remembering

45

this, will enable you to look on with intellectual coolness upon
the bustling tumult of raging passions as upon schoolboys at
play. Thus, if the predisposition be to melancholy, remember
that these gloomy feelings have no foundation in reality, but are
the product of your own organization; that but for this hereditary predisposition, the same circumstances would produce opposite feelings; that, in short, all your trouble is self-made, and
without foundation, and this will enable you to dismiss them.
And so of any predisposition that may beset you.

Of course all those directions just prescribed for the prevention
and cure of nervousness, apply with redoubled force to insanity.
Of course, too, all forms of dissipation and vice, and whatever fires
up the passions, are to be most sedulously avoided. None who
lead right hygienic and moral lives need ever fear insanity, no
matter how predisposed to it all their relatives may have been.

SECTION VI.

ACUTE DISEASES, WOUNDS, CONVALESCENCE, ETC.

130. — TREATMENT OF ACUTE AND CONTAGIOUS DISEASES.

GUARD AGAINST them. They are not causeless, but *caused;*
and that by precursors as potential as they are violent. They
generally gather a long time before they finally burst, and are
usually the most violent in those whose constitutions are the
strongest; because such unload disease as fast as it is generated,
till some sudden cold stops up the outlet, when their powerful
constitutions grapple right in resolutely with their disease, and
the two struggle for the mastery so violently that one or the
other must conquer promptly.

ALL SUCH can get well if they give the life-force a fair chance.
A constitution able to set up so fierce a struggle, is therefore
able to win a victory. Let them fight it out.

HEROIC medicines are positively dangerous in all such cases.
Superadding the inflammations created by these medicines to
those of the disease, endangers a sudden snapping of the cords
of life. Let the life-force alone and it will struggle through; for
it would not grapple thus resolutely unless it had the power to

overcome. It would take hold less resolutely and cast out more gradually if it needed to. All Nature's provisions warrant this conclusion.

PREVIOUS CARE, however, will stave off the battle. A sharp eye can always tell beforehand that the thunder cloud of disease is gathering, and about how long before it will naturally burst. It is always preceded by a dark, livid red about the face and eyes; too much general inflammation; a bad and haggard, or else a wild, glaring look, along with other signs of inflammation; including passional irritability. Let such beware how they violate the health laws much longer; for retribution is knocking at the door, preparatory to their arrest.

MOTHERS should watch these and other signs presaging sickness in their children, and take patients in season, put them on short dietetic rations, soak their feet in hot water and put them to bed early, covered up warmly, with a dose of strong catnip tea, so as to start the perspiration.[114]

ACHING BONES, violent, sharp, darting pains, local or general, an irregular appetite, or none at all, restlessness, and bad dreams during sleep, &c., signify that the gathering disease storm is about to burst.

BEGIN IN SEASON. Be especially careful not to take cold, to which you are now especially predisposed in proportion as you are loaded with disease. Keep well housed and warmed, but *eat nothing*. Let your system live on its *accumulated* carbon.[120] Lay a wet cloth on your stomach nights. Motherwort tea to open your bowels will help. These and like means will probably stave it off.

TAKE YOUR BED as soon as the struggle fairly commences. Give up work before you fully feel that you need to, so as not to aggravate your malady. *Doctor yourself. You* are the one to live or die. Or if you call a doctor, insist on *knowing* what he gives, and what effects are expected to be produced.

BREATHE, *breathe.* Breathe deep and fast, besides keeping your room well aired, and struggle resolutely against disease by will-power. By all means secure as much skin action as possible.[93] If you are thirsty, drink, drink, drink, so as to give your friend, fever, materials to hustle out corrupt matter; and keep well covered up, so as to prevent more colds. If your fever proves to be chronic, take it patiently, assured that Nature will work just as fast as she is able, and do whatever is possible for your recovery, but she *will not* be hurried. Probably a few days will suffice to completely restore you, and leave you a *great deal* better than if you had not been sick.[114]

A SICK ROOM needs common sense more than any other place, yet usually has less. Good ventilation is especially important; so is an even temperature; but *cheerfulness* in its nurse and attendants is more so. A sad, sorrowful, plaintive, whining attendant is awful. None should, by whispers, action, or manner, imply that there is any danger; for this unmans the patient, even though a child, and this discourages or alarms the will-power, which is the great remedy.[114] Apprehension of death does more than all else to induce it, as hope and clasp on life do to avert it. Sympathy implies danger. Let the hopes and wills of attendants tone up those of the patient.

CONTAGIOUS diseases are easily managed, and need rarely prove fatal. Small-pox can be so treated as completely to rid the system of all its morbid matter, and give a twenty years' extra lease of life. Proceed thus : —

1. AFTER EXPOSURE, and before it sets in, eat but little, and take two or three good sweats by the hot bath, steam bath, Turkish bath, or drinking hot water or teas, going to bed, and covering up warm. Meanwhile avoid all exposures to colds.

2. WHEN it sets in, *do but little* except to be *very* careful not to get cold, or any set back.

3. A flour poultice on your face after the pits begin to head, will prevent all pits and marks, and help their forming. It should be worn constantly till they are healed. Never touch a scale till it falls off of itself.

4. After your disease has turned, and your appetite is restored, be extra careful not to over-eat, or eat what is injurious, or over-do.

5. If any part fails to fill out well, lay a wet cloth on it, wrung from cold water, and keep changing it often.

6. Keep a deep and fast breathing continually.

7. Trust to Nature, and allow no fears.

131. — CONVALESCENCE, RELAPSES, WOUNDS, BOILS, BURNS, ERUPTIONS, SORES, ETHER.

How one gets up, is most eventful for good or evil. If you "get up" right, you will be regenerated, physically and mentally, "by the sick spell," and live many years longer than you otherwise could have lived.

RELAPSES are always more dangerous than the original disease, and often fatal, and by all manner of means to be avoided. Yellow-fever patients usually die of them, but rarely of the fever proper. There is no earthly need of them. Right care and nursing, always more important than doctoring, will prevent them. Remember that the system is *exhausted*, and hence very susceptible.

CHILDREN, by tens of thousands, get up from measles, scarlet fever, &c., so poorly that they are ever afterwards ailing; whereas, a little care after the disease had turned, would have left them better than before.

DON'T GET ABOUT too soon. You will feel that you are able to do more than you can do without injury. Be sure to always keep far *within* your strength, and are on the side of safety. Twice in his life the Author did his constitution almost irreparable damage by resuming work too soon, once after the varioloid, and once after the typhoid pneumonia.

DON'T OVER-EAT, and be careful as to *what* you eat; but eat often, and always leave off hungry.

COLDS are your worst enemy. Look out for them. Remember what a herculean task your skin has just achieved, and how weak and susceptible to colds it must therefore be.

A LONG FURLOUGH from business is now most desirable. It will let you get *right* well before you harness up, and enable you to make many times more money in the long life run with than without.

MOTHERS and nurses will find directions for keeping children well, and managing sick ones, in Part VIII. of "Sexual Science." [637]

132. — TUMORS, ERUPTIONS, SCALDS, BURNS, &c.

These should be left unchecked. Rely for their cure on washing and obviating their cause. As long as that corruption which causes them continues to gather, this outlet of it should be allowed

to remain open ; else its inward accumulation will clog and cripple
all the other parts. Open sluice-ways, for its free exit is your
salvation, and to be encouraged, till you can reach its fountain
and stop its manufacture.

CUTANEOUS eruptions are governed by this same law, except
what are "catching." Don't put on anything to *dry up* such
eruptions. Every pimple is a blessing. It is better to have
neither corruption nor pimples ; but as long as the corruption remains, please allow pimples to eject it. Meanwhile look around
sharply for its cause, and cure your pimples by obviating that
laboratory of corruption in which they originate, besides taking
more care of your skin. ·

SCALDS, BURNS, &c., should be at once immersed in water, cold
or warm, as is most agreeable, and kept there till their smart
ceases, then cover with flour, and *let alone.* The fact that after
half or more of one's skin has been scalded or burnt, they must
die, is full of meaning, and shows how absolutely essential is the
office of the skin ; but if those scalded by hot water or steam, or
badly burnt, will jump into cold water, clothes and all, or can
have pails of cold water dashed on them, they will instantly stop
their hot clothes from burning any more, and take out the burn
more effectually than by any other means. Or, if a hand, arm,
foot, or any locality is thus burnt, either hold the parts in water,
or else bind on a wet bandage, or lay on a thickness of cotton cloth,
and pour on cold water, gently but steadily, till the pain ceases.

THE *cold* probably effects the cure, because, as soon as the flesh
heats the water the burn aches ; whereas, *moving* it in the water,
that is, keeping *cold* water next to the burnt skin, eases and
cures it.

CUTS AND BRUISES should be done up in their own blood, before
they stop bleeding, and then *let alone;* or, if they pain you, keep
them wet with cold water. *Blood* is the best dressing in the
world. It coagulates and dries, thus forming an *air-tight covering*, which *seals up* the wound while Nature goes on to heal it.
Do salves or plasters carry off waste matter or insert new flesh?
They are better than nothing, because they keep out the cold, protect it, &c., but do that far less effectively than a blood poultice.

·POWDERED CHALK on all kinds of sores and raw places is most
excellent. It unites with the exudations to form a perfect coating,
under which the healing progresses finely.

DRESSINGS irritate, and must be avoided as much as possible. Of course, when suppuration is in progress, the yellow, corrupt matter thus formed must have an outlet, which can easily be made through this blood overcoat.

EVERY TOUCH pains, because it injures. Let our involuntary shrinking from touch warn all to *let them alone*.

RUPTURED ARTERIES must of course be taken up and tied, but this belongs to surgery, that wonderful art in modern hands, which we leave to surgeons. But they often amputate limbs they could save.

TUMORS may, and may not, need the knife. If not, keep a cold wet cloth on them, and let them alone; meanwhile asking yourself how, by violating what law, you are generating this corruption, and head off its manufacture, but not its formation.

CANCERS may, but may not, be curable by cundurango. If it really proves efficacious, of which there seems recently some doubt, if it dissolves and neutralizes the cancerous ingredient in the blood, it will be a great public blessing; for there is an incalculable amount of *internal* cancerous diseases, especially in females, which creates cancers in the stomach, intestines, &c.

STUFFING is probably the best cure. By a recent discovery, all the affected parts can be completely stuffed off, when the wound readily heals.

INFLAMMATIONS are usually due to an accumulation of fibrine, and obviously a healing or formative process. They are governed by that curative law already applied to fevers.[114] Rejoice that the part inflamed has sufficient vitality to *institute* inflammation.

COLD WATER is your best restorative. It will probably give a feeling of comfort, and whatever *feels* good *is* good.[50]

AN ACHING FOREHEAD can be relieved by wearing a wet cloth nights. All who use their intellects right briskly by day, will find a wet cloth worn on their foreheads by night a great relief. They will sleep much better that night, and can work their brain all the harder the next day without injury. It will also greatly promote memory of all kinds, intellectual acumen, clearness and vigor, and mental snap in whatever you engage. Editors whose foreheads are usually hot from incessant and long-continued intellectual effort, — and if any man earns his living it is a good editor and author, — and minds sometimes loath to come right up to their full work, will find their greatest personal relief and very best aid to consist in wearing this wet compress. Teachers, clergymen, and all who apply their minds incessantly, will be similarly benefited, and for a like reason. It will allow them to put forth double and treble their wonted intellectual effort with ease, relieve cerebral congestion, and work "*like a charm.*"

ETHER, or laughing gas, now extensively used in surgical operations, deserves notice. The Deity understood Himself and His work when he created pain, but has graciously superadded destructiveness to resist it. By resolutely bracing up against it, we can "grin and bear" almost any amount of pain and disease. This mental resistance to pain is quite analogous to that "will-cure already presented.[118] The provisions of *God in* Nature are the best possible, and worthy of adoption. Those who make up their minds to endure heroically whatever pain is inflicted, had better dispense with these destroyers of pain which suspend consciousness. There are cases in which it becomes suddenly fatal, and many others in which the nervous system more fully regains its former susceptibility. One had better bear any amount of pain than to blunt this sensory *capacity* itself. Each and all should judge for themselves, but at least inform themselves beforehand. Its administrators should give as little as possible, and its takers should give extra attention to their health for days before and after. The Author, speaking only for himself, would do without taking it just as long as possible, and then take as little as would barely suffice. It must needs do only damage in childbirth, because it simply *suspends* pain and all the other functions about equally, besides necessarily affecting the nervous system of the infant.

133. — FEMALE WEAKLINESS; ITS CAUSES AND OBVIATION.

FEMALE HEALTH concerns every woman, man, and child more deeply than any other public problem, and unborn generations more still. Robust, healthy women are more desirable, yet rarer than any other commodity. The woman's rights question is nowhere, as to practical importance, in comparison with woman's health. To attempt to say how infinitely important it is to every woman herself, is to attempt the impossible. And it is about as important to every man as woman. And still more so to children, and to those yet to be born. The most "society" suffers more to-day from the acknowledged feebleness of the female sex than from all other evils put together. Let the individual experiences of nearly all say how much.

AMERICAN "society" suffers by far the most. In no nation on earth are women as weakly, yet in none is female health as desirable. Woman and man, come go with me into the solution of this portentous problem.

How feeble are nearly all, and how sickly are most American ladies, it is not our present purpose to say; nor to discuss their special ailments as such; but only to inquire after the *causes* and the remedies of the present weakliness and physical debility of, especially, cultivated women ladies.   .

BY NATURE the female sex is as healthy as the male. German and Irish women are about as healthy, and almost as robust, as German and Irish men; and squaws as Indians. That this modern and American debility is due to the *habits* and usages of civilized life, is demonstrated in the palpable fact that the female sex, among the peasantry and uncultivated, is about as strong and robust, and as uniformly healthy, as the male. This shows that modern female weakliness is easily avoided; that they originated in *style*, not in Nature — in *fashion*, not necessity. Female drudges are healthy. Only ladies are weakly and sickly. Mark this universal *fact*, and learn the lesson it teaches.

MUST MAN, then, put up with either a strong, robust, healthy, coarse-grained, uncouth woman for a wife, or with a weakly, nervous, sickly one? Has he no alternative? For if not, his lot is as hard as that of woman herself in being doomed to drudgery or feebleness. The trouble is not inherent. God has made all things wisely and well, but "*society*" has sought out many foolish inventions.

A HEALTHY *lady* is not impossible, yet is so *very* rare. But if any can be healthy *and* refined, of course *all* can. Why need refinement blight the female physiology? It need not. The two are not antagonistic, but were made to accompany each other. She is unfortunate who has either without the other. Woman certainly needs refinement,[356, 362] but she needs good health still more, both as a human being,[29] and as a female.[603] Both are natural concomitants. Only false sanitary usages separate them.

In the good time coming, men will be blessed with wives who are both fine-grained, delicate, intensely emotional, and exquisitely tasty, not occasionally, but *generally;* not by now and then one, but by *millions;* and be infinitely blessed therein. And *some* readers will live to see that glorious day. It may tarry, but it will certainly come. And come just as soon as men choose to prepare its way.

WHAT CIVIC USAGES, then, render ladies so uniformly weakly or else sickly? The causes to a fact thus uniform, must needs be perfectly apparent, and very aggravated.

VIOLATION OF THE LAW OF BALANCE,[34] is the great cause. That law is both absolute and universal. It governs woman as well as man. All degrees of its violation are punished with proportionate severity. Modern female education, which, to be rightly named, should be modern female *ruination*, consists in a steady, persistent and intense taxation of the *brain* and nervous system, from the very cradle. The little girl must learn to read before she has fairly learned to walk, and be confined in school, and made to sit still, while yet a mere little tottler. She needs and desperately craves exercise; but no, poor, dear sufferer, she must enter from her cradle upon her lady-modelling martyrdom, just as her Chinese sister in sorrow must put on the ever pinching shoe; and both deserve equal pity. Cannot both customs be abrogated? She needs and craves exercise; let her take her fill. Her first great specific "ruination" consists in the *conjunction* of these two things : preventing bodily development, but stimulating mental, to its very highest possible pitch. And this error is kept up throughout her miscalled educational, but really ruinational, career.

STUDY is not what hurts her; for she could study all she now does, and much more, without injury, *provided* she also *exercised* proportionally. Neither separately, but both *together*, work all this physical ruin. Give her the full liberty of yards and fields, and she will grow up both talented and robust, healthy and refined. Her romping desire grows on her till three years after puberty; but no, she must *primp* up, dress up, pretty up, and be so very precise and *proper* in every word and action. Her gushing girlish *nature* must be as effectually cramped and dwarfed, as a Chinese lady's foot is by her tight shoe, worn night and day.

THE BEAUX both tickle her already feverish excitability up to fever heat. She talks of them, and of little else, by day, and thinks mainly of them by night, and perhaps suffers nervous paralysis from analogous amatory excitements. Of course sitting still retards her growth, and interferes with the formation of a good constitution, perhaps even undermines it. At length her ambition is roused to become a premium scholar. She not only studies, but she *worries* day and night to get her lessons, and for fear she might miss one question or word; her anxieties straining her nerves even more than her studies.

NOVELS AND MAGAZINES, with a love affair or two thrown in, now finish off her nervous ruination, which really is by this time becoming complete. Yet we have already mentioned them under a kindred head.[127] Cultivated or fashionable female life is one dead strain on the brain and nerves all the way up from the cradle to the death, which therefore usually transpires early. Why cannot fashion-makers get up those fashions which will *promote* female health instead of ruining it? and why will women follow and impose on one another these ruinous fashions? The woman is by far too precious and too lovely to be thus offered up on the altar of the fashions. They are not worth the sacrifice.

FEMALE APPAREL is another cause of female feebleness. Its construction is wrong, and constitutionally destructive of health from first to last, and head to foot. All this false rigging of the head and compression of the arms and shoulders; this lacing of the waist and loading of the hips; these visceral displacements, caused by the perpetual dragging down of clothes, including consequent local overheating; the narrow, pinched-up shoes, to make the foot look genteel and prim, thin soles and thin hose included, are, collectively, enough to ruin the constitution of an alligator, much more of a woman naturally weakly, and then overtaxed mentally, and cramped physically. Female health demands, all men, and especially all prospective children, demand a complete *revolution* in the female toilet, and the recent dethroning of the queen of fashion renders this a most auspicious time to begin this greatest of all reforms. Its inconvenience, in tangling the feet in walking, and especially in ascending stairs, should alone doom it to oblivion. Woman's rights righters, come right up to this most irksome of woman's wrongs, a ruinous toilet. And it ruins the female *spirit* the most.[308]

OUT-DOOR EXERCISE is now woman's special need. *Confinement* to the school-room, the house, and the nursery is her greatest curse. She needs something to care for, nurse, and do in the open air. .To *do* anything about house is ungenteel, and to walk abroad is unlady-like. To remain *within* is her fashionable doom. Some excuse for going abroad, something out of doors to call and keep her more in the open air and sunshine, is her great requisition.

FLOWERS AND BERRIES furnish this needed excuse. To admire and nurture them, thank God, is yet "genteel." Do, ladies, make one grand rush for flower-beds and flower-pots. Besides showing your gardener, take hold with your *own* hands. Yet your apparel is really a great hinderance.

A STRAWBERRY bed, a berry patch, and a vegetable garden increase woman's range of out-door excuses; and so does skating in winter; but she requires some genteel *play*, some laughter-promoting *sports*, which shall furnish a great deal more of muscle-developing *exercise* than croquet, and yet allow both sexes to participate.

FEMALE TOURISM bids fair to do something in this direction during July and August; but something much less expensive and fitful, and more consecutive, is needed, which is available the year round.

Ladies, come, awake to your own emancipation, and then summon men to your aid. And let men and women join heads and hands in promoting this greatest American desideratum — FEMALE HEALTH. Fashionable *exercise* is the main prerequisite and restorer, as excessive cerebral taxation is the main debilitator.

134. — THE AUTHOR'S PERSONAL HEALTH EXPERIENCES.

FROM YOUTH, all along up till now, the Author has had his attention directed quite as much to the human Physiology as Phrenology; because it plays quite as important a part in human weal and woe, and in whatever appertains to life. His profession has kept thrusting this problem perpetually upon his attention, in one continuous round of ever-ranging aspects, which he has been eager to observe, and assiduous in deciphering.

AN EXPERIMENTAL CAST of mind was his hereditary endowment. This trait made him a Phrenologist. He was bound to *see and know experimentally* whether *facts* sustained or contradicted the assertions of this science; and found they did in every particular.

HEALTH EXPERIMENTS enlisted his attention, *pari passu*, with phrenological. He began them when he started for college, and partly as a matter of necessary economy. His boyhood was quite like that of other boys born in log cabins, and helping a father clear off a new and very stony farm, on which he did *all* the ploughing among roots and stones together, from his tenth year to his seventeenth; and, of course, working very hard.

THE COLLEGE MESS constituted his first dietetic experiment — a dozen students uniting, agreeing about how high we could afford to go, appointing a contractor, who hired a room and cook, bought the provisions, and was captain-general of the mess. The Author joined those which averaged from sixty to eighty cents *per week*, for food alone, and had enough; though he sometimes boarded himself cheaper, by living mostly on bread and milk; yet not living well enough then for health.

He accepted President Hitchcock's abstemious views, already quoted from,[68] which he carried somewhat too far; considering that he took a great amount of exercise all through college, by sawing dry hickory wood in two twice, and backing it up four and *five stories* for only *seventy-five cents per cord*, thus earning most of his collegiate expenses. But over-working with under-feeding wore in upon an excellent constitution. He violated the law of *proportion*.[34]

In 1835 he began his vegetarian experience, with results already detailed.[68] Whether, on general average, it improved or injured him, its beginning was certainly most beneficial; whilst his return to a mixed diet was about equally so.

AGAINST ONE of his habits — writing nights — he must warn all concerned. The composition of every one of his early books caused a sickness, more or less severe, on its completion; probably consequent on *night* writing. Unable to write during the day, because continually interrupted by professional calls, he wrote nights, and often till daylight. His day labors were enough for any man, and, when supplemented by night, became too much. On retiring, a fitful, dreamy state precluded sufficient sleep. This obtained up to 1869, and prevented his writing but one work between 1850 and 1869.

In 1841 a severe attack of the varioloid, caught in the practice
of his profession, almost ended his life. Unaware that he had
been exposed, he worked on till it had actually broken out. He
felt very badly for a day or two, administered to himself a
Thompsonian course, Thursday, P. M., lectured Thursday evening, that night went to a new home, for the first time so sick that
he sent for Dr. Lee, of Buffalo, who pronounced it small-pox;
kept his bed ten days, suffered terribly in the head meanwhile;
steadily refused to take medicines; adopted the let-alone-pathy,
excepting the external use of wet bandages; was pronounced
hopeless Saturday night, but ordered a tub of cold water brought
to his bed, and a dozen cloths kept soaking in water, and changed
every five minutes all night; broke the back of the disease that
night; was prescribed wine whey Sunday, which he refused, for
he wanted only to rest and breathe; found his appetite returned
Monday, and Wednesday most foolishly and wickedly began the
revisal of "Matrimony," which brought on an intense pain in his
forehead, that lasted and tormented him incessantly till 1865; all
of which pain would have been avoided simply by waiting a week
or two before resuming his pen.

From 1835 to 1849 he ate two daily meals, then only one till
1865, was benefited by changing from three to two, and also by
changing from two to one; but still farther improved by returning to two, which both observation and his own experience have
convinced him as by far the best, and taken before beginning, and
often finishing, the day's work.

AN INHERITED weak stomach, and consequent dyspepsia, was
his perpetual plague and enervator from 1827 to 1865, since
which it has disappeared wholly, leaving instead the digestion
seemingly of an ostrich; though it has been gradually improving
since 1835.

A TERRIBLE TYPHOID PNEUMONIA in 1860, contracted by the
striking in of the perspiration incident to sea-sickness, while
crossing the Bay of Fundy, where the tide rises and falls sixty
feet, after lecturing all summer, and continuing to redouble it by
lecturing instead of giving up to it, came within an ace of ending
his life and labors together. Lecturing first between two open
windows, and then with a window open at his back, was the immediate occasion of the attack. Three doctors pronounced death

inevitable, but missed.   The special danger lay in diarrhœa super-
vening on the turning of the disease ; which was averted by using
water enemas, with a little Cayenne pepper.

After becoming convalescent, his doctor said six months was
the soonest time possible for resuming lecturing, yet he resumed
in less than six weeks ; but a relapse was induced by lecturing in a
cold hall, which induced a terrible cough and consumptive attack,
compelled another five weeks' suspension, and left his nervous
system extremely feeble, which took two years for recovery.
He serves this absolute injunction on all typhoid patients — to
wait several months after they think themselves perfectly restored
before again resuming work.

But this typhoid gave the death blow to his dyspepsia, which
an important adjunct in 1865 completely routed and annihilated,
followed by a morbid improvement in every aspect of health and
intellectual vigor ; and in 1868 that expectoration already mentioned routed the last remnant of his inveterate headache, and
prepared the way for the resumption of his pen.   But for his
wickedly resuming work too soon after both his sicknesses, no
such intermission need or would have occurred.   Let all similarly
circumstanced take warning.

SEVERE PAIN in the forehead supervened almost immediately
on resuming his night authorship, accompanied with fitful dreams
on first retiring ; to obviate which he wore a cold wet towel on
the forehead during sleep, which took out every night the inflammation engendered by the previous day's and night's work.   Night
writing is unmistakably bad.   You who enjoy morning papers
little realize the wear and tear of brain and constitution which
serves up this intellectual breakfast ; and those who write nights
must sleep abundantly and keep a cool forehead.

"SEXUAL SCIENCE" occupied just one year in preparation and
proof-reading.   Its amount of thought will bear inspection.   To
prepare a *philosophical* page, requires much more deep thought
and adjusting of ideas than any other.   To *average* three such
pages *per day*, and to revise, costs more labor than to originate
— to lecture twice per week on the average, summer and winter,
and do all the requisite agency, and then transact all the *office*
besides, would soon break down most young men, much more
old.   His usual day's routine was, in summer, to rise before the

sun, write till after ten, breakfast, wait on professional calls, read proof, answer correspondence, and rest till seven P. M., then write with all steam on till eleven; but in cold weather, to rise at eight, but write from seven P. M., to two A. M., and never going out of doors except to lecture. How he endured all his severe and varied labors without breaking down is to him unaccountable, unless it be in the efficacy of the doctrines he preaches. Their effects for good on those who desire or require to perform great brain labor are certainly wonderful.

A HEARTY APPETITE he has found uniformly accompanies severe and protracted brain labor, whether professional or in authorship. Severe brain action uses up organic material quite as fast and effectually as severe muscular. Right brain work *promotes* digestion, instead of retarding it. Vigorous health is as compatible with severe and protracted study as work. The Author regards his ability to sustain severe and protracted brain labor as something marvellous, and as proving the efficacy of his doctrines in his own person.

He attributes this power chiefly to three things : —

1. To having taken a very great amount of muscular exercise all the way along up from boyhood till after fifty.

2. To having kept well slept up. Sleep he *will have*, and knows how to get, and gets mornings what he fails to get nights.

3. To uniform correct habits, and total abstinence from alcoholic liquors.

He certainly never before felt as well, or as well able and willing to work, or as little fatigued by it, and now has every prospect of being able to continue to work on hereafter as heretofore, till after "three score years and ten." To know how to pile on and endure any desired amount of work decade after decade, without breaking down, is certainly no mean *practical* recommendation of one's doctrine. They will be found to be much more efficacious in *practice* than in theory.

135.—RULES FOR PRESERVING AND REGAINING HEALTH.

FORMULAS are given in arithmetic, and all the natural sciences, or short laconic rules, for attaining desired results. Whatever is governed by laws has these rules. Health is thus governed,[31] and has its summary rules, or short but explicit direction for preserving and regaining this best of all acquisitions. We propose to conclude this work with a few of them; accompanied with their reasons.

1. STUDY THE SCIENCE AND LAWS OF HEALTH.

The Deity, in bestowing health, has written certain conditions accompanying it, which all are sacredly bound to *know*, that they may fulfil,[19] and *study*, that they may know.[22] Get what aid you please and can from books, conversation, experience, observation, &c., and then make their summary *results* a matter of *personal* investigation, and right hard searching inquiry. All through life you will need to know for your own *self* what will promote and what impair this sacred treasure in yourself. So post yourself the more, especially since you your own *self* is the main one to be benefited thereby, and the one *personally* concerned in the matter.

2. OBSERVE THE EFFECTS of these things and conditions, and of those upon yourself.

Constitutions differ. "What is one's meat is another's poison." Cold water applications may benefit you and injure another; or warm water may be best for you, but injurious to another. What you especially desire, is to know just what kinds and quantities of food, how much sleep, what kinds of external applications, &c., are best for yourself first, others afterwards. *Experience* is immeasurably your best of teachers, for she has a way of enforcing peculiarly impressive. She is sometimes dear, but always thorough. Note especially her chastisements. They never come unless in reproof for some great health outrage. Never allow yourself to be punished twice for the same offence. Learn the first time, so as to escape a second suffering. Be quick to take the hint. Keep your eyes wide open, whenever you do suffer, to spell out its cause, and ever after avoid it.[21] An elephant, in passing a bridge twenty years ago, broke through, and was lifted out only after suffering considerable pain. Lately he came to the same bridge, but absolutely refused to cross it. No persuasions, no punishments could get him on to it. Remember the bridges which carry you over safely; but be at least as wise as the elephant, in absolutely refusing to expose yourself to a second health catastrophe from the same cause.

NOTE also you own changes. What your constitution could

47

weather and turn to good account twenty years ago may break it to-day. Keep well posted as to the *current* requirements of your health market.

TRY EXPERIMENTS and note their effects on yourself, being careful to prosecute any which are injuring you. Eat this for a time, then that, and note their different effects.

3. LEARN FROM OTHERS.

THIS neighbor has a terrible fever or fit of sickness. He will gladly tell you all about it, for he loves to talk about himself; you meanwhile spelling out warnings and directions by which to escape the pit into which he stumbled.

A TYPHOID fever has attacked this, that, the other member of a neighbor's family. For years some one in it has sickened, possibly died, perhaps all taken about the same time of year, and their sickness quite alike. If that family is your own, "step around" right lively till you ascertain what causes it, and look sharply when others suffer.

IF A DARK BED-ROOM is in the house, you need look no farther. Breathing over and over again, night after night, the same poisonous effluvia, has loaded the systems of those who sleep in it down with corruption, and induced this attack. It may be caused by a cesspool close by the window, by vegetables decaying in the cellar, a leaky roof, stagnant water to the windward, &c., &c. Scan all like conditions. If they are all right look farther.

THE HEALTH HABITS of that family may be wrong. They uniformly eat hot saleratus bread, and buckwheat cakes swimming in butter, or eat voraciously, or later suppers, &c.

A DARLING CHILD sickens and dies. Something caused that death.[21] See if you cannot spell it out, and take warning from it not to lose your own by a like means. In short, learn all you can from other people's sicknesses; and equally from their health.

4. BE REGULAR IN EVERYTHING.

A bad habit regularly followed is better than a poor one irregularly. Lay down certain rules, and follow them up assiduously. We have already specified some, but there are many others about equally important. To retire, and rise, and eat, and work, by the clock, is highly promotive of health, even though at wrong hours. *Periodicity* is one of the laws of Nature, instituted by the Maker of the sun and seasons, which we are bound to observe. All old people, without any exception, are just as regular as clockwork. If they do not regulate the sun, the sun certainly regulates them; for both are always in concert in all things.

BE PARTICULAR what habits you do form. To form right ones is immeasurably better than to form wrong. If you chew, or smoke, or drink, or all, have your "appointed times" for each, and indulge in them only at those times; but you had by far better form no such habits; and if formed, *break them up*. Your system may bend to them, but you had better not bend it.

FOR CHILDREN, regularity is still more important; but mothers will find this point discussed in Sexual Science.[638]

5. WASH your face and hands every morning, and limbs and body alternately every other morning.

But be especially careful to establish a subsequent reaction and glow. So modify your bath that you can withstand all colds from it, and secure only benefits.

6. CHANGE YOUR UNDER GARMENTS DAILY.

NEVER SLEEP at night in what you wear by day; but wear and air each every twenty-four hours. They absorb a great amount of putrefaction while on you, so give the air a chance to take it out.

AIR BEDS and bedding often and well.

7. DO SOMETHING WORTHY OF YOURSELF.

WORK UP your constantly accumulating vital forces. Inertiæ is terribly paralytic. Few things are equally so. Have some great *motive*, some paramount life *object*, some mental or physical *work* in hand, worth accomplishing, and if possible, something in which you are thoroughly, deeply *interested*, so that you really love your work. On no account hibernate. If you have money enough, set up some other object or idol; but if you want more money, set about making it; and *stick right tight to* it. What is worth doing at all, is well-worth doing *well*. Do nothing "just for now," but everything thoroughly, so as to last. It is better to wear out than to rust out. Nothing is more wholesome than *work* of some kind. Choose head-work, or hand work, and the kind of either you like best, but select something, and then pitch right in. You will sleep the better, feed the better, be the stronger, live the longer and faster, and be every way the better the harder you work, provided you do not overdo.

8. KEEP WELL RESTED UP AND SLEPT OUT.

There is little danger of your over-doing, provided you rest out daily. Your clock of life will not run down if you wind it fully up every day. Make it a fixed rule never to begin any day's work till that of the preceding day is squared off by laying in the next day's stock before you begin its use. By resting till noon, if needs be, you can do the more work in the afternoon than if you had worked all day, tired; while the latter draws on the *constitution*, the former improves it.[28]

9. KEEP YOUR BODILY MACHINERY IN GOOD RUNNING ORDER.

As SOON AS anything gives out, stop at once, and repair damages. If you still work on, expect a wholesale "smash up." Remember the importance of all to each. Life will not go on without all its functions.[34] The better you keep your machinery repaired, and in good running order, the more and better work it will do.

10. NURTURE AND FAVOR ALL WEAK FUNCTIONS.

STRONG ones will generally look out for themselves, but weak ones need balancing up. Be especially careful not to violate Nature's law of balance.[34] Be doubly careful not to over-tax weak organs. Examine your machinery, to see which is being worked too hard, or too steadily, and give it the more time to rest the harder it is worked. If you are consumptive, favor your lungs; if dyspeptic, your stomach, &c.; and if your business taxes your muscles only, intersperse study; but if it is all brain labor, take daily and vigorous exercise.

The more so if your brain and nerves greatly exceed your muscles by *constitution*. Nature *will have* balance, or punish you for want of it. Watch your children lest they *grow* up unbalanced.

11. FOLLOW NATURE, by eating when hungry, drinking when thirsty, sleeping when sleepy, &c., but then *only*.

INSTINCTS to eat, sleep, &c., were created to be *followed*. They either are, or are not, reliable guides. God made them expressly to direct us. We should see that they are not perverted, but should implicitly obey their calls. As far as they are normal, they constitute a *perfect* guide. Nature's calls are few, but loud. Hear and attend to them.

12. SUPPLY YOUR SYSTEM WITH WHATEVER IT REQUIRES.

Nothing it needs is too good for it, while its denial saps the life entity at its fountain head. As you would feed your hard-working horse, so feed your hard-working organism, not with bread and meat merely, but with breath, exercise, sleep, and whatever else it requires.

13. RETIRE WITH WARM FEET.

Good sleep is not possible while they remain cold. Nature must keep you awake till she can warm them, which may take her hours. Warming and keeping them warm by their exercise, friction, &c., is far better than by artificial heat. To warm them by hot water, bricks, stones, &c., is better than retiring with them cold; yet it is to them what laziness is to the muscles, or nailing a tin to a wall is to its trunk — weakening.[34] This is equally true of all use of the warming-pan. If necessary, *toast* them well before you retire; but rely as far as possible on *natural* warmth.[90]

14. NEVER GET OUT OF BREATH.

BREATHING must always keep even pace with your exertions; but *never fall behind* them. Nature *will not trust.* She must *get* energy before she can expend it. Nothing draws on the constitution as does working beyond breathing. Let those awful feelings, consequent on panting for breath, attest its hurtfulness. If you must run a long way, or work with all your might, *keep your wind.* Do not do or run so fast the first few minutes as to labor for breath afterwards, so that you give out on the last heat, and lose the effort.

15. BEGIN AND CLOSE OUT ANY POWERFUL EFFORT MODERATELY.

WHAT FOLLY to work so hard in the morning as to break down before noon, and lose all the afternoon's work! Start in leisurely, and increase effort gradually, doing two thirds of your day's work in the afternoon; but slacken off gradually towards the close; being especially careful not to expose yourselves to colds, or any thing injurious, till well rested up. Few of Nature's operations are sudden, except what are destructive. Sunlight waxes and wanes gradually to and from your strength, and work along up to its meridian. Begin far below, but never stop anything suddenly. Texans never stop to feed during the day. Any horse had better be put right through his day's work at one heat, than make "two bites of a cherry." One *full* effort, and then lay off.

Otherwise make two days of one by one exhaustive work, a rest, a meal, and then another day's work in the afternoon.

A like plan will enable INVALIDS thus to get well — two days in one by a midday sleep.

This law is equally applicable to ·all intellectual efforts, public speaking, writing for the press, and the labors of a lifetime. Many men throw so much more energy than is needed into the first few years of business, as to unfit themselves for sustained effort ever after. By the time they have worked up a business, they must leave it. As soon as they get fairly started in life, their working power is used up.

16. BE DOUBLY CAREFUL WHEN ABOUT FIFTY.

RECUPERATION begins to wane about that age. Self-abuses before that are soon made up; but after that Nature demands respite and favoring. Slacken off effort in the afternoon of life, as towards the close of the day. Favor yourself by working easily, and husbanding your strength, and you may work on twenty-five years longer; otherwise not. See how many men die, or else give out, between fifty and sixty, and take warning.

STILL LATER in life, when Nature gives warning that she does not intend to do much more repairing on your organism, be doubly careful to *need* but little. Octogenarians and septuagenarians, be extra careful of yourselves.

17. AVOID ALL PASSIONAL EXCESSES all through life.

THINGS PERISH with their using. Many men *burn out* one or all of their passions early in life; so that ever after they "have no pleasure in them." This doesn't pay. This sensory principle is well worth preserving for future use.[448] All the passions are good in their place, but must not be allowed to run tandem.

VIOLENCE of passion sears the nerves. It is to them what looking at the sun is to vision. Too much light blurs all after vision. All excesses must·be paid for at a heavy discount. Make no such drafts.

18. BE PATIENT, PLEASANT, CHEERFUL, HAPPY.

"FRET NOT" thyself for anything or anybody. Obviate all the ills you can, and then patiently *endure* what you cannot cure. Nothing promotes health equally with cheerfulness and serenity of mind; yet nothing wears, corrodes, paralyzes, and shortens life and all its functions equally with anger, hatred, envy, malice, grudges, and vindictiveness. Those who really deserve to be hated are not worth hating, and do not merit the life-ammunition fired in hating them. Leave Nature to punish those who wrong you; assured that in her own time she will do it up brown. Perhaps *you* are the one to blame. All wrong doing punishes itself.[21] At least, don't hurt *yourself* by indulging any bad moods, sad, sorrowful, hating, or other like feelings.

IF RELIGIOUS faith and resignation will enable you to smother wrath, or dispel the blues, or bear life's ills (punishments[21]), cultivate them. As a medicine, they are as much better than nothing as calomel is worse,[112] which is considerable, and *not* hard to take. Genuine piety, not long-faced, moody, sanctimonious, is an excellent tonic and nervine, and the best of all the pathies. None need ever fear an over-dose or relapses.

MAKE EVERY DAY A HAPPY HOLIDAY. Those who enjoy "the most are the best fellows." Seize and turn all you touch, and all surroundings, into occasions of enjoyment. Lay good, bad, and indifferent under contribution — tax everything — to promote your comfort. That good old-fashioned idea of *comfort* is the one great thing. Make yourself just as *comfortable* in mind and body as possible. Let "Sufficient unto the day is the evil thereof" be our motto, and another, "Hope on, hope ever, for the best." This gives you a double enjoyment in everything: once in expecting it, the other in its fruition.

FOLLOWING THESE RULES, and the other directions and doctrines of this book, will keep you well, if well, and get you well if sick. None can at all realize their efficiency or beneficial effects till taught them by *experience*.

GOD BLESS every reader! And every reader and practitioner of these doctrines will be immeasureably blessed in and by following every *single* one of its directions.

Subsequent volumes will prove equally life improving.

FINIS.

PROSPECTUS OF O. S. FOWLER'S

COMPLETE REVISED WORKS ON MAN.

LIFE; its Science, Laws, Faculties, Organs, Functions, Conditions, Philosophy, Improvement, etc.; including the Organism, Health, Social Affections, Moral Faculties, Intellect, Memory, Miscellany, etc.; as taught by Phrenology and Kindred Sciences, in six volumes, as follows: —

I. PHYSIOLOGICAL SCIENCE; or, HEALTH, its Value, Laws, Organs, Functions, Conditions, Restoration without Medicine, etc. $2.00.

II. PHRENOLOGICAL SCIENCE; its Principles, Proofs, Temperaments, Cerebral Organs, Mental Faculties, Teachings, etc., as applied to Self-Culture. With a Steel Engraving of the Author. $3.00.

III. SEXUAL SCIENCE; or, MANHOOD, WOMANHOOD, and their Mutual Interrelations: LOVE, its Laws, Power, etc.; SELECTION, and Mutual Adaptation; COURTSHIP, or Love-making; MARRIED LIFE made Happy; REPRODUCTION, and Progenal Endowment, including Paternity, Maternity, Bearing, Nursing, and Rearing Children; PUBERTY; GIRLHOOD; SEXUAL AILMENTS Restored, and FEMALE BEAUTY Preserved and Regained, etc., etc.

IV. RELIGIOUS SCIENCE; or, MAN'S MORAL NATURE and Relations, as proving the existence of a SUPREME BEING, His Attributes, the True Theology, etc.: IMMORTALITY, its Proofs, Conditions, and Relations to Time; NATURAL RELIGION, its Doctrines, Duties, etc.; Worshipping God in Nature, and by Obeying His Natural Laws; Future Rewards and Punishments; the Law of Love, "Faith," "Prayer," Rites, "Total Depravity," "Conversion," Forgiveness, etc., etc., as taught by Phrenology. $2.00.

V. INTELLECTUAL SCIENCE; or, MEMORY, REASON, and their Culture; including "The Senses," Intellectual Faculties, Schooling, Self-Education, Mental Discipline, etc. $2.00.

VI. AUTOBIOGRAPHY, Progression, Republicanism, Miscellaneous Writings, etc. $2.00.

NATURE is infinitely philosophical and perfect, because the embodiment of all the Attributes, Laws, and Works of her Divine Creator.

MAN IS THE EPITOME of Nature, and of her Author, — the compendium of *all that is;* so that human science expounds all the principles and facts of the universe — *everything everywhere* — and, by unfolding the Creator's crowning work, expounds UNIVERSAL THEOLOGY, thus immeasurably transcending all other studies, besides being most ennobling and perfecting.

THE HUMAN MIND is the summary of man, and therefore of all things, because that for which all else was created; yet it can be studied scientifically and practically *only through its organism,* as manifesting and modifying its action.

PHRENOLOGY analyzes man's mind, and is its only text-book, besides being that *chit* from which emanate the tap-root, rootlets, trunk, limbs, and fruit of all reform and progress; for, by unfolding man's mental constitution, it shows wherein any and all have departed from this perfect type, besides revealing the pathway of return; and must therefore soon become and remain *the great study* of the race, "till time shall be no longer."

A STANDARD WORK on Phrenology, which shall condense whatever is valuable in former writings, superadd its history and all its recent discoveries and improvements, and become a repository of whatever is known on this science of the mind, besides adapting its teachings to our congenial institutions, is therefore a philanthropic desideratum to mankind.

PROF. O. S. FOWLER is now issuing a complete series of exhaustive volumes, as above, based on these principles, embodying all his former writings, revised, condensed, systematized, enlarged, illustrated, and every way improved, including the results of his *forty years* of thought and professional observations, on four generations and in both hemispheres; devoted to the *Brain and Organism* as influencing the mind, and indicating character; to recording its facts, amply illustrated by eye-teaching *likenesses,* and applying its doctrines to all the varied aspects of human life; yet never pandering to popular prejudices: for human *science,* sitting enthroned in dignified majesty above all else, should *direct and reprove* all, but *temporize never.* Philanthropists, Philosophers, and Students of human nature, do not each and all of these works deserve your patronage?

TERMS. — As they are published by subscription, each or all can be obtained ONLY by remitting their price, $12 by those who already possess "Sexual Science," or $15 for the entire series, when they will be mailed, bound and prepaid, as fast as issued, and all completed before the close of 1873. Address

Prof. O. S. FOWLER, 514 Tremont Street, Boston, Mass.

PHYSIOLOGICAL SCIENCE,

(VOL. I. OF THE "SCIENCE OF LIFE,") OR

HEALTH,

Its Value, Functions, Organs, Conditions, and Restoration.

BY PROFESSOR O. S. FOWLER.

HEALTH IS LIFE; while life itself, with all its powers and pleasures, consists only in healthy functions and organs. Health is the "GREATEST GOOD" of every human being. What can we do, become, or enjoy without it? But *how* much with it? Its preservation, improvement, and restoration, therefore, become the paramount *self-interest* of every laborer, trader, scholar, voluptuary, Christian, and philanthropist, — of all in all conditions.

HEALTH LAWS govern health. Therefore, all will enjoy perfect health in proportion as they observe its laws; while breaking them destroys it. To all who observe them, Nature guarantees perfect health, beyond anything we now behold or can imagine. A knowledge of these laws, therefore, becomes immeasurably important. To expound them is the "chief end" of this work. All works on this subject omit the true *principles* and chief means of physical vigor and recuperation.

KEEPING WELL, that greatest art of life, is here expounded, and also applied to preserving the lives and constitutions of children.

RESTORING LOST HEALTH is as important as life itself. Nature's recuperative powers are *so* wonderful that all, not disorganized, can enjoy good health. This book shows invalids how to *restore themselves*, less by medicines, than by *right health habits*. Its perusal will promote the health and happiness of all readers, however well or ill.

HEREDITARY DISEASES can be cured, or kept at bay; and this volume shows how to do both, besides discussing those ailments "flesh is heir to."

THE WATER CURE, WILL CURE, SUN CURE, EARTH CURE, LET ALONE CURE, BREATHING CURE, MOVEMENT CURE, and other cures, are here expounded.

EXCELLENT ENGRAVINGS illustrating the human anatomy sufficiently for all practical purposes are here given.

WHATEVER THE AUTHOR KNOWS about health from forty years of experience and professional observation, he here tells his readers, not in Greek, but in plain understandable English.

TERMS. — It is now published, and can be obtained only by subscription, containing about 450 octavo pages, is well printed and bound, and will be mailed to subscribers, prepaid, on receipt of $2. Post-office orders preferred.

Address *PROFESSOR O. S. FOWLER,*

514 TREMONT STREET, BOSTON, MASS.

N. B. — Price when sent in numbers, $1.50.

PROSPECTUS OF

PHRENOLOGICAL SCIENCE,

Its Principles, Pro:fs, Temperaments, Cerebral Organs, Mental Faculties, Teachings, etc., as applied to Self-Culture. With a Steel Engraving of the Author.

(VOL. II. OF THE "SCIENCE OF LIFE." PRICE $3.)

BY PROFESSOR O. S. FOWLER.

THE HUMAN MIND, — its faculties, structure, philosophy, improvement, etc., — has engrossed the researches of the most gifted men of the race, throughout all ages. And well it may; for all human interests converge in this, their focal centre.

PHRENOLOGY alone unfolds this mental structure and philosophy, and propounds the only *science* of the mind in the analysis of its faculties, and their right and wrong outworkings. In doing so, it *defines* right and wrong, shows what actions and feelings are virtuous, and what vicious, and becomes an infallible guide in conducting life aright. In short, it is the science of sciences, and as far transcends all other subjects, even all the other sciences, as its subject-matter, man's mind, surpasses all else terrestrial.

PROFESSOR O. S. FOWLER understands Phrenology. What is known of it, *he* knows. To an eminently observing and reflective cast of intellect, he superadds *forty years* of study, and just that *kind* of *professional practice* of this science, throughout various climes and countries, which fits him to furnish a correct, embodied, and complete exposition of its philosophies and practical outworkings. All his talents, strength, and experience, together with a strong native desire to benefit every reader in every page, he brings to the composition of this work.

It will be *enriched* — not merely embellished — by engravings, not piled in just for show, but *teaching the art* of reading character by means of this science of the organism.

In short, no labor, no expense, will be spared to render it a *standard* modern work on Phrenology. Gall's works are valuable as giving the origin, history, and facts of this science; and Spurzheim's still more so, as adding materially to its analysis and facts; and Combe's superadd to both; while " Fowler's Phrenology " redevelops this science, especially in its facts; but this volume superadds to all the excellences of all its predecessors whatever advances have been made by *forty years* of subsequent phrenological research, along with all their applications to self-improvement contained in " Self-Culture."

Reader, does not *such* a work commend itself to your patronage, and very *self-interest*. Can you afford to do without it?

TERMS. — It will contain about 700 octavo pages, be mailed during 1872, well printed and bound, and prepaid to all who inclose $3 to

PROFESSOR O. S. FOWLER,

514 TREMONT STREET, BOSTON, MASS.

N. B. — Price, when sent in numbers, $2.00. Those who send $15 will receive this entire *series* of six volumes. See general prospectus.

SEXUAL SCIENCE, AND RECUPERATION:

Including Manhood, Womanhood, and their Mutual Inter-relations; Love, its Laws, Power, etc.; Selection, or Mutual Adaptation; Courtship, or Love Making; Married Life made happy; Reproduction, and Progenal Endowment, or Paternity, Maternity, Bearing, Nursing, and Rearing Children; Puberty, Girlhood, etc.; Sexual Ailments restored, and Female Beauty perpetuated, etc., as taught by Phrenology.

BY PROF. O. S. FOWLER.

A RIGHT MALE AND FEMALE LIFE constitutes the master problem, as yet unsolved, of every human being. "Sexual Science" expounds this problem, and thereby utters a divine mandate to lovers, and the married, and especially to prospective parents, to learn and fulfill Nature's sexual laws. No other knowledge is equally important, because no other duties are as imperious; nor is ignorance of any other so fatal. Reader, would not such knowledge have converted your *own* present sexual or marital sufferings into enjoyments? By expounding and applying Nature's sexual ordinances to these subjects, this work becomes a great public benefaction. Do not the following subjects, among many other kindred ones which it discusses, go right home to the heads and hearts of all who have either?

Part I. Manhood and Womanhood, or the constituent *elements* of male and female perfection. Dignity and utility of sexual knowledge. Reproduction Nature's *paramount* work. "Each after its own kind," throughout every minute particular of body, mind, instinct, everything. Sexual attraction its means. Amativeness confers procreative capacity, and conjugal talents. Is located at the seat of physical life, and apex of every mental organ. Is in sympathetic rapport with every iota of all, that it may transmit all to progeny. Gender wields supreme control over the voice, walk, dance, beauty, complexion, eyes, courage, talents, temper, spirits, morals, happiness, and every element of body and mind. A right sexual state impairs, while a wrong one crushes, the entire being. Hybrids show what parts are derived from the male, and what from the female. What each sex likes and dislikes in the other, and why. Woman loves originality, power, firmness, courage, passion, etc., in man, but dislikes their converse, because the male originates life, and most things human, and confers these elements on offspring; while man loves purity, exquisiteness, affection, maternal love, piety, taste, prudence, ton, in woman, because mothers stamp these attributes on children. How all women can obtain much more than their "rights." How ladies and gentlemen should treat each other. Signs of a strong and weak, healthy and impaired, sexuality. Male and female forms contrasted, and criticised. Only maternal excellences create female beauty. Why men admire the female bust. Analysis of the fashions, etc.

Part II. Love. Its analysis in all its different aspects. Its magic power over the entire being. Its right state improves, but wrong impairs, the form, walk, countenance, muscles, circulation, health, longevity, expression, tones, laugh, manners, mental faculties, energy, industry, ambition, self-trust, morals, hopes, worship, kindness, taste, wit, memory, music, language, sense, agreeableness, — every function of body and mind. Makes or breaks all. Is life's "master passion." Marriage is its natural sphere. Pairing innate. Mating before twenty-one for women, and twenty-three for men, a solemn duty. Its poor substitute. Old-bachelorism, old-maidism, and their excuses. One love *vs.* free-love. Marriage creates families and homes. All sexual vices originate in disappointed or perverted love. How to moralize young men, heal "broken hearts," redeem sexual sinners, restore one's own self to purity, etc. Seducers most accursed. Self-abuse, its prevalence, and terrible effects. It exhausts, inflames, and destroys the entire body and mind. Is as sinful as fornication. Its prevention by knowledge, conscience, commingling of the sexes, etc. Boys and girls, mixed schools, fathers and daughters, mothers and sons, brothers and sisters, ladies and gentlemen, public and parlor amusements, &c.

Part III. Selection, or the natural *laws* of sexual attraction and repulsion. Founding a family. Nature's true *time* to mate, and wed. Similar and different ages. A right choice life's casting die. Mutual rights of parents and children in their own and each other's selection. *Self* the final umpire. Courtship's first stage. *General* marital prerequisites. Healthy rs. invalid. and housekeeping rs. fashionable, consorts. Wealth rs. worth. A poor *man rs.* a rich *thing.* Habits, temperance, sexuality, etc. Marrying cousins. What traits each requires in the other. Superb offspring the determining condition. When and why those similar, and dissimilar, should, and must not, marry. Combining the greatest *aggregate* number and amount of excellences. How to find one thus adapted. Phrenology aids a right choice. Intuition. The proposal, acceptance, and vow. Parental consent, relatives, elopements, dismissals, breaches of promise, etc.

PART IV. COURTSHIP, its fatal errors, and right management. None should love until engaged. Loving is marrying. Love-spats. Flirtations. Liberties. Presents. Disclosing faults. Day rs. night. and Sabbath-evening, courtships. Sudden loves. RIGHT courtship. Its first prerequisite. Duration, etc.

PART V. MARRIED LIFE. Establishing a perfect love. The wedding, honey-moon, honey-marriage, first year, etc. Love-making rules. Be perfect gentlemen and ladies. Mould and be moulded. Coöperate in all things. Promote each other's happiness. Nurture each other's affections more than during courtship. DISCORDS, their amount, causes, and obviation. Toleration. Burying old bones, etc. DIVORCES. When, and when not, allowable, etc.

PART VI. REPRODUCTION. The ultimate end of everything sexual. Intercourse its only means. All temporary parental states transmitted. Platonic love the great prerequisite. It creates the *mind.* Love and intercourse natural concomitants: therefore marrying one while loving another is double adultery. Amativeness and the sexual organism in sympathetic rapport. Female passion necessary. It inspires man. Why intercourse without it becomes insipid, injurious, and most infuriating. Its promotion by health, love, etc. Amorous husbands, and passive wives, reproved. Woman may control her own person. Conjugal rapes. What creative states promote, and what prevent, parental pleasure, and progenal endowment. Promiscuosity. Frequency. Advice to those just married. Mutual adaptations of the sexes. The life-germ ; its creation, progress, wants, and their supply. The female creative office. The womb, and its appendages. The ovum, and its fecundation. Predetermining the sex. Twins and triplets. Promoting and preventing conception. Barrenness, onanism, etc., etc.

PART VII. MATERNITY and childbirth. The effects, on offspring, of different antenatal states. Ishmael, Samuel, Samson, Christ, James I., Bonaparte, the giant maniac, etc. Why children should be loved before their birth, and bad tempered ones be pitied, etc. Diseases, marks, hydrocephalus, etc., their causes and preventives. Intercourse during pregnancy. Maternal vitality, sleep, food, breathing, tight-lacing, exercise, fear, fortitude, inanity, culture, etc. The first six months, and the last three. How to render children natural divines, poets, scholars, thinkers, business men, artists, etc. Maternity should take precedence. Pregnancy healthy. Rendering childbirth easy by health, muscular culture, resolution, water treatment, etc. What forms may, and must not, intermarry. Drugging, bleeding, milk sickness, promoting lactition, etc.

PART VIII. CHILD-REARING, its laws, and details. Modern education empirical. Value of infants. Their nursing, "complaints," teething, worms, scarlet-fever, crying, weaning, diet, habits, sleep, ablution, clothing, going barefoot, schooling, etc. Their nutritive, muscular, and growing epochs. Play and playmates. Precocity. Governing them by moral suasion rs. the rod. Directing will, not crushing it. Example rs. precept. Patience rs. scolding. Love, the mother's magic wand, etc.

PART IX. SEXUAL RECUPERATION. The amount, causes, and cures of sexual disorders. Right and wrong love states. Continence. Seminal losses. Prematurity. Impotence. Aversions. Health habits, exercise, etc. Local applications of water, electricity, etc. Female complaints, their causes and cures. Girlhood. Right and wrong merging into womanhood. Sexual inertia. Female ruination, misnamed education. Abortion, and sexual frauds. Prolapsus, its effects and cure. Visceral manipulations. Fluor albus. Miscarriages, and their prevention. Menstruation, its office, and promotion. Surplus fat, and labored breathing, their causes and cures. Barrenness, its causes and obviation. Female beauty. Its conditions. A full bust, how lost, and regained. Rules for promoting sexual vigor. Concluding appeal.

Reader, can you get a tithe as much life-long value, with five dollars, as by procuring this volume?

Address Prof. O. S. FOWLER, 514 Tremont Street, Boston, Mass.

PROSPECTUS OF VOL. IV. RELIGIOUS SCIENCE;

Or MAN'S MORAL NATURE, and Relations; A GOD and His Attributes, the True Theology etc.; IMMORTALITY, its Proofs, Conditions, and Relations to Time; NATURAL RELIGION, its Doctrines, Duties, etc.; Worshipping God in Nature, and Obeying His Natural Laws; Future Rewards and Punishments; The Law of Love, Faith, Prayer, Rites, "Total Depravity," "Conversion," "Forgiveness," etc., etc., as taught by Phrenology. $2.00.

Did all that is, come by chance? or exists there, in very truth, a God, the Great Creator and Governor of this magnificent universe? And if so, what of His attributes, laws, government, works, worship, and the allegiance due from man to his Maker? That is, *What is the true* THEOLOGY?

Is death our last? or is man indeed immortal? And if so, what of that immortality? Are this life and that to come antagonistic? And if so, should we sacrifice the pleasures of this life on the altar of the best interests of that, or those of that for those of this? Or are both states so interrelated that whatever promotes or curtails the pleasures of either, thereby similarly affects the other also? And if so, *what* life is best for us both here and hereafter?

Is man totally depraved by nature? And if so has this depravity any antidotes or palliatives? Must he be born again? What of Faith, Prayer, Worship, Rites, Forgiveness, etc.?

These and like problems, O man, which have puzzled the race throughout all ages, are among the most practically important mankind can ever ask or answer, because there impinge upon them eventualities so much farther reaching, and more momentous than upon any others whatsoever, that it becomes us, as intelligent, self-interested beings, to obtain answers so absolutely reliable that we can well afford to live and die by them.

But where can we find answers thus reliable because *scientific?*

In the structure of the human MIND. Since man is the epitome of all that is, and the grand summary of the universe, and since the human mind is the ultimate end of all things, and therefore adapted to everything else in nature; therefore if there is a God, and if man is immortal, the mind of man will be adapted to both. And if it is thus adapted, they of course exist.

But where can we find this mind so expounded as to solve these and like problems scientifically?

In and by the science of PHRENOLOGY. Its analysis of the mental faculties expounds all their adaptations and dependencies, together with all those ranges of truths they involve. In short, man's mind is the storehouse of all truth, religious included, which Phrenology unlocks, and which this volume applies to its moral and religious elimination. Its author understands both this science, and that subject to which he thus applies it. Its line of argument discusses the following among many kindred subjects : —

Man is created with moral and religious faculties. This, his religious department, must have its laws, which render religion one of the natural and demonstrable sciences. Religious truth is the same throughout all times and places. Hence the thousand and one conflicting religious creeds and sects prove that all but one are wrong. The location of these moral organs on the top of the head proves that these faculties control human character and destiny, and should be supreme in conduct; while their joining the reasoning organs shows that both should be exercised *together*, not by proxy, but by every one being his *own* priest.

VENERATION, the centre organ of this group, worships a Supreme Being; therefore a God exists, adapted to this worshipping instinct. All are born worshipful, and therefore bound to worship. Devotion yields man his richest pleasures, besides sanctifying all his other enjoyments. Promoting piety by studying God in His works, and obeying His natural laws. Loving Him renders us like Him. Analysis of the Divine Attributes. Prayer benefits us, not Him. How it is answered. Religious creeds, rites, the Sabbath, etc. Sects accounted for. A new sect proposed. The true theology.

SPIRITUALITY. Immortality proved. A mental faculty adapts man to it. The law of progress, general and individual. Age ripens, improves, and spiritualizes. Death, as proving a life to come. Our future life is a continuation of this. All we do and are here affect us forever, just as youthful conduct influences all after-life. Memory never forgets, — is "fact tight." Life is a system of causes which produce eternal effects. Little things are most eventful. What causes here produce what effects there. Phrenology furnishes an infallible guide to that best life, both here and there.

CONSCIENTIOUSNESS. Right and wrong *inherent*. Created by natural laws. Obedience to them a divine duty, and infinitely obligatory on all. Right rewards, and wrong punishes, irrespective of faith, prayer, or persons. Christians should obey the natural laws. Use of punishment. All evil causes good. Penitence demanded, implies forgiveness, and stops further sin and suffering. The teachings of Phrenology harmonize with those of Christ. Summary application of this whole subject, etc.

Should not the purely *scientific* discussion of these and analogous subjects from the standpoint of the structure of the human mind, command the attention of Christian, savant, infidel, and nothingarian?

TERMS. Published *only by subscription.* A sample No. of 62 octavo pages, 25 cts. The entire work, near 500 pages, bound, mailed, and prepaid, during 1872. Address prepaid subscriptions to Professor O. S. FOWLER, 514 Tremont Street, Boston, Mass.

INTELLECTUAL SCIENCE;

(VOL. V. OF THE "SCIENCE OF LIFE,")

OR

Memory, Reason, and their Culture:

INCLUDING

The Senses, Intellectual Faculties, Mental Discipline, Self-Education, Schooling, etc.

BY PROFESSOR O. S. FOWLER.

MIND controls matter. *Knowledge* is power; and *reason* is man's constitutional guide and governor in all things. Those alone may justly exult who install *sense* as their ruler. *Mental discipline* is man's highest attainment; because it crowns all others. Teaching men the natural laws, and the consequences of their obedience and infraction, enlists their very *self-interest* in leading right lives.

MEMORY is one of man's most valuable possessions. What *rent* could a lawyer, a business man, a scholar, everybody, well afford to pay, to be enabled to recall and apply to any case in hand *all he ever knew?* How many daily losses are consequent on a poor memory, which a good one would convert into gains?

REASON is still more valuable, while eloquence and the other intellectual endowments are scarcely less so. To show how to redouble these and all other intellectual capacities and accomplishments, as well as how to conduct self-education, musical, scientific, conversational, etc., schooling, including writing, and other talents, the scholastic education of children, mental culture in general, is this work written. Reader, can you expend two dollars as profitably as in its purchase? By disclosing Nature's true educational *principles*, it shows parents, teachers, and individuals how to advance their children's mental culture many times faster than now. It analyzes and shows how to cultivate each mental faculty and kind of memory, and thus expounds the true educational *system.*

TERMS. — It will contain about 450 octavo pages, be well printed and bound, be published in 1872, only by subscription, and mailed as soon as issued to subscribers who remit $2 to

PROFESSOR O. S. FOWLER,

514 TREMONT STREET, BOSTON, MASS.

N. B. — Price when sent in numbers $1.50. Fifteen dollars will secure the author's entire writings. See general prospectus.

A Correct Phrenological Examination

Is indispensable to Self-Knowledge and Self-Culture, Life's greatest work; for, by admeasuring each mental faculty, it points out your own and children's *constitutional* excesses, errors, defects, etc., and shows how to obviate them; reveals natural talents, and thereby in what business, sphere, or pursuits you and they can, and cannot, succeed, thus preventing failures, and guaranteeing success and happiness; directs *specifically* just what physical functions and mental faculties either may require to cultivate and restrain; shows how to *make the most* of whatever inborn capacities and virtues either may possess, as well as the best way to influence and govern each; and is your *very best* means of personal and juvenile improvement possible. In short, Phrenology embodies the whole science of human life, which a correct delineation applies throughout all your every-day affairs and feelings. It is therefore worth a hundred-fold its cost.

PROFESSOR O. S. FOWLER, OF BOSTON,

(Formerly of New York,) has devoted *forty years* to the study of this science, and its application to human culture. His professional opinions are SCIENTIFIC, and therefore a *sure* guide in the management of yourselves and children. He answers all questions, and gives all needed advice — and who but requires both? — as to your and their *health, best business, marriage,* etc.; takes a *personal* interest in each applicant; and furnishes, when desired, a full *written out* description, which perpetuates all, and re-impresses, by reperusal; can be shown or printed; and furnishes incomparably the best record.

As he may not suffer his professional services much longer, because he retires from practice to write, many who do not apply soon will be *too late;* yet he can now be consulted, never in the New York, but only at his new *Boston* establishment. Though he founded the New York firm of " FOWLERS & WELLS," yet he withdrew from it in 1854, as did his brother, L. N. FOWLER, in 1863, and both now forbid the continued use of the Fowler name by Wells; while common justice demands that each branch seeks its patronage by its *own* name and merits, without misleading unwary patrons. Let those who prefer an examination by Wells, the old firm's *financier*, not examiner, or by his employés, pay their money *understandingly,* while those who prefer one having the *genuine* O S. FOWLER *ring* in its metal. can obtain it at his Boston residence. 514 Tremont Street, where he has purchased, and located for life.

N. B. — Those who cannot consult him *in person* will find their next best substitute in sending to his address a " three-quarter " or else a front and profile likeness, with six dollars, and their address plainly written. age, business, complexion, height, weight, education, the avocation preferred, and any other facts concerning themselves they please; and will receive in return a FULL WRITTEN DESCRIPTION of themselves, the avocation and sphere for which NATURE has fitted them, and of the one to whom they are adapted in marriage, etc., together with any warning and advice required by their phrenological organization.

Or if any gentleman desires to ascertain whether, wherein, and how far, he is or is not adapted in marriage to a given lady, or she to him; or if any lady desires similar information; or if two, as regards each other; they will be told with SCIENTIFIC ACCURACY, by inclosing the likenesses and personal descriptions of both with $5, addressed to

O. S. FOWLER, 514 Tremont Street, Boston, Mass.